DINÉ BAHANE
THE NAVAJO CREATION STORY

Diné bahane'

The Navajo
Creation Story

Paul G. Zolbrod

University of New Mexico Press / Albuquerque

ISBN-13   978-0-8263-1043-9

This publication has been supported by the
National Endowment for the Humanities, a
federal agency which supports the study of such
fields as history, philosophy, literature,
and languages.

Library of Congress Cataloging in Publication Data
Zolbrod, Paul G.
      Diné Bahane'.

Translated Navajo origin myths.
Bibliography: p.
1. Navajo Indians—Religion and mythology.
2. Indians of North America—Southwest,
New—Religion and mythology.
I. Title.
E99.N3Z65   1984   299'78   84-6920
ISBN 0-8263-1043-5

CONTENTS

ACKNOWLEDGMENTS

Preparing this volume took a long time, and conventional literary scholarship provided few examples of what I hoped to do. So I am all the more grateful to those who have helped me in one way or another.

I begin as I must by mentioning the late Charles Crow, my teacher in college and graduate school at the University of Pittsburgh. As he did with so many of his students, he taught me to trust my own judgment and to work doggedly to support my convictions. Never having entertained the possibility himself that there was such a thing as American Indian poetry, he read the first essay I wrote on the subject with characteristic open-mindedness and then urged me to continue my research. Along with him, another former teacher and now a close friend deserves special mention. Richard C. Tobias supplied early encouragement and has remained resolute in providing help and advice through the completion of this work. Likewise, I hasten to single out my Allegheny College colleague and good friend, Bruce Clayton, who over the years listened patiently and offered useful suggestions as I attempted to formulate my ideas and struggled to transform them into a finished manuscript. And I must also acknowledge the generous support of Lawrence Lee Pelletier, past president of Allegheny College, who was instrumental in helping me to acquire funds to cover the cost of doing early research in the field. He, too, offered encouragement, especially at the outset.

While I know that there are many individuals whose names I neglect to mention, I wish to single out others for their invaluable help. My thanks go to Professor James Barbour of the University of New Mexico, whose curiosity about my work was a welcome reinforcement in the early going. My thanks, too, go to Professor Ekkehart Malotki of Northern Arizona University for listening to my ideas about transcription and translation and for sharing his with me while he was working on Hopi narratives. Likewise, I owe thanks to Karl Luckert of Southeast Missouri State University for his guidance in locating necessary resources in the field and for his bold and lucid interpretations of Navajo material. And I extend a special word of appreciation to Katherine Spencer Halpern, who read an early draft of my entire translation along with two separate versions of the introduction, alternately encouraging me to pursue my ideas about the relationship between poetry and culture and prompting me to be more accurate, sometimes by locating material I would not otherwise have found, and sometimes by spotting mistakes I had made. Hers is clearly the superior knowledge.

Dorothy Jean Smith and Donald Vrabel, reference librarians at Allegheny College, rendered ongoing assistance by obtaining valuable resource material. Mary Blumenthal, curator of the Clinton P. Anderson collection in the Zimmerman Library of the University of New Mexico, helped me to identify key sources, as did Katherine Bartlett, archivist at the Museum of Northern Arizona, and her colleague, Dorothy House, museum librarian. I am grateful to those three in particular for their hospitality and their ready knowledge of local material. Besides Dr. Halpern, Professor Herbert Landar of California State University at Los Angeles, Professor Andrew Welsh of Rutgers University, and Professor James Bulman of Allegheny College all read early drafts of my work in part or entirely and provided useful guidance. Professor Barre Toelken, University of Oregon; Professor Jarold Ramsey, University of Rochester; and Professor Robert Young, University of New Mexico, read all or portions of a later draft, as did Professor Carter Revard, Washington University, whose comments and criticisms were especially helpful. And I make a special point of mentioning Elizabeth C. Hadas, Senior Editor at the University of New Mexico Press, in appreciation for her patience and her firm editorial hand.

I acknowledge as well the hospitality of the University of New Mexico, particularly the English Department there, which provided me with workspace and a stimulating intellectual environment during the 1971–72 academic year. I also appreciate the use of resources at Northern Arizona University in Flagstaff during the 1978–79 academic year. Irvy Goosen, then Professor of Modern

Languages there, kindly allowed me to participate in his course on the Navajo language. He also assisted me with the orthography of Navajo proper nouns in addition to helping me considerably with my conversational Navajo. Likewise, I thank Hermann K. Bleibtreu, then Director of the Museum of Northern Arizona, and Susan McGreevy, then Director of the Wheelwright Museum in Santa Fe, for making the resources of those two institutions available to me; and I thank the various members of their respective staffs for their generous assistance. And I also acknowledge the support of the National Endowment for the Humanities during the 1978–79 academic year in the form of a research fellowship that enabled me to assemble a great deal of material in a single year.

In a study like this one, all sources cannot be identified by citing written works, whether published or unpublished. I must also recognize the help I received from native informants. In addition to Martin Vigil, whose unforgettable four-hour session with me at Tesuque Pueblo late in the summer of 1969 made everything else seem possible, I wish to thank these others. Roseann Sandoval Willink, originally of Pueblo Pintado, New Mexico, was my first Navajo teacher. With the help of her patience and friendship, I managed to fathom some of the subtle features of the language and the culture. Her cousin, Arthur Sandoval, of Pueblo Pintado, was the first of many who explained some important aspects of tribal life to me. Mescalito, an old storyteller from the same region, permitted me to record a long story which he performed at the local Bureau of Indian Affairs school in the late winter of 1972, during storytelling season. I have listened to that tape over and over, so that I know the sound of his voice well. I spent countless hours with Avery Jimerson and his wife, Fidelia, of the Allegany Seneca Reservation in Salamanca, New York, listening to them sing and talk, observing them dancing both in their kitchen and at the Cold Spring Longhouse, or watching them direct the Seneca Youth Dancers in concert. They demonstrated to me by their example that there is a place in scholarship for the unrecorded knowledge that accompanies long, informal visits with people from another culture who become good friends.

Harry Bilagody, Jr., of Tuba City, Arizona, spent several long sessions with me discussing particular details of the Navajo creation story in his family's ceremonial hogan over a warm evening fire during the winter of 1979. Those conversations were some of the finest, most intense discussions of poetry I have ever had. I also wish to thank Dr. William Morgan of Fort Defiance, Arizona, who is more or less the official lexicographer of Navajo. He helped generously with some archaic Navajo terms which I never could have otherwise understood or transcribed. I also appreciate the assistance of Ethelou Yazzie of the Little Singer School, Bird Spring, Arizona, for her help with linguistic details. And I wish to make special mention of Danny Blackgoat of Flagstaff, Arizona, for his invaluable help in translating some very difficult old passages.

I am grateful to numerous other Navajos, some of whose names I never learned, who in small but significant ways helped me to acquire valuable knowledge. I regret my clumsy intrusions, but at the same time I appreciate the hospitality I received everywhere on the reservation. Likewise, I acknowledge the generous hospitality of various people at Old Oraibi and Walpi on the Hopi Reservation; of the Pueblo communities of Acoma, Taos, Tesuque, and especially Santo Domingo; of the Seneca communities of Jimersontown and Cold Spring in upstate New York; and of the people of the Tuscarora Reservation at Niagara Falls.

Of course, none of the individuals, groups, or institutions I have named are responsible for my errors. Without their help I would have made many more; and it is to them above all that I would hasten to apologize for the mistakes I have made. That is particularly true of the Native Americans who assisted me; all told, they taught me a valuable lesson: in places where preliterate traditions survive, personal contact can have the same impact on a researcher as books have in a library.

I save for last the tribute I must pay to my family: my wife, Joan, my daughter, Lisa, my son, Aaron, whose lives have been closely bound to this work over a long period of time. On three separate occasions they accompanied me to the Southwest for extended and sometimes unsettling stays in strange places far from home. Much too often they endured my absence for many days while I worked in the field, at times completely out of touch. More often still, they suffered my absent-minded preoccupation while I was at home working on this manuscript or thinking about it. All the while, however, they struggled to understand what I was doing and rooted for me as I worked my way to completion. In the last analysis that kind of help is best of all. I thank them for it, and I dedicate this book to them with my gratitude and my love. That is the very least I can do to repay them for all they have given me.

PRONUNCIATION KEY*

1. There are four basic vowels in Navajo:
   a as in *art*
   e as in *met*
   i as in *sit*
   o as in *note*
2. Vowels may be short or long, length being indicated by a doubling of the letter. The quality of the vowel is not affected by length except that long "i" is pronounced as in *seen* or *machine*.
3. Vowels may also be nasalized. The nasalized pronunciation is indicated by a hook underneath the affected vowel, as in *Mą'ii*.
4. A tone marker over a vowel, as in *Tó* or *dine'é* indicates a rise in pitch. Long and short vowels alike can be high tone or low.
5. Navajo has the following diphthongs that require special mention:
   ai as in *kite*
   ei as in *day*
   oi as in *buoy*
6. While many Navajo consonants are unfamiliar, they can be reasonably well approximated by a casual reader. There are two characters in the Navajo alphabet, however, which do not appear in the standard English alphabet. They include the glottal stop ('), as in *Mą'ii* or *dine'é*, and the voiceless glide (ł), as in *Niłch'i*. The former is pronounced like the break between the two elements of the familiar English expression, "oh, oh." The latter is pronounced by unvoicing the "l" familiar to speakers of English. Or it can be roughly approximated by pronouncing it as if it were "sh" in a word like *push* or *shoot*.

*This is a simplified guide for readers of this volume who wish to approximate the Navajo terms used here. For a more detailed guide, see Goosen; Young and Morgan 1943; or Young and Morgan 1980.

INTRODUCTION

This project began as an experiment in text retrieval, since my
original intention was to present an English version of the Navajo
creation story as evidence of an ongoing pre-Columbian literary
tradition in North America. What it has become, however, is an
expanded view of poetry and poetics, or an uncertain one. For now
I marvel that we have come to take written texts so much for
granted. More extravagantly, I question afresh whether we know
any more about poetry now than was known at the proverbial
dawn of civilization.

I

Back in the early sixties, soon after I began teaching literature to
undergraduates, I found myself wondering whether a significant
body of preliterate poetry existed. It was a possibility that I had
never considered before. I was working then on my dissertation—a
detailed study of Renaissance poetics—looking primarily at Sir
Philip Sidney's *Defence of Poetry*, a work that summarizes the
literary theory of that period as well as any document written
during the sixteenth century. For all that Sidney had said in behalf
of printed literature, he admits that he had once found the lyrics of
a particular ballad especially appealing: "I have never heard the old
song of Percy and Douglas that I found not my heart moved more
than with a trumpet," he wrote. "And yet it is sung but by some
blind crowder, with no rougher voice than rude style; which being
eveil apparelled in the dust and cobwebs of that uncivil age, what
would it work, trimmed in the georgeous eloquence of Pindar?"

That passage impressed me. I had grown up on the southern edge of Pittsburgh, where at night the sky was red with burning slag. As a child in a working-class neighborhood I had heard memorable stories on front porches and at streetside about life and death in the old country. Immigrants and refugees who had not yet learned to read and write English somehow wanted us young boys to know of earlier times, and in retrospect it seems that they had a way of impressing us. For the memory of their voices and of the things they recited have always lingered with me. During the course of my studies, as I acquired literary experience, I managed to remain more or less aware of an implicit poetic element in the speech of those informal gatherings of young and old. In college and in graduate school, however, it never occurred to me to associate what I had heard from neighbors during the late Depression and the early years of World War II with the poems I was learning to read out of textbooks.

Then, during a casual and quite accidental 1967 visit to an Indian museum at Browning, Montana, I happened upon *By Cheyenne Campfires*, a volume of Cheyenne narratives compiled by George Bird Grinnell in 1928. While reading it, I suddenly found myself receptive to the possibility of studying oral traditions. My dissertation was completed by then, my degree assured. Why not determine whether a significant corpus of Native American poetry existed? As I was to learn, the serious study of Native American literature had been going on for well over a century, but that fact had been pretty much ignored by mainstream literary critics, at least in the academic realm. Certain biases engendered by the long-standing prominence of print in Old World cultures might have helped to keep such work obscure. And those biases might have been intensified by the more direct forms of racist and pseudo-Darwinian mind-sets. Or vice versa.[1] Whatever the reasons, though, nowhere during my formal education had anyone I encountered even hinted that there was such a thing as American Indian poetry; and I suspect that I was typical of students of literature in that regard.[2]

As an English professor I had been trained to deal with printed material in a fairly well-prescribed way. I learned how to analyze published texts and to examine unpublished manuscripts, how to distinguish folio from quarto sheets, how to reconstruct the process by which a literary work was edited and published in the early days of commercial printing, how to do close and careful reading. Without realizing it, I was being conditioned primarily to *see* language; and during the early part of my career as a teacher I was conditioning undergraduate students primarily to see it as well. If I heard it at all, I heard it only secondarily, silently re-creating its sound in my mind and occasionally reading it aloud thereafter. Certainly I was not encouraged to think consciously about the relationship between the graphics of print and they dynamics of speech and song. There had been some cursory training in linguistics, of course, but among my colleagues then that was considered a distant adjunct to the real thing, the printed page.[3]

Perhaps my conditioned bias in favor of print is what made me so naïve, but once I made up my mind to explore Native American material I actually believed that I needed only to identify a tribe somewhere, become acquainted with its language, and then unearth submerged elements of an oral tradition. I could subsequently transcribe and translate a major sample of the tribe's poetry and present it. Simple!

But an impulse is by no means a workable plan. To begin with, it was not easy to find informants, especially since I was without any of the elaborate preparation that anthropologists acquire. I learned by my own dumb experience that you just don't drive into an Indian community and ask someone to start reciting something. In the summer of 1969, I traveled to New Mexico and drove quite alone and uninformed up and down the Rio Grande Valley, visiting one Pueblo community after another without so much as consulting an ethnographer. After being turned away at village after village, I finally met Mr. Martin Vigil, who at that time was governor of Tesuque Pueblo, near Santa Fe. When I told him what I had hoped to do, he looked at me incredulously and asked, "Do you have fifty years? Because that's how much time you will need just at this village." He knew, of course, how intricate the esoteric oral traditions of the various Keres and Tewa Pueblo communities in the valley were. And, although I did not realize it then, the same could be said of any other Native American culture.

Still, he was willing to tell me a little bit about life at Tesuque and among other groups and tribes in the region, if only to get me to appreciate the magnitude of what might lie ahead for me if I really wanted to learn about Indian poetry. Many of the Pueblo communities observed secret ceremonies in the kivas, which were frequently restricted. Some villages were unwilling to share any material with researchers, while others refused to permit their language to be written down. Bitterness toward whites was stong nearly everywhere. And Pueblo languages varied so much from one village to the next that linguistic communities were too small to permit generalizations about whatever data a researcher might be able to gather. Perhaps it would be better to inquire among the Navajos, he suggested, since theirs was the largest tribe and since they spoke a fairly uniform language from one part of the reservation to another. Also, they were less unwilling to share their traditions with outsiders than the more conservative Pueblo tribes were.

Something like what I wanted to do could be accomplished, then, but not without difficulty—at least for someone like myself, untrained in ethnography and folklore and knowing nothing about field research. So after I retuned I began a tentative investigation by reading printed material entirely new to me. Since its inception well over a century and a half ago, for example, the Bureau of American Ethnology has fostered a great deal of direct research among Indian tribes all over North America and has published numerous transcriptions of prayers, songs, and narratives in its numbered bulletins and reports. Many are straightforward literal translations of what might actually have been poetry of a sort. They were seldom assembled as an exercise in Native American literary history or in primitive poetics, but these volumes at least indicated that Native Americans everywhere on this continent had traditions not generally acknowledged outside such academic disciplines as folklore, ethnography, or linguistics. By reading as much as I could find and absorb, I acquired a sense of how adequate or inadequate most printed versions of Indian "literature" then were.[4] And I began to appreciate the range of material that might actually be available, the hurdles translators and interpreters had to overcome, and the implicit assumptions that prevented literary scholars and critics from taking full measure of native poetry.

II

Eventually, though, I had to locate some primary sources, or at least learn enough of a language to evaluate printed material at closer range. So I decided to spend a sabbatical year, 1971–72, at the University of New Mexico, in Albuquerque. Mindful of

Governor Vigil's suggestion, I began studying Navajo, seeking out native speakers and reading what I could find in regional journals and among local archives. I discovered that Washington Matthews (1843–1905) had done pioneering research among the Navajos during the last two decades of the nineteenth century. Among his published work was a volume titled *Navaho Legends*, which contained, in addition to two shorter narratives, one of the earliest renditions of the Navajo account of the creation and the most comprehensive English text of that particular cycle I had yet found. Even now it may be among the most complete renditions of its kind from any Native American language, and that possibility becomes all the more significant when one realizes that the creation story is an important genre in many preliterate traditions.

The story tells of the emergence of the insect-like *Nitch'i dine'é* or "air-spirit people" from a primal domain deep within the earth. It describes how they gradually make their way to the surface of the world, where they evolve into *nihookáá' dine'é* or "earth surface people" and then into an aggregate of human clans ready to form an intricate society. It may seem to glib to compare this narrative with the Bible, although I am sometimes tempted to do that because I can think of no other analogue to offer someone who knows nothing about tribal poetry. The story resembles the Old Testament in that its origins reach deep into the inscrutable loam of a primeval past. Also, it articulates a distinct sense of the sacred for those who share a familiarity with it. It displays more unity than the Scriptures, however, resembling Hesiod's *Theogeny* in that respect, although it seems to draw more eclectically from a wide array of sources. The central theme is the attainment of *hózhǫ́*, a fairly untranslatable term which can only be approximated in English by combining words like *beauty, balance,* and *harmony.* As the people grow more complex biologically, psychologically, spiritually, and socially, they learn how to mitigate evil with good by developing a relationship with the supernaturals and among themselves. The pivotal element in achieving that intricate set of relationships is the fundamental relationship between male and female, represented first by *Áłtsé hastiin* or First Man and *Áłtsé asdzą́ą́* or First Woman, and later by *Asdzą́ą́ nádleehé* or Changing Woman and *Jóhonaa'éí* the Sun. The inability of the former two to get along causes evil by bringing about the generation of the *Naayéé'* or Alien Gods. The union of the latter couple represents the first step leading to the destruction of the evil monsters. But full harmony cannot be established until Changing Woman and the Sun achieve a fully equitable relationship; and not until then does the actual creation of the Navajo people occur. Everything that happens throughout the story relates directly or indirectly to the notion of delicate balance between male and female.[5]

Representing narrative poetry at its richest, the cycle displays an awareness of human complexity different from anything in our own literature. The emotions it identifies are as intense as those found in *Oedipus Rex* or *Othello*, although motives are not as easily identified. Yet somehow the main characters display the kind of distinctiveness associated with a Dickens or a Balzac. While First Man and First Woman start out virtually as abstract prototypes of male and female, we come to recognize in them impulses basic to being a husband and a wife cast into a relationship which at once ties them and repels them. Their first quarrel is both sexual and egocentric; she accuses him of sharing the meat he hunts only in exchange for sex with her. His counter accusation is that he serves her well with no genuine recognition for what he does. It is difficult to think of one particular title in our own tradition where man and woman embroil themselves quite like this in a conflict caused equally by hurt and anger, wounded pride and foolish obstinacy, and tragic blindness combined with comical stubbornness. Their quarrel suggests the sexual urgency of *Lysistrata*, the ugly fervor of Strindberg's *The Father*, and the cloying irony of Shaw's *Candida*. Yet there seems to be less self-conscious artistry in the way the incident is told. What divides First Woman and First Man seems both logical and ludicrous. They do not at first contrive to hurt one another, but their mutual anger somehow functions as a destructive consequence of their sexuality. Because of their origin as ears of corn they remain as basic as germinating seeds. But since they acquire distinct personalities of their own, they assume proportions that can easily be associated with the quintessential human spirit. And as they gain experience and wisdom they take on god-like proportions: their intelligence grows with their wisdom, they accumulate power that seems magical, and they finally manifest a grasp of the destiny that lies ahead for the as yet uncreated human race. The whole story, then, occurs in a setting that combines the real and the earthy with the mystical and the cosmic, where spirits and humans interact in a way not duplicated in any one of our own familiar literary works save perhaps those like the Homeric epics or Ovid's *Metamorphoses*. Reflected is a poetic intricacy that would certainly surprise many of us, because—or so I suspect—most of us have inherited assumptions that Indians do not have a "high" culture, in spite of the current fashion of our professing sympathy for them.

The Navajo creation story is not an isolated work in a culture with no other poetry. The Navajos have always had a dynamic oral tradition, and it thrives to this day. But in preparing his translation Matthews did not succeed in replicating a poetic idiom appropriate to that tradition. He wrote up his English version in fairly ordinary, discursive prose intended to transmit the story's content and to convey information about Navajo beliefs. So his text reflects little of the art of preliterate storytelling in any native language. How he acquired his material never became entirely clear to me, and limited to the evidence presently available we may never know exactly what procedure he used in assembling his text. It does seem certain, though, that he gathered material for it piecemeal—perhaps over a span of a dozen years or more—and that the process of acquiring it was slow and difficult. He first arrived at Fort Wingate, New Mexico, in 1880, having already published a monograph on one Indian tribe, the Hidatsa. He remained there until 1884, when he was transferred to Washington, by then having published various articles on Navajo culture and on his experiences among the Navajos. While stationed in Washington, he continued writing about them, making an unspecified number of trips back to the Fort Wingate area, where he remained until shortly after suffering a paralytic stroke in 1902, when he was summoned back to Washington for a medical discharge. Not until after that, it seems, did he begin actually preparing the manuscript for *Navaho Legends*.[6]

Thus the work might very well have been assembled primarily from notes originally acquired from informants like Old Torlino, Jake the Silversmith, or Hataalii nez—Navajos whom Matthews got to know during his years of association with the tribe and whom he mentions in his introduction (pp. 50–51). But he could also have worked from memory when he actually prepared the manuscript, and from a sense both of the language and of the overall story that grew familiar to him over the years as he made one foray after another to attend Navajo ceremonies and to compile data in whatever way he could. He speaks in occasional letters of Navajo friends and acquaintances, sometimes with fondness and always with a respect that apparently resulted from his unopinionated, objective observations. He never romanticizes, however, and his painstakingly acquired knowledge of the Navajo language becomes more and more obvious when his notes and letters are read in chronological order. Well before the time he left Fort Wingate at the end of his second tour of duty there, he could very easily have become a fluent conversationalist in that language, possessing a sense of the nuances of its puns and peculiarities, the characteristic style of its songs and prayers, and the subtle features of its storytelling. His published and unpublished writings alike indicate that he had a special gift for observing minute details, while his letters suggest that he also had a good memory. So it is likely indeed that what finally appears in print as "The Navaho Origin Legend" in the 1897 volume represents a retrospective compilation of notes and recollections collated as a unified text and edited intentionally or unintentionally to demonstrate to an English-speaking audience that Navajos did indeed have literary traditions comparable to those of the Greeks.

Nevertheless, his version is not fully representative of the poetic effects intrinsic to Navajo oral recitations. For all his gifts as a translator, Matthews appears to have grown partially deaf before he finished recording everything he eventually transcribed. Yet he was struggling to master a complex tonal, holophrastic language with particles of tense and mode having no precise counterparts in any Indo-European language he knew. Furthermore, he managed to learn Navajo without any of the formal linguistic training he might get today and with none of the convenient equipment now available to anyone wishing to gather linguistic data.

More significantly, though, he was schooled to think of poetry primarily as a printed art, very much the way we are. The assumption that all literature is composed alphabetically on a page is one so fully taken for granted that until recently we have seldom if ever questioned it. For him—as for us today—the long prose passage was a basic typographical unit. Only when a verbal passage is set in some deliberate arrangement of type or handwritten script on a page do we have something that can be called poetry. Conditioned to accept such a tacitly fixed bias, Matthews seems not to have listened to Navajo informants recite narrative as attentively as he might have, at least when gathering the data that he would eventually transform into what was published as "The Navaho Origin Legend." In this regard he is probably no different from other early ethnographers who translated and transcribed. Ironically, he observed some of the features of poetic performance in what he heard when he listened to the stories: " . . . the original was often embellished with pantomime and vocal modulation which expressed more than the mere words," he writes in his introduction to *Navaho Legends* (p. 53). He obviously knew what oral discourse was all about. Likewise, he displayed a poet's sensitivity when he transcribed and translated passages which he felt could be presented as verse. Consider the text and interlinear translation of a portion of Torlino's prefatory asseveration which he includes in his notes to that volume (p. 258), or his interlinear transcriptions and translations of some of the songs and prayers associated with the creation cycle (pp. 261–72). When he prints such material he treats it poetically. By contrast, he includes a transcription and an interlinear translation of the opening passage of his version of the origin legend and sets that up as prose, filling each line from margin to margin with no attempt to identify discrete poetic units (pp. 258–61). Somehow he failed to replicate the innately poetic quality of narrative in a final printed text the way he could replicate the poetic quality of a prayer or a song on the printed page. "No letters can express those extemporized onomatopes," he goes on to say, inadvertently revealing the barrier that literacy seems to have created between speech and the printed word by then.

What he heard his informants recite when he listened to narrative, then, he wrote as prose; or else he composed his final manuscript in prose, seeing no reason to do otherwise. In either case, it makes his version of the creation story seem dense and distinctly unpoetic. Not fully sensitive to the immediate difference between the printed word and the spoken, he assumed that the sound of a narrator's voice should in all respects be subordinated to print. To prove to members of a highly print-oriented culture that the Navajos did in fact have a "literary" tradition he had to do no more than that, or so it may have seemed to him and his contemporaries. Missing from Matthews's text, then, is the full effect of repetition as an important stylistic device, just as he failed to preserve other features of oral delivery such as the long pause, the abrupt phrase, the whispered statement, the delicate sense of timing a storyteller brings to an audience to establish a certain intimacy with it.

In short, Matthews divided all texts into *prose* or *poetry*, with no "Ossianic" in-betweens, and when he recorded examples of songs and prayers he composed such material on the written page as verse. In one letter he acknowledges and praises the rhythm basic to those kinds of discourse, and the lyrics he transcribed and translated stand today as some of the finest examples of Native American verse we now have. He may very well have been one of the first Euro-Americans to illustrate the poetic technique— common in prayers, chants, and songs of many Indian tribes—that Francis E. Gummere identifies as "incremental repetition" and Nellie Barnes examines in her innovative study of Native American poetics.[7] When Matthews listened to a chant or a prayer, he did not hesitate to duplicate its stylistic features by carefully arranging it in printed lines of fixed length enclosed in larger stanzaic units. But whenever he listened to a storyteller recite, he worked in conventional paragraph units, failing to record the more subtle patterns of pitch, stress, and pause. Thus he overlooked the poetic devices employed by storytellers, especially after his hearing began to fail. And because he had such a strong influence on subsequent translators, the understated poetic features of Navajo storytelling style have gone more or less unnoticed until very recently.

Matthews's "Navaho Origin Legend" remains an imperfect rendering of a Native American poetic narrative for yet another reason. It appears that Matthews arbitrarily deleted passages dealing overtly with sex. The explicit sexuality in other versions I have found suggests that he must have encountered such allusions himself. And wherever such passages occur, they add to the understanding of the delicate balance between male and female intrinsic to the Navajo world view. In Navajo thought, the nature of sexual harmony and the way of achieving and maintaining it are central. Such harmony epitomizes the pattern of *hózhǫ́* manifest everywhere in the universe. It does not just govern male-female relationships; directly or indirectly it is reflected in the harmony of relationships between all sorts of counterparts in the broad cosmic scheme: earth and sky, night and day, mortals and supernaturals, summer and winter. That harmony is also reflected in relationships among humans and animals here on earth, and it predicates the way members of clans and individual families regard each other. Sexuality as it is understood in ideal human behavior among the Navajos reveals why certain events occur as they do in Matthews's account of the creation. Likewise, when sexual imbalance or aberration occurs, the breakdown of *hózhǫ́* is explained. Thus, explicitly sexual passages remain important.

For example, the quarrel between First Man and First Woman which leads to the temporary separation between men and women acquires an added dimension of understanding from a fragment, found elsewhere, that describes how First Woman created male and female sensuality. She decides to make sex gratifying to both partners so that couples will stay together. Whether or not Matthews even heard such an account of the origin of the penis and the clitoris, he did not include it in his text. Likewise, when *Mąʾii* the Coyote wins *Asdzáni shash nádleehé* the Changing Bear Maiden as his wife, he consummates his success by tricking her into having intercourse with him. I learned of the actual seduction in an unpublished version of that episode which Matthews either ignored or never learned.[8] In it their sexual relationship is explicitly described, and she receives her evil power from him by permitting him to insert his penis into her.

Sex, in fact, is a very important motif throughout the creation story; but sex is a subject Matthews apparently shunned as much as he possibly could. Therefore, he damaged a lot of what he meant to preserve. Today that lapse may seem flagrant, but Matthews, we must remember, published his work when so-called Victorian taste would scarcely have sanctioned an English version of the Navajo creation story preserving the blunt sexual allusions present in the original. In what he saw fit to put into print, Matthews was overly judicious when measured by standards current now. But he was no more prudish than anyone else writing at that time.

Bowdlerized and unpoetic as it turned out to be, however, his translation relieved me of the nearly impossible task of acquiring a complete version of my own in the field. My impression now is that while the storytelling tradition remains vibrant among the Navajos, less and less of the creation cycle has come to be performed during this century. I doubt if anyone could now recover as much of it as Matthews managed to acquire. I was satisfied enough with the overall accuracy and fullness of his translation to build upon that rather than starting from scratch. Other translations and transcriptions subsequently printed made it possible for me to verify his work and to add missing fragments. And I managed to locate several Navajo informants who agreed to help me by reciting portions which they knew or by sharing interpretations of passages I found obscure. Meanwhile, I studied Navajo to acquire a sense of what a performance might have sounded like originally.

That way I hoped to recast the story in a text that would surpass the limitations of Matthews's impacted, unrepresentative prose. But as I grew familiar with the language I found the problem a difficult one to solve. Navajo has features that give a storyteller options which either do not exist in English or, if duplicated, sound disconcertingly stilted or artificial. The language is a holophrastic one with an extremely complicated verb system whose intricate morphology contrasts dramatically with the relatively simple forms of English verbs. In effect, a sentence in Navajo is a repetitive syntactic unit with the nouns and certain adjectival and adverbial elements duplicated in the verb part, where they reappear as a string of pronominal particles leading up to an abstract unit of meaning that identifies a category of motion. Navajo is also a language easily given to certain kinds of puns and to what can be loosely identified as assonance, alliteration, and dissonance. So it provides a wide range of possibilities for special effects. Because each oral vowel has a nasalized counterpart, for example, Coyote can be made to sound like he is talking through his nose if his words are grouped in a certain way.[9] Complex sentences with strings of recurring relative or subordinate clauses can sound particularly distinctive, since the Navajo particle which introduces them permits a very rigid sort of parallelism resembling the sort of structure we find in the familiar verse about the house that Jack built. The result can be a sentence containing a string of clauses that echo each other in a decidedly chantlike way. These clauses can easily be broken down into individual sentences almost identical to each other. By changing a syllable or two in every line of such a passage, a singer or a storyteller can shift the meaning slightly from sentence to sentence, the result being a semi-repetitive sequence growing progressively into a complete, self-contained statement. Then, by matching such a systematic, sequential passage with one less rigidly constructed, he can simultaneously reiterate what he has already said and create a stark phonemic and syntactical contrast. Sound and word order alter drastically while content is repeated.

For example, consider this short passage from a chantway prayer:[10]

Shikee' sháádiłił	My feet for me restore.
Shijáád sháádiłił	My legs for me restore.
Shats'íís sháádiłił	My body for me restore.
Shíni' sháádiłił	My mind for me restore.
Shiné sháádiłił	My voice for me restore.
Jįįdisdzįį naalíl shá'adilel	This very day your spell for me remove.
Naalíl sha'anéinla'	Your spell is now removed for me.
Shitsadzhe ts'i'ndinla'	Away from me you have taken it.
Nizhágo nastłįį	Far off it is gone.
Hozhógo nadedishdááł	Happily I will recover.

The first five lines with their parallel syntax differ sharply from the second five, which display no such parallelism. Yet each set identifies the desired effect of recovery. Notice the orderly progression expressed in the first five lines from feet to legs to body to mind to speech—speech, incidentally, being the highest human faculty in the Navajo hierarchy of such things. Once the voice is "restored," the patient/speaker is capable of freer, less constrained expression. Thus restoration of the highest human faculty in its proper turn equals full recovery—removal of the "spell."

This is but one small illustration, of course, and it remains to work out a systematic, comprehensive demonstration of Navajo poetics, which I cannot do here.[11] But perhaps the example demonstrates the dynamic sense of balance so prevalent in Navajo poetry but subtly applied so often. For all the contrast between the rigid syntactical structure of the first five lines and the looser structure of the second, the whole passage comes full circle, the speaker demonstrating at the conclusion by his manner of verbal expression what he evidently asks to possess as the statement begins.

What I am trying to demonstrate in that short example is evident in the design of the whole creation story. The cycle opens with a highly patterned description of two rivers crossing at a central point and flowing indefinitely toward each of the four cardinal directions. Soon thereafter the story describes a social conflict, with the original inhabitants of the region where the rivers meet squabbling among themselves and being expelled by the gods. But the text concludes with a more loosely narrated account of

disparate bands assembling from various points to live
harmoniously together at at highly localized central point. Overall,
it is a balanced display of dispersal and reunion, physically as well
as spiritually, just as the short illustration above is a balanced,
cyclical display of how harmony once lacking is restored. The long
narrative is far more complex, of course, but it reflects the same
dynamic sense of balanced design evident in the example just
given, with style giving way to content. In such a manner
throughout the Navajo creation story motion is played off against
emotion, comedy gives way to pathos, life is measured against
death, and fear is mitigated by reassurance as opposites clash and
are reconciled. At the very end the people have regained the trust
of the supernaturals by treating each other generously and learning
to live in harmony. Every detail reflects that broad rhythm of ebb
and flow, and the Navajo language is capable of sustaining such
cyclical balance throughout the story and within any digression,
right down to individual sentences and portions of sentences
whose syntax makes manifest unique orderliness or tricks us
with the illusion of contrast. Hearing an oral performance in
Navajo must be something like looking at a Navajo rug or a
sandpainting, which characterizes the dynamic symmetry of
Navajo design so well.[12]

Once I had acquired such understanding and had assembled the
necessary material, I returned home to Pennsylvania to begin
experimenting with ways of revising Matthews. In the words of
Mary Austin, I hoped to create a Native American text "with its
intrinsic values unimpaired" (1931, p. 428). I wanted my English to
duplicate the parallel structure of the language a Navajo storyteller
employs. I wanted the diction to be characteristically simple
without being child-like; too many adaptations from Native
American traditions are presented as children's stories, which is a
gross, unfair misrepresentation. I also wanted to feel free to use
mildly archaic English terms and phrases to preserve the
conservative diction of traditional Navajo stories, but I did not
want my version to sound deliberately quaint. I knew that the
rhythmic effects of a native performance could not be easily
retained without sounding artificial; yet I wanted to preserve
something of the steady but leisurely pace of a recitation. Least of
all did I want something that looked like prose, where the sound of
a human voice was subordinated to the information being
conveyed. Somehow I wanted to appeal to a reader's ear, so to

speak, hoping that he or she would imagine hearing the story in some authentic way.

But the sharp contrast between the two languages and the two cultures seemed at first to get in my way. Dennis Tedlock's translation of ten Zuni narratives (1972a) provided some help. He had worked closely with native informants over a period of years, taping storytelling sessions and then monitoring the recordings carefully with the help of a native speaker. As a result, he concluded that prose so-called "had no real existence outside the written page" (p. xix).[13] Thus he sharpened my awareness that the story I wanted to retell grew directly out of the reality of the spoken voice. But he had acquired his material under very different circumstances. It would be impossible for me to duplicate as many of the contours of Navajo speech as he had done with the language of Zuni performers. At best I could work out a modified form of prose that might suggest some of the general features of Navajo storytelling and reflect the narrative's preliterate origins. But I could not manipulate print the way he had done any more than I could reproduce the features of Navajo syntax in English. Tedlock was recasting stories that he had actually heard in Zuni, first in performance and then over and over again on tape. He could be more certain of his choice of type, his sometimes drastic spacing, and the other radical techniques of employing print so that it obviously became distinct from ordinary prose. Furthermore, the stories he translated were shorter. My impression is that they were also less ceremonially performed than some of the Navajo stories I knew about which belonged to the creation cycle. Except possibly for the last two sections in his volume, the Zuni narratives did not tell of origins in the very distant *inoote* or long-ago, "when the world was soft" (pp. 221–22). Overall, then, his style did not seem to suit my purpose, which was to present a long, comprehensive story about the beginnings of things with its poetic features distributed more subtly over a greater length.[14]

Armed with Tedlock's suggestion that the printed page had to be carefully managed, however, I turned to some resources that were close at hand for the guidelines I was seeking. I knew of a small Seneca reservation in upstate New York, just a few hours from my home. For several years I managed to go there fairly often and listen to speeches, songs, and stories that still circulated in something of a preliterate setting. That way I could test Tedlock's suggestion that written prose is inaccurate "for representing spoken narrative" because "it rolls on for whole paragraphs at a time without taking a breath: there is no silence in it" (p. xix). I was able to observe firsthand how oral performances made use of the melodic and rhythmic aspects of language. I actually saw that storytellers rely heavily on pitch and cadence. When they repeat sequences their voices are often more markedly measured than print can always allow. I saw, too, a kinesthetic dimension in oral delivery not evident in print, which might include a heavy gesture at one point and motionlessness at another, the deliberate use of eye contact and grinning, mimicking and mime, a hushed whisper or an unexpected shout. I gained a sense that I had never consciously acquired before of how many effective poetic devices can occur in a preliterate performance.

While I had no illusions about reproducing the kinetic activity of a native storyteller in print (to say nothing of re-creating the distinct sound of his voice), at least I could observe that a performance consists of more than words as they are recorded on a page; furthermore, I could make that observation in an unfamiliar setting where certain things were easier to notice. That way I increased my awareness of all that my version of the Navajo creation story would have to represent. Just listening to some of the old timers sing at festivals or tell about their lives helped me to associate the way they talked with features of their culture. When they told traditional stories there was a distinct cadence. As a rule they recited with what I would call a ceremonial voice. Speech was more deliberate. I noticed an added vocal tenseness marked by a slight rise in pitch. One old man held his eyes closed when telling serious stories; but when telling funny ones he would glance mischievously around the room, exaggerating the nervous movement of his eyes.

In addition, I designed and helped to produce a televised oral history in a rural county in Northwest Pennsylvania—a project that took nearly four years while I continued revising the "Navaho Origin Legend." Monitoring over two hundred hours of audio- and video-taped narration and listening to perhaps another two hundred hours of untaped testimony permitted me to observe some of the more subtle features of oral recitation among native speakers of English, too, and to consider how they might be projected onto the printed page. I learned, for example, that many of the people we interviewed enjoyed telling of certain events over and over again, and that without necessarily realizing it, some of them had acquired a certain stylized way of reciting their favorite stories. Sometimes they used recognizable formulaic expressions. Sometimes their bodies moved in a patterned way. One woman would begin to recite in a distinct cadence whenever she repeated something she had narrated before. There was also a man who would pause longer between sentences while retelling a story he had recited earlier. Another woman had a very effective way of softening her voice to tell a favorite anecdote, and the rhythm of her speech became quite pronounced. She also had a habit of crossing her hands in her lap and wrapping the fingers of her left one tightly around the right at high points in her narrative. And when we studied her interview on videotape we discovered that her body movement synchronized closely with the rhythm of her speech. She was an especially good storyteller; whenever she started to talk members of the production crew would gather around to listen. "I don't know what it is," observed one of them, "but she really has a way about her." What "it" was, I now believe, turned out to be a whole set of features being more or less subconsciously orchestrated. All these features, however, are such familiar components of ordinary conversation that we tend to overlook them, just as we can easily overlook some of the poetic features of ordinary prose because they grow familiar. There really was a storytelling class among the people we interviewed, although in our print-oriented culture we have either forgotten how or not yet learned to notice it. And much of what made their delivery effective might be transferred into print by means of carefully arranged stylistic devices just as subtly and just as thoroughly as good storytellers can blend poetic technique into their speech and gestures when they recite.

All of this convinced me that what was needed for my text was a middle course between the prosaic extreme of Matthews's dense translation and the typographical extreme of Tedlock's renderings. Paragraphs would have to be short, as a rule, with space separating them as a reminder that, in oral performance, pause is essential to the timing of the speaker. To retain much of the poetry inherent in good oral rendition I worked carefully with the syntax of individual sentences, patterning my prose to reflect the cadence of a well-told anecdote recited in English by someone like the elderly people I had interviewed in Crawford County. I also wanted it to reflect the importance of repetition in Navajo poetry, and I found that certain stylistic features like parallelism were easily transposed. That seemed the best way to impart many of the features of Navajo design—with its characteristic tension, balance, and symmetry—without creating any unseemly distortion of written English. Instead of struggling to re-create all the features of a Navajo performance by one orthographic means or another, I tried to preserve something of the sense of the original by replicating certain elements of the native style in a fairly natural idiomatic written English. Although I had never actually witnessed a performance of the entire cycle, as Matthews apparently had, I could apply what I had perceived in English-speaking storytellers to what I had learned about traditional Navajo storytelling. And I could do so without departing too radically from the conventions of printed prose.

After six years of listening to spoken narrative and revising Matthews, I returned to the Southwest in 1979–80. There I found over three dozen manuscripts deposited at the Museum of Northern Arizona in Flagstaff that confirmed much of what I had come to suppose. Compiled earlier in this century by two outstanding ethnographers, Father Berard Haile and Gladys Reichard, they consisted for the most part of transcriptions in what was then essentially the standard Navajo script along with very literal translations of very old narratives. Some of them contained fragments of the creation cycle that I had encountered nowhere else. Some included variants of episodes I had come to consider standard, while others included elaborate embellishments.[15]

Both Reichard and Haile knew Navajo well and had gained the confidence of conservative storytellers and medicine men. Apparently they managed to transcribe the Navajo-language versions of sacred performances, perhaps in actual ceremonial settings in some cases. But in transcribing what they recorded, Reichard and Haile had repeated Matthews's mistake of filling every page with long, dense paragraph-like units that tended to obscure many of the poetic features they might otherwise have preserved. By inspecting those transcriptions I found that there was indeed a poetic style common to Navajo storytelling in general, and that each singer displayed particular stylistic traits unique to himself as well. All of the informants observed certain conventions of syntax, emphasized special details, and relied more or less on a fixed manner of expression at crucial points. But where one used a more formal archaic diction, another would recite in a simpler, more ordinary idiom. Such a difference could be as marked as that which separates Emerson's prose from Poe's verse. Still another would perform almost exclusively in dialogue, actually miming the role of certain characters, while yet another narrated discursively. Given the general uniformity of storytelling techniques, there was still plenty of room for an individual performer to assert a distinct artistic identity, just as any good writer should be able to do.

Furthermore, those manuscripts fully demonstrated that the Navajo creation story was not, strictly speaking, a single story anymore than the Bible is. It turns out to be a kind of boundless, sprawling narrative with a life of its own, so to speak, fixed in its actual limits only by what might be recited during a particular performance. From telling to telling it could change depending upon the singer, the audience, the particular storytelling event, and a very complicated set of ceremonial conditions having to do with illness, departure, return, celebration, or any one of a number of other social occasions. Incidents lifted from one telling might be included in another. Discovering "fragment" after "fragment," I concluded that any written text would have to be arbitrary in its length and in the extent to which dialogue might be included or details added or deleted.[16] If what Matthews wrote out was "incomplete," that was because any particular telling of any particular portion of the story was but a finite manifestation of an entire tradition infinite in the possible ways it could be disclosed. The Navajo creation story was the soul of a distinct Navajo identity that found shape under a particular set of social or ceremonial conditions. It could never be written down in its entirety, just as we could never put the whole story of the Trojan war and its aftermath into a single book, or just as we could never encapsulate the whole Arthurian tradition in one unified, definitive volume or set of volumes.

Suddenly I found myself struggling with the enormity of what I was trying to do. Who was I to decide what to include and what to leave out? I am not even sure I could ever get very many Navajos to agree on a "standard" text. As someone working with print, I would ultimately have to make perfunctory decisions, perhaps according to a set of artistic standards alien to those by which portions of the story are performed. No text could ever fairly represent this fluid, all-encompassing narrative cycle, and unlike a purveyor of an oral tradition, I could never even tell the story a second time. At best a printed work like this one would be to the whole dynamic tradition what a fossilized pawprint would be to some giant prehistoric creature typical of its species and total environment. And as I attempted to complete the project to some degree of satisfaction, I began thinking of the overall implications of just what it was I had been doing. The results, I believe, are worth summarizing.

III

To begin with, no oral tradition should be diminished by referring to it as folk art. To use that label can be condescending and, I believe, inaccurate. By the most cautious means of reckoning such things, the bias of the literate goes back at least as far as the Renaissance; the earliest explorers to the New World apparently brought it with them.[17] Yet the capacity of the collective memory among nonliterate peoples to reach far back into the past is greater than the white man ever supposed. Likewise, the capacity for artistic achievement in oral performances among so-called primitive cultures is as great as the artistic capacity we associate with printed poetry. It should go without saying that people who do not read and write what we call poetry are not necessarily unpoetic in the deeper sense of that term. The voice of the storyteller can be every bit as much of an artistic medium as print can be.

Obviously I was not the first to explore poetry in conditions of preliteracy, nor the first to participate in the process of transforming oral narrative into carefully composed print, any more than was Dennis Tedlock or Washington Matthews. That kind of endeavor has a long history in the New World, beginning with a handful of Spaniards soon after the discovery of America who saw fit for one reason or another to record what native informants were willing to recite to them.[18] It has an even longer history in the Old World. It is actually as old as alphabetical technology itself—traceable as far back as the early cuneiform etchings of the *Gilgamesh Epic* on stone tablets. In fact, the process is really commonplace. For centuries and centuries literate individuals have converted chants, narratives and songs into texts. In some instances the conversions have been highly polished, as with the *Iliad* and the *Odyssey*, perhaps, or with *Beowulf*. In others, there may have been a cycle of repeated redaction, wherein a relatively crude initial transcription was reworked so that it evolved gradually into something finally accepted as literature. I speculate that the various works loosely identified as Arthurian tradition could provide illustrations. So could the entire Faust cycle, where the process actually takes hundreds of years. It could have started with hearsay and unscripted puppet shows or with itinerant dramatic presentations; it could then have progressed through crudely written accounts and the unsophisticated *Faustbuch* to the brilliant *Dr. Faustus* we associate with Marlowe; and it could have culminated in the highly polished printed texts of Goethe and Mann. Or maybe it will never "culminate" as long as someone somewhere thinks that the story will bear yet another retelling, not only in print but on film or videotape or on the stage once again. Consider the tradition of Reynard the Fox or the *Fables Choisies* of La Fontaine traceable back to Aesop and beyond. Chaucer, too, has deep roots in preliterate traditions that actually span many centuries, and to overlook this fact is to ignore a great deal about what poetry actually is and what it means to (and can tell us about) peoples all too easily dismissed as illiterate folk.[19]

Obviously we could look beyond the European evidence on such movement from oral to literate work. We might speculate, for instance, about the fundamental poetic origins of the Sanskrit texts of what we now call the *Mahābhārata* and the *Rāmāyana*, about the very first alphabetical renderings of the Old Testament, and about how the Homeric epics actually came to be written down. Similarly, when their backgrounds are examined, works like *La Chanson de Roland, La Poema de Mia Cid, Der Nibelunge Not* and *Volsung Saga,* or the various printed versions of the English and Scottish ballads demonstrate that not everything that finds its way into our pantheon of printed works suddenly materializes into manuscript form out of an individual writer's imagination or a simple, perfunctory decision on the part of a single scribe to write something down and call it a literary masterpiece. The art of poetry has its roots in speech and song, not in print.

But the connection between oral tradition and written texts is complex. If I did not fully appreciate that complexity when I began this work, I came to realize it as I asked various Navajos for help. While most of them cooperated, many were hostile to the idea of having it written down. More than once I was told that if the old culture was indeed dying out the traditional stories should die with it. Some complained that print was an undesirable medium for stories that should properly be recited; words on a page were silent and unalive. Among individuals from various parts of the reservation there was strong disagreement over what might properly belong in a written-out version and what should be omitted. Likewise, I sensed a general inclination to reject any version that did not reflect the authority of appropriate medicine men, especially among traditional Navajos. And often I sensed a general bewilderment that writing something like this narrative down should matter so much in the first place, especially to a non-Navajo.

If I encountered such reactions to the idea of recording something belonging to an oral tradition, others before me who attempted to do that must have as well. Thus the ways in which speech and print intersect can raise vexing issues. What prompts someone to put such a narrative into writing to begin with? Is the transformation a self-consciously artistic attempt or does it merely represent an impulse to record? How much self-expression occurs in what the scribe writes down? What mutations actually take place when a singer or storyteller's vocal inflections or his physical gestures are replaced with alphabetical symbols? How much of the change is deliberate? To what extent do the social and cultural values of the performer and his audience clash with the assumptions of the scribe and *his* audience?

I know that many critics would insist that such questions are moot. All that should matter is the text as it has survived in its printed form and a reader's capacity to appreciate it at face value, whatever that may be. Perhaps so, but only from one established point of view. I have become all too aware of how much the Navajo creation story means to the people whose lives are fixed in the tradition it defines.

I have heard Navajos talk about *Asdzą́ą́ nádleehé* the Changing Woman or *Naayéé' neizghání* the Monster Slayer the way some of my neighbors discuss characters in a soap opera. In a session that seemed almost like gossip, I once had a long conversation with a middle-aged Navajo man about the philandering ways of *Jóhonaa'éí* the Sun that led to a discussion of marital infidelity. His strong views on the subject were forged by his understanding of the narrative. In more than one talk, I found that Navajos who recalled World War II had gained their grasp of Hitler by associating him with the voracious monster *Yé'iitsoh*. Navajos commonly point to landmarks on the reservation made prominent by episodes in the creation story. This seems especially true of young people, whose enthusiasm for it is as obvious as that of my children for a favorite television show. "There's the dried-up blood of Big Giant," I was told more than once by a Navajo who happened to be riding with me on Interstate 40 between Albuquerque and Gallup or along the unimproved road from Pueblo Pintado to Prewitt, New Mexico. Then he or she would gesture toward the black lava deposits scattered among the western foothills of Mount Taylor. Or as the features of the San Francisco Peaks became more distant south of Cameron or Gray Mountain, Arizona, along U.S. Route 89 on the way from Tuba City to Flagstaff, I would be told, "*Shash* the Bear is up there somewhere. He helped the children of Changing Woman get from California to the reservation." Especially if they had been away for any length of time, studying or working in a city like Phoenix or Albuquerque, my passengers would shift excitedly in their seats as they spoke of sites important to the story. If Navajos relate to their landscape in a special way it is because one version or another of the creation cycle is immediate and familiar to them, whether they are young or old, modern or traditional.

Under special circumstances, it might even be possible to get an old Navajo—maybe even a medicine man—to talk about the deeply sacred dimensions of the story. Throughout the seventies there was a legal controversy over whether a commercial ski facility on the San Francisco Peaks, or *Dook'o'oosłííd*, was to be expanded. Like their neighbors, the Hopis, they objected and agreed to testify against the plan. During the litigation process, attorneys gathered depositions from a number of Navajos, who reluctantly referred to the creation story, insisting that certain episodes therein stood as proof that it would be sacrilegious to install an additional ski lift or pave over any ground in the vicinity of the Arizona Snow Bowl.[20]

Thus, along with an aesthetic application not easily recognized by outsiders, the Navajo creation story has social and religious applications even more difficult for us to apprehend, and its importance transcends the arcane artistic value that an academic literary critic might assign to an established poetic text. Some of the people who finally agreed to cooperate with me did so only because it seemed to them that I might salvage portions in print that would otherwise disappear. That way, they reasoned, the culture was less likely to vanish. To this day the narrative gives individual Navajos an important ethnic identity that elders are anxious to preserve. It defines a meaningful relationship between

each member of the community and between the community and
the whole surrounding cosmos. Such a relationship is still very real
among traditional Navajos, and it is very important. By respecting
the full cultural context of a story like this one, we can know more
about the people who tell it. We might also reach a fuller
understanding of what we call the literary process. And we can
learn to consider the relationship between literate cultures and
preliterate ones. Isolated from its cultural setting, the text alone
may not say in its own behalf all that a reader should know. Or at
least that qualification applies to works that can be associated with
preliterate origins. We have, after all, no guarantee that the
Beowulf manuscript, surviving as it does with manifestly Christian
overtones, does not represent something of a denial of an older
Germanic religion. How can we be sure that some old Anglo-Saxon
storyteller—wary of a scribe's eagerness to put things in
writing—did not choose to hold something back? Nor do we have
any assurance that the text records the full range of social
functions served by that narrative poem about monster slaying and
ring giving. Perhaps somewhere in the process of transforming an
oral performance into a written text some Christian scribe might
even have bowdlerized *Beowulf* the way Matthews seems to have
bowdlerized the Navajo creation story.

A writer recording a verbal artifact in print for the first time
might be the agent of a tyrant knowingly suppressing some
essential features of a despised culture. He or she might be a
bungler who fails to understand and hence fails to safeguard the
spirit of the prototype. He or she might be insensitive to nuances
essential to the original. The print technician might be a
headstrong proponent of an alien set of aesthetic standards,
imposing mutations by reflecting his or her own taste at the
expense of what others may like. That individual might be
someone too sedentary or too provincial to realize that a particular
performance might vary from one region of a linguistic community
to another. Yet the result of converting a narrative to print could
ultimately become known as a literary classic to generations of
readers, indelibly fixed as *the* way a story was told or sung. In
many respects, then, a text is a mute, lifeless artifact—as cold and
silent as a statue or, better still, a potsherd.

Although a text cannot always be trusted to speak fully for the
culture it purports to represent, however, neither should it be
considered exclusively—as the dominant critics of our century

have argued—as a self-sufficient artistic unit, divorced from everything else. Nor should it be evaluated exclusively in terms of any reader's own response. In my research I encountered a direct relationship between the elements of Navajo poetic tradition and the way Navajos conduct their daily lives. The separateness of art that marks our own culture simply does not apply in Navajo culture, and Navajo poetry in particular cannot be isolated from its social context or its moorings in the broader frame of life. Furthermore, art in general is integrated into the Navajo way to an extent that sometimes seems beyond our comprehension. It is no oversimplification to assert that in Navajo society a genuinely poetic recitation must accompany the building of a new house, the treatment of a broken leg or of insomnia, the resolution of a dispute, the unwanted intrusion of a stranger, or the announcement of a pregnancy. Without the appropriate performance, in fact, certain everyday tasks cannot be accomplished.[21]

To this day, then, the Navajo creation story gives individual Navajos (including many illiterate ones) an important ethnic identity. It defines meaningful relationships among members of the community and between the community and the entire cosmos. Such relationships are still very real among traditional Navajos, and very, very important.[22] To try to monitor Navajo poetry without acknowledging the details of its social and cultural matrix is like trying to study law in America without acknowledging the United States Constitution and British constitutional history. Indeed, it would be like trying to study Christianity without knowing the Bible. All of which never should have taken me so by surprise in the first place, any more than I should have been surprised while a graduate student to discover that in studying Dante's *Divina Commedia* I had learned a great deal about early Florentine culture, or that I could scarcely overlook the history of the Protestant movement while I was reading *Paradise Lost*. What does surprise me now, or at least disappoints me a little, is that in this half of the twentieth century we have carried specialization so far.

Somehow we have established an academic system that has encouraged many of us to isolate an individual poem from its fuller context, an object of art from the broader fabric of values and customs that influenced it in one way or another, or a laboratory experiment from its ultimate impact when the theory it generates finds its way to the marketplace. Such a system finally threatens to isolate us from one another. Maybe the isolation has already set in. Maybe that's why scarcely anybody in literary study noticed the very important discoveries of Franz Boas or Washington Matthews as the nineteenth century gave way to the twentieth, or the stimulating ideas of Paul Radin as this century got under way. Perhaps that's why the poetic traditions of the New World went relatively unexplored in spite of attempts of scholars earlier in the twentieth century to broadcast them. Until very recently, ethnographers have gone their way and we in literary study have gone ours, which helps to explain the fate of all too many texts as they find their solitary way into a cultural vacuum.

Such are some of the conclusions I have reached and the questions I now raise as a result of trying to assemble a suitable English version of the Navajo creation cycle. What began innocently enough as an exercise in reinstating a preliterate narrative in an appropriate printed form turned out to be a broader, more speculative enterprise.

Here is my text in any case, along with a set of endnotes, in which I deal in greater detail with some of the issues just raised, and explore others not mentioned thus far: for instance, the age of the narrative, or its origins. I hope that the story can speak for itself as a worthwhile literary experience, of course. I hope, too, that it indicates a dimension of American poetry not yet fully recognized. For readers in general, I would also hold up this text as an example of what may yet be recovered if oral traditions are taken seriously as a source of poetry by more readers. For students of Native American cultures, I would present it at face value as one more document that may yield additional understanding. To the ethnographer, I would submit it as an added means of exploring another culture: perhaps the poetry of a particular people can serve as a useful supplement to conventional field work and to the analysis of ordinary research data.

But I would also hope that the text addresses a set of issues which transcend any one established academic discipline or any one verbal medium such as print. Given the relationship between Navajo poetry and the wider sectors of Navajo life, I would hope, too, that it introduces readers of poetry to Navajo culture. Better still, it might revive interest in the broad set of relationships that link a particular specimen of poetry with its cultural matrix. It might even stimulate readers to consider the likelihood that print is not poetry but merely one medium for that art. Poetry's pervasive presence extends well beyond the printed page and serves to manifest the essence of human communities with or without alphabetical systems. What I would ultimately hope for, then, is that humanists and social scientists might be stimulated to work together to explore the implications of such a likelihood.

IV

As for me, I am only beginning to fathom a few of the emerging implications. Take, for example, some basic terms that are familiar but still manage to elude precise, comfortable definition. To start with, there is the word *poetry* itself. Conventionally, it is understood to mean a certain kind of literature distinct from prose or, say, drama and fiction, even though a given play or novel might be considered poetic. Often *poetry* denotes lines of print that clearly rhyme, show set patterns of rhythm, or are carefully placed on a page in some distinct, deliberate spatial pattern. And when literary critics and scholars speak strictly of poetry they generally remove it from its social context, isolating it from any possibility that it may function to bond individuals in any kind of community or to achieve some other useful social end. If we could grant that the rhyming jingles and cadenced sales pitches common to radio and television commercials might represent poetry in that conventional sense, we might gain some agreement that in this electronic age it might at least function to promulgate some of the values of commerce. But whether or not we can call such verse poetry is open to question.

Regardless, I would rather use the word as a more widely applied generic term, very much as Aristotle uses it in *The Poetics*, where he takes it to mean that art form whose principal medium is language. Other critics use the term that way, too, but not consistently; they might very well turn right around and use the same term in the smaller sense when it suits them to do so. But *poetry*, as I think we should speak of it, might be made to signify more or less what is commonly meant when the term *literature* is used today.[23] To what Aristotle says about poetry being the verbal art, I would add that when I use the term I do not implicitly distinguish between that which is written down or that which is recited or performed. If I wanted to make such a distinction, I would try to forge a more secure definition of the term *text*, or I would speak explicitly of *written poetry* or of either *performed poetry* or *spoken poetry*. Perhaps we are not too far from the time when we will want to subclassify *spoken* or *performed poetry* into two smaller subgroups, distinguishing further between the live performance on the one hand and the electronic performance on the other, familiar to videotapes, films, audiotapes, or discs. I would add, too, that the very existence of performed or written poetry posits the existence of a community including at the very least the poet and his or her immediate audience. In other words, poetry is actually a highly social art, or should be more widely recognized as such by the establishment of literary critics who nowadays sanction "good taste" and fix the boundaries of artistic acceptability. In the broad human scheme, though, poetry exists for those who hear it or read it and not just for its own sake; and it might very well exist to help them attain an important communal sense, consciously or otherwise.

I also now prefer to speak deliberately of something I call *narrative*, which is a work of poetry either written or performed that has as its chief property a plot. It relates events occurring in a given time sequence suggesting some sort of continuum. In that way *narrative* is somewhat distinct from, say, *drama*, which is identifiable by the fact that events are expressed through dialogue. It is also distinct because of the preeminence of someone who knows the story and is obviously telling it. A speaker in a *drama* may narrate in a given dialogue, but his or her presence as the storytelling agent throughout the work is not ordinarily felt.

The term *literature*, I now believe, has outlived its usefulness as a broadly applied generic term and ought to be replaced by the word *poetry*. Too many verbal artifacts already exist by virtue of electronic media for the word to function with very much accuracy anymore. In its conventional application, the term *literature* limits poetic activity to the medium of print and fails to record the origins of poetry in performance. For some, it may imply an unwarranted aesthetic distinction between what is acceptable as art and what is not. If it is to survive usefully at all, perhaps the term can best serve us by being applied more specifically. At least in my printed version of the Navajo creation story, I would propose that the word *literature* be understood as that poetry which exists typographically by virtue of its original composition in some written form, by virtue of a deliberate transcription of something originally performed, or by virtue of any other means of storing it alphabetically. In that sense and in that sense alone, my main purpose has become that of transforming a work of Native American poetry fully into a literary text, and of exploring some of the implications that accompany such a process. By doing that, I mean to reassert what a relatively small number of unheeded critics and scholars have been trying to say for quite some time: American poetry is more variegated and has deeper roots than most of us have suspected.[24]

DINÉ BAHANE'
THE NAVAJO CREATION STORY

PART ONE

The Emergence

One

Of a time long, long ago these things are said.

It is said[1] that at *Tó bił dahisk'id* white arose in the east and was considered day. We now call that spot Place Where the Waters Crossed.

Blue arose in the south. It too was considered day. So the *Níłch'i dine'é*, who already lived there, moved around.[2] We would call them Air-Spirit People in the language spoken today by those who are given the name *Bilagáana*, which means White Man.

In the west yellow arose and showed that evening had come. Then in the north black arose.[3] So the Air-Spirit People lay down and slept.

• • • •

At *Tó bił dahisk'id* where the streams came together water flowed in all directions. One stream flowed to the east. One stream flowed to the south. One stream flowed to the west. One stream flowed to the north.[4]

Along three of those streams there were dwelling places. There were dwelling places along the stream that flowed east. There were dwelling places along the stream that flowed south. There were dwelling places along the stream that flowed west. But along the stream that flowed north there were no dwellings.

• • • •

To the east there was a place called *Dą́ą́'*. In the language of *Bilagáana* the White Man that name means food. To the south there was a place called *Nahodoolá.* It is unknown what that name means. And to the west there was a place called *Lók'aatsoh sikaad.* In the White Man's language that name means Standing Reed. Nothing is said about a place to the north.

Also to the east there was a place called *Ásaa'łáá'ii,* which means One Dish. And also to the south there was a place called *Tó hadziłtił,* which means A Big Amount of Water Coming Out in the language of *Bilagáana.* And also to the west there was a place called *Dził łichíí' bee hooghan.* That name means House of Red Mountain. To the north there are no places that have been given names.

Then there was a place called *Leeyaa hooghan* to the east. In his language the White Man would give it the name Underground House. And there was another place called *Chiiłchintah* to the south. In the language he speaks *Bilagáana* would give it the name Among Aromatic Sumac. And there was another place called *Tsé łichíí' bee hooghan* to the west. In the language of his people the White Man would give it the name House of Red Rock. We hear of no places with names to the north.

•   •   •   •

In those early times dark ants dwelled there. Red ants dwelled there. Dragonflies dwelled there. Yellow beetles dwelled there.

Hard beetles lived there. Stone-carrier beetles lived there. Black beetles lived there. Coyote-dung beetles lived there.

Bats made their homes there. Whitefaced beetles made their homes there. Locusts made their homes there. White locusts made their homes there.[5]

Those are the twelve groups who started life there. We call them *Niłch'idine'é.* In the language of *Bilagáana* the White Man that name means Air-Spirit People. For they are people unlike the five-fingered earth-surface people who come into the world today, live on the ground for a while, die at a ripe old age, and then leave the world. They are people who travel in the air and fly swiftly like the wind and dwell nowhere else but here.

•   •   •   •

Far to the east there was an ocean. Far to the south there was an ocean. Far to the west there was an ocean. And far to the north there was an ocean.

In the ocean to the east dwelled *Tééhoołtsódii*, who was chief of the people there. In the White Man's language he can be called The One That Grabs Things In the Water. In the ocean to the south lived *Táłtł'ááh alééh*. His name means Blue Heron. In the ocean to the west *Ch'ał* made his home and was chief of those people. In the language of the White Man he would be called Frog. And in the ocean to the north dwelled *Ii'ni' jiłgaii*. In the White Man's language that name means Winter Thunder. He was chief among whoever those people were who lived there, it is said.[6]

Two

It is also said that the Air-Spirit People fought among themselves. And this is how it happened. They committed adultery, one with another.[7] Many of the men were to blame, but so were many of the women.

They tried to stop, but they could not help themselves.[8]

Tééhoołtsódii The One That Grabs Things In the Water, who was chief in the east, complained, saying this:

"They must not like it here," he said.

And *Táłtł'ááh álééh* the Blue Heron, who was chief in the south, also complained:

"What they do is wrong," he complained.

Ch'ał the Frog, who was chief in the west, also complained. But he took his complaint directly to the Air-Spirit people, having this to say to them:

"You shall no longer be welcome here where I am chief," is what he said.

"That is what I think of you."

And from his home in the north where he was chief, *Ii'ni' jiłgaii* the Winter Thunder spoke to them also.[9]

"Nor are you welcome here!" he, too, said to them.

"Go away from this land.

"Leave at once!"

• • • •

But the people still could not help it: one with another they
continued to commit adultery. And when they did it yet another
time and then argued with each other again, *Tééhoołtsódii* The
One That Grabs Things In the Water would no longer speak to
them. *Táłtł'ááh álééh* the Blue Heron would no longer speak to
them. Likewise *Ch'ał* the Frog would say nothing to them. And
Ii'ni' jiłgaii the Winter Thunder refused to say anything.

Four days and four nights passed.

Then the same thing happened. Those who lived in the south
repeated their sins: the men with the women and the women with
the men. They committed adultery. And again they quarreled
afterward.

One woman and one man sought *Tééhoołtsódii* The One That
Grabs Things In the Water in the east to try to straighten things
out. But they were driven away. Then they went to *Táłtł'ááh
álééh* the Blue Heron in the south. But they were again driven
away. And they looked for *Ch'ał* the Frog in the west. But they
were driven away again. Finally they went to the north to speak
with *Ii'ni' jiłgaii* the Winter Thunder. He, too, drove them away,
breaking his silence to say this to them:

"None of you shall enter here," he said to them.

"I do not wish to listen to you.

"Go away, and keep on going!"

• • • •

That night the people held a council at *Nahodoolá* in the south.
But they could not agree on anything. On and on they quarreled,
until white arose in the east and it was again day. *Tééhoołtsódii*
The One That Grabs Things In the Water then spoke to them:

"Everywhere in this world you bring disorder," he said to them.

"So we do not want you here.

"Find some other place to live."

But the people did not leave right away. For four nights the
women talked and squabbled, each blaming the other for what had
happened. And for four nights the men squabbled and talked. They,
too, blamed one another.

At the end of the fourth night as they were at last about to end
their meeting, they all noticed something white in the east. They

also saw it in the south. It appeared in the west, too. And in the north it also appeared.

It looked like an endless chain of white mountains. They saw it on all sides. It surrounded them, and they noticed that it was closing in on them rapidly. It was a high, insurmountable wall of water! And it was flowing in on them from all directions, so that they could escape neither to the east nor to the west; neither to the south nor to the north could they escape.

So, having nowhere else to go, they took flight. Into the air they went. Higher and higher they soared, it is said.

Three

It is also said that they circled upward until they reached the smooth, hard shell of the sky overhead.[10] When they could go no higher they looked down and saw that water now covered everything. They had nowhere to land either above or below.

Suddenly someone with a blue head appeared and called to them:

"Here," he called to them.

"Come this way.

"Here to the east there is a hole!"

They found that hole and entered. One by one they filed through to the other side of the sky. And that is how they reached the surface of the second world.

•　•　•　•

The blue-headed creature was a member of the Swallow People. It was they who lived up there.

While the first world had been red, this world was blue. The swallows lived in blue houses, which lay scattered across a broad, blue plain. Each blue house was cone-shaped; each tapered toward the top where there was a blue entry hole.

At first the Swallow People gathered around the newcomers and watched them silently. Nobody from either group said anything to any member of the other. Finally, when darkness came and the exiled Air-Spirit People made camp for the night, the blue swallows left.

In the morning the insect people from the world below decided that someone should explore this new world. So they sent a plain locust and a white locust to the east, instructing them to look for people like themselves.

Two days came and went before the locusts returned. They said that they had traveled for a full day. And as darkness fell they reached what must have been the end of the world. For they came upon the rim of a great cliff that rose out of an abyss whose bottom could not be seen. Both coming and going, they said, they found no people, no plants, no rivers, no mountains. They found nothing but bare, blue, level ground.

Next the two messengers were sent south to explore. Again, two days came and went while they were gone. And they again reported that after traveling for a full day they reached the end of the world. And they reported again that neither in going nor in coming back could they find people or plants, mountains or rivers.

They were then sent to the west. And after that they were sent to the north. Both times they were gone for two days, and they reported each time that they reached the end of the world after traveling for a full day. They also reported that again they could find neither people nor plants and neither mountains nor rivers.

To the others they had only this to say:

"It seems that we are in the center of a vast, blue plain," was all that they could say.

"Wherever we went in this world we could find neither company nor food; neither rivers nor mountains could we find."

After the scouts had returned from their fourth trip, the Swallow People visited the camp of the newcomers. And they asked why they had sent someone to the east to explore.

This is what the insect people from the lower world replied:

"We sent them out to see what was in the land," they replied.

"We sent them out to see if there were people here like ourselves."

Then the swallows asked this:

"What did your scouts tell you?" they asked.

To which the newcomers replied this way:

"They told us that they reached the end of the world after traveling for a full day," they replied.

"They told us that wherever they went in this world they could find neither people nor plants. Neither rivers nor mountains could they find."

The swallows then asked why the insect people had sent their scouts to the south. And they were told that the locusts were sent south to see what was in the land. And when the swallows asked why scouts were sent to the west, they were told again that the locusts were to see what they could find in this blue world. Which is what they were told when they asked why scouts were sent to the north.

To all of which the Swallow People then had this to say:

"Your couriers spoke the truth," they then said.

"But their trips were not necessary.

"Had you asked us what the land contained, we would have told you.

"Had you asked us where this world ended, we would have told you.

"We could have saved you all that time and all that trouble.

"Until you arrived here, no one besides us has ever lived in this world. We are the only ones living here."

The newcomers then had this suggestion to make to the swallows:

"You are like us in many ways," they suggested.

"You understand our language.

"Like us you have legs; like us you have bodies; like us you have wings; like us you have heads.

"Why can't we become friends?"

To which the swallows replied:

"Let it be as you say," they replied.

"You are welcome here among us."

So it was that both sets of people began to treat each other as members of one tribe. They mingled one among the other and called each other by the familiar names. They called each other grandparent and grandchild, brother and sister; they called each other father and son, mother and daughter.

For twenty-three days they all lived together in harmony. But on the night of the twenty-fourth day, one of the strangers became too free with the wife of the swallow chief.

Next morning, when he found out what had happened the night before, the chief had this to say to the strangers:

"We welcomed you here among us," was what he had to say to them.

"We treated you as friends and as kin.

"And this is how you return our kindness!

"No doubt you were driven from the world below for just such disorderly acts.

"Well, you must leave this world, too; we will have you here no longer.

"Anyhow, this is a bad land. There is not enough food for all of us.

"People are dying here every day from hunger. Even if we allowed you to stay, you could not live here very long."

When they heard the swallow chief's words, the locusts took flight. And all the others followed. Having nowhere else to go, they flew skyward.

Into the air they went. Higher and higher they soared. They circled upward until they reached the smooth, hard shell of the sky overhead, it is said.

Four

It is also said that like the sky of the world below, this sky had a smooth, hard shell. And like the sky of the world below this one seemed to have no opening. When the insect people reached it they flew around and around, having nowhere to land either above or below.

But as they circled, they noticed a white face peering at them. This was the face of *Nílch'i*. In the language of *Bilagáana* the White Man he would be called Wind. And they heard him cry to them:

"Here!" he cried.

"Here to the south you will find an opening.

"Come this way."

So off they flew to the south, and soon they found a slit in the sky slanting upward in a southerly direction. One by one they flew through it to the other side. And that is how they reached the surface of the third world.

•　•　•　•

While the second world had been blue, this world was yellow. Here the exiles found no one but Yellow Grasshopper People, who lived in yellow holes in the ground along the banks of a river which flowed east through their yellow land.

At first the Yellow Grasshopper People said nothing. They gathered silently around the newcomers and stared at them. Nobody from either group spoke to anyone from the other. And when darkness finally came and the people from the world below made their camp, the grasshoppers left.

In the morning the wanderers sent out the same two locusts who had explored the second world.

First they flew to the east where they were gone for two days altogether. Then they flew to the south where they were gone for two more days. Then they flew to the west, where they were gone for another two days. And they flew to the north where for two additional days they were gone. Each time they returned with the same report.

For a full day they had journeyed, until by nightfall they arrived at the rim of a cliff that rose from some unseen place far, far below. And neither in going forth nor in coming back could they find people or plants, mountains or waters. The river along whose banks the Grasshopper People lived soon tapered off toward the east until it was a dry, narrow gully. Otherwise there was nothing to see in this world except flat, yellow countryside and the yellow grasshoppers who lived on it.

When the messengers returned from their fourth journey the two great chiefs of the Grasshopper People came to visit. And they asked the newcomers why they had someone fly to the east and to the west, to the south and to the north.

To which the insect people from the world below replied:

"We sent them to see what was in the land," they replied.

"We sent them to see if they could find people like ourselves."

Then the grasshopper chiefs asked:

"And what did they find?" they asked.

Answered the newcomers:

"They found nothing but the bare land," they answered.

"They found nothing but the cliffs that marked the edge of this world.

"They found no plants and no people. They found no mountains and no rivers.

"Even the river along whose banks your people live here in the center of this world tapers off until it is only a dry, narrow gully."

Replied the grasshopper chiefs then:

"You might have first asked us what the land contains," they replied.

"We could have saved your messengers all that trouble.

"We could have told you that there is nothing in this land but what you see right here.

"We have lived here for a long time, but we have seen nothing that you have not seen. And we have seen no other people until you came."

The insect people from the world below then spoke to the grasshopper chiefs as they had spoken to the Swallow People in the second world, saying these things to them:

"Come to think of it, you are somewhat like us," they said to them.

"Like us you have heads. Like us you have wings. Like us you have bodies. Like us you have legs.

"You even speak the way we speak.

"Perhaps we can join you here."

The grasshoppers consented, and the two groups quickly began to mingle. They embraced each other, and soon they were using the names of family and kin together. They called each other mother and daughter, father and son, brother and sister, grandparent and grandchild. It was as if they were all of the same tribe.

As before, all went well for twenty-three days. But as before, on the night of the twenty-fourth, one of the newcomers treated the chief of the grasshoppers exactly as the swallow chief had been treated in the second world.

When he discovered how he had been wronged, the grasshopper chief spoke this way to the insect people:

"No doubt you were sent away from the world below for such transgressions!" is how he spoke.

"No doubt you bring disorder wherever you go. No doubt you lack intelligence.

"Well, here too you shall drink no more of our water. Here too you shall eat no more of our food. Here too you shall breathe no more of our air.

"Get out of here!"

So the insect people took flight again. And again they circled round and round into the sky until they arrived at the smooth, hard shell of its outer crust, it is said.[11]

Five

It is also said that they again had to circle around for quite some time, looking in vain for some way to get through the sky overhead. Finally they heard a voice bidding them fly to the west and look there. And they noticed a red head peering at them. The voice they heard and the head they saw belonged to *Nílch'i łichíí'*. In the language of *Bilagáana* the White Man he would bear the name Red Wind.

Doing as they were told they found a passage which twisted around through the sky's other surface like the tendril of a vine. It had been made this way by the wind. They flew into it and wound their way to the other side. And that is how they reached the surface of the fourth world.

Four of the grasshoppers had come with them. One was white. One was blue. One was yellow. And one was black. To this very day, in fact, we have grasshoppers of those four colors among us.

•   •   •   •

The surface of the fourth world was unlike the surface of any of the lower worlds. For it was a mixture of black and white. The sky above was alternately white, blue, yellow, and black, just as it had been in the worlds below. But here the colors were of a different duration.

In the first world each color lasted for about the same length of time each day. In the second world the blue and the black lasted just a little longer than the white and the yellow. But here in the fourth world there was white and yellow for scarcely any time, so long did the blue and black remain in the sky. As yet there was no sun and no moon; as yet there were no stars.

When they arrived on the surface of the fourth world, the exiles from the lower worlds saw no living thing. But they did observe four great snow-covered peaks along the horizon around them. One peak lay to the east. One peak lay to the south. One peak lay likewise to the west. And to the north there was one peak.

The insect people sent two scouts to the east, who returned at the end of two days. Those two said that they had not been able to reach the eastern mountain after an entire day's flight. And although they had traveled far indeed they could see no living creature. Neither track nor trail could they see; not one sight of life were they able to detect.

Two scouts were then sent to the south. And when these two returned at the end of two full days they reported that after an entire day's flight they managed to reach a low range of mountains on this side of the great peak which lay in that direction.

They too had traveled very far. They too could see no living creature. But they did observe two different kinds of tracks the likes of which they had never seen before. They described them carefully, and from that description the tracks seemed to resemble those made these days in our own world by deer and turkey.

Two scouts were sent next to the west. And after two full days they returned, reporting that they could by no means reach the great peak which lay in that direction, no matter how fast they could fly in a single day and no matter how far. Neither in going forth nor in returning could they see any living creature. Not one sign of life were they able to see.

Finally, two scouts were sent to explore the land that lay to the north. And when they returned they had a different story to tell. For they reported that they had found a strange race unlike any other. These were people who cut their hair square in front. They were people who lived in houses in the ground. They were people who cultivated the soil so that things grew therein. They were now harvesting what they had planted, and they gave the couriers food to eat.[12]

It was now evident to the newcomers that the fourth world was larger than any of the worlds below.

•   •   •   •

On the very next day, two members of the newly found race came to the camp of the exiles. They were called *Kiis'áanii*, they said, which in the language of *Bilagáana* the White Man means People Who Live in Upright Houses. And they wished to invite the exiles to visit their village.

On the way they came to a stream which was red. The *Kiis'áanii* warned their guests not to wade through it. Otherwise the water would injure the feet of the newcomers. Instead they showed the insect people a square raft made of four logs. One log was of white pine. One log was of blue spruce. One log was of yellow pine. And one log was of black spruce. On this raft they all crossed to the opposite bank, where the people who had arrived from the third world visited the homes of the people who dwelled here in the fourth world.

The exiles were given corn and pumpkins to eat. And they were asked by their new friends to stay. For quite some time, in fact, they stayed in the village of the upright houses. There they lived well on the food that the *Kiis'áanii* gave them. eventually they all lived together like the people of one tribe. Soon the two groups were using the names of family and kin between themselves. They called each other father and son, mother and daughter, grandparent and grandchild, brother and sister.

The land of the *Kiis'áanii* was a dry land. It had neither rain nor snow and there was little water to be found. But the people who had been dwelling there knew how to irrigate the soil to make things grow, and they taught the newcomers to do so.

Twenty-three days came and went, and twenty-three nights passed and all was well. And on the twenty-fourth night the exiles held a council meeting. They talked quietly among themselves, and they resolved to mend their ways and to do nothing unintelligent that would create disorder. This was a good world, and the wandering insect people meant to stay here, it is said.

Six

It is also said that late in the autumn of that year the newcomers heard a distant voice calling to them from far in the east.

They listened and waited, listened and waited. Until soon they heard the voice again, nearer and louder than before. They continued to listen and wait, listen and wait, until they heard the voice a third time, all the nearer and all the louder.

Continuing to listen, they heard the voice again, even louder than the last time, and so close now that it seemed directly upon them.

A moment later they found themselves standing among four mysterious beings. They had never seen such creatures anywhere before. For they were looking at those who would eventually become known as *Haashch'ééh dine'é*.[13]

In the language of *Bilagáana* the White Man, that name means Holy People. For they are people unlike the earth-surface people who come into the world today, live on the ground for a while, die at a ripe old age, and then move on. These are intelligent people who can perform magic. They do not know the pain of being mortal. They are people who can travel far by following the path of the rainbow. And they can travel swiftly by following the path of the sunray. They can make the winds and the thunderbolts work for them so that the earth is theirs to control when they so wish.

The people who were then living on the surface of the fourth world were looking upon *Bits'íís łigaii*, which name means White Body. He is the one that the Navajo people who live in our own world would eventually call *Haashch'éélti'í*, which in today's language means Talking God.

And they were looking upon *Bits'íís dootł'izh*. That name means Blue Body. He is the one that the Navajo people in our own world would eventually come to know as *Tó neinilí*, which means Water Sprinkler.

And they were looking upon *Bits'íís łitsoii*, or Yellow Body. He is the one that the Navajo people today call *Hashch'éoghan*. Nobody can be sure what that name means in today's language. Some say it means Calling God; some say that it means House God; and some say that it means Growling God.

And they were looking upon *Bits'íís łizhin*. In the White Man's language that name means Black Body. He is the one that the Navajo people living in this world would eventually come to know as *Haashch'ééshzhiní*, which means Black God. Sometimes he is also called the God of Fire.

Without speaking the Holy People made signs to those who were gathered there, as if to give them instructions. But the exiles could not understand their gestures. So they stood by helplessly and watched.

And after the gods had left, the people talked about that mysterious visit for the rest of that day and all night long, trying to determine what it meant.

• • • •

As for the gods, they repeated their visit four days in a row. But on the fourth day, *Bits'íís łizhin* the Black Body remained after the other three departed. And when he was alone with the onlookers, he spoke to them in their own language. This is what he said:

"You do not seem to understand the Holy People," he said.

"So I will explain what they want you to know.

"They want more people to be created in this world. But they want intelligent people, created in their likeness, not in yours.

"You have bodies like theirs, true enough.

"But you have the teeth of beasts! You have the mouths of beasts! You have the feet of beasts! You have the claws of beasts!

"The new creatures are to have hands like ours. They are to have feet like ours. They are to have mouths like ours and teeth like ours. They must learn to think ahead, as we do.

"What is more, you are unclean!

"You smell bad.

"So you are instructed to cleanse yourselves before we return twelve days from now."

That is what *Bits'íís łizhin* the Black Body said to the insect people who had emerged from the first world to the second, from the second world to the third, and from the third world to the fourth world where they now lived.

• • • •

Accordingly, on the morning of the twelfth day the people bathed carefully. The women dried themselves with yellow corn meal. The men dried themselves with white corn meal.

Soon after they had bathed, they again heard the distant voice coming from far in the east.

They listened and waited as before, listened and waited. Until soon they heard the voice as before, nearer and louder this time.

They continued to listen and wait, listen and wait, until they heard the voice a third time as before, all the nearer and all the louder.

Continuing to listen as before, they heard the voice again, even louder than the last time, and so close now that it seemed directly upon them, exactly as it had seemed before. And as before they found themselves standing among the same four *Haashch'ééh dine'é*, or Holy People as *Bilagáana* the White Man might wish to call them.

Bits'íís dootl'izh the Blue Body and *Bits'íís lizhin* the Black Body each carried a sacred buckskin.[14] *Bits'íís ligaii* the White Body carried two ears of corn.

One ear of corn was yellow. The other ear was white. Each ear was completely covered at the end with grains, just as sacred ears of corn are covered in our own world now.

Proceeding silently, the gods laid one buckskin on the ground, careful that its head faced the west. Upon this skin they placed the two ears of corn, being just as careful that the tips of each pointed east. Over the corn they spread the other buckskin, making sure that its head faced east.

Under the white ear they put the feather of a white eagle.

And under the yellow ear they put the feather of a yellow eagle.

Then they told the onlooking people to stand at a distance.

So that the wind could enter.

Then from the east *Nílch'i ligai* the White Wind blew between the buckskins. And while the wind thus blew, each of the Holy People came and walked four times around the objects they had placed so carefully on the ground.

As they walked, the eagle feathers, whose tips protruded slightly from between the two buckskins, moved slightly.

Just slightly.

So that only those who watched carefully were able to notice.

And when the Holy People had finished walking, they lifted the topmost buckskin.

And lo! the ears of corn had disappeared.

In their place there lay a man and there lay a woman.[15]

•　•　•　•

The white ear of corn had been transformed into our most ancient male ancestor. And the yellow ear of corn had been transformed into our most ancient female ancestor.

It was the wind that had given them life: the very wind that gives us our breath as we go about our daily affairs here in the world we ourselves live in!

When this wind ceases to blow inside of us, we become speechless. Then we die.

In the skin at the tips of our fingers we can see the trail of that life-giving wind.

Look carefully at your own fingertips.

There you will see where the wind blew when it created your most ancient ancestors out of two ears of corn, it is said.[16]

Seven

It is also said that the two people created thus were *Áłtsé hastiin* and *Áłtsé asdzą́ą́*. In the language of *Bilagáana* the White Man they would be called First Man and First Woman.

The gods told the people to build a shelter of brushwood for the couple. And as soon as their home was ready, *Áłtsé hastiin* the First Man and *Áłtsé asdzą́ą́* the First Woman entered their home. And the Holy People had this to say to them:

"Live here together," they said to them.

"Live here as husband and wife."

At the end of four days, *Áłtsé asdzą́ą́* the First Woman gave birth to twins.[17] But they were neither entirely male nor entirely female. They were what the Navajo people call *nádleeh*, which in the language of *Bilagáana* means hermaphrodite.

Four days later a second set of twins was born. But this time one of them was entirely male, while the other was entirely female. These two reached full maturity in four additional days, and from then on they lived with one another as husband and wife.

Four more days passed, and *Áłtsé asdzą́ą́* the First Woman bore yet another set of twins. Like the set born just before them, they too were either entirely female or entirely male. And they too reached maturity in four days and then resolved to live together as husband and wife.

Two additional sets of twins were born to *Áłtsé asdzą́ą́* the First

Woman, so that she and her husband *Áłtsé hastiin* had five pairs of twins all told. Among those five pairs, only the first were neither entirely male nor entirely female. Only the first did not resolve to live together as husband and wife after becoming fully mature in four days.

Four days after the last pair of twins was born, *Haashch'ééh dine'é* the Holy People came again. They took *Áłtsé asdzą́ą́* the First Woman and *Áłtsé hastiin* the First Man away with them to their own dwelling place on the eastern mountain and kept them there for four days. Then they returned the couple to the brushwood shelter which was their home. In turn each set of twins was likewise taken by the Holy People to their dwelling place on the eastern mountain and kept there for four days.[18]

•   •   •   •

Soon after *Áłtsé hastiin* and *Áłtsé asdzą́ą́* the First Man and the First Woman and all of their children had gone to the eastern mountain and returned, it was observed that they occasionally wore masks something like the masks worn by *Haashch'éélti'í* the Talking God and by *Hashch'éoghan* who is sometimes called House God and sometimes given the name Calling God or Growling God.

Whenever these masks were worn, those who wore them prayed for the good things and the necessary things. They prayed for such things as the steady rain, or for things like abundant crops.

But it also seems that during their visit to the eastern mountain the people learned terrible secrets, too. For witches also possess masks like these, and they too marry their close relatives.

As for the four sets of brothers and sisters who had at first chosen to live together as husband and wife, when they returned from the eastern mountain they separated. They were now ashamed, it seems, of their incest.

However, they kept their shameful marriages a secret and then remarried. The brothers married women of the *Hadahoniye'dine'é* or Mirage People as they would now be called. And the sisters married men of the same people. They also chose to keep secret the mysteries they had learned on the eastern mountain.

•   •   •   •

Áłtsé asdzáá the First Woman was glad that her children had married among *Hadahoniye'dine'é* the Mirage People. For now their incest would stop. But she grew worried when she realized how easily they had renounced their first marriages, even if those marriages were shameful.

Marriage is useful, thought she. For there is a lot of work to be done. The people must hunt. They must plant food and they must harvest it. They must gather wood. They must prepare what they eat. It is best that they marry and divide the work between them.[19]

By marrying, thought *Áłtsé asdzáá* the First Woman, the people can also be assured of having children. But their marriages should last, so that harmony can prevail. It had been all too easy for a man or a woman to commit adultery. A woman could leave her husband all too easily; all too easily a husband could leave his wife.

As she thought of it, she resolved that she would take these matters into her own hands. It ought to be more difficult for a man to leave his wife once he has married her. It should also be difficult for a woman to forsake her husband once she has married him. There should be a bond between man and woman. There should be a bond between woman and man. That bond should be strong; it should endure.

So thought *Áłtsé asdzáá* the First Woman. And so she would continue to think until she could determine what might be done.

•　　•　　•　　•

Meanwhile, the descendants of *Áłtsé hastiin* the First Man and *Áłtsé asdzáá* the First Woman established a great farm. They built a dam and dug a wide irrigation canal. They feared that the *Kiis'áanii* might destroy their dam, though, or that they might injure the crops. So they put one of the nonchildbearing *nádleeh* in charge of the dam. And they bid the other twin guard the lower end of the field.

With nothing else to do, the hermaphrodite twin who watched the dam invented pottery. First he made a plate. Then he made a bowl. Then he made a ladle. And the people all admired the work he had done. They knew at once how useful those implements would be.[20]

As for the twin who stood guard over the lower field, he too had time enough and skill enough to design something useful. So he invented the wicker bottle. The people all admired what he had done, too, for they could see immediately how useful that implement would be.

Others among the people made scythes out of split cottonwood boards which they used to clear the land. Still others made hoes from the shoulder blades of deer. And others made axes out of stone. From the *Kiis'áanii* the people got seeds. And so they flourished as people who farmed the earth.

Once they killed a young deer, and somebody among them had the idea of making a mask out of the skin of its head. Then they could approach a live deer disguised as one of them when they hunted. That way they could catch a full supply of game. But when they tried to make such a mask they failed. Somehow they could not get it to fit their own faces.

They argued about how that might properly be done. For four days, it seems, they could do nothing else or discuss anything else. Try as they might, they could not succeed. Try as they might, they could not agree.

Then, on the morning of the fifth day they heard a voice calling to them in the distance. From far to the east it came.

They listened and waited, listened and waited. Until they heard the voice again, just as they had heard it before. They continued to listen and wait, listen and wait, until they heard the voice a third time, all the nearer and all the louder.

Continuing to listen, they heard the voice again, even louder than the last time, and so close now that it seemed directly upon them.

It was the *Haashch'ééh dine'é* who had been calling. It was *Bits'íís łigaii* the White Body. It was *Bits'íís dootł'izh* the Blue Body. It was *Bits'íís łitsoii* the Yellow Body. And it was *Bits'íís łizhin* the Black Body. And when they appeared they were seen carrying heads of deer and antelope along with them.

Then they showed the people how to make the masks they wished to have. They showed the people how to fit them. They showed them how to cut the eye holes and how to imitate the motions of deer. To the people they explained all the mysteries of those fine animals.[21]

Next day the hunters went out and killed a few deer. From these they made more masks. And with the newly made masks they were able to add several more men to the party of hunters. From then on the people had plenty of meat. Moreover, they cured the hides and made garments out of them. So everyone had warm clothing to wear, it is said.

Eight

It is also said that while all of those things were happening, *Áłtsé asdzą́ą́* the First Woman had continued to think about how she might strengthen the bond between men and women. And after considering the matter carefully, she came up with a plan.[22]

Men and women should have the power to attract each other for a lifetime, thought she. So she fashioned a penis of turquoise. Then she rubbed loose cuticle from a woman's breast and mixed it with yucca fruit, which she put inside the turquoise penis. And she named the organ *'aziz*.

Next she made a vagina of white shell. Into the vagina she placed a clitoris of red shell. Then she rubbed loose cuticle from a man's breast and mixed it with yucca fruit, which she placed in the clitoris. And she combined herbs with various kinds of water and placed that mixture deep inside the vagina. That way pregnancy would occur. She then named the organ *ajóózh*.

She placed the vagina on the ground. Next to it she placed the penis. Then she blew medicine upon both of them from her mouth. And she spoke these words to the penis:

"Now think!" she said to it.

"Think about the one to your left."

The penis did as it was told, and its mind extended a great distance. Whereupon *Áłtsé asdzą́ą́* the First Woman said this to the vagina:

"You think, too!" she said to it.

"Think about the one to your right."

The vagina also extended. But it extended only half the distance the penis had gone. Then it returned to the place where it first lay. That is why a woman's longing does not travel as far as a man's.

And to both of them *Áłtsé asdzą́ą́* the First Woman said these words:

"Now shout!" she said to the two of them together.

"Shout, both of you.

"Penis, shout so that your partner can feel the might of your voice.

"Vagina, shout so that your partner can feel the touch of your voice."

Penis shouted very loud. But vagina had only a weak voice. So *Áłtsé asdzą́ą́* the First Woman spoke to them again:

"Do it once more," she said to them.

"Touch one another and shout once more.

"Penis, shout again so that your partner can feel it.

"Vagina, shout again so that your partner can feel it."

So they both tried again. This time, though, penis could not shout as loudly as he had the first time. Vagina, however, had a good voice this time.

Áłtsé asdzą́ą́ the First Woman was satisfied with her work. Now men and women would learn to care for each other. They would be eager to have children. They would share the labor evenly. And they would each more willingly tend to the other's needs.

She commanded that upon reaching a certain age, every girl and every boy should be given such a vagina and such a penis as those she had fashioned: a penis for the male and a vagina for the female.

•　　•　　•　　•

One day soon thereafter, while the elders were giving a penis to a boy who had come of age, and while they were giving a vagina to a girl who had come of age, the people saw the sky swooping down. It seemed to want to embrace the earth. And they saw the earth likewise looming up as if to meet the sky.

For a moment they came in contact. The sky touched the earth and the earth touched the sky. And just then, at exactly the spot where the sky and the earth had met, *Mą'ii* the Coyote sprung out of the ground.[23] And *Nahashch'id* the Badger sprung out of the ground.

It is our belief that *Mą'ii* the Coyote and *Nahashch'id* the Badger are children of the sky. Coyote came forth first, which leads us to suppose that he is Badger's older brother.

Nahashch'id the Badger began sniffing around the top of the hole that led down to the lower world. He finally disappeared into it and was not seen again for a long time.

Mą'ii the Coyote saw at once that people lived nearby. So he

came immediately to their village. He arrived among them just as
the boy was receiving his penis, and just as the girl was acquiring
her vagina.

As the male organ was being placed, *Mą'ii* the Coyote pulled
some of his beard away from his face and blew on it. Then he
placed it between the legs of the boy.[24] And this is what he
had to say:

"It looks pretty nice there between that boy's legs," he said.

"But I can make it look nicer."

And as the female organ was being placed, *Mą'ii* the Coyote
pulled more of his whiskers out of his chin and blew on them.
Then he put them between the legs of the girl. And this is what he
said:

"As nice as it looks there between that girl's legs, it can be made
to look even nicer," he said.

"Watch and see if you don't think so."

Everyone agreed. Coyote had made the boy and the girl more
attractive. But *Áłtsé asdzą́ą́* the First Woman now feared that
women and men would be too easily drawn to one another.

So she ordered the boy to cover himself at once. And she ordered
the girl to cover herself also. She ordered them to dress that way in
the company of others.

Likewise, she ordered all the people to cover themselves in the
company of others. Which is why the people have clad themselves
modestly ever since, it is said.

Nine

It is also said that eight winters passed since the people had
migrated from the third world. And for eight years they prospered,
acting intelligently and doing nothing to create disorder.

Áłtsé hastiin the First Man had become chief of all who lived in
that world, except for the *Kiis'áanii*. As their chief he taught the
people the names of the four mountains which rose in the distance
and marked the four cardinal points.[25]

Sisnaajiní lay to the east, he taught them. Exactly what that

name means is unknown, but now the mountain is called Sierra
Blanca Peak. *Tsoodził* lay to the south, he taught them. In the
language of *Bilagáana* that peak is called Mount Taylor. To the
west lay *Dook'o'oosłííd*, he taught them, which means, Never Has
Thawed on Top; but that mountain is now called San Francisco
Peak by the White Man. And to the north lay *Dibé nitsaa*, which
in English means Big Mountain Sheep.

   Those four names have been kept in the present Navajo world,
too. And *Áłtsé hastiin* the First Man taught the people that
Haashch'ééh dine'é the Holy People lived in those mountains. He
explained to them that they were a different sort of people. For
they were intelligent people who could perform magic. They could
travel swiftly and they could travel far. They know how to ride the
sunbeam and the light ray, and they knew how to follow the path
of the rainbow. They felt no pain, and nothing in any world could
change the way they were.

So it was that *Áłtsé hastiin* the First Man taught the people the
names of things and the ways of the gods. So it was that he taught
them what to do and what not to do. So it was that the people grew
to respect him. And so it was that they came to obey him.

●　　●　　●　　●

Áłtsé hastiin the First Man became a great hunter in the fourth
world. So he was able to provide his wife *Áłtsé asdzą́ą́* the First
Woman with plenty to eat.

As a result, she grew very fat.

Now one day he brought home a fine, fleshy deer.

His wife boiled some of it, and together they had themselves a
hearty meal. When she had finished eating, *Áłtsé asdzą́ą́* the First
Woman wiped her greasy hands on her sheath.

She belched deeply. And she had this to say:

"Thank you *shijóózh* my vagina," she said.

"Thank you for that delicious dinner."

To which *Áłtsé hastiin* the First Man replied this way:

"Why do you say that?" he replied.

"Why not thank me?

"Was it not I who killed the deer whose flesh you have just
feasted on?

"Was it not I who carried it here for you to eat?

"Was it not I who skinned it?

"Who made it ready for you to boil?

"Is *nijóózh* your vagina the great hunter, that you should thank it and not me?"

To which *Áłtsé asdzą́ą́* offered this answer:

"As a matter of fact, she is," offered she.

"In a manner of speaking it is *jóósh* the vagina who hunts.

"Were it not for *jóósh* you would not have killed that deer.

"Were it not for her you would not have carried it here.

"You would not have skinned it.

"You lazy men would do nothing around here were it not for *jóósh*.

"In truth, *jóósh* the vagina does all the work around here."

To which *Áłtsé hastiin* the First Man had this to say:

"Then perhaps you women think you can live without us men," he said.

"Maybe you need only *nihijóózh* your vaginas.

"*Nihijóózh* your great huntresses.

"*Nihijóózh* your tireless workers."

Quickly came this reply from *Áłtsé asdzą́ą́* the First Woman:

"All things do not exist thanks alone to you," she replied quickly. "We could live alone if we wanted to.

"We are the ones who till the fields, after all.

"We are the ones who gather the food, after all.

"We can live on the crops that we grow. We can live on the seeds that we gather. We can live on the berries that we find and on the fruits that we bring.[26]

"Things exist thanks as much to us as to you. We have no need of you men."

On and on they argued that way, *Áłtsé hastiin* the First Man permitting himself to grow angrier and angrier with each reply his wife made; *Áłtsé asdzą́ą́* the First Woman permitting herself to grow more and more vexing with each reply she offered.

Until at length he stalked out of the shelter where they had lived together as man and wife. Out he stalked and jumped across the fire in front of their home, where he remained all that night with only his anger to keep him company.[27]

• • • •

Early next morning he walked to the center of the village and called loudly so that everyone could hear:[28]

"All you men!" he called.

"Gather round me.

"I wish to speak to you.

"I wish to instruct you.

"As for the women, let them stay where they are.

"Not one woman do I wish to see.

"I have nothing to say to any woman around here."

Soon all the males were assembled around *Áłtsé hastiin* the First Man. And he repeated to them what his wife had said the previous night. Then he told the men this:

"The women think they can live without us," he told the men. "They think that things can continue to exist thanks as much to them as to us.

"Well, let us see if all that is true.

"Let us see if they can hunt and till the fields, with only *jóósh* the vagina to help them. Let us see what sort of living they can make, with only *jóósh* to assist them.

"We will cross the stream and live apart from them. And from *jóósh*.

"We will keep the raft with us on our side of the water, so that even when they long for us they may not have us.

"If they seek companionship, let them seek it with *jóósh* the vagina.

"And if *jóósh* wishes to shout, let her shout to herself.

"Let us see what *jóósh* the vagina brings forth when she hears the sound of her own voice. We will see what happens when they try to sustain life without help from us."

●   ●   ●   ●

So it was that all the men gathered at the river.

Áłtsé hastiin even summoned the twins *nádleeh*, who were neither entirely male nor entirely female. They were covered with meal when they arrived, for they had been grinding corn.

This is what *Áłtsé hastiin* the First Man asked them:

"What do you have that you have made all by yourselves?" he asked them.

"What is there that you have made without the help of any woman?"

Answered the twins *nádleeh*, who were no more female than they were male:

"We each have a set of grinding stones that we have made," they answered.

"We have cups and bowls. We have baskets and other utensils.

"We have made those things by ourselves with the help of no woman."[29]

To which *Áłtsé hastiin* the First Man had this to say:

"Go fetch those things and bring them here; for you must come with us," he said.

"You are as much men as you are women. And you have made those things with no woman's help.

"Let the women learn what it means to live without the help of any man.

"Let them learn to live without anything that has been made by someone who is even part of a man."

•   •   •   •

So the men ferried across the river, taking the nonchildbearing twins *nádleeh* with them. They crossed over to the north bank. And with them they carried their stone axes, their wooden scythes, their hoes of bone, and the utensils that the twins had invented. In fact, they took anything that they had made themselves.

After they had crossed, they sent the raft downstream, inviting the men of the *Kiis'áanii* to join them, from whom six clans did join. They too had allowed their women to anger them.

As some of the young men rode across the stream they wept at having to part with their wives.[30] They had not been angered by anything the women had said. But they had become used to doing whatever *Áłtsé hastiin* had told them to do.

The men left behind everything the women had made by themselves. And they left behind everything the women had helped them to make or to raise. They took only what they had produced without the help of any woman.

•   •   •   •

Once they reached the north bank of the river, some of the men set out to hunt. For the young boys needed food. Others set to work cutting willows for huts. For the young boys also needed shelter.

It seems that they managed very well. Within four days they had plenty of food, and they built strong homes for themselves and the boys. Within four days they were sure that they could get along without women.

They were sure they would thrive without women to make them angry. And their spirits were high, at least at first, it is said.

Ten

It is also said that the women, too, were in high spirits at first.

That winter they had plenty of food. They worked and they ate. They sang songs and they told stories. Often they came down to the bank of the river where the men could hear them and see them. And there they taunted them.

One of them would pull her sheath over her head and shake her bare body. Another would do likewise; then she would turn her back toward the men, and bend forward, and wiggle her buttocks.

"Hey you men," called yet another meanwhile. "Look over here. Look at that!"

"Don't you see what you're missing?" shouted still another.

Others would then similarly bare themselves to the men. All together they would laugh and cry out. Thus they teased the men, alternately calling them obscene names and coaxing them suggestively. They used their bodies to tempt the men until they were sure that the men longed for them as much as they longed for the men.[31]

• • •

In the spring the men prepared a few small fields and managed to raise a little bit of corn. Still, they did not have much of it to eat, and they had to depend on hunting for most of their food.[32]

Meanwhile, the women cultivated their entire farm. But without hoes they could not work the soil properly. And without scythes they were unable to harvest well. So that during their second winter alone they were forced to live on a smaller crop. They did not sing as much or tell as many stories as they had done the previous winter.

The women planted less the second spring, while the men cleared more land than they had cleared the year before. So the crops of the men increased while those of the women decreased. And during the winter that followed, the women began to suffer for want of food. Some of them had to gather the seeds of wild plants to get enough to eat.

During the autumn of the third year of the separation many women jumped into the river and tried to swim over to the north shore where the men lived. But they were carried away by the current and were never seen again.

By the end of the fourth year the men had more food than they could eat. Corn and pumpkins lay untouched in the fields while the women starved.

But the separation was still having a bad effect on the men, even if they had raised enough crops for themselves. For during the entire time that they lived apart, the men longed for the women just as badly as the women longed for them. That longing grew, in fact, on both sides of the stream.

So strong did it become that members of both sexes indulged in the practice of masturbation. The women sought to satisfy themselves with long stones and thick quills. They attempted intercourse with cactus or with bone. The men, meanwhile, tried to relieve their longing with mud, or else they used the flesh of freshly slain game.

There was one in particular called *K'íídeesdizí*, whose name means Man With Wrappings On in the White Man's language. One morning he went out hunting alone and found a place far from the village where nobody would see him. Once out there he killed a deer just as the light of day began to wane.

He then made a brush circle and lit a fire therein, according to the manner of doing such things in those times. Into the fire he placed a piece of venison from his quarry, meaning to eat a little of it and then to spend the night there, satisfying his longing for the companionship of his wife. He would return the next morning with the rest of his game and share it with the others.

As darkness fell, he ate the meat. And while he watched the sky darken, he began thinking about his wife on the opposite bank of the river.

The more he thought of her, the more he longed for her. The

greater his longing, the more he desired her, especially as the sky in the west darkened and gave way to black night.

"It was not I who was angered by a woman," thought he. "It was not my wife who said she could get along without us men."

And as he reflected on such things, he found himself longing all the more. In the darkness he pictured the women standing on the far shore of the river beckoning to the men. He pictured them cupping their hands under their breasts suggestively. He pictured them as they shook their naked bodies to tease the men. He imagined he could see them wiggling their buttocks at them.

Surely his own wife was among the women who desired the company of their husbands.

Full of such thoughts, and longing so for her, he took the liver from the body of the slain deer and cut a slit into it. then he placed it by the fire to warm.

"So be it," said he when the liver felt as warm as his wife had felt whenever he and she would lie close together. "I have no quarrel with my wife or any woman.

"No quarrel whatsoever."

Upon saying which, he placed the liver carefully below himself where his legs joined.

But just then *Né'éshjaa'* the Owl cried out. He had come unseen upon Man With Wrappings On.

"Wu'hu'hu'hu'," cried he from somewhere just outside the brush circle.

"Wu'hu'hu'hu'," he was heard to cry.

"Stop, *K'íídeesdizi!* Stop that.

"Do nothing with that liver if you do not intend eating it!"

Startled, Man With Wrappings On returned the liver to the fire. Then he stepped outside the brush circle and walked around, looking in vain for whomever had just spoken.

Finding no one, he came back to the fireside, lay down, and tried to sleep, attempting at first to put his wife out of his mind and to forget his longing.

Well into the night he lay there unable to sleep. Try as he might, he could not stop thinking of her, and the more he thought of her the more he missed her. The more he missed her the more he desired her. Until he finally reached for the liver again, which still lay warm by the fire. Taking it into his hands again, he listened carefully for the cry he had heard earlier. But he could hear nothing.

"Ah," thought he. "Now's the time."

"Come, wife-liver.

"Come to me now!"

Upon thinking which, he again positioned the liver below himself.

But hardly had he done so when again he heard the cry of *Né'éshjaa'* the Owl.

"Wu'hu'hu'hu'," he heard him cry.

"Stop, *K'íídeesdizi!* Stop that.

"Eat that liver; do not have intercourse with it!"

Startled again, Man With Wrappings On quickly returned the liver. Then he curled up and tried again to sleep, doing what he could to forget that he missed his wife. But he was unable to do so. On into the night he lay there, missing her. The more he missed her, the more he desired her. The more he desired her, the more easily he imagined that she lay there close to him. Thus he waited, listening for any sound that might break the silence and stop him. Hearing nothing, however, he once more longed for the warm liver.

"Now perhaps that meddling fool is gone," he thought as he took it in his hands and once again placed it against himself.

"Now," he whispered hoarsely.

"Let it be now, no matter who's out there."

His having hardly said so, the voice again broke the silence.

"Wu'hu'hu'hu'," cried the voice.

"*K'íídeesdizi*, stop! Stop that.

"If you do not intend to eat that liver, keep it away from yourself."

With a start, *K'íídeesdizi* replaced the liver by the fire. Again he tried to rid himself of his desire and sleep. Unable to do that, though, he lay there until the eastern sky began to show the gray light of the oncoming dawn. He lay there desiring his wife, longing for her all the more as he thought of her, all the more anxiously imagining that she lay close beside him, nestling her warmth against the full length of his great longing. He lay there in the silence until he could contain himself no longer, and until he cried out, scarcely in control of himself.

"I don't care," he gasped.

"I don't care who's out there. I don't care where he may be. It's got to be now. It must be now." And he grabbed the liver and thrust it against his penis.

No sooner than which the voice of *Né'éshjaa'* the Owl rang out. *"K'íídeesdizi!* you must stop that. Stop!

"Do not have intercourse with that liver; leave it alone."

Man With Wrappings On then threw the liver back to the fire and sprang to his feet. "Who are you, anyway?" he demanded. He faced one way, then another. He stalked to the outer edge of the brush circle and paced around it, first one way, then the next twice around, then back again the way he originally went. "Where are you?" he asked.

"Can't you leave a person alone?

"Or can't you at least face a man and explain yourself as someone ought to do?"

Whereupon *Né'éshjaa'* the Owl suddenly appeared. And he softly spoke these words.

"I really mean you no harm, grandchild," spoke he.

"But I also insist on what I am telling you.

"What you are trying to do is altogether out of place. You cannot make things normal by treating the liver of a slain deer as if it were your wife."

K'íídeesdizi took a moment to consider.

Indeed, the liver was not his wife.

Nothing he might do with it would bring her to him. Nothing he did with it would take him to her.

"Wait right there, granduncle," he said to *Né'éshjaa'* after a short pause. Then he returned to the center of the brush circle and built a fresh fire. From the carcass of the slain deer he cut a choice tenderloin. He sliced it thin and cooked it together with the liver. Taking that for himself to eat, he offered the steak to Owl.

"Here, granduncle," he said, handing it to *Né'éshjaa'*.

"You eat this while I eat the liver."

"Thank you, my grandchild," said he. "But turn your back to me. I do not eat in anyone's plain sight."

Thus he ate behind the back of *K'íídeesdizi* the Man With Wrappings On, promising that after he finished he would explain himself, which indeed is as much as anyone ought to do.

• • • •

"It has been nearly four years, now," explained *Né'éshjaa'* the Owl, "since you men left the women over there on the other shore, as you yourself certainly know.

"Whether the women are to blame or the men, no good can come of the separation.

"Fewer of the women now remain than you menfolk left behind. Many of them have plunged into the water and disappeared. As for those who remain, they are abusing themselves any way they can in the absence of you men. They have intercourse with long stones. They seek to satisfy themselves with thick quills. Some insert cactus into themselves. Some handle the bones of animals as if they were their husbands.

"What is more, they grow hungry for want of food.

"Suppose that those who remain eventually threw themselves into the water because they are in such misery? That will leave only you men living on the surface of this world. Do you think you can sustain life by yourselves? Will the liver of a slain deer bear your children?

"I do not know how long they can endure over there, meanwhile. Just yesterday I overheard *Áłtsé asdzáá* the First Woman lament to her followers. She grieved for those who had disappeared into the water, and she pitied those who have survived only to long for their husbands on empty stomachs. She even confessed that she wished to hear the voice of her husband *Áłtsé hastiin* the First Man once more.

"I mention all of that for your sake, grandson. And for the sake of the others.

"Somehow you must contrive to have the women brought across the river so that they can rejoin the men. Otherwise this disorder will continue until the world we now know comes to an end. Even the sky will disappear, and with it all the work that has been done so far. Life can go on only if the women and the men reunite.

"Now I must go, grandson," concluded *Né'éshjaa'* the Owl to *K'íídeesdizi* the Man With Wrappings On. " I have nothing more to say.

"Except that I leave it to you to devise a way to bring the men and the women together again."

•   •   •   •

K'íídeesdizi thought carefully about what he had been told, and then he returned to the village. Once there he started straight toward *Áłtsé hastiin* the First Man to repeat outright what *Né'éshjaa'* had said. But he thought the better of that, remembering how angry he had been after his quarrel with *Áłtsé asdzáá* the First Woman.

Instead, he assembled several of the older men and began to reason with them.

"Think about it," he reasoned, after he had explained what he had heard. "Over there our women are starving. What good is our food over here if they have little to eat?

"One by one they plunge into the water. Or else they abuse themselves with long stones and thick quills, or with cactus and the bones of animals. Suppose that they were all to perish while we survived? Could we possibly sustain life without them? Can mud bear our children? Can the livers of slain deer nurture our offspring?

"If life is to go on, we and the women must rejoin each other. Otherwise this disorder will continue until the world as we know it disappears.

"Who knows?

"Even the sky could come to an end, together with all the work that has so far been done."

Thus he spoke to various men, getting them all to agree. And together they decided to induce *Áłtsé hastiin* the First Man to change his mind and initiate a reunion.

One by one they managed to get him to reconsider.

"Did you hear plaintive voices over there on the other shore last night?" someone would ask him early one morning.

"Unless I'm mistaken I believe that yet another woman jumped into the river," someone else might say. "Over there across the water. Where they struggle to survive."

"How terrible it must be on the opposite bank," said still another. "No food to eat. No men for companionship."

Said yet another: "Perhaps I was dreaming, but all night long I thought I heard a woman pleading. I cannot be sure—after all, I have not heard her voice up close for four years now—but it sounded like *Áłtsé asdzáá* the First Woman. But then why should that matter to me? She insisted that the women can get along just fine without us men, after all."

•   •   •   •

By the end of the fourth year of the separation, *Áłtsé hastiin* the First Man did indeed wonder whether he had acted wisely. So he called the men together and asked them what they thought. And this is what one of them said:

"Over there our women are starving," he said.

Added another:

"What good is our food on this side of the river if our women starve on the other side?" he added.

And another spoke these words:

"One by one they leap into the water. Meanwhile, those who remain abuse themselves with long stones and thick quills, or with cactus and the bones of animals," were his words.

And asked still another:

"Suppose we survived while they all perished?" he asked. "Could we possibly sustain life without them? Can mud bear our children? Can the livers of slain deer raise our offspring?

"If this present disorder continues, the world as we know it will come to an end.

"Who knows?

"Even the sky would disappear, along with everything else that has so far been created."

    •   •   •   •

Áłtsé hastiin the First Man thought carefully about what the men were saying. And he finally sent one of them down to the river. He instructed him to call across the stream and ask if *Áłtsé asdzą́ą́* the First Woman was still there. If so, would she be willing to come to the water's edge and hear something her husband had to say?

When she received that message she gladly came to the river. Whereupon *Áłtsé hastiin* asked her this question:

"Do you still think you can live alone?" he asked her.

To which she gave this response:

"I no longer believe that I can," she responded.

"I do not think that any woman here can live alone.

"And I now regret the things I said to you."

That is what she told him.

And this is what he replied to her:

"And I am sorry that I let the things you said make me angry," he replied.

    •   •   •   •

So it was that the men and the women put their quarrel to an
end. *Áłtsé asdzą́ą́* the First Woman instructed her followers to
gather at the bank of the river on their side. And *Áłtsé hastiin* the
First Man instructed his to gather at the bank on their side.

He then sent the raft over to the women's side, where they were
ferried across to the opposite shore. There they were told to bathe
and to dry their bodies with meal.[33] The two sexes would remain
separated until nightfall. Then they would rejoin each other and
resume their lives together, it is said.[34]

Eleven

It is also said that soon after the women rejoined the men three
of them were found to be missing. A mother was missing and so
were two of her daughters.

By that time the day was nearly over.

After darkness fell the people heard the voices of the missing
three, crying out from the opposite bank. Left behind somehow,
they now begged to be carried across the stream. They too wanted
to rejoin the men and the boys.

It was now too dark to cross, the men explained to them. They
would have to wait until morning. Then the raft could be sent and
someone would fetch them.

The three did not want to wait, however. So they jumped into
the river and tried to swim over in the dark. The mother managed
to reach the north shore, where she found her husband. But the
two girls were seized by *Tééhoołtsódii* the Big Water Creature, who
dragged them down into the water where they disappeared.[35]

For three nights and for three days the people searched for the
two maidens. But they found no trace of them and gave them up
for lost.

Then, on the morning of the fourth day, they heard a voice
calling to them from far to the east. They listened and waited until
they heard it again, nearer and louder. They continued to listen and

to wait until they heard it a third time, all the closer and all the louder. Continuing to listen and to wait they heard the voice again, so close upon them that it seemed to come from where they now stood.

And after the fourth call *Bits'íís łigaii* the White Body appeared, holding up two fingers and pointing to the river. It seemed to the people that he was trying to tell them something about the missing girls. So some of the men took the raft across the stream and looked for the tracks of the maidens.

They traced their footprints to the water's edge but no further. While the men continued to search, *Bits'íís łigaii* the White Body went away. But he soon returned with *Bits'íís dootł'izh* the Blue Body. He carried a large bowl made of white shell, and his companion carried a large bowl made of blue shell. They beckoned for a man and a woman to follow them and then went down to the river.

At the water's edge the two gods placed both bowls on the surface and caused them to spin around. And where the bowls spun the water opened.

The opening made by the spinning bowls led to a large house underground that contained four rooms. The room in the east was made of dark waters. The room in the south was made of blue waters. The room in the west was made of yellow waters. And the room in the north consisted of waters of all colors.

The man and the woman who had followed *Bits'íís łigaii* the White Body and *Bits'íís dootł'izh* the Blue Body climbed through the hole in the water and entered the large house. They did not realize that *Mą'ii* the Coyote had been following them all this time; unseen by everyone he too had entered the underwater house.

First they went into the east room, but they found nothing there. Then they went into the south room, but they found nothing there, either. Then they went into the west room where they again found nothing. And finally they went into the north room, where they found *Tééhoołtsódii* the Big Water Creature.

There he sat.

Next to him on one side sat two infant children of his own. And next to him on the other side sat the two girls he had stolen.

The man and the woman demanded their two girls. And since *Tééhoołtsódii* the Big Water Creature said nothing in reply, they took the two and walked away. But while all four of them were

leaving, *Mą'ii* the Coyote seized the two water babies. And
unnoticed by everyone he carried them off under his robe.

Coyote always wore his robe folded close around him. He even
slept with it folded against his body that way. So nobody was
surprised to see him wearing his coat folded like that as he came
out of the water with the others. Least of all did anyone suspect
that he had just stolen the children of *Tééhoołtsódii* the Big Water
Creature, it is said.

Twelve

It is also said that on the very next day something took the
people by surprise. For they saw *Bįįh* the Deer pass right in front of
them. And they saw *Tązhii* the Turkey pass quickly before them.
And they saw *Jádí* the Antelope rushing past. They saw all three
fleeing headlong from the east to the west.

Meanwhile, other animals came running into their village
seeking refuge. *Atseełtsoii* the Yellowtail Hawk came, along with
his mate and their offspring. *Hazéétsoh* the Squirrel came with his
mate and their offspring. *Dah yiitįhí* the Hummingbird came with
his brood. And so came *Jaa'abaní* the Bat.

For the rest of the day, and during the three days which followed,
other animals either came running through the village or stopped
there and begged for shelter. Something had frightened them all.

On the morning of the fourth day, when the white light of dawn
made its way up the wall of the eastern sky, the people noticed a
strange white glimmer along the horizon. So they sent the locust
couriers to find out what was happening.

Before dark the locusts returned and told the people that a great
tide of water was rushing in on them from the east.

When they heard this news the people all assembled in a great
crowd, including the *Kiis'áanii*. Some of them cried out. Some
wept. Some tried to run away and then returned soon afterwards,
realizing that there was no where to go. For a great tide of water
was also coming in on them from the west. And water was now
coming in from the south, and likewise from the north. Some of
the people ran off in panic and were never seen again.

All night long the people who remained cried and moaned, argued and talked. No one among them slept that night, so fearful were they, it is said.

Thirteen

It is also said that the next morning the white light of dawn arose in the east as it had done in mornings past. But now it arose with a steady roar that sounded distant at first and then grew louder. And the people soon saw water high as mountains encircling them across the horizon all around.

It came upon them from the east. It came at them from the south. It also came upon them from the west. And from the north it came at them. Only in the west was there a small break in that tidal wall. But it was too small to allow them all to escape.

As fast as they were able, the people packed up all their goods and took refuge high on a nearby hill. But they knew that they were only temporarily safe there.

On that knoll they held a council to try to decide what they should do next. Someone then suggested that perhaps *Hazéétsoh* the Squirrel and his wife might somehow help. Said they:

"We will try," they said.

"We will do what we can."

Whereupon one of them planted a pinyon seed while the other planted a seed of juniper. Both seeds grew so fast that the people could actually see them getting taller.

They grew so fast, in fact, that some of the people hoped they might rise beyond reach of the floodwater. But they grew upward only a little way further. And then they branched out and got no higher.

Then the frightened people called on *Dlǫ́'ii* the Weasel and his mate to help somehow. Said they:

"We will try," they said.

"Whatever we can do we will do."

Whereupon one of them planted a spruce seed while the other

planted a seed of pine. Both seeds grew as before: both grew so fast that the people could see them becoming taller.

In fact, they grew so fast that some of the people believed that the newly grown trees might actually rise beyond the reach of the flood. But as with the pinyon and the juniper that *Hazéétsoh* the Squirrel and his mate had planted, they grew only a little way more. Then they branched out and became wide rather than tall.

Now the people were more frightened than they had ever been. For the waters had continued to rush in on them from east and from west, from north and from south. They all believed that they would soon perish. Then suddenly two men appeared on the hill on which the people all stood, it is said.

Fourteen

It is also said that one of the two men who suddenly appeared was old and grayhaired. The other, who walked in advance of the elderly one, was young and limber. His hair shone and little rays of light sparkled from his eyes.[36]

The two spoke to no one as they climbed the hill. They passed quietly through the crowd and made directly for the summit. Once they had reached the very peak, the young man sat down. Then the old man took a seat directly behind him. And for no reason that anyone could understand, *Wóóneeshch'įįdii* the Locust sat directly behind him. All three of them faced the east.

Then the old man took seven bags from under his robe and opened them. Each contained a small amount of soil. This soil, he then proclaimed, had been gathered from the sacred mountains that marked the limits of the fourth world. Whereupon a few of the people spoke words like these:

"Ah, perhaps something can yet be done," spoke one.

"Perhaps our grandfather can help us," said another.

"Perhaps we can find another world to live in," another said.

To which the old man replied:

"I myself can do nothing more than what I have done," replied he.

"But maybe my son here can help you."

Whereupon the people begged the young man with the shiny hair and the sparkling eyes to do something. And this is what he said to them:

"I can do something to help you, yes," he said to them.

"But there are two things that you must do, too. Likewise, there are two things you must not do.

"You must all move away from where you stand. And you must all face the west.

"But you must not look at me until I call for you. And you must not ask me any questions.

"Nobody is to see me working. And nobody is to know what I have done or how I have done it."

The people all agreed to do what he told them to do. And they agreed not to do what he said they must not do.

They moved away from where they stood. They all faced the east. None of them looked at him. And no one asked him a question. And in a few minutes he called for them to return to the place where they had all been standing.

When they returned, they saw that the youth had spread the sacred soil on the ground. And they saw that in it he had planted thirty-two reeds, each of which had thirty-two joints.

They looked at the reeds, and as they gazed at them they saw that they took root in the ground and that the roots spread downward rapidly. They also saw that the reeds themselves grew upward rapidly. And in another moment all thirty-two joined together to form one giant stalk with an opening in its eastern side, it is said.[37]

Fifteen

It is also said that the young man then told the people to enter the reed through the opening. When they were all safely inside, the opening disappeared. And none too soon, for scarcely had it closed before the people inside heard the terrible sound of the surging water outside: "Yin! yin! Yin! yin!"

The water rose rapidly. But the reed grew faster. It grew so high, though, that the people inside feared that under their weight it might break and topple into the water.

Luckily, though, *Bits'íís łigaii* the White Body and *Bits'íís dootł'izh* the Blue Body were in the reed with them. *Bits'íís łizhin* the Black Body was also inside, and he blew a great breath out through a hole in the top of the reed, and a heavy dark cloud formed around it and kept it steady.

And still the reed grew. Higher and higher it grew, higher and higher. Until it began to sway again, and until the people were again seized with fear. But then *Bits'íís łizhin* the Black Body blew a second great puff of breath, making another cloud to steady the towering reed.

By the time that darkness was about to fall, the reed had grown clear up to the crown of the sky. It swayed and bowed so much that the people could not steady it. Until finally *Bits'íís łizhin* the Black Body, who was now uppermost inside the reed, took the plume out of his headband. And he stuck it through the top of the cane and fastened it to the sky. Which is why that reed is plumed to this very day, it is said.

Sixteen

It is also said that the people stayed inside the reed all night long. And when the white light of day filled the sky next morning they looked outside. But they could see no hole in the sky.

So the people sent *Atseełtsoii* the Hawk to look for a way through to the other side. Out he flew and immediately began to scratch at the sky with his claws.

He scratched and scratched until he was lost from sight. And sometime later he returned to say that he had dug his way into the sky overhead to see some light shining through from the other side. But he was tired now and could dig no more.

Next they sent *Wóóneeshch'įįdii* the Locust to dig. He too was gone for a long time. But he finally came back, and when he did he had this story to tell.

•   •   •   •

He had dug through to the upper world on the other side of the
sky. There he emerged on a small island in the middle of a large
lake. When he set foot on that soil he saw a black loon approaching
him from the west. And he saw a yellow loon approaching from
the east.

"Who are you and where have you come from?" one of the loons
asked him. Whereupon *Wóóneeshch'įįdii* made no reply.

"Between us two," the other loon then said, "we own half of this
world.

"The east belongs to me. And the west belongs to my cousin
here.

"So listen to this.

"If you can do what we do, we will give you the other half of this
world. We will give you the north and the south.

"But if you cannot do what we do, you will die."

Each loon had an arrow made of the black wind. And each passed
his arrow through his body. Each passed it from one side to the
other, piercing it straight through his heart.

And after he had finished, each of the two loons flung his arrow
down at the feet of *Wóóneeshch'įįdii* the Locust.

He in turn picked up one of the arrows. And he ran it through his
own body. He ran it from side to side and pierced his own heart,
just as he had seen the loons do.

Then he picked up the other arrow and ran it through his body. It
too he ran from side to side so that it pierced his heart. And when
the loons saw him perform this task so easily they dove into the
water and swam away from the island. One swam to the east and
the other swam to the west. And they troubled *Wóóneeshch'įįdii*
the Locust no more.

When they had gone, two more loons appeared. A blue one came
out of the water from the direction of the south. And a shining one
came out of the water from the direction of the north.

They spoke to *Wóóneeshch'įįdii* the Locust exactly as the other
two had spoken to him. And they confronted him with the very
same challenge.

Again he passed two arrows through his body from side to side so
that each pierced his heart. And again no harm came to him.
Whereupon the two loons swam away as the others had done,

troubling *Wóóneeshch'įįdi* the Locust no more. They left the land entirely to him.[38]

To this day, incidentally, you can see holes in the side of a locust if you look carefully at him. Those are the holes made by the arrows which he passed from one side of his body to the other.

As for the opening that had been made in the sky, it was still too small for many of the larger people to climb through. So *Nahashch'id* the Badger was sent to make it larger.

When he came back from doing his work, his legs were stained black with the mud that fills the inside of the dome of the sky that covers the fourth world. And that is why all badgers have had black legs ever since.

Finally, *Áłtsé hastiin* the First Man and his wife, *Áłtsé asdzáá* the First Woman were able to lead the people through the hole. One by one they all followed the pair. And the people, safe at last, climbed through the hole to the surface of this the fifth world, it is said.[39]

All these things happened a long, long time ago, it is said.

PART TWO

The Fifth World

One

Of a time long, long ago these things too are said.[1]

It is said that high cliffs bordered the lake that surrounded the island. And great plains extended out in every direction from the tops of those cliffs. Mountains tower above that lake now, but they were not yet there when the people emerged into the fifth world.

At first the people could find no way to get across the water from the island to the other shore. So they called on *Bits'íís dootł'izh* the Blue Body to help them.

It seems that he had brought four stones with him from the world below. And he now threw one of them toward the east. Then he threw one toward the south. And he threw one toward the west. And toward the north he threw one.

When a stone landed against each of the cliffs it made a hole in the rock. And through each of the holes the water flowed off in four different directions.

But the lake did not drain entirely. Enough water flowed off, though, so that in one place the bottom showed. And there was now a lane that connected the island with the land on the other side.

At first the people were afraid to walk over that land because it was muddy and because the mud looked so deep. So they asked *Níłch'i dilkǫǫh* the Smooth Wind to help them.

So he blew steadily all day long. And before darkness fell the mud dried. So that on the very next day the people easily walked over to the other shore.

While they had waited for the mud to dry, the *Kiis'áanii* camped on the east side of the island. There they built a stone wall that stands to this very day. They wished to have something to lean

against and to shelter them from the wind. The others built
shelters of brushwood. These were built on the west side of the
island.

While the people all waited the women erected four poles. Over
the poles they stretched a deerskin. And under the skin they played
tsindił. In the language of *Bilagáana* that game would be called
stick dice.[2] The women brought it with them from the world
below. To this very day women like to play that game while they
are waiting around.

·   ·   ·   ·

When everyone at last reached the mainland, the people all
wanted to know what would become of them. So someone threw a
hide scraper into the water and had this to say.

"If it sinks we will eventually perish. But if it floats we shall all
go on living."

It floated, and everyone was glad.

But then *Mą'ii* the Coyote stood up. And he had this to say:

"Wait a minute here. Let me do this," he said.

And before anybody could object he picked up a stone and spoke
this way:

"If it floats, we will all live forever. But if it sinks, everybody
will die sooner or later."

Of course the stone sank, and everyone grew angry. They called
Mą'ii names and they cursed him. Some of the people even
threatened to throw him in the water. But he cried out, and this is
what he said.

"Wait!" he said.

"Listen to me."

"If we all go on living, and if the women keep having babies,
there will be too many people. There won't be any room.
Nobody will be able to move around. There will be no space to
plant corn.

"Isn't it better that each one of us should live here for just a
while, until old age slows us down?

Not just until we can't hunt. Not just until we can't plant and
harvest. But until we can't think. Until we can no longer speak.

"Then we ought to move on. Leave everything behind for the
young. Make room for the next generation."[3]

When the people heard what *Mą'ii* the Coyote had to say, they recognized the wisdom of his words. Grudgingly they agreed that he was right. And one by one they grew silent.[4]

●　　●　　●　　●

Later that day, the people had two visitors. *Náshdóítsoh* the Mountain Lion visited them. And *Mą'iitsoh* the Big Wolf visited them.

They had this to say:

"We have heard that some new people have come here," they said.

"We have heard that they came out of the ground over there on that island.

"We are here now to see them," they said.

And they looked at the newcomers. For a long time they looked them all over. And from among the unmarried women *Náshdóítsoh* the Mountain Lion took himself a bride, it is said.

Two

It is also said that four days passed. The white light of day arose in the east four times. And four times the black darkness of night fell. Then, on their fifth day in this new world, one of the people crossed back over to the island where they had all emerged.

He went to the hole through which the people had escaped from the flooded fourth world. And, looking into it, he noticed water welling and churning inside. It rose steadily he noticed. Already it was nearly to the top of the hole. And with each moment it seemed to get higher!

The man ran back to tell the others what he had seen. And at once a council was called, so that the people could discuss this new danger.

For a while the people talked and argued, but they were unable to decide what should be done. But then *Áłtsé hastiin* the First Man got up to speak. Before he said anything he looked around until he saw *Mą'ii* the Coyote. And as First Man's eyes met his own, Coyote looked down at his feet.

Whereupon *Áłtsé hastiin* the First Man pointed to *Mą'ii* the Coyote and had this to say:

"There!" said he.

"There's the rascal who's to blame!

"Something is wrong with the way he's been behaving.

"He never takes off his robe. Even when he lies down. I have been watching him ever since we arrived here. And now I am sure that he has something hidden under that cloak of his.

"Something that he has stolen, maybe?

"Let's search him!"

So they all fell upon *Mą'ii* the Coyote and tore the robe from his shoulders.

Sure enough! two strange looking creatures dropped to the ground. They looked something like tiny buffalo calves, except that they were covered over with spots of different colors. They were the babies of *Tééhoołtsódii* the Big Water Creature: his very own children, stolen by *Mą'ii* the Coyote.

At once the people ran over to the island and threw the infants into the hole from which they had emerged. And in an instant the waters inside stopped welling and surging. With a deafening roar they were drawn back to the lower world.

•   •   •   •

Late the next day, after darkness had fallen, one of the nonchildbearing twins, *Nádleeh*, stopped breathing. Afraid, the people left her alone all the night. And when morning came *Mą'ii* the Coyote proposed that they lay her to rest among the rocks.

This they set out to do. But when they returned to the spot where they had left the twin, they could not find her body. Wondering what had become of her, they all started to look.

They searched in all directions. They looked to the east. To the south they looked. They looked in the west, also. And they also looked in the north. But they could find no trace of the vanished twin *Nádleeh*.

Finally, two men wandered nearby the hole through which they had escaped from the fourth world. And it occurred to one of them to peer inside.

He leaned forward as far as possible and gazed down into the fourth world. And there, far below, he spied the dead one sitting by the side of the river combing her hair.

He called for his companion to come and look. Together the two of them gazed down. Then they returned to their people to tell them what they had seen.

But four days later, these two men also died.

From then on the people refused to look at a corpse. Never again would they seek the dead. And that is why the Navajo people have always been afraid to stare at a ghost ever since then, it is said.[5]

Three

It is also said that the *Kiis'áani* built their camp close by. And word soon got around that they had an ear of corn. It seems that they had brought it with them from the lower world to use for seeds.

Some of the younger, more unruly men proposed going over to the *Kiis'áani* camp and taking the corn. But the older, more moderate men insisted that taking it would be wrong.

After all, the *Kiis'áani* had suffered as much hardship as the wind-spirit people had. If they had the foresight to bring seeds of corn with them, so much the better for them.[6]

In spite of that advice, however, a band of the young roughnecks went to the *Kiis'áani* camp and demanded the ear of corn. After some angry talk on both sides, the *Kiis'áani* made an offer. One of them had this to say:

"We will break the ear in two," he said.

"We will give you whichever half you choose. That way, both groups will have seeds."

The young men agreed to this bargain. So the woman who had owned the ear in the first place split it in the middle and laid the pieces on the ground for the others to choose.

The young men looked carefully at the two half-ears. They looked first at one piece and then at the other. Then they huddled together to discuss their choice.

Meanwhile, *Mą'ii* the Coyote, who unseen by everyone had followed the young men to the place where the *Kiis'áani* were encamped, grew impatient. While the others were carefully choosing their piece of corn, he simply picked up the tip end and made off with it.

Whereupon the *Kiis'áani* insisted that the choice was now made. The people had picked the more meager end with its small, uneven kernels. And they, the *Kiis'áani*, were to have the butt end, with its larger, more evenly spaced kernels. Which is why the Pueblo Indians have always grown better corn than the Navajos to this very day.

•   •   •   •

As for the *Kiis'áani*, they were offended by the threats and curses of the young men who had come to demand the corn in the first place. What would stop them from coming back some other time and demanding something else?

So they moved away from their neighbors and built their village further off. Which is why the Navajos and Pueblos have lived far apart from one another to this very day, it is said.

Four

It is also said that soon after the *Kiis'áani* moved away *Áłtsé hastiin* the First Man and *Áłtsé asdzą́ą́* the First Woman decided to embellish this new world.[7]

So together with *Bits'íís łizhin* the Black Body, and with *Bits'íís dootł'izh* the Blue Body, they first set out to build the seven mountains sacred to the Navajo people to this very day. They built those mountains out of things they had brought with them: things they had taken from similar mountains in the fourth world below.

In the east they made *Sisnaajiní*, or Sierra Blanca Peak as *Bilagáana* now calls it. In the south they made *Tsoodził*, or Mount Taylor. In the west they made *Dook'o'oosłííd*, or San Francisco Peak as it is now called. And in the north they fashioned *Dibé nitsaa*, or Big Mountain Sheep.

Those four mountains they built at the four cardinal points. They placed them where the water flowing from the fourth world gathered after it seeped up through the holes *Áłtsé hastiin* had made when he threw four stones in the four directions.

Also they made three mountains in the middle of the land. They made *Dził ná'oodiłii*, or the mountain that *Bilagáana* would call Travelers Circle. They made *Ch'óol'į'į* or the mountain that some would now call Giant Spruce while others claim that the meaning is obscure. And they made *Ak'i dah nást'ání*, or the mountain that the White Man calls Butte Piled on a Butte in his language.

•   •   •   •

Through *Sisnaajiní* in the east they ran a bolt of lightning to fasten it to the firmament.[8] Then they decorated it with white shells. They decorated it with white lightning. They decorated it with white corn. They decorated it with the dark clouds that produce the harsh and sudden male rain.

On the summit of *Sisnaajiní* in the east they placed a bowl of shells. In that bowl they placed two eggs belonging to *Haabídí* the Gray Dove, for they wanted feathers on the mountain. They then covered those eggs with a sacred buckskin so that they would hatch. Which explains why there are so many wild pigeons on that mountain to this day.

All that they had placed on *Sisnaajiní* in the east they now covered with a sheet of daylight. And from small stone images which they had carried with them from the world below they fashioned *Tséghádi'nídínii ashkii* the Rock Crystal Boy and *Tséghádi'nídínii at'ééd* the Rock Crystal Girl.[9] These two they stationed there to dwell forever as the male god and as the female god of *Sisnaajiní*, or Sierra Blanca Peak as it would be called today in the language that *Bilagáana* the White Man speaks.

•   •   •   •

From top to bottom through *Tsoodził* in the south they ran a great stone knife to fasten it to the firmament.[10] Then they adorned it with turquoise. They adorned it with dark mist. They adorned it with many different animals. They adorned it with the heavy mist that brings the slow, gentle female rain.

On the peak of *Tsoodził* in the south they placed a large bowl of turquoise. In that bowl they put two eggs of the *Dólii* the Bluebird, for they also wanted feathers on that mountain. They next covered those eggs with a sacred buckskin to make them hatch. Which explains why so many bluebirds dwell there to this very day.

All that they had placed on *Tsoodził* in the south they now covered with blue sky. And from a portion of substance which they had brought with them from the world below they fashioned *Dootł'izhii náyoo'ałí ashkii*, the Boy Who Is Bringing Back Turquoise. And they fashioned *Naadą́ą́'lą'i náyoo'áłí at'ééd*, the Girl Who Is Bringing Back Many Ears of Corn. These two they stationed there to dwell forever as the male god and as the female god of *Tsoodził*, or Mount Taylor as it is called in the language that *Bilagáana* speaks.

• • • •

They used a sunbeam to fasten *Dook'o'oosłííd* in the west to the firmament. Then they decorated it with haliotis shell. They decorated it with a variety of animals. It too they decorated it with the black clouds that produce the harsh, sudden male rain.

On the top of *Dook'o'oosłííd* in the west they placed a large bowl of haliotis shell. Into that bowl they placed two eggs of *Tsídiiłtsooí* the Yellow Warbler, for they also wanted plenty of feathers on this mountain. Then they covered those eggs with a sacred buckskin to be sure that they would hatch. Which explains why so many yellow warblers live on that mountain to this day.

All that they had placed on *Dook'o'oosłííd* in the west they covered with a yellow cloud. And from material which they had obtained before they left the world below they fashioned *Naadą́łgaii ashkii* the White Corn Boy and *Naadą́łtsoii at'ééd* the Yellow Corn Girl. These two they stationed to dwell there forever as the male god and as the female god of *Dook'o'oosłííd*, or San Francisco Peak as it would now be called in the language that the White Man speaks.

• • • •

They fastened *Dibé nitsaa* in the north to the firmament with a rainbow.[11] Then they adorned that mountain with black beads.

They adorned it with many different kinds of plants. They adorned it with many different animals. And it too they adorned with the gray mist that brings the slow, gentle female rain.

On the highest point of *Dibé nitsaa* in the north they placed a large bowl of black beads. Into that bowl they placed two eggs of *Ch'agii* the Blackbird, for they believed that there should also be feathers up there. Which explains why so many blackbirds fly around on that mountain to this very day.

All that they had placed on *Dibé nitsaa* in the north they covered with a blanket of darkness. And from a bundle of things that they had gathered while they were living in the world below they fashioned *Tádídíín ashkii*, the Pollen Boy and *Nahachagii at'ééd* the Grasshopper Girl. These two they stationed to dwell there forever as the male god and as the female god of *Dibé nitsaa*, or the Place of Big Mountain Sheep as it would today be called in the language spoken by *Bilagáana* the White Man.

●　　●　　●　　●

After they had secured the mountains that marked the four cardinal points, they built the three central mountains.[12]

Dził ná'oodiłii they fastened to the firmament with a sunbeam. They decorated it with all kinds of things, including the dark clouds that bring the male rain. They put nothing on the summit, for they wished to keep it empty so that warriors might be able to fight there. But they placed *Yódí neidiitsi ashkii* the Boy Who Produces Goods there, and they placed *Yódí neidiitsi at'ééd* the Girl Who Produces Goods there to dwell forever as gods.

Ch'óol'į'í they fastened to the firmament with a streak of falling rain. Then they decorated it with pollen and with the dark mist that brings female rain. On its summit they placed *Choozhgháálii* the Bullock Oriole, which is like those that are plentiful there to this day. And there they also put *Nitł'iz neidiitsi ashkii* the Boy Who Produces Jewels and *Nitł'iz neidiitsi at'ééd* the Girl Who Produces Jewels to dwell forever as male god and female god.

And finally they fastened *Ak'i dah nást'ání* to the firmament with a sacred mirage stone.[13] It they decorated with many different plants, and with the black clouds that bring the male rain. On its summit they placed *Nahachagii* the Grasshopper, whose descendants are abundant there to this day. And there they also placed *Tsé hadahoniye' ashkii* the Mirage Stone Boy and *Yoo'łichí'í at'ééd* the Carnelian Girl to dwell there forever as gods, it is said.[14]

Five

It is also said that the darkness overhead alternated with three feeble shades of light, just as it did in the four lower worlds. So *Áłtsé hastiin* the First Man and *Áłtsé asdzą́ą́* the First Woman decided to make the fifth world brighter than any of the four lower worlds had been.

They thought about it for a while. And for a long time they talked about what kind of light they wanted.[15] Until they finally decided to make a sun and a moon.

First they fashioned the sun.[16] They made an object round and flat, something like a dish, out of a clear stone called *tséghádi'nídínii* or rock crystal, as *Bilagáana* would call it today.

They set turquoise around the edge of this dish. And just beyond the turquoise they placed rays of red rain. Beyond that they placed bars of lightning. And beyond those they placed shimmering swirls.

At first they thought that they might put four points on it, as they later did with the stars when they made them. But at the last minute they changed their minds and decided that the sun should be round.

Then they fashioned the moon. They made another object round and flat, something like a dish but smaller than the first one they had made. This they made out of *tsésǫ'*, or rock-star mica as the White Man would call it.

They bordered it with white shells. And on its face they placed sheet lightning, along with a holy mixture of spring water, rain water, snow water, and hail water. Into this mixture they added water they had fetched from the east, from the south, from the west, and from the north.

They looked at what they had done so far. And they thought about it some more and continued to talk about it. For they needed to decide where the sun ought to rise and how it should set.

Niłch'i ha'a'aahdę́ę́'go the East Wind begged to have it brought
to his land so that it could begin its journey there. So the people
carried it to the edge of the world where he made his home.

Now they needed to give life to the sun that they had made. And
they needed to give it a purpose, so that it would serve *Nihookáá'
dine'é*, the Earth Surface People who would eventually be created.
Likewise they needed to give life to the moon they had made. And
likewise they wished to make it useful, also.

So they decided to place the sun in the keeping of the limber
young man with the shiny hair and the rays of light sparkling in
his eyes. This was the youth who had spread sacred soil on the
ground in the fourth world below: the same young man who had
planted thirty-two reeds in the ground so that the people could
escape the flood and make their way up to this world. And they
said that henceforth he should be the carrier of the sun.

Similarly, they placed the moon in the keeping of the grayhaired
old man who had appeared with the youth in the world below.
This was the man who had brought the soil which the younger
man was to scatter. And the people said that henceforth this old
man would be the carrier of the moon.

Until now these two men had no names. But now, said *Áłtsé
asdzą́ą́* the First Woman and *Áłtsé hastiin* the First Man, the
carrier of the sun would be known as *Jóhonaa'éí*. In the language of
Bilagáana that name means The One Who Rules the Day.

And now, said *Áłtsé hastiin* the First Man and *Áłtsé asdzą́ą́* the
First Woman, the carrier of the moon would be called *Tl'éhonaa'éí*.
In the White Man's language that name means The One Who
Rules the Night.[17]

When *Jóhonaa'éí* the Sun and *Tl'éhonaa'éí* the Moon were ready
to depart to begin the work that would always be theirs, the people
grieved. For everyone had come to love these two. But *Áłtsé
hastiin* the First Man consoled them, having this to say:

"Do not mourn for them," he said.

"For they will not really be gone from us. You will see
Jóhonaa'éí the Sun in the sky each day. And on many nights you
will see *Tl'éhonaa'éí* the Moon.

"Nor is that all.

"Everyone who dies will eventually be placed in the keeping of
these two as a fair exchange for the work done here in this
world."[18]

That is what *Áłtsé hastiin* the First Man said.

• • • •

In those earliest of times this world we now live in was much
smaller than we find it today. The mountains that marked the
limits of our world were not as far apart then as they are today.
And when *Jóhonaa'éí* the Sun followed his path in the sky
overhead he passed nearer to the earth's surface than he does
today.[19]
So that on the first day of its travels the sun was intolerably hot.
In fact the people nearly burned to death. So they prayed to the
four winds that each should pull his mountain further from the
center of the world.

Accordingly, *Níłch'i ha'a'aahdę́ę'go* the East Wind pulled. And
Níłch'i shádi'aahdę́ę'go the South Wind pulled. Likewise *Níłch'i
e'e'aahdę́ę'go* the West Wind pulled. And so did *Níłch'i
náhookǫsdę́ę'go* the North Wind pull.

They all pulled at the same time, as the people prayed they
might do. And the seas that bounded the land receded before the
mountains. The next day came, and when *Jóhonaa'éí* the Sun
followed his path through the sky the earth was still too hot, even
if the people did not nearly burn to death as they had done the
day before.

Again the people prayed to the four winds. And again each of the
four pulled his mountain further from the center of the earth. So
that on the third day the world was somewhat cooler. Still, the
people were a little hotter than they wanted to be.

As before, the people prayed to the four winds. And as before
each of the four pulled his mountain further from the center. So
that at last, on the fourth day, the people found the weather
pleasant. They did not have to ask again to have the face of the
earth changed.

• • • •

After four nights had come and gone, *Áłtsé asdzą́ą́* the First
Woman and *Áłtsé hastiin* the First Man saw that the sky was too
dark. More lights were needed up there for those who wished to
travel by night, especially when the moon did not shine.[20]

So they gathered as many fragments of rock-star mica as they could find. For those could be made to shine in the sky and give extra light. Then *Áłtsé hastiin* the First Man sketched a design on the ground, so that he could work out a plan for lighting up the heavens. Once he was satisfied with his scheme, he began to carry it out.

Working very slowly and very carefully, he placed one fragment of mica in the north. There he wished to have a star that would never move. By it those who journeyed at night could set their course.

Then he placed seven more pieces of rock-star mica. Those became the seven stars we now see in the north.

Next he placed a bright piece of mica in the south. Likewise, he placed one in the sky to the east. And he put another one in the sky to the west. He did so very carefully and very thoughtfully.

So it was that he slowly built several constellations. For he wanted the results of this work to be perfect. But while he was laboring, along came *Mą'ii* the Coyote.

For a while he watched *Áłtsé hastiin* the First Man as he worked. Then he looked down at the pieces of mica that had been gathered. There he found three red fragments. And when he noticed them he had this to say:

"I will take these for my very own stars," he said.

"And I shall place them where I please."

So saying, he put them exactly where we now see three large red stars among the white ones that shine above us in the darkness every night.[21]

Meanwhile, *Áłtsé hastiin* the First Man continued his work as carefully as before. One by one he positioned each star according to his original plan. And *Mą'ii* the Coyote watched him, observing the results of First Man's slow progress.

Until at last he grew impatient and cried out, having this to say:

"Never mind doing it that way!" he said.

"Why must I wait this long for your work to be done?

"Let the stars sit wherever they will."

So saying, he gathered all of *Áłtsé hastiin* the First Man's pieces of rock-star mica in his paw. Then he threw them up into the air, blowing a strong breath at them as they flew. Instantly they stuck to the sky helter-skelter in random bunches.[22]

At least those stars which *Áłtsé hastiin* the First Man had already placed remained in their proper positions. So some constellations were carefully fixed. Otherwise the stars were scattered across the sky in uneven clusters.

To this very day, those who look at the sky on a dark night can see the unevenly placed stars. And by looking at them they can observe the everlasting disorder created by *Mą'ii* the Coyote in his impatience, it is said.

Six

It is also said that with more room in the fifth world the people began to travel. First they journeyed east. And after one day's walk they reached *Ni'hahoogai* or White Spot on the Earth as *Bilagáana* the White Man would call it.

There they camped. And during that night a young woman gave birth.

She was a beautiful maiden who, during the separation of the men and the women in the world below, had reached the age where she longed for the company of a man.

So early one morning she had torn off an antelope horn, which was fuzzy at the time as growing antelope horns usually are. And after warming it all day long in the light, she had inserted it into herself as darkness fell. With it she spent the whole night trying to make *bijóózh* her vagina shout.

Now she was bringing forth the fruit of that self-abuse: an offspring that looked nothing like an ordinary child. Instead, this infant was a round, misshapen creature with no head.

When the people saw, they were frightened and ashamed. So they held a council and decided that this baby should be abandoned. They threw it into a gully and left it there to die.

Nonetheless it lived, as they were to learn. It would grow up and become a terrible creature *Déélgééd* the Horned Monster. And eventually he would destroy many of the people.[23]

The very next day they traveled farther to the east. And as the yellow light of dusk filled the sky they made camp at *Tset'ą́ą́'yisgah*, or Rock Bending Back as *Bilagáana* would call it.

There they rested. And during that night another young woman brought forth a child.

She was a comely maiden who, during the separation of the men and the women in the world below, was among those who wanted a man.

So early one morning she had plucked a feather from an eagle's wing. Its stem was thick and coarse at the time, as a newly grown eagle's feather would be. And after warming it all day long in the light, she had inserted it into herself as darkness fell. With it she spent the entire night getting *bijóózh* her vagina to shout.

Now she was experiencing the result of that self-abuse: a child that did not look as an offspring should look. This infant was a round, headless, misshaped creature with broad, feathered shoulders.

The people were more frightened and more ashamed than they had been the day before. They held a council and decided that this baby too should be abandoned. They threw it into a nearby alkali pit and left it there, thinking that it would die.

But nonetheless it lived, as they were to learn. It would grow up and become the fearsome creature *Tsé nináhálééh* the Monster Eagle. Eventually he carried away many people who would never again be seen.

•   •   •   •

The following day the people continued traveling east. And when the sky grew yellow with the light of dusk they stopped to camp at *Tsé bináhooteel*, or Broad Flat Area Surrounds the Rock as it would be translated into the White Man's language.

There they slept. And during the night to a third young woman a child was born.

She was a pretty maiden who had found, during the separation of the men and the women in the world below, that she longed to have a man close beside her.

So early one morning she grabbed a smooth, elongated stone. It was crusty and hard as such a stone should be. And after warming it all day in the light, she had inserted it into herself when darkness fell. With it she spent the entire night evoking the shout of *bijóózh* her vagina.

Now she was learning the effect of that self-abuse: a child that looked nothing like ordinary offspring. This infant was a long, headless creature with hard skin whose neck tapered to a crusty, flinty point.

The people were even more greatly frightened and more deeply ashamed. They met in council and decided that this baby should also be abandoned. They threw it into a fissure among the jagged edges of the cliff, and they sealed the fissure with rocks, hoping that the child would die there.

But nonetheless it lived, as they were to learn. It would grow up and become the merciless creature *Tsé dah hodziiłáłii* The Monster Who Kicks People Down the Cliff. Eventually he would cause many people to be crushed among the rocks in the deep canyons.

• • • •

On the day that followed they continued their travels eastward. And when the yellow light of dusk was upon them they stopped and camped at *Tséghálzhinii*, or Black Hole Rock as it would be called in the language of *Bilagáana* the White Man.

There they spent the night. And while they did so for the fourth time a young woman gave birth.

She was a lovely maiden who had found herself torn with desire for the closeness of a man's body during the separation of the men and the women in the world below.

So early one morning during that time she had uprooted a sour cactus and whittled it to a point. It was moist and solid as a fully grown cactus would be. And after warming it all day long in the light, she had inserted it into herself when darkness fell. With it she spent the entire night heeding the shouting voice of *bijóózh* her vagina.

Now she was discovering the consequences of that self-abuse: children that looked nothing like ordinary offspring. These infants were twin mutants instead. They were roundish, headless creatures whose one end tapered to a point, who had no limbs, and who bore two depressions near their topmost extremity that looked somewhat like eyes.

The people grew panicky with fear and were overcome with shame. They gathered and declared that these infants had to be abandoned. So they threw them as far as they could and left them in the dust of the bare earth to die.

But the terrible twin babies did not die. Somehow they took shelter in a nearby pile of brush and lived. They would grow up and become the relentless *Bináá' yee agháni* the Monsters That Kill with Their Eyes. Eventually they would paralyze many of the people with their deadly stare.

•　　•　　•　　•

Which explains how monsters came to exist in this world, bringing disorder wherever they went. Such creatures were the fruit of the transgressions that took place in the fourth world, where the men and the women were separated.

Like the men, the women could not endure living apart. And for as long as they lived separately on opposite banks of the same stream, both groups had made a mockery of marriage by masturbating.

As the march to the east continued, other monsters were likewise born. They too were the result of the foolish quarrel that had taken place between *Áłtsé hastiin* the First Man and *Áłtsé asdzą́ą́* the First Woman.

Still other monsters sprang from the blood that was shed during the birth of the first four. And all of them would likewise grow up, as the people were soon to learn.

They would all become enemies and destroyers. Soon they would begin to lurk under rocks and along cliff-paths. They would spring upon passersby and kill them. Then they would devour them. And because of all those monsters the people would live in daily fear, it is said.

Seven

It is also said that the people now turned west and traveled in that direction. They continued on until they came to a place called *Tó nts'ósíkooh*, or Mancos Canyon as it is called today in the language of *Bilagáana* the White Man.

There they remained for thirteen years. They settled and farmed the land at that place, planting corn, beans, pumpkins, and squash each spring and harvesting them each fall.

In those times all the animals were like people. The four-footed beasts, the flying birds, the coiling snakes, and the crawling insects behaved the way that earth-surface people who occupy the world today behave.[24]

They built houses and lived as neighbors the way people do today. As people do today they married and increased their numbers. As people do today they worked and tended to their affairs. In those times the difference between human and nonhuman was not nearly as great as it is now.

But while the walking and crawling and coiling people built their homes on the ground, the birds erected their dwellings high on the cliffs, where many of them remain to this day. It must have been the birds: how could anyone without strong wings reach those homes away up there?[25]

•   •   •   •

At first all went well at *Tó nts'ósíkooh*. But by and by the monsters began to prey on them, killing them and devouring them.

So they left that place and moved to *Tsé łigaii íí'áhí*, or Standing White Rock as it would be called in the language of *Bilagáana*.

At that place too they settled and farmed the land. As they had done before, they planted corn and beans, pumpkins and squash. Each spring they planted those crops and each fall they harvested them.

But by and by the monsters found them. And again they began to prey upon them, killing them and devouring them. So after thirteen years they were forced to leave once more. They moved to *Tsé bee hoolgaií*, or Whiteface Cliff as it would be called in the language of the White Man.

Also at that place they tried to settle and farm the land. As they had done before, they planted corn and they planted beans; they planted pumpkins and they planted squash. Each spring they planted them and each fall they harvested them.

But as before the monsters caught up with them. And as before they began to prey upon them, killing them and devouring them. Sadly, after another thirteen years, they were forced to leave again. And this time they moved to *Kin nteel*, or Broad House as *Bilagáana* the White Man would call it in the language he speaks.

Kin nteel is in Chaco Canyon, and the ruins of that great village still stand for anyone who wishes to go there to see them. But when the wanderers arrived there that selfsame pueblo was only then being built. It was, in fact, far from completion.

Indeed, how the great pueblo at *Kin nteel* came to be built in the first place is well worth hearing, it is said.

Eight

It is also said that what happened as a result is likewise well worth hearing.

Here, then, is the whole story.[26]

Some time before the arrival at *Kin nteel* of those from whom the Navajo people descended, a gambling god descended among the Pueblos already living there. His name was *Nááhwíiłbįįhí*, which means He Always Wins in the language of *Bilagáana* the White Man.

When he arrived he challenged the Pueblos to all sorts of games and contests. And in all of them he was successful.

So successful was he, in fact, that before long he had won all their property. Then he won all their women. Next he won their children. And finally he won many of the men themselves.

But he promised them that he would return some of what had been lost to him as payment, if those who were still free would agree to build a great village for him. So the Pueblo men got busy. For they were eager to regain their kinsmen and their women, their children and their property.

They were also told to build a race track and a playing area. For *Nááhwíiłbįįhí* wanted to challenge people from other villages to match their skill with him at games. Some of the Pueblo men got busy on those projects, too.

That was when the people in flight from *Tsé bee hoolgaii* came to *Kin nteel*. And when they arrived they found the Pueblo men hard at work. They found them building the great village that *Nááhwíiłbįįhí* the gambler had demanded. And they found them building the race track and the arena that he wanted.

• • • •

Soon some people from the neighboring pueblo of *Kin dootł'izh*,
or Blue House as it would be called in the language of *Bilagáana*,
heard about *Nááhwíiłbįįhí* and his great desire to play games.

So that when they thought they were ready to match their skill
with his, and when they had given him four days notice, twelve
men came from that village to compete with the gambler. As the
people had done at *Kin dootł'izh*, they offered themselves as
stakes. And as the people at *Kin dootł'izh* had done, they lost after
only a few brief contests.

Again, after four days notice, twelve more men came from *Kin
dootł'izh* to match wits and skill with *Nááhwíiłbįįhí*. They were
all kinsmen of the original twelve players. They too offered
themselves as stakes. And they too lost after only a few brief
contests.

Then, four days later, after notice was again sent from *Kin
dootł'izh*, another group of twelve came to test the skill and
strength of the great gambler. This time there were women among
the contestants. But they too lost, just as the others had done. And
as soon as he won the new players from the neighboring village
Nááhwíiłbįįhí put them to work on the mighty building he wished
to erect.

But people still came from *Kin dootł'izh* to try to win back their
kinsmen. After four more days the children of some of those who
had already lost came to regain their parents. But they too
succeeded only in adding themselves to the number of slaves
Nááhwíiłbįįhí the game-player had already taken.

Then, four days after that, twelve elders of the village came to
play. But they too lost. And four days after that on another
agreed-upon gambling day, twelve more men came, including some
of the most highly esteemed leaders. These men also staked their
own freedom on winning back their tribesmen. But they too lost.

What with the labor of all those slaves he had won,
Nááhwíiłbįįhí the great gambler had succeeded in having the
dwelling at *Kin nteel* finished in no time at all.

• • • •

Meanwhile the wandering Air-Spirit People from whom the
Navajos were eventually to descend had remained onlookers. They

refused to take any part in the games; they refused to get involved in any way. They simply did their work each day and tended to their own affairs.

One day, though, they heard the voice of the kindly god *Haashch'ééłti'í* calling from a distance.[27] This was the god who in the fourth world had been known by the name of *Bits'íís łigaii* the White Body.

"*Wu'hu'hu'húú,*" he called, his voice barely reaching them at first.

They listened and waited, listened and waited, until soon they heard the voice again, nearer and louder than before. They continued to listen and wait, listen and wait, until they heard the voice a third time, all the nearer and all the louder.

Continuing to listen, they heard the voice again, even louder than the last time, and so close it seemed directly upon them.

That was when *Haashch'ééłti'í* the Talking God appeared. He became visible at the doorway of a dwelling where a young couple with no children lived. And he communicated in sign language, which this couple managed to understand.

He told the young man[28] and his young wife that the people of *Kin dootł'izh* the Blue House village had lost everything. And among all the other things they had lost to *Nááhwíiłbįįhí* the gambler were two great shells. These were the greatest treasures of the village.

What is more, he told the young man and his young wife, *Jóhonaa'éí* the Sun had coveted those very shells, although he was satisfied to let them remain in the keeping of the people of *Kin dootł'izh*. But when *Nááhwíiłbįįhí* the gambler took possession of the shells, *Jóhonaa'éí* the Sun asked the gambler to give them to him.

And what is more, said *Haashch'ééłti'í* the Talking God to the young woman and her husband, *Nááhwíiłbįįhí* the gambler had refused the request of *Jóhonaa'éí* the Sun.

Now, said *Haashch'ééłti'í* the Talking God to this young husband and his wife, *Jóhonaa'éí* the Sun was very angry.

As a consequence of that anger, continued *Haashch'ééłti'í* the Talking God, certain ones from among *Haashch'ééh dine'é* the Holy People would gather in twelve days. They would gather in the mountains at a place designated by *Jóhonaa'éí* the Sun.

They would assemble there to hold a great ceremony. And they would conduct that ceremony to determine what might be done to put a stop to *Nááhwíiłbįįhí* the gambler, who had chosen to disregard the wishes of *Jóhonaa'éí* the Sun.

The young husband was being summoned to attend that ceremony, said *Haashch'ééłti'í* the Talking God. Whereupon he then disappeared.

• • • •

So the young man carefully counted the passing days. And on the twelfth day he appeared at the place where the ceremony was to be held.

There he found a large assembly of *Haashch'ééh dine'é* the Holy People. He found *Haashch'ééłti'í* the Talking God, along with *Hashch'éoghan* the Growling God.[29] This was the god who in the fourth world had been known by the name of *Bits'íís łitsoii* the Yellow Body.

He found *Hashch'éoghan* the Growling God's son *Níłch'i* which name means Wind in the language of the White Man, along with *Níłch'i* the Wind's good friend *Chahałheeł*, the name for the word Darkness in the language that *Bilagáana* the White Man speaks today.

He found *Jaa'abaní* the Bat along with *Tł'iistsoh* the Great Snake. And he found *Tsįįłkaałii* the Woodpecker along with *Na'azísí* the Gopher. Many of the gods and holy spirits were there.

He found a large assembly indeed. For in fact many pets and domestic animals had also come. These were creatures who now belonged to *Nááhwíiłbįįhí* the gambler, who had won them from the people of the two pueblos.

But they were unhappy at being someone else's property. They wanted their freedom, and when *Níłch'i* the Wind[30] had told them about this meeting, they agreed to come.

They promised to do whatever they could to help in the conspiracy against *Nááhwíiłbįįhí* Who Always Wins. And they would gladly take their proper share of the winnings, of course, in the event that their new master could be beaten at his own games.

All night long the gods and their guests danced and sang. They performed the appropriate rites to give *Hashch'éoghan* the Growling God's son *Níłch'i* the Wind gambling powers equal to those which *Nááhwíiłbįįhí* the Gambler had.

When morning came they all bathed *Níłch'i* the Wind. Then they dried him with meal, dressed him exactly the way

Nááhwíiłbįįhí dressed himself, and made him look as much like the gambler as they could.

Next they set out to learn how *Nááhwíiłbįįhí* felt about having refused *Jóhonaa'éí* the Sun those two great shells.

"I can do that myself," volunteered *Nílch'i* the Wind.

"For I can penetrate everywhere. I can make my way through anything. Yet for all that, nobody can see me."

But the others objected.

"No," they replied.

"You had better not try. It is true that you can go everywhere. But you cannot travel without making noise and disturbing people.

"Let your companion *Chahałheeł* the Darkness go instead.

"Like you he manages to go wherever he wants. But unlike you he travels in silence."

That is what the others said.

So it was that *Chahałheeł* the Darkness made his way to the home of *Nááhwíiłbįįhí* the gambler. Then he entered his sleeping body, searched his mind carefully, and came back to report to the others.

"*Nááhwíiłbįįhí* is sorry for what he has done," said *Chahałheeł* the Darkness to them.

But *Nílch'i* the Wind did not believe his friend. So he too made his way to the home of *Nááhwíiłbįįhí* the gambler. He too entered his sleeping body and searched his mind carefully. And he too came back to report to the others.

"*Nááhwíiłbįįhí* is sorry for what he has done," he too reported. "It is as my companion *Chahałheeł* the Darkness tells you."

Then they talked about how they might outwit the gambler. And they began to think of games that they could play with him.[31]

One of the games they decided to play was *tsidił táá'ts'áadah*, or thirteen chips as we would call it today in the language of *Bilagáana* the White Man. That game is played with thirteen flat pieces of wood which are red on one side and white on the other. Who wins depends upon how many chips thrown into the air fall with their white sides up.

"Leave *tsidił táá'ts'áadah* to me," said *Jaa'abaní* the Bat.

"For I have made thirteen chips that are white on both sides. I will hide myself in the roof of his dwelling. And when *Nílch'i* the Wind throws his chips up, I will catch them and throw mine down."

Another game they decided to play was *na'azhǫǫsh*, or hoop and pole as we would call it today in the language of *Bilagáana*. That game is played by rolling a hoop along the ground and then throwing two long sticks after it to stop it. One stick is marked with red and the other is marked with black. A long string with many tails called a turkey claw is fastened to the end of each of the poles.

"Leave na'azhǫǫsh to me," suggested Tł'iistsoh the Great Snake. "For I will hide myself inside the hoop and make it fall wherever it must for Níłch'i the Wind to win."

Another game they decided to play was tsin bétsił, or push the wood as we would call it today in the language of the White Man. In that game the contestants push against a tree until it is torn from its roots and falls.

"Leave tsin bétsił to me," volunteered Na'azísí the Gopher. "For I will gnaw the roots of the tree when it is Níłch'i the Wind's turn to push so that he can easily make it fall."

And they also decided to play jooł, or hit the ball as today it would be called in the language of Bilagáana the White Man. In that game the object was to hit the ball as far as possible so that it would fall well beyond a certain line.

"Leave jooł to me," offered Tsįįłkaałii the Woodpecker. "For I will curl up inside the ball so that I cannot be seen there. And then, once it is hit, I will fly with it wherever I want to go. Níłch'i the Wind won't even have to hit it very hard. He'll only have to give it a light tap, and I can do the rest."

Meanwhile the pets and farm animals advised Níłch'i the Wind to blow hard. Then they would have an excuse to give their master for not keeping a close watch and warning him of any oncoming danger. And in the morning there was in fact a strong gale.

Meanwhile, the whole party of conspirators had left the mountain at dawn. They came down to the brow of the canyon where Nááhwíiłbįįhí made his home. And they waited for the sunrise, fully prepared to match their wits and their skill with his at the games he liked to play.

•　　•　　•　　•

It so happened that Nááhwíiłbįįhí had two wives. And they were the prettiest women anywhere. Wherever each of them went, she carried a stick in her hand with a talisman fastened to the end of it to signify whose wife she was.

It was the custom of one of these two wives to go to a neighboring spring each morning to get water. So that when the sun rose in the east on this particular morning a woman came out of the gambler's house bearing a waterjar on her head and the wand in her hand with the mark of *Nááhwíiłbįįhí* the gambler on it.

At that moment those who were watching from the canyon's rim knew that it was time to put their plan to work. So they made a signal which *Nítch'i* the Wind would understand. Whereupon the son of *Hashch'éoghan* the Growling God descended into the canyon, following the woman to the spring where she customarily drew water.

He watched her silently while she filled her jar. And she did not notice him until she was ready to turn and go back home.

Then, when she did see him, she at first mistook him for her husband, since he was dressed to look like *Nááhwíiłbįįhí* the gambler. So she allowed him to approach her.

Then she realized her mistake. But she could not bring herself to say anything to him. She turned to leave and he followed her. And since she made no attempt to stop him, he stayed with her all the way home. He even followed her inside.

Jealous to see a stranger enter their dwelling with his wife, *Nááhwíiłbįįhí* looked up angrily. But he immediately disguised his scowl, managed to control his rage, and said nothing. He realized that to appear calm he would have to say something sooner or later. So he asked the newcomer quietly if he cared to gamble.

But *Nítch'i* the Wind did not answer.

"Have you come here to gamble?" repeated *Nááhwíiłbįįhí* Who Always Wins, a little more pointedly this time.

"No," replied *Nítch'i* the Wind, saying nothing else.

"Haven't you come here to gamble with me?" asked *Nááhwíiłbįįhí* the gambler, slightly more irritation now showing in his voice.

"No," repeated *Nítch'i* the Wind again, still adding nothing else to his answer.

"I said, are you here to gamble with me for some sort of prize?" asked *Nááhwíiłbįįhí* the winner of games, no longer trying to hide his irritation.

"No," repeated *Nítch'i* the Wind, still refusing to add anything else to what he had already said.

The more the stranger refused, the more eager *Nááhwíiłbįįhí* became to play with him, thinking that he was simply afraid to accept his challenge. He forgot his jealousy by now. He wanted only to beat this stranger at a few games and put him in his proper place. That way he would drive him away in disgrace.

So he began to challenge him to try his luck, taunting him and tempting him more and more recklessly. Until soon he was making extravagant boasts indeed.

"I'll bet everything of mine against everything of yours," he boasted at length.

But *Nitch'i* the Wind continued to refuse, which drove *Nááhwíiłbįįhí* to tempt him outrageously.

"Why I'll even bet myself against yourself," he finally declared.

"I'll bet my feet against your feet, I'll bet my legs against your legs. I'll bet my body against your body. . . ."

On and on he continued that way, naming his every limb against every corresponding part of the stranger's.

". . . I'll bet my hands against your hands.

"My arms against your arms.

"My shoulders against your shoulders. . . ."

On and on he continued, on and on:

". . . I'll bet my neck against your neck. My head against your head. My mind against your mind. My voice against your voice. . . ."

Meanwhile, unnoticed by *Nááhwíiłbįįhí* the gambler, who by now had worked himself into a frenzy for playing no matter what the stakes, *Haashch'ééh dine'é* the Holy People were quietly filing into his home.

They had been watching everything from their perch up on the canyon's rim. They could see him and they could hear him, and they knew that by now he was determined to play against *Nitch'i* the Wind.

So they made their way down into the canyon and entered the dwelling, along with people from the neighboring pueblos who had heard that the greatest set of games ever was about to start.

Among those who came in were two boys dressed up like women. They were wearing clothes very much like the clothes that the wives of *Nááhwíiłbįįhí* the winner of the games were accustomed to wearing.

And no sooner had these two boys entered than *Nitch'i* the Wind finally spoke up and accepted *Nááhwíiłbįįhí* the gambler's challenge. He had this to say:

"I'll tell you what," said he.

"I will accept your challenge. I will accept as stakes all of the things that you have named so far.

"Every one of them I will accept.

"And I will even raise the ante beyond that.

"In addition to what you offer, I will bet my two wives standing here against your two wives standing over there.

"What do you say to that?"

That is what *Nítch'i* the Wind had to say at last. And this is what *Nááhwíítbįįhí* the gambler said to him in reply:

"Agreed, agreed," said he in reply.

"It is agreed!

"You have all heard this intruder!" he cried to the onlookers who had by now assembled in his house.

"All the things that I have named so far are to be accepted as stakes.

"Every one of them he has accepted.

"And beyond that he bets his two wives standing right here against my two wives standing over there.

"You have heard what he offers.

"So there is now no way he can back out when he loses."

That is what *Nááhwíítbįįhí* the gambler had to say to the offer of *Nítch'i* the Wind. And as he spoke the two masquerading boys and the two proper wives were placed side by side in a row.

And then the games began.

First the contestants played the game of *tsidił táá'ts'áadah,* or thirteen chips as it might now be called. As he had promised he would, *Jaa'abaní* the Bat assisted the son of *Hashch'éoghan* the Growling God. So *Nítch'i* the Wind soon won the game and thus claimed the wives of *Nááhwíítbįįhí*.

But the gambler was unwilling to give them up so soon. This is what he had to say.

"Not yet! Not yet!" he said.

"First we must play more.

"You cannot play just one game.

"You cannot expect to win but once and claim to be the winner. I suggest that we move outdoors and try our hand at several other games."

That is what *Nááhwíítbįįhí* the gambler said. And to that *Nítch'i* the Wind agreed. So out they went to play more games.

They began with the game of *na'azhǫǫsh,* or hoop and pole as it might now be called. The track that *Nááhwíítbįįhí* had always used lay east to west. But now *Nílch'i* the Wind insisted on having another one made that ran north to south. He also demanded that he should play with the red stick.

The son of *Hashch'éoghan* was to play first. So he threw the hoop. For a while it looked like it would fall on the gambler's pole, where it appeared to become tangled up in the turkey claw. But much to *Nááhwíiłbįįhí*'s great surprise it somehow worked its way free, rolled further on, went still further than that, and fell on *Nílch'i*'s pole instead.

When it landed, *Nílch'i* the Wind ran quickly to pick up the ring, lest his opponent do so and discover *Tł'iistsoh* the Great Snake hiding inside and lest he might even hurt him.

As for *Nááhwíiłbįįhí* the gambler, he threw his stick away in an outburst of anger when he saw what happened.

For that he forfeited the game. But he remained confident that he would do better in the next contest. Which was to be the game of *tsin bétsił*, or push the wood as it might now be called.

For this game *Nááhwíiłbįįhí* chose two modestly small trees. But when *Nílch'i* saw the trees he had chosen he insisted on playing with larger ones. And after looking several trees over very carefully, they agreed on playing with two good-sized ones that grew close together.

This time it was *Nááhwíiłbįįhí* the gambler's turn to go first. He stood over the tree for a minute, and then he began to push. He pushed and he pushed. He grunted and he strained.

With all his might he pushed and strained.

But the tree would nqt budge. Until finally he gave up and bid his opponent have a try. Whereupon *Nílch'i* the Wind shoved his tree over easily, its roots having all been gnawed loose by *Na'azísí* the Gopher as he promised he would do.

•   •   •   •

And so the match went. They played game after game, game after game. And for all of these games *Nááhwíiłbįįhí* the winner of men had staked his wealth: his shells, his precious stones, his houses, his slaves, his wives, and even his limbs from head to toe.

And in game after game, *Nílch'i* the Wind continued to win.

The last contest between them was *jooł*, the game of hit the ball.

Everyone assembled on the line over which the ball had to be hit. On one side stood those who still remained the property of *Nááhwíiłbįįhí* the gambler. On the other side stood those who had already been freed, along with those who had come to bet themselves against their kinsmen who were still captives.

It was on this final game that *Nááhwíiłbįįhí* had bet the last of his slaves and his very self. That was all that was left for him to wager.

His turn coming first, the gambler hit his ball a hard blow, and it appeared to sail mightily through the air. But it did not quite reach the line.

Then came the stranger's turn. He hit his ball very lightly, hardly seeming to strike it at all. But *Tsįįłkaałii* the Woodpecker lay hidden inside as he promised he would. And with the tap of *Nilch'i*'s bat he flew with all his might and carried the ball far beyond the line.

Thereupon the remaining captives jumped from their side of the line over to the other side where their free kinfolk and tribesmen had been standing.

Meanwhile, *Nááhwíiłbįįhí* sat off to one side all alone.

There he sat, saying bitter things about his losses. At first he mumbled and muttered. But soon he was cursing so that all could hear him. He called everyone his enemy and threatened them all. He had such things as this to say:

"I will kill you all with lightning," he said.

"I will send war upon you.

"I will inflict you with sickness. I will bring disorder into your lives."

But he was not satisfied with just those oaths.

He had other things to say, and he shouted and cursed at anyone who would listen or anyone who would dare to look at him. Such things as these he also said:

"May the waters drown you!" he also said.

"May the cold weather freeze you all!"[32]

"May the fires burn you. May the lightning strike you all!"

"Listen to him carry on so," whispered *Nilch'i* the Wind to his father *Hashch'éoghan* the Growling God, who had been watching the games along with other *Haashch'ééh dine'é* the Holy People.

"Yes," replied *Hashch'éoghan* the Growling God to his son *Nilch'i* the Wind.

"But he has said enough. Do what you will to put an end to his
angry words."

So the son of *Hashch'éoghan* called *Nááhwíiłbįįhí* the gambler
to him. And to him he spoke these words:

"Remember that you bet your very self," were the words
he spoke.

"And admit that you have lost.

"Just as others had once been your slaves, you are now mine. So
you must follow my orders.

"I can do with you as I wish.

"I hope you realize by now that you are not one of the Holy
People. By no means are you a god. You are merely one of the
Nítch'i dine'é, the Air-Spirit People.

"You may have gained power over some of your own kind. But
you have no such power over us. Not here in this world."

That is what *Nítch'i* the Wind had to say to *Nááhwíiłbįįhí* the
winner of men. And so saying, he drew a magic bow which he
owned called *ałtįį' diłhił*. That name means bow of darkness in the
language of *Bilagáana* the White Man.

He bent the bow upwards, arching it so much that its string
touched the ground. Then he ordered *Nááhwíiłbįįhí* to stand on
the string and place his neck against the arched bow. And without
another word he shot the gambler into the sky as if he had been
nothing but an arrow.

Up and up went the hapless *Nááhwíiłbįįhí*.

Up and up he went, growing smaller and smaller to the gaze of
all those who watched him sail. Up and up he went, until he faded
silently and became a mere speck. Until he finally disappeared
altogether.

At first he could still be heard muttering and cursing angrily. But
his voice grew fainter as his body appeared smaller and farther off
in the distance of the sky. Soon he was too far away for anyone
to hear him at all. Even as he began his ascent nobody could really
make out what he was saying, so incoherent had he become in
his anger.

Up and up he flew, farther and farther into the blue of the sky
overhead. Until he arrived at last at the dwelling of *Begochídí*,
whose name in the language of *Bilagáana* means One Who Grabs
the Breasts of Women.[33]

Some people think that *Begochídí* the Grabber of Breasts was
born because early one morning the first rays of *Jóhonaa'éí* the Sun

touched a certain flower. Soon that flower became pregnant and gave birth to him.

Other people think that *Begochídí* keeps a close watch on *Tl'éhonaa'éí* the Moon.

And still others think that he has the power to bring game to those hunters he favors and that he can spoil the aim of those hunters he dislikes.

Nearly everyone agrees, however, that *Begochídí* the Breast Grabber is a great mischief-maker among the gods. But he often takes pity on those who fall upon hard times, especially because they have made the gods angry. Even when they bring their misfortune upon themselves with disorderly behavior *Begochídí* takes pity upon them and treats them with kindness.

So when he saw *Nááhwíiłbįįhí* appear, he gently asked him this: "Who are you?" he gently asked.

"How is it that you have come to my dwelling place?"

Whereupon *Nááhwíiłbįįhí* the erstwhile winner told his story. He accounted for every detail of his misadventure in the fifth world. And he was even willing to admit that he had come to think of himself as one of the Holy People, so powerful had he grown among the Air-Spirit People.

"And so it is that I have become a poor man," said the gambler as he concluded. "And that is why I have come to you."

To which *Begochídí* made this reply:

"Well you will be poor no longer," he replied.

"I will provide for you.

"The gods conspired against you, which was unfair of them. But I will make up for whatever they did.

"I will make you rich again. And I will make you powerful again.

"I will give you animals the likes of which nobody has yet seen in the fifth world. And I will give you fabrics as yet unfamiliar to those who live in that world."

Whereupon *Begochídí* the Grabber of Women's Breasts set about making pets for *Nááhwíiłbįįhí* the gambler, and whereupon he made domestic animals different from any he had owned where had formerly lived.

He made sheep for *Nááhwíiłbįįhí*, and he made burros for him. He made pigs and he made goats. He made horses that could run farther and faster than any creature yet seen. He made birds whose plumage was brighter than the colors of the sun as it shimmered against the rocks and the waters.

He also made bayeta, which was softer and more colorful than any fabric seen anywhere. He made cotton cloth and wool more beautiful than anything *Náahwíiłbįįhí's* slaves were ever able to weave at *Kin nteel.*

Begochídí even made a new people for *Náahwíiłbįįhí* to rule. For he made the *Naakaii dine'é,* whose name in the language of the White Man means Mexican people.

Having done all those things, *Begochídí* the Breast Grabber then sent *Náahwíiłbįįhí* the gambler back to this world again. But he saw to it that he descended at a place far to the south of his former home, where he established himself in the place called *Naakaii bikéyah,* the name that means Old Mexico in the language of the White Man *Bilagáana.*

There *Náahwíiłbįįhí* who always wins prospered, and there his people increased their numbers and their wealth. And after a while they began to move northward, building their villages along the river now called the Rio Grande.

Náahwíiłbįįhí came with them until they arrived at a place north of what we now call Santa Fe. Once that far the ceased migrating any further north, and he returned to Old Mexico to live out his days in this world. Having died there soon after his return, he dwells there to this very day as god of *Naakaii dine'é* the Mexican people.

• • • •

As for the young Navajo bridegroom who was invited by *Haashch'éélti'í* to witness the ceremony of the Holy People as they conspired against *Náahwíiłbįįhí,* he remained with them until the gambler was shot into the sky.

Then he returned to his people and told them plainly what he had seen. He warned them never to behave contrary to sacred wishes. And he warned them above all never to despise the poor and the humble.

"Those whom you despise," he warned them, "may in fact be favored by the gods. While they may appear weak and of no account today, tomorrow you might discover that they possess more power than they seem to have at the moment."[34]

After giving them that message, he went back to *Tséyi',* which is the home of the gods. In his language *Bilagáana* now calls that place Canyon de Chelly, it is said.

Nine

It is also said that those from whom the Navajo people were to descend did not stay long at *Kin nteel*. Soon after *Nááhwíiłbįįhí* was shot into the sky and disappeared, they left.

From *Kin nteel* they moved to *Tó nidoots'os*, which means Where the Stream Becomes Narrow in the language of *Bilagáana* the White Man. And it was there that *Mą'ii* threw his lot in with them. For he married one of their women.[35]

He stayed with his wife's people for nine days. Then he went to visit *Dahsání* the Porcupine. During that visit, *Mą'ii* the Coyote saw his friend scratch his nose with a piece of bark until blood flowed all over it. Then he watched him put the bloody bark over the fire, and he watched him roast it slowly and evenly until it turned into a fine morsel of cooked meat.

Dahsání the Porcupine then spread some clean herbs on the ground. Over these he laid the roasted meat, and he bid *Mą'ii* the Coyote help himself.

Coyote was delighted. He accepted the invitation and ate his fill. Never before had he had such a fine meal, he declared. And before he left he invited his host to come and visit him.

One day came and went, and on the day after that *Dahsání* the Porcupine turned up at Coyote's hut. Greeting his guest warmly, *Mą'ii* bid him have a seat. Then he rushed out to find a nice piece of bark. And in a few minutes he returned with what looked to him like a good chunk.

With that bark he scratched his nose bloody as he had seen *Dahsání* the Porcupine do two days before. Then, as he had also seen Porcupine do, he let the blood flow over the bark. And just as *Dahsání* had done he placed the blood-soaked bark over the fire, thinking that he would roast it slowly and evenly.

Within a minute, though, it burst into flames. Soon nothing was left of it but powdery ashes. Humiliated, Coyote hung his head in shame while *Dahsání* the Porcupine went home hungry.

•   •   •   •

Soon afterward, *Mą'ii* the Coyote visited his cousin *Mą'iitsoh* the Wolf. And while Coyote was there, Wolf reached up into the rafters of his dwelling and pulled two reed arrows with wooden heads. They were the old-fashioned kind such as the ones used by the Navajos in the old days.

Mą'iitsoh the Wolf then took the wooden points off of their shafts as *Mą'ii* the Coyote watched. Then, as *Mą'ii* continued to watch, *Mą'iitsoh* rolled the points against his thigh, moistened them in his mouth, and buried them in the hot ashes beside the fire.

After waiting a little while and chatting amiably with his guest, Wolf raked out from the ashes where he had buried the arrow points two fine cooked puddings of mincemeat.

Mą'iitsoh the Wolf then spread some clean herbs on the ground. Over these he laid the two cooked puddings, and he bid *Mą'ii* the Coyote to help himself.

Delighted, Coyote accepted the invitation and ate until he was fully satisfied. Only rarely did he ever taste such a fine meal, he insisted. And before he left he also insisted that his host should come soon and visit him.

Another day came and went, and on the day after that who should turn up at Coyote's hut but *Mą'iitsoh* the Wolf? Telling his guest how please he was to see him, *Mą'ii* invited him to sit down.

Then, as he had watched Wolf do two days before, he drew two arrowheads from their shafts. And as he had also watched *Mą'iitsoh* do, *Mą'ii* rolled the points against his thigh, moistened them in his mouth, and then buried them in the hot ashes beside the fire.

After waiting a while, he raked the ashes and found that nothing was left of them but two pieces of charred wood.

But this time *Mą'ii* did not display his disappointment as he had done with *Dahsání* the Porcupine. Instead he said nothing about the mishap. He merely sat and continued talking with his guest as if nothing out of the ordinary had happened.

Finally, *Mą'iitsoh* the Wolf, seeing no sign that dinner would be offered, grew hungrier and hungrier. Until he got up and went home without getting anything to eat, it is said.

Ten

It is also said that in those days *Atseełtsoii* the Chickenhawks and *Dah yiitįhí* the Hummingbirds were on friendly terms. They shared the same village and they hunted together as one people. As hunters they were widely admired.

One day *Mąʼii* the Coyote decided to visit their village. When he arrived, he walked boldly into one of the dwellings of *Dah yiitįhí* the Hummingbirds.

There he found two beautiful Hummingbird maidens, gayly dressed with rows of deer-hoof pendants adorning their skirts and draped over their shoulders. Without acting in the least like a stranger, *Mąʼii* lay down inside the lodge and spoke to the two young females, asking this of them:

"Where is everybody today?" he asked them.

"I had heard that many people dwelled here. *Atseeltsoii* the Chickenhawk people lived here, I had heard. And *Dah yiitįhí* the Hummingbird people lived here, I had heard. But the place seems deserted right now.

"Why is this so?"

That is what Coyote asked of the two maidens.

"You are right," replied one.

"Many people live here, including *Atseeltsoii* the Chickenhawk people and including *Dah yiitįhí* the Hummingbird people. But the men are all out hunting today, and the women are out doing their different chores."

Now do not forget that in those long, long ago times *Mąʼii* the Coyote was a dandy. He did not look then the way he looks now.

He carried a nice otter-skin quiver, and his face was painted. He wore a rich and shiny coat of fur, and his tail was long and thick and fluffy.

Once the maidens got a look at him, they bent their heads together and remarked to one another how handsome he was. This is what they whispered, one to the next:

"Look at him," whispered one.

"Notice how well dressed he is. Notice the richness of his fur."

"Yes," whispered the next.

"Notice how he carries himself! Notice how his eyes sparkle!"

"Truly he must be a person of great importance," said the first.

"Truly he must be," repeated the second.

So *Mąʼii* was welcome to spend the rest of the day with the two maidens, chatting and joking and telling them wonderful tales, especially about himself.

"Would you like to know who I am?" he asked them eventually.

And without waiting for them to answer, he continued, telling them this:

"I am the god of *Dził naajiní* the Sleeping Ute Mountain," he told them.

"Consequently I do not have to spend my hours hunting as your people do. For me, getting game is no problem at all.

"All I need do is think of the animal I would like to catch. All I need do then is will its death, and it curls up at my feet and dies.

"With me around, you know, your people would no longer have to wear themselves out hunting game every day. With me around, they would get all the meat they wanted without any effort at all.

"Just think.

"With me around, you men could lie here just as I am doing. With me among them they could spend their days right here like this, chatting and joking and telling stories."

• • • •

At nightfall, when the hunters returned, the two maidens ran out to meet them. They wanted to tell them all about this wonderful visitor who could hunt without any effort at all. They wanted to tell them what easy lives they could lead with this visitor living among them.

When the maidens finished telling their story, the chief of the hunters directed one of the young men to go over to the lodge where Coyote now sat alone.

"Peep in through the doorway," directed the chief. "And let us know what this stranger looks like."

So the young man made his way silently over to the lodge where *Mą'ii* the Coyote sat waiting. And unobserved by him, the youth looked in.

"The maidens certainly are right," observed the young hunter to himself.

"This stranger is a fine-looking fellow indeed."

And with that he slipped away and hurried back to tell the others what he had seen.

"Perhaps he really is a god," he told them.

"Perhaps he is one of *Haashch'ééh dine'é* the Holy People."

To which their chief had this to say:

"It may very well be as the maidens insist," he said.

"Perhaps what the stranger says about himself is true.

"And indeed, we all know how hard we must work to secure

food. We know how we must travel far each day to look for game. We know how we must labor to skin and cook and cure. We know how we must endure heat in the summer and cold in the winter.

"This newcomer might very well be able to save us from all that hardship.

"Let's be kind to him."

That is what the chief of the hunters had to say to all of the men in his village. And to one of the two maidens he also had this to say:

"Go to him," he said.

"Go back to the lodge.

"Serve this guest.

"Treat him kindly.

"Make him comfortable.

"Give him all that he asks for."

That is what the hunter chief instructed one of the two Hummingbird maidens.

Eager to do what she had been told to do, the youngest of the two women ran back to the lodge. And she had this to say to *Mąʼii:*

"I have come to serve you," she said to him.

"I am told to treat you kindly.

"I am told to make you comfortable.

"I am told to give you all that you may ask for."

That is what she had to say to Coyote.

As she spoke, *Mąʼii* the Coyote looked at her. He observed her very carefully. He observed that her clothing was ornamented with pendants of bone and hoof that tingled softly with each movement she made.

He liked the way she looked. He liked what she said. He liked the sound of her voice. Most of all, he liked the sound her ornaments made whenever she moved.

So he gave her a name.

Chʼikééh naʼazílí is what he called her. In the language of *Bilagáana* the White Man that means Tingling Young Woman.

•   •   •   •

On the very next morning, *Chʼikééh naʼazílí* the Tingling Young Woman went to the lodge where her kinfolk dwelled. There a good breakfast was being prepared.

She filled a large dishful of food to take to her guest, and as she was about to leave, her people instructed her to tell Coyote nothing about her disorderly neighbors.

"After all," they warned. "He might take a notion to visit them and to work his wonders for them rather than for us."

But the warning had come too late!

She had already told *Mq'ii* the Coyote about those neighbors. And he had already made up his mind that he would visit them.

After he had finished his morning meal, *Mq'ii* noticed that *Ch'ikééh na'azílí* the Tingling Young Woman kept glancing outside.

Presently she turned to Coyote and spoke to him, saying this:

"It appears that the menfolk are now going out to hunt," she said, not without sadness.

"I will go, too, then," he replied.

So it was that he joined the hunting party. So it was that he went off with them.

They all traveled together until they reached the top of a high hill which overlooked a vast expanse of countryside. Here *Mq'ii* the Coyote bid the others hide while he went to flush out game.

"You stay here," he bid them.

"Stay out of sight.

"In the meantime I'll make my way across that plain down there. I'll round up plenty of game for you down there. And I'll drive it all up here. The rest will be up to you."

When he was gone from their sight, he tied a long fagot of shredded cedar bark to his tail. Then he set the bark on fire. And with the burning wood fastened to his tail he ran across the countryside, where many antelope were grazing.[36]

Running as fast as he could, he traveled in a wide arc, circling clear around the grazing animals. And with the blaze at the end of his tail he set fire to the grass he ran across. That way he raised a circle of flame and smoke around the antelope herd.[37] And frightened by the fire, many of them stampeded out of the flaming ring which gradually surrounded them and up the hill where the hunters lay waiting.

So the men were able to kill antelope upon antelope as the fleeing animals made their way to the top of the ridge. And by day's end they headed back to their village laden with meat. When they arrived, they had nothing but praise for their new companion.

"What is said about our guest is true," they proclaimed.

"He certainly makes hunting easy for us."

On the next day they went out again. And again the hunters lay hidden atop the hill. Meanwhile *Mą'ii* again tied a blazing fagot of cedar bark to his tail and ran. And with the fire at the end of his tail he again raised a circle of flame and smoke around the grazing antelope herd. So that once again the hunters were able to kill antelope upon antelope as they stampeded up the hill to escape the fire. And so that once again they returned to their village at nightfall proclaiming that Coyote was indeed a great hunter.

On the following day they again went out. And for a third time *Mą'ii* the Coyote made a ring of fire to trap the grazing antelope. And for yet a fourth time they went out. And once again he led them on a successful hunt. So that by this time when they all returned the men were fully convinced that this newcomer among them was indeed one of *Haashch'ééh dine'é* the Holy People.

Could such a great hunter be anything less?

•　　•　　•　　•

On the fifth day of hunting with Coyote, however, as the men on the hilltop watched the arc of fire that he was making while he circled across the plain, they noticed that it looped clear around to where it began. He had made a complete circle and then somehow disappeared.

As before, antelope came running up the hill in droves where the ambushing hunters could easily kill them. But this time their new companion did not return. So the men set to work cutting up the meat and cooking it without him.

•　　•　　•　　•

As for *Mą'ii*, he had gone looking for the bad neighbors that *Ch'ikééh na'azílí* the Tingling Young Woman had spoken of. Untying his brand of burning cedar bark at the point where he had made a complete circle of fire, he headed in a different direction to begin a search.

After traveling for a while he came to two large trees growing close together. One of these was a spruce tree. The other was a pine. Chattering birds filled both trees. In the spruce were the birds called *Ch'íshiibeezhii*, which in the language of *Bilagáana* means Chickadees. And in the pine were the birds called *Tsídiisháshii*, which in the language of the White Man means Cedar Waxwing.

All of those birds were busy playing a game that Coyote had never seen before. They would fly at each other and then pluck each other's eyes out. They they would toss the eyes upwards toward the treetops and cry out, "Drop back, eyes! drop back!" And as the eyes would fall back down, their respective owners would catch them in their sockets.

Coyote watched the birds play this game for a long time, growing more and more fascinated with it. Until at length he called to *Tsídiisháshii* the Cedar Waxwings, saying this to them:

"*Héí! Héí!*" he said to them.

"Hello up there!"

"I want to play that game, too.

"Somebody pluck out my eyes for me. Then throw them up and let me catch them."

"*Ńláahdi naniná!*" replied the birds.

"Go away!"[38]

"We want nothing to do with you. Go away and leave us alone."

"*Héí! Héí!*" repeated *Mą'ii* the Coyote. "I say to you up there!

"Me, too! I want to play, too!

"Let somebody pluck my eyes out and throw them up so that I can catch them"

"Can't you hear?" replied the birds.

"Go away! *Ńláahdi naniná!*

"Go away and leave us to ourselves."

"But I really want to play!" insisted *Mą'ii.*

"Why can't somebody pluck my eyes out, too? And then throw them up so that I can catch them, too?"

"Don't you understand?" repeated the birds.

"We don't want to play with you. We don't want to be bothered. Go away! Go away!"

"I won't go!" declared Coyote.

"I'm going to stay right here.

"I can watch if I want to. And I'm going to stay here and watch until one of you plucks out my eyes. And until one of you throws them up so that I can catch them.

"Just like you are doing."

So *Mą'ii* the Coyote sat there.

There he sat, asking and pestering while they played. Until finally several of the birds flew down to where he had placed himself. And with sharp sticks they gouged out his eyes.

Then, just as he had seen them do with their own eyes, they threw his up into the treetops.

"Drop back!" cried *Mą'ii*, just as he had heard the birds cry.

"Drop back, eyes!"

And when they fell back down, just as the eyes of the Chickadees and of the Cedar Waxwings had fallen, he caught them in his sockets and could see again as well as ever.

Coyote was delighted.

"Do it again," he begged the birds. "Come on! Let's play it again."

"Now you listen here," replied the birds.

"We have no desire to play with you. We have already done enough for you. We do not wish to have anything else to do with you. We just want you to get out of here."

But *Mq'ii* the Coyote just sat there where he sat. And he continued to whine and beg and beg and whine. Until at last several other birds pulled his eyes out again, and threw them up into the treetops again. And again he called them to drop back.

Four times his eyes were plucked out that way. And four times they were thrown up. Likewise he called for them to fall back to him four times. And four times he caught them in his head where they originally belonged.

But when he asked for a fifth time to have his eyes thrown up into the air, the birds flew away. And they held a council where he could not hear what they said. They all agreed that this time they would remove *Mq'ii*'s optic nerves along with his eyes.

So when they returned they pulled out his eyes as they had done before, carefully plying out the nerves as they had agreed they would do. And when they threw his eyes up into the trees they threw the optic nerves along with them, still fastened to them the way they had been fastened inside his head.

Which is why, when Coyote's eyes were again flung upwards, they got tangled on one of the high branches. And there they remained, dangling by the cords whenever the wind blew.

Poor *Mq'ii!*

Poor, poor Coyote!

"Drop back, eyes! Drop back!" he cried again and again as he waited for them to return.

And each time he called for them he felt less and less as though he were still playing a game.

"Eyes!" he cried out again and again, again and again.

"Drop back, eyes! Drop back!"

But they would not fall.

So *Mq'ii* the Coyote sat there with his empty sockets, with his nose pointed up toward the treetops, with his whole body wrapped in the darkness he now felt, and with no companionship but the sound of his own voice. For he began to howl as he sat there and begged his eyes to return to him.

"Please, eyes!" he cried out.

"Drop back here, eyes! Drop back here!"

At last the birds took pity on him.

"He has suffered enough," said one of them.

"Yes," said another. "Let us make new eyes for him."

"Perhaps we should," said another. "But remember how he bothered us a while ago."

"If we make new eyes for him," said another, "we should also teach him a lesson."

So they agreed to make a couple of partly dried pieces of yellow pine gum and roll them into two balls.

That would have to do for *Mą'ii*'s new eyes.

These they stuck into his empty sockets. And while they were certainly not as good as his original bright and handsome eyes, they gave him enough sight to make his way. Although they were yellow and dull, ugly and unappealing, they provided him with some vision.

And that is why all coyotes have unattractive eyes and poor vision to this very day.

•　　•　　•　　•

Meanwhile, during Coyote's absence from the place where his erstwhile hunting companions had stopped to butcher and cure the meat they had gotten, a messenger had turned up from a nearby village. He had come to advise *Atseełtsoii* the Chickenhawks and the *Dah yiitįhí* the Hummingbirds to be on the lookout. Someone who called himself *Mą'ii* the Coyote had left his home recently, and he was headed this way.

"Beware of him," warned the messenger.

"He is an idler and a trickster. One way or another, he will bring disorder into your lives. One way or another, he will deceive you and embarrass you."

•　　•　　•　　•

As for *Mą'ii*, he crept as best he could to where the hunters had made their camp. There he found them cutting meat and cooking it.

Saying nothing, he sat down facing the fire. But soon he realized that his gum eyes were growing soft because of the heat. As a precaution he gave his body a sidelong twist so that he did not look directly at the flames.

The hunters accepted his return without seriously considering the warning they had received earlier. They were eager to give this stranger the benefit of the doubt. After all, they wanted to believe that he possessed a magic skill that would make hunting easier for them. So they chose not to suspect him. And after he had placed himself comfortably in front of the fire, they gave him a piece of raw liver, assuming that he would cook it himself as menfolk customarily do on hunting trips.

But Coyote was afraid to face the fire outright, lest his eyes should melt completely. So he threw his piece of liver on the coals without looking. And when he thought it would be done he tried to reach into the fire and feel for it with his paw. But all he managed to grab was hot, burning coals.

Not wanting to attract too much attention, he tried to treat what was happening to him as a joke. Each time he reached for his piece of liver and picked up nothing but a hot coal, he called to it playfully, singing out, "Don't burn me, liver. No there. Don't you burn me!"

But those who were sitting around the fire with *Mą'ii* the Coyote grew suspicious.

"He doesn't act the way he acted at first," whispered one to another.

"No," said another, speaking to still a third. "Something about him seems different."

And said the third to a fourth, "Sidle over there next to him. Look him over carefully and see what is wrong with him."

Doing as he was instructed to do, the fourth hunter saw the melting gum running out of *Mą'ii*'s eyes.

When they all saw his face, the hunters realized who he was.

"This is no hunting god," declared one of them.

"This person must be *Mą'ii* the Coyote, the idler and the trickster we were warned about," said another.

"Yes," said still another. "That's who it must be. And it seems that he has been playing with *Ch'ishiibeezhii* the Chickadees and *Tsídiisháshii* the Cedar Waxwings."

"So it seems," said a fourth. "And he has lost his eyes."

Once they recognized Coyote, they started back to their village,

leading the blind stranger along with them. And as they made their
way home they devised a plan for getting rid of him.

•   •   •   •

When they got back to the village, they took the rattling dress of
Chikééh na'azílí the Tingling Young Woman away from her,
giving her an ordinary one to wear for the time being. And, flying a
little distance above the ground just beyond *Mq'ii* the Coyote's
reach, one of the birds shook the dress in front of him, making
certain that it could be heard.

Mq'ii, thinking that *Chikééh na'azílí* was standing before him,
and seeking to comfort himself with her, took several eager steps
toward the soft clattering noise. But as he moved forward, the
chickenhawk managed by flying skillfully to remain just out of
Coyote's reach. And all the while he continued shaking the dress
so that Coyote could easily hear it.

Thus it was that *Mq'ii* the Coyote continued moving forward in
spite of his blindness, following the sound that had pleased him so
much. Until he had actually made his way to the very ledge of a
steep canyon.

Here the hawk shook the dress one more time. But he shook it
just beyond the edge of the cliff, managing to keep it only slightly
out of *Mq'ii*'s grasp.

And Coyote made a final eager leap toward the noise. But
needless to say, he did not touch the dress. Instead he sailed
headlong off the ledge and fell swiftly through the air to the
bottom of the canyon, where he was dashed to pieces.

•   •   •   •

But for all that, *Mq'ii* the Coyote did not die.

Do not suppose that this creature *Mq'ii* is like other creatures
known to us.

For his life-force does not reside in his chest like that of ordinary
mortals, where it can so easily be destroyed.

Instead he keeps one-half of it in the very tip of his nose. And he
keeps the other half of it at the most remote tip of his tail, where
nobody would expect to find it. And where it remains invulnerable
to falls and to blows that would kill other creatures.[39]

Thus it was that after a time Coyote regained his senses,

reassembled himself, treated his bruises and his cuts, and recovered what he could of his dignity. Following which recovery he made his way back to the village of *Dah yiitį́hi* the Hummingbirds and *Atseełtsoii* the Chickenhawks where he asked for *Ch'ikę́ę́h na'azílí* the Tingling Young Woman.

Whereupon he was told that she had gone away.

And whereupon he was told angrily that he too would have to leave.

For the people of that village now knew who he really was. He was a worthless fraud. He was an idler. He was a trickster. He was *Mą'ii* the Coyote. Surely he would bring disorder into the lives of the Hummingbirds and the Chickenhawks, if in fact he hadn't already done so.

Which is why those people never wanted to see him in their village again.

So Coyote went away and resumed his wanderings, it is said.

Eleven

It is also said that he roamed the countryside until he happened to hear of a maiden famous for her virtue and her beauty.[40]

She was a model among women, this maiden was. She prepared abundant meals. She wove strong baskets. She kept a clean, well-ordered household. And she attended the menfolk in her family with care and skill.

The only sister of twelve brothers, she lived with them in a dwelling abundant with meat. For those brothers were the best hunters anywhere.

Likewise they were good ranchers. They husbanded rare game and they had acquired their own livestock. As a consequence many people would come to visit them or to barter with them for food.

Some of those visitors would stay for days or even for months. So there grew up around their home a cluster of temporary shelters such as the Navajo people build today when they bring their herds of sheep to summer pastures to graze temporarily.

In fact, if the truth is fully to be known, many of the huts erected in that neighborhood were occasionally occupied by suitors of the maiden. They had heard tell of her beauty and her industry, her virtue and her devotion. And as a consequence they would come one after the other to seek her as a wife.

These suitors even included some of *Haashch'ééh dine'é* the Holy People. They declared that she above all the other womenfolk of *Nilch'i dine'é* the Air-Spirit People was worthy of marriage to a god. Even *Jóhonaa'éí* the Sun is reputed to have sought her to win her.

But she had refused every man who wished to marry her. She had established conditions for the man whose wife she was to become. After all, she was the best of all women, as her brothers would remind her over and over again. Why shouldn't she have the best husband to be found?

As for *Mq'ii* the Coyote, that was the kind of woman he longed to have. So he resolved to seek her out and to win her by one ruse or another. And at last he found her after searching and looking, looking and searching. And when he saw her at last, he was overcome with desire for her.

When the two of them met, *Mq'ii* greeted her with the dignity and the respect he thought her beauty deserved. This is what he said to her:

"Tell me, lovely maiden," he said to her, placing himself in front of her submissively.

"Why have you refused so many offers of marriage? You have even refused offers of marriage from men of the Holy People themselves. Why?"

"It would make no difference to you," she replied.

"For you could not meet even one of the demands that I have established for the man who is to become my husband."

That is the answer given to Coyote by the maiden. And this is what he said to her in reply:

"Well tell me this," he said to her in reply.

"Tell me what it is that you demand of the man who is to become your husband."

"Why should it make any difference to you?" she asked in turn.

"For surely you could not meet any of those demands that are to be met by the man who is to become my husband."

That is how the maiden replied to him. And this is what *Mq'ii* said back to her:

"How can you say such a thing to me?" he said back to her.

"How can you say that I could not meet any of your demands when you have not yet told me what those demands are?"

To which the maiden then had this to say:

"You scarcely look like someone who could meet them," she said.

That is what she said to *Mą'ii* the Coyote, and this is how he replied.

"You have made up your mind about me too soon," he replied.

"You have made up your mind that I cannot meet any of your demands. Yet you have not as much as told me what one of them might be."

To which the maiden then said this:

"If you must know, then," she then said.

"I will marry no one who has not at least slain one of the *Naayéé'*, the alien monsters who prey upon so many of the people, killing them and devouring them. And I can see at a glance that you are not the kind of person capable of doing that."

That is what the proud maiden said to *Mą'ii*.

And he, hearing her reply, had no answer to give.

Absolutely nothing did he say.

He simply raised himself onto his four paws, looked at her for a moment, turned away silently, and left her standing alone where she stood. For all that she could tell, he left her dwelling to resume his aimless wanderings.

•   •   •   •

But in reality he had a plan.

Which explains how it came to pass that Coyote made his way to the dwelling of *Yé'iitsohíbáhí*, or Gray Giant as he would be called today in the language of *Bilagáana*. This creature was one of the *Naayéé'* who killed and devoured. Half as tall as the tallest pine tree anywhere, *Yé'iitsohíbáhí* was evil and cruel indeed.

And this is what *Mą'ii* the Coyote said to him:

"Big brother," said he to him.

"I want to be your servant.

"Because I think I can help you.

"Especially when it comes to hunting.

"You really ought to know that you do not manage to catch more people because you are not very fast.

"On the other hand, look at me.

"I can outrun *Náshdóítsoh* the Mountain Lion if I have a mind to.

"I can jump over four bushes at a time.

"I can catch anybody I hunger for.

"That's why I always have enough to eat.

"Would you like me to show you how I acquired such great speed?"

That is what *Mą'ii* the Coyote said to *Yé'iitsohíbáhí* the Gray Giant. And this is what he answered:

"Little brother," he answered.

"I sure would like you to show me how.

"For I am as slow as you say I am. And I am always hungry.

"Tell me what I must do to become as fast as you are, and I shall do it."

That is what *Yé'iitsohíbáhí* the Gray Giant said to *Mą'ii*.

Whereupon Coyote instructed him to build a sweat lodge, and to get it ready for a nice hot fire.[41]

Which the monster did.

And while *Yé'iitsohíbáhí* the Gray Giant was hard at work, Coyote set out on an errand. For he needed the bone of some big animal which his cousin *Mą'iitsoh* the Great Wolf had slain and eaten. At length he found just the sort of bone he wanted: a long thighbone which suited his purpose perfectly.

Concealing it under his shirt, he took it back with him.

By the time he returned, *Yé'iitsohíbáhí* the Gray Giant had finished the sweathouse. With *Mą'ii* the Coyote's help he then built a fire in front of the lodge, heated some large stones in the fire, and spread a carpet of leaves upon the ground.

Mą'ii then hung four blankets of sky over the doorway. He hung one white blanket. He hung one blue blanket. He hung one yellow blanket. And he hung one black blanket.

Next he carried the hot stones into the lodge. Then he went back outside and told *Yé'iitsohíbáhí* the Gray Giant that everything was ready. So the two of them undressed, hung their clothes on a neighboring tree, entered, and sat down.

But unnoticed by the monster, Coyote managed to smuggle the thighbone into the sweathouse with him.

Mą'ii the Coyote then spoke to *Yé'iitsohíbáhí* the Gray Giant. And this is what he said:

"Now, my friend," he said.

"If you want to become a fast runner like me, you must do what I am about to show you.

"First you must cut the flesh of your thigh. Cut it all the way down to the bone.

"Then you must break the bone itself. Break it clear through.

"In a moment it will heal, though. Don't be afraid.

"And when it does heal you will be stronger and swifter than before. You will catch and eat whomever you like.

"Each time you repeat the procedure your strength will grow. Your speed will grow.

"As for me, I often do it. That's why I keep getting faster and faster.

"In fact, I am about to do it again. Right now. Watch for yourself and see how easily and how quickly it is done."

Upon saying which, *Mą'ii* produced a great stone knife and pretended to cut into his own thigh, wailing and crying as if he were suffering great pain. Then he placed the old thighbone on top of his real thigh, held it by both ends, and cried out.

"At last!" he cried out.

"At last I have reached the bone.

"Feel it, cousin. But hurry!

"Hurry! I am enduring great pain, and I wish to finish this ordeal as quickly as I can."

Yé'iitsohíbáhí the Gray Giant reached and felt the bare bone, convinced in the steamy darkness of the sweat lodge that it was indeed Coyote's thighbone that he felt.

Mą'ii then shoved the giant's hand away and struck the bone hard with the edge of his knife several times until it split. Then he bid his companion feel the fractured ends. Next he threw the old bone aside, rubbed some spittle on his thigh, prayed and sang so as to be easily heard, and finally bid the monster feel his sound thigh. Then he had this to say:

"See?" he said.

"My limb is sound again.

"It is as sound as ever. In fact, I do not even feel pain any longer.

"Now, my kinsman, try it yourself while I instruct you.

"Then let us go outside and see how much more swiftly you will be able to run. After that you can put an end to your hunger.

"You can end it once and for all."

Whereupon *Mą'ii* the Coyote handed *Yé'iitsohíbáhí* the Gray Giant the great stone knife. And whereupon the giant in turn slowly cut into his own thigh as he thought Coyote to have done, wailing and crying with pain. And as he believed Coyote to have done, he severed the bone that lay under his flesh until its two ends were entirely disjointed. That much accomplished, he pieced the two severed ends together as Coyote appeared to have done, spat upon the place where they joined, and prayed and sang as he had heard Coyote do.

Needless to say, the severed ends would not unite.

"Heal together, bone! Heal together!" he commanded, thinking that his great size and strength would give his voice authority. But size and strength do not persuade broken bones to mend, and his femur would do nothing of the kind.

"Little brother," he called out to Coyote.

"Little brother, help me heal this leg!

"Tell me what I have done wrong, that the two ends of my thighbone do not join as yours have done. Tell me why it will not heal as you promised it would!"

But Mą'ii the Coyote said nothing.

Absolutely nothing did he say.

He sat there silently while Yé'iitsohíbáhí the Gray Giant wailed and cried with pain, until at last he was sure that the monster's strength was sufficiently diminished. Then, when he thought that the right moment had come, he ran outside, seized his bow, went back inside the sweathouse, and shot every single arrow he had into the body of the hapless Yé'iitsohíbáhí.

Whereupon the giant died, it is said.

Twelve

It is also said that Mą'ii the Coyote scalped his victim and tied the scalp to the top of a cedar branch which he broke from a nearby tree.

He knew that the maiden would recognize that scalp. For in those days the fearsome Naayéé' all had yellow hair such as no other people had.

But just to make sure, he also took the giant's quiver and arrows with him when he set out for the dwelling of the young woman he longed to have.

When he got there, he presented his spoils to her, having this to say:

"Here," he said.

"Here is the scalp of the mighty *Yé'iitsohíbáhí*. Surely you are aware that he is one of the *Naayéé'* who kill and devour so many of the people wherever they go. Now it would seem that you must marry me."

That is what *Mą'ii* said to the maiden. And this is what she replied:

"It is not necessarily so," replied she.

"You have met only one of the demands which I have established for the man who wishes to become my husband."

To which the Coyote had this to say:

"Then you must tell me what the other demands are," he said.

To which she replied:

"The man who wishes to become my husband must die four times.

"Four times he must be killed. And four times he must come back to life.

"Those are the other demands."

To which he next had this to say:

"Have you told me all that I need to know to count myself among your suitors?"

To which she answered:

"I have told you all that you need to know to be included among those who seek me as a wife.

To which he now asked this of her:

"I must be sure that you have told me all that must be done. I must be sure that you are telling me the truth."

That is what the wary Coyote asked of the cautious maiden. And this is what she responded:

"I speak the truth," she responded.

"I have told you everything."

"Here I stand, then," said *Mą'ii* the Coyote.

"I am ready to die for you. But you must kill me yourself. If I am to die for you four times, you and only you must kill me each time."

Thereupon the maiden took him a short distance from her dwelling. And she laid him on the ground. And there she beat him with a great club until she thought she had smashed every bone in his body. And she then left him for dead.

However, she did not smash the tip of *Mq'ii*'s nose or the end of his tail where the two halves of his life-force reside.

Believing that she was now rid of him, though, she hurried back to her dwelling. For she had work to do. After all, she was the only woman in a family of thirteen. She had food to cook. She had clothing to make. She had seeds to gather. She had baskets to weave.

At this particular time she was busy making four such baskets. And she was eager to resume that task. So when she returned home she sat down and got busy.

But she had not worked long before she realized that someone was standing in the doorway staring at her. And looking up she saw Coyote.

"Here I am," he said to her.

"We have played one game already. And I have only three more to win now."

Whereupon the maiden took *Mq'ii* further than she had taken him before; and there she pounded him to pieces with a club; and there she scattered those pieces in different directions; and thinking that now he was dead she hurried home to finish weaving.

But she did not make very many stitches in her basket before Coyote again appeared in the doorway. "We have played two games," he said. "And I have now only two more to win."

Again she led him away silently, taking him still further this time. Again she pounded him until his body became a shapeless mass but with a heavier club this time. Again she disposed of what was left of him, but this time by scattering the remains on a hot rock in the burning sun. And again she returned home to finish her work, but not before she pounded what remained of him again just to be certain that he was dead this time.

Thinking that at last she could finish her work without seeing him anymore, she sat quietly and wove for a while. But again *Mq'ii* the Coyote appeared in the doorway. "We have played three games," he said. "And I now have only one more to win."

This time she led him further away than ever, to a place so far off that it was strange to her. And this time she not only mashed him to pieces, but she mixed the pieces with earth, ground the mixture between two large stones as corn is ground until it became a fine powder, and scattered this powder far and wide to the winds. And this time she returned to her work absolutely sure that she was rid of him once and for all. But this time she still neglected to crush the point of Coyote's nose and the tip of his tail.

Once she was back in her dwelling, she was able to continue stitching undisturbed for awhile. At last, she reflected, he is done for. But no sooner had she said that to herself than she looked up. Again, there stood *Mǫ'ii* in the doorway, saying this:

"Now," he said.

"We have played four games. Now here I am to declare myself your husband. Now here I am to declare you my wife."[42]

Having sworn to him that there was nothing else he needed to do to claim her, she could not now send him away. Yet she was by no means eager to accept him as her husband. So she answered him by declaring this:

"No!" she declared.

"I cannot be your wife after all."

"But after all," answered he.

"I have just killed *Yé'iitsohíbáhí* the Gray Giant, exactly as you instructed me to."

"Even so," answered she.

"It is not right.

"By no means would it be suitable for the likes of you to marry me."

"Have I not allowed you to kill me four times?" asked he. "Just as you stipulated that I should?"

"That is true," answered she to him.

"But still I cannot marry you. My brothers would never permit it to be so, even if I myself should."

"Have I not come back to life four times?" protested he. "Just as you directed that I should."

"That, too, is true," admitted she.

"Still I must refuse you. My brothers would have it no other way."

"But after all you have told me," persisted he to her, "how is it that you can refuse me?"

"Very well, then," replied she to him.

"You may wait here until my brothers return. At the very least you may do that. Then at the very least we can discuss the matter with them."

So said she to *Mǫ'ii* the Coyote, thinking that when they came back her brothers would drive him away. Then at long last she would be rid of him.

Once and for all he would then be gone.

By that time it was nearly dark, and she got ready for bed at the far side of the room. Meanwhile, *Mą'ii* lay down on the floor near the door, making as if he too would fall asleep.

As she lay down on the thick, warm robe on which she usually slept, he watched her out of the corner of his eye. The last few rays of light filled the room, and the fire still glowed. But even though there was still some warmth inside the lodge, Coyote made his teeth chatter. And he said this:

"My," he said, sucking his lips and shivering.

"It's cold in here."

As for her, she made no reply.

"Brrrr. . . . " he said, sucking his lips again and shivering once more. "It certainly is cold in here."

She, in turn, said nothing. She only pulled a warm buckskin counterpane over her shoulders.

"Oh . . . oh . . . ohhhh!" said he, sucking his lips, shivering and rattling his teeth.

"It is a cold winter night and I'm freezing."

For her part, she made no reply. She only closed the buckskin tightly about herself and turned so that her back was to him.

"Oh, brrrr. . . . Ohhhh, br!" repeated he.

"It's unbearable. How cold it is tonight! How frozen I am!

"My dear friend, let me at least lie over there at the fringe of your robe, please."

"Well, all right," said she.

So he crossed the room and lay just at the very edge of the robe. There he lay for several minutes, saying nothing at first. But then again he began to shiver.

And then again he spoke.

"My sister," spoke he then.

"My dear sister. How cold I still am. At the very least, let me move a little closer. At least let me move close enough so that the fringe of your blanket covers me."

"Well, I suppose that would be all right," said she.

So he pulled the fringe over himself. And there he lay for several minutes more, saying nothing at first. But then he again began to shiver. And then he again spoke.

"Goodness!" he said.

"The frost is awful! Awful! And I am freezing, my dear sister.

Can't I lie closer? Can't I place myself beside you so that I can at least get warm?"

"Well, if you are cold," said she, "I guess that would be all right."

So he placed himself closer to her, pulling the blanket over so that it covered both of them equally. And there he lay, quietly at first; but soon he brought his body closer still to hers. For a few minutes more he lay without moving; but then again he stirred, bringing his body still closer so that his stomach and foreparts were curved fully around her hindparts.

For some minutes they lay that way, until he felt her breath coming faster and harder. Then he placed one arm around her and they lay that way for a while. She breathed still harder and he could feel the added warmth in her. And then again he spoke.

"My dear sister," is what he said.

"My dearest wife.

"I am a little warmer now. I am nearly warm enough. But if I could only get just slightly warmer. . . . How about it, my dearest, dearest wife? Just let me put my hand there.

"There!

"There where it is oh so warm."

And after putting his hand there he lay quite still again. Very still he lay. But in the meanwhile he could feel her turning slowly towards him. Slowly she turned until she now faced him, he with his hand there as steadily as he could keep it.

"How about it, my dearest sweet wife? Just let me point it up. There! Just like that! Let me just keep it there that way."

"Yes," she said. "Yes. That's quite all right."

And after just pointing it up he left it there. Erect he left it. Then after a minute or so he spoke.

"My dearest wife. My sweetest wife. How about it? Just let me put it in; let me just insert it.

"There! There!

"Just like that. Let me just keep it in there that way."

"Oh, yes!" she said. "Oh, yes! yes! That's quite all right. That's good."

Having inserted it, he left it there inside her, erect. Then in no more than a minute he spoke again.

"My sweetest, sweetest wife! My dearest, dearest wife! How about it? Shall I turn over on top of you and hump myself? Shall I hump myself just once?"

"Oh, yes, yes!" she said.

"Twice?"

"Yes! Yes! Yes!"

"Three times my dearest, dearest wife?"

"Yes, yes, yes, yes!"

"Four times! Four times let me hump dearest wife!"

"Yes yes yes yes yes!"

"Five times! Shall I hump five times dearest dearest wife!"

"Ohhhh yes! yes yes yes yes yes yes!"

"Six times?"

Oh, yessss! yesyesyesyesyesyesyessssss. . . ."

"Seven times my dear wife! My dearest, dearest, dearest, dearest wife. . . ."

"Yesyesyesyesyesyesyesyessss! Yesyesyesyesyesyesyesyessss!"

"Seven, seven, seven, seven, seven, seven, seven!" cried he.

"Seven, seven, seven, seven, seven, seven, seven!" he cried again.

"Seven! seven! seven! seven! seven! seven! seven! seven!" repeated she. "Seven seven seven seven seven seven seven seven!" she repeated.

"Yesssssssss. . . . "

• • • •

And that's what they did.

They did it beyond the possibility of counting. They just kept doing it that way off and on all night long. And so it was that *Mą'ii* the Coyote became her husband and she became his wife without ever discussing it with her brothers.

• • • •

Next morning when they awoke and got up. Coyote was pleased with himself.

So happy was he that he sprang up and ran outside. Back and forth he ran, urinating wherever he went. From a cottonwood that grew alongside the spring north of the lodge he ran. And there he urinated. To a small cedar that grew to the west he ran, urinating there also. He ran to a pinyon that grew south of the lodge and he urinated there. And then he ran to a spruce that grew to the east, urinating there also. Then he scampered around the lodge in a circle. Around and around he raced, around and around, urinating everywhere.[43]

Finally he returned inside where she lay waiting for him. And he placed himself beside her and lay with her, fondling her again. All day long they lay together, those two, she neglecting her duties and thinking only of him and how nice it was. So completely distracted was she that she gave no thought to her brothers, until suddenly she heard them approaching as the sun began to set.

"My brothers are coming!" she then said. "You must hide. Some of them will surely be angry when they find you here. No, that's not entirely true. They will all be angry. They will want to harm you. So you had better stay out of sight. At least for now!"

Whereupon she hid him behind a pile of skins on her side of the lodge, where she usually stored the belongings that were hers.

No sooner than which the menfolk filed into the room, one by one. And one by one they greeted her.

"Hello, little sister," said the eldest.

"We bring you some fat young venison," said the next eldest.

"Put it down to boil," said the next. "And put some of the fat into a pot for us."

"For our faces are burned by the wind and the sun," said another of the brothers.

"Yes," said another. "And we want to rub them down."

Thus each one of them spoke to her, until at last the youngest had this to say. He was the sloppiest of the twelve, and the one with the least ability. But he was a good-hearted youth.

"It is good to see you again, little sister," he said to her. "Especially at the end of a tiring day. We are lucky to have someone like you to look after us."

Meanwhile, she had put the pot over the fire as she was told. And as she was told she placed fresh sticks over the embers so that they would flame up quickly.

When the fire began to burn well, and when the water began at first to steam and then to boil, the room grew warm. As it grew warmer, the smell of coyote urine filled the air.[44]

"It smells like some wild creature has been in the woodpile," said one of the brothers. And with that he picked up some of the sticks his sister had brought in. "Let's throw some of these away," said he.

"Yes," said another. "Let's get some fresh logs from the bottom of the pile."

Several others helped the first two. They even took some of the burning wood out of the fire and threw it away. And they went outside, broke fresh branches from some nearby trees, and built a new fire.

But the odor would still not go away.

"Perhaps the smell comes from the water," said the eldest brother. "Tell us, little sister, where did you get that water?"

"At the spring," replied she. "Where I always get it."

"Well throw it out and get some that is fresh," said the next eldest.

So she picked up the pot, took it outside, emptied it, and filled it up again. Then she placed it over the fire until it began to boil once more. Again it began first to steam and then to boil until the room grew warm; and again the smell of a wild animal filled the air. In spite of all the extra work, the stench was as strong as ever.

At length the eldest brother turned to his sister and asked this question:

"What causes that terrible smell?" he asked.

"It does not come from the wood. It does not come from the water. Where then does it come from?"

She, however, made no effort to reply. Instead she averted his stare, turning silently away.

"Didn't you hear him?" asked a second brother.

"What is the source of that terrible smell? If it does not come from the wood, and if it does not come from the water, where does it come from?"

As for her, she did not look at him either. And again she made no effort to reply.

"We are asking you a question," demanded a third. "What makes that terrible smell? The wood is not making it. The water is not making it. So what is making it?"

But she refused to look at him, too. And she made no more of an effort to answer him than she made to answer the other two.

"This is the last time we will ask you," threatened a fourth brother. "Tell us what causes that stench that none of us can stand. The wood does not cause it, and the water does not cause it. Surely you know what causes it, and you must tell us."

Whereupon Coyote jumped out of his hiding place at the sister's side of the room and strode over to the middle of the lodge.

"I am what you smell!" he proclaimed.

"*Mạ'ii* the Coyote is what you smell.

"And you might as well know right now that you are going to get used to that odor.

"For I have taken your sister as my wife.

"Which means that I am a member of your family."

To which the eldest brother replied:

"I will never accept that odor," he replied.

"Nor will I," replied the second eldest.

"Nor I," repeated the third.

"Nor I," said the fourth.

"It is that way with me, also," said the next.

"So get out of out house," said the next.

"Get out now," said the next.

"Before you feel the pain of our blows," said still another.

"As for you," said the first of the four youngest to their sister. "If you really are his wife, you must also go."

"Under such a circumstance this is no longer your home," said the next of the youngest four.

"You cannot be a wife to him and a sister to us at the same time," said the next of those four.

And then the eldest brother spoke up again, saying this:

"You have done wrong," said he.

"For you have chosen a spouse without consulting any of your kin.

"Because of that you will have to leave!"

So the two of them, Coyote and the young woman, left the place that had been her home. They left the men who had been her brothers. But not before *Mạ'ii* darted over to the fire and snatched a glowing brand from it. And with it he lit a new fire in a grove of trees that grew nearby the dwelling. Then he build a shelter for himself and his bride.

That done, he returned to the lodge of the brothers and walked boldly in. And without saying so much as a word to any of them, he took what had been her belongings. He took her pots. He took her skins. He took her baskets. He took four awls that had been hers. All that was in fact rightfully hers he took while the brothers looked on in dumb silence. And he carried those belongings to their sister's new home.

•   •   •   •

"Go out tonight and watch those two," bid the eldest brother to the youngest one, the sloppy one.[45]

"Find out what kind of a brother-in-law we have acquired. Hide somewhere outside their shelter and observe them. And do not let them see you."

So the young brother did what he was told. He went to a place where he could peep in and see by the light of the fire. His hiding place was close enough to Coyote and his wife so that he could hear nearly everything they said. And he watched and waited.

Presently the woman placed her hand across *Mǫ'ii* the Coyote's knees affectionately. But he thrust it away.

He did so without speaking.

She waited for a while and again placed her hand across his kneè, again looking at him affectionately. But again he thrust it away without speaking.

As before she waited for a while, and as before placed her hand across his knee, looking at him as she had looked at him before. But as before he thrust it away, saying nothing.

Once more she waited for a few minutes. Once more she placed her hand where she had placed it before. And once more she gave him the same affectionate look that she had given him before. But once more he thrust it away without saying anything. Without as much as a single word he thrust it away.

Until at length she spoke to him, asking him this:

"Why do you refuse me that way?" she asked.

"Because I have sworn never to take a woman as my own until I have killed her," answered he.[46]

"Four times she must be killed before I will take her. And four times must she come back to life.

"Only then will I accept her."

For what seemed like a long time, the woman gazed silently at the fire. Until at length she sighed, stood up, looked at him meekly, and had this to say:

"Here I stand, then," she said.

"I am ready to die for you. Do what you will to slay me."

Whereupon *Mǫ'ii* took her a short distance from their shelter. And whereupon he laid her on the ground. And whereupon he beat her with a great club until nothing in her body stirred. And whereupon he then left her for dead.

He then returned to the shelter and waited, wondering where the vital spirit resided in her body and wondering if he had indeed destroyed it. But he did not have to wait long before she appeared in the doorway.

"Here I am," she said to him. "We have played one game already. I need submit to your blows only three more times now."

Whereupon Coyote led her to a place farther away than the place he had taken her before; and he pounded her to pieces with a club; and he scattered those pieces in different directions just as she had done with his bodily remains earlier; and, leaving her for dead, he returned to the shelter and waited, wondering if he had indeed destroyed her vital spirit this time.

But he did not wait long before she appeared in the doorway again. "Here I am," she said. "We have played two games. And I need now submit to your blows only twice more."

Again *Mą'ii* the Coyote led her away silently, but into the darkest part of the thicket. And he pounded her until her body became a shapeless mass, but with a heavier club. She was surely dead by now, he was convinced, but he took the added precaution of placing her remains on a large rock. And there he beat them into still finer pieces, but he did not stop until what was left resembled a mass of paste. Then he returned to their shelter and waited, but not without reflecting that it would be difficult indeed for her life-force to endure what he had just done to her.

But it wasn't long until she appeared again in the doorway. "Here I am," she said. "We have played three games. And now I need submit to your blows only once more."

This time he led her further away than ever, deep into a canyon where the light of no star reached. And he not only smashed her to pieces; he mixed the pieces with sand from the canyon floor, ground the mixture between two stones like corn until it became a fine powder, and scattered that powder far and wide until it disappeared into the utter darkness. Then he returned to their shelter to wait, worrying that he had indeed destroyed her life-force this time.

And he waited for a considerably long while, listening carefully in the dark silence for the slightest sound of her return, afraid that she had been unable to survive what he had done to her. But at last she appeared, just as the fire had burned to its last glowing ember.

Saying nothing, she placed herself on a couch of pine boughs that he had made, and she lay down there. He followed her there and placed himself beside her. And they spent the rest of the night together accepting one another as man and wife.

But *Mą'ii* never did learn how or where she had managed to preserve her life-force.[47]

•   •   •   •

Meanwhile, the sloppy youngest brother had remained hidden in his tracks, witnessing nearly all that had gone on between Coyote and his sister. He had managed not only to see what had occurred in the shelter but to hear all that was said between them save for a few scraps of long, low murmurings while they lay together for the remainder of the night. And at the first sign of dawn he went home to report to his brothers all that he knew.

"What went on between them?" asked the eldest of the brothers.

"What have they said? asked another.

"What have they done?" asked still another.

"What are they up to?" asked a fourth.

"Much of what I have to tell you," replied the youngest brother, the sloppy one, "you would scarcely believe. And quite a bit of what they said I could not plainly hear.

"But this I can surely tell you.

"Beware of those two.

"For a great deal of what I did hear was magic. Bad magic. And a great deal of what I did see was also magic.

"Bad magic indeed."

And the brothers could tell that he was worried by what he had witnessed, it is said.

Thirteen

It is also said that on that very morning the twelve brothers prepared to go hunting. And as they were getting ready, *Mq'ii* the Coyote entered their dwelling and asked to join them.

"No, certainly not," said one.

"You may not come," said another.

"Stay home with your wife," taunted another.

"Help her with her work," teased still another.

"She might get lonely," another one said.

"She might want someone to keep her company," another said.

And all of them chased him away.

As they were about to leave, however, *Mq'ii* came back and

begged them to take him along. But they all laughed at him and made him go away. Then they left.

They had not gone far, though, before Coyote overtook them, asking again if he couldn't come. But they only made fun of him.

"Who will stay back there with your wife?" one of them jeered.

"Who will fetch water for her?" laughed another.

"Who will bring it to a boil?" teased another.

"Who will help her cook the meat?" another one taunted.

"Leave the job of hunting to those who know how to hunt," one of them said.

"You go back there and help your wife weave," said another.

Saying such things to him, they drove him off.

They traveled until they came to the edge of a deep canyon bounded on both sides by sheer cliffs that dropped vertically from the plateau above to the bottom far below. Here they noticed that *Mạ'ii* the Coyote had been following them right along. There he was, skulking behind, sometimes plainly seen and sometimes dropping out of sight. And when he knew that they had actually spotted him, he insisted again that they let him come along.

Once more they were inclined to refuse. But this time the sloppy young brother disagreed.

"Perhaps we ought to take him with us," he observed. "He is fast and he is cunning. Maybe he can round up game for us and drive it our way."

The brothers talked about it for a while and finally decided that their little brother might be right. And at last they agreed to let *Mạ'ii* come after all.

At the edge of the canyon they made a bridge of rainbow so that they could cross to the other rim. But before they all reached the opposite side, Coyote leaped over to it from halfway across the arch. And once he reached the other side he began to frisk and prance.

"Hurry up!" he cried. "Come on over as fast as you can. This is a nice place to play."

"We haven't come all this way to play," scolded the eldest brother. "We have come to hunt. So mind your ways."

They traveled further on, and after a while they came to a plateau which protruded out of a lower plain. A narrow bridge of level land connected the mesa to the plain. It was a mesa much like that on which the three eastern towns of the Hopi people stand. Its sides were high and steep, its entrance narrow. On that neck of land they observed the tracks of four Rocky Mountain sheep who had apparently gone over to the opposite mesa but had not returned.

At the neck they built a fire, sat down beside it, warmed themselves, and then talked about how they might trap those sheep.

"I have a plan," the eldest brother said.

"Our brother-in-law, *Mq'ii* the Coyote, can go over there, circle around to the far side, frighten the sheep, and then drive them back here, where we will lie hidden."[48]

It was obviously a good plan, and Coyote performed his part well. For soon after he started out alone the quarry came stampeding out over the neck of land within easy range of the hunters. All four sheep were killed easily, and presently *Mq'ii* returned, tired and out of breath.

Now in those ancient times the horns of Rocky Mountain sheep were fat and fleshy and could be eaten. Some say in fact that no part of that particular animal tasted better. They were considered a prize, to be enjoyed by the best hunter in a hunting party.

"I will take the horns as my share of the kill," said the oldest brother, as they all prepared to eat.

"No you will not," said Coyote. "The horns will be mine. Give them to me."

"The horns shall be my share of this day's catch," the eldest repeated.

"I am the one who drove the sheep into easy range for you to kill," declared Coyote. "It is only fitting that I get the horns. So give them to me."

"I am the one who instructed you to drive the sheep out toward us," replied the brother. "So the horns should be mine."

"What good are your ideas unless you have the speed and the strength to carry them out?" Coyote asked.

"What good are speed and strength without the good sense to know how to use them?" replied the brother. And so saying he drew his knife and began to cut one of the horns away from the carcass that held it.

But no sooner had he done so than *Mq'ii* the Coyote cried out saying this:

"*Ts'in nánídleehí! Ts'in nánídleehí!*" he cried.

"Turn to bone, horns! Turn to bone!"

And with the sound of *Mą'ii*'s voice the horns became hard, so that the eldest brother could not separate them from the head of the mountain sheep.

The brother slashed and hacked, but he was unable to make his knife work for him. The harder and more furiously he tried to cut, the harder the horns became, as Coyote continued to shout.

"*Ts'in nánídleehí!*" he shouted. "*Ts'in nánídleehí!*

"Turn to bone!" he repeated. "Turn to bone!"

Finally the eldest realized that his knife was of no use. The horns were now like stone and would not be fit to eat by anyone, even if they could be cut away from the sheep.

"*Ch'įįdii!*" he cried to *Mą'ii* the Coyote. "*Ch'ińdáásh!*

"You devil!" he cried. "You evil traveling companion!"[49]

There he stood, squatting over the sheep, slashing and hacking first at one horn and then at another, going furiously from animal to animal only to learn that each set of horns might just as well have been rocks.

And all the while he cursed *Mą'ii*.

"You trickster!" he cursed. "You devil! You sorcerer! You worthless evildoer!"

But nothing that he did and nothing that he said could make the horns of the sheep any softer or any more edible.

And that is how the horns of the Rocky Mountain sheep came to be as hard as they now are, it is said.

Fourteen

It is also said that the hunters gathered all the meat into one pile. And somehow they reduced it to a very compact bundle, which they bound so firmly that it could be easily carried by one person. Then they gave it to *Mą'ii* the Coyote and instructed him to take it home.

"Travel around by the head of the canyon we crossed this

morning," they bid him. "But do not go through it, whatever you do. Troublemakers dwell down there along the canyon floor, and they will surely do you mischief.

"And whatever you do, do not open the bundle until you are safely home."

Then they lifted the pack onto *Mq'ii*'s back and helped him secure it there, he assuring them that he had listened to everything they had told him, and promising them that he would indeed do what he was being instructed to do.

And then he started home.

But no sooner was he out of their sight than he slipped the bundle from his back and lowered it to the ground. He wanted to see how his brothers-in-law had managed to make such a small package out of so much meat.

So he opened it.

And at once the meat expanded and became as large a heap as it originally was. Needless to say, Coyote could not tie it up the way it had been tied by the brothers. And of course he could not carry it all since it was no longer tied.[50]

So he hung some of the meat on the trees and bushes.

He stuck part of it into crevices he found among the rocks.

A portion of it he simply left scattered on the ground.

And as much of it as he could manage he tied into a new bundle, which he then hoisted up on his shoulder.

And with this bundle he resumed his journey.

•   •   •   •

When he reached the edge of the forbidden canyon, he looked down and saw some birds playing a game he had never seen before. They were rolling great stones down a slope, which extended from the foot of the cliff all the way to the bottom of the valley. Before the others pushed a boulder into motion, one of them would climb on top of it. And once it began to move, he would remain upon it all the way down, carefully balancing himself so that he stayed on his feet unhurt until the stone came to a full stop.

Fascinated, *Mq'ii* the Coyote stood and watched.

Not one bird fell. Not one lost his balance. Not one slipped. Not one was injured in even the slightest way. And the sight of this pastime so pleased Coyote that he descended into the canyon in spite of what he had been warned. And he begged the birds to let him join them.

Saying nothing to welcome him, several of the birds chose a stone for *Mą'ii* and rolled it gently. As soon as it started moving he jumped on. Then, as the boulder picked up speed, he began to work his feet and legs. He handled himself so nimbly that he reached the bottom of the slope without getting hurt at all.

Delighted with this game, he begged the birds to let him try again, which they reluctantly permitted him to do. And again he got on a stone after the birds gave it a gentle shove to get it started. Again he maintained control all the way to the bottom of the slope, nimbly working his feet and legs so that he remained upright to the very end.

"I really enjoyed that," cried Coyote.

"Let me try again."

Without bothering to conceal their impatience with him, the birds grudgingly agreed. And once more he jumped onto a stone after it was gently placed in motion, and once more he remained upright upon it, nimbly working his feet and legs to the very end.

"What fun that was!" he cried. "Let me do it once more, please?"

But by now their impatience had turned to anger. So this time the birds hurled a stone with such force that Coyote lost his footing the minute he landed on it. He and the stone rolled headlong down, the one tumbling over the other, clear to the bottom of the hill, *Mą'ii* the Coyote crashing and stumbling all the way down.

●   ●   ●   ●

Not wishing to stay with the birds after that, *Mą'ii* wandered around along the canyon floor, having by now fully forgotten what the brothers had warned.

On he continued, sometimes following the stream, sometimes exploring the cliffs and the slopes that rose above them. Until he came upon *Tábąąstíín dine'é* the Otter People playing the Navajo game of *na'azhǫǫsh*, or hoop and pole as it would be called today.

They were betting their skins against each other as stakes. But when one of them lost his skin he would simply jump into the water and splash around. Then he came out wearing a new hide.

"What about letting me play?" asked Coyote, stepping forward to approach *tábąąstíín* the otters.

Having heard all about him by now, the otters refused, telling *Mą'ii* the Coyote to go away and keep company with himself. But there he stayed, right where he stood. And he begged and pleaded to be allowed to play.

Realizing that he would not leave, *tábąąstíín* the otters talked it over among themselves and at last agreed to let him join them in the game, but only for a while.

Mą'ii promptly bet his skin and lost it in the first round of play. The moment he lost, the otters all rushed at him to tear his hide off.

"No, don't!" Coyote begged.

"Please don't take my skin!"

But they paid no attention to his pleas, and they tore the hide from him, stripping it off clear from the root of his tail to the vital spot at the end of his nose. And all the while *Mą'ii* the Coyote wailed and groaned.

"Ahh," he wailed. "Ahh, oh, oh, oh!"

"Aii," he groaned. "Aii yii yii yii!"

When he finally found himself entirely stripped of his hide, fur and all, he jumped into the water as he had watched the otters do. But his skin did not come back to him.

So he clambered out, leaped onto shore, shook himself, and jumped in again. But still no skin returned.

Again he darted out of the water and then jumped back in. But again no skin! And once more he jumped back out and in again, but still no skin! No skin whatsoever. Each time he came out of the water he emerged as bare as he was when he leaped in.

Over and over he jumped in and out of the water, until at length he grew thoroughly exhausted and lay down in the stream, frightened and ashamed. Whereupon *tábąąstíín* the otters took pity on him and pulled him out. Then they dragged him to a badger hole, threw him into it, covered him over with earth, and left him there.

As we know, *Mą'ii*'s fur had been smooth and beautiful until then. But when he dug his way out of the badger hole he discovered that he was once again covered with hair; however, he realized that it was coarse, rough hair, much like the coat *Nahashch'id* the Badger wore. And such a pelt, alas, all coyotes have worn ever since.[51]

Sad as this experience was, it did not deter Coyote. Least of all did it teach him not to butt in on other people.

So he returned to the place where *Tábqqstíin dine'é* the Otter People had been playing. And he challenged them to yet another round of hoop-and-pole, fully prepared to bet his hide again.

"But your skin is worthless now," they replied.

"Who would want it? Who would bet anything on it?

"Go away and leave us. Get out of here!"

But *Mq'ii* the Coyote insisted. Again and again he asked to play, again and again getting the same reply, the otters repeatedly reminding him how ugly his fur was and how worthless.

Until at length *Mq'ii* became angry and withdrew to what he considered a safe distance. And there he began to taunt *tábqqstíin* the otters with insults, crying things like this:

"You are brutes!" he cried.

"You are smart alecks!

"You think you are brave, but you're cowards.

"You think you're better than other people, but you are nobody special."

On and on he prattled that way, adding one insult to another.

"Your women are as bad as you are!" he added.

"They are ugly too.

"Their heads are flat like yours. Their eyes are beady and small like yours are. Their teeth stick out like yours do. They smell bad just like you do."

Then he shook his foot at them to taunt them all the more. He wanted them to chase him, for he knew he could outrun them easily.

Step by step he drew closer to them, shaking his paw at them until they made as if to pursue him. And at that moment he would jump backwards and again place himself out of their reach.

When they settled down and resumed their game, he again skittered toward them, shaking his foot once more. And again they would lunge toward him as if to go after him. But just then he jumped back where they could not reach him.

Whereupon they went back to their game, gradually becoming absorbed in it and forgetting all about him. But then he would approach them again and again interrupt their play. And they would feign pursuit again, hoping to drive him off once and for all.

But he merely drew back again. And then he would start all over, reviling them and insulting them.

Until he finally perched himself on a cliff overlooking *Tábąąstíín dine'é* the Otter People where they could see him as plainly as he could see them, and where they could hear him as plainly as he could hear them. And there he repeated his insults to them and even added some new ones.

"Idlers and braggarts!" he shouted.

"Puny cowards!

"Nervous rodents!

"No-account sissies!

"Take a good look at yourselves. Better yet, take a good look at your women. Look at your wives and your daughters. Look at your mothers and your sisters.

"Notice their flat heads. Look at their beady little eyes. Observe their protruding little teeth. Study their oily nostrils.

"Consider how ugly they are, and then think about how you must look!"

By now the otters could no longer ignore Coyote. And they were no longer willing to endure his abuse. So they decided that something would have to be done to put a stop to such a nuisance.

They talked it over among themselves and decided on a plan. One of them would send word to *Na'ashjé'ii dine'é* the Spider People, their good neighbors who lived a short distance downstream. The messenger would tell them what was going on and ask for their help.

So unknown to *Mą'ii* the Coyote, the obliging spiders crept up the side of the bluff where he sat, circled around him as he continued cursing and scolding the otters, and wove strong webs in the trees and bushes behind him. Then, when they finished their work they sent word back that all was ready. Whereupon *tábąąstíín* the otters now began climbing the cliff to attack *Mą'ii*.

Confident that he was much faster than they were, he sat unconcerned on his perch above them, continuing to hurl insult upon insult at them.

"Stupid cowards," he went on.

"Husbands and sons of beady-eyed, fang-toothed, snotty-nosed, flat-headed women.

"No wonder you are so ugly.

"No wonder you are such fools."

As he shouted and cursed he let them come closer and closer, sure that he could wait until the very last moment before he turned to run from them. For he was eager to say as much as he could to anger them.

Finally, just before they drew to within easy reach of him, he turned tail, chuckling to himself that he could get away from them so easily.

But scarcely had he made six strides before he found himself tangled in the network of webs that *na'ashjé'ii* the spiders had woven.

So it was that *Tábąąstíín dine'é* the Otter People caught him and seized him.

Then they dragged him down the hillside, he howling and screaming all the way; he clinging in resistance to the grasses and the shrubs as he was dragged along; he clinging in fact so hard that he pulled junipers and pinyons out by their very roots as the otters dragged him along.

When they got him to the bottom of the hill by the water's edge they set out to destroy him. They knew that they wanted to kill him. Nothing less than his absolute death would they settle for.

They bit him.

They tore at him with their claws.

They clubbed him with stones.

And as they beat him and pummeled him they reviled him four times more furiously than he had insulted them. They showered him with their spittle as they screamed their curses at him. Many of them even lashed at one another for a turn to strike him.

Until there he lay at last, motionless and lifeless.

And when the otters were finally exhausted from beating *Mą'ii* the Coyote, they sent for their neighbors *táshchozhii* the cliff swallows, who then flew down from the high canyon walls and set upon his body.

They peeled his skin away in narrow strips. Then they tore his remains into pieces. These they carried off to their nests, down to the last few morsels of gristle and bone. Until all that remained of *Mą'ii* were a few drops of blood which soon soaked into the ground and disappeared.[52]

The strips of skin that they pealed off of Coyote's body the swallows made into bands, which they tied around their heads before they flew away. Which accounts for the band worn by the cliff swallow on its brow to this very day, it is said.[53]

Fifteen

It is also said that at sundown the twelve brothers returned home. And they saw that *Mq'ii* the Coyote had not come back.

They wondered what might have happened to him. But they were by no means bothered by his absence, and they made no pretense at worrying.

As for their sister, *Mq'ii*'s wife, she had awaited him eagerly all day long. And now she observed her brothers file into their lodge without so much as a word to her about him. So she approached the dwelling and peered in through the door, watching them seat themselves calmly.

After hesitating for a moment, she finally entered and looked at them.

"Where is my husband your brother-in-law?" she asked. "And what have you done to him?"

But no one replied.

She stood there, weighed their silence, stared at each one of them separately, and then repeated the question.

"Where is my husband your brother-in-law, and what have you done to him?" she repeated.

But again no one answered her.

Enduring their silence for a minute or two, she continued to look straight at them, fixing her gaze first on the eyes of one and then on the eyes of another, until she had stared at each of them. Then she repeated the question again:

"What have you done with my husband your brother-in-law?" she questioned. "And where is he?"

But as before, no one answered.

Waiting for several minutes for one of them to break the silence, she gazed intently into the eyes of first one brother and then the next until she had glowered at each of them. Then she repeated the question once more.

"Tell me," she insisted once more. "Tell me now! What have you done with my husband your brother-in-law, and where is he?"

Finally the eldest brother spoke. And he had this to say to her:

"Go back to your shelter," he said to her.

"Go to bed without your husband.

"Do not concern yourself with that worthless fool. Truly we do not know what has been done with him.

"As you can see, he is not with us.

"For all we know he has gone into the canyon where we warned him not to go. For all we know he has been killed there.

"Perhaps he has been killed by *tsénoolch'óshii* the rockbirds. Or by *tábąąstíín* the otters. Or by *na'ashjé'ii* the spiders. Or by *táshchozihii* the swallows. Maybe all of those people together have killed him for all we know.

"Or for all we care."

Upon hearing which, Coyote's wife turned in anger and went out of the lodge saying nothing.[54]

•　　•　　•　　•

Before the twelve brothers lay down to sleep later that evening, they sent the youngest brother, the sloppy brother, to hide where he had hidden before.

Eavesdrop on their sister, they instructed him. Learn what she intended doing. From his hiding place he was able to see that she only pretended to go to sleep. She had lain down and turned her back toward his gaze. But when all grew silent, she arose and walked around her lodge four times.

Next she placed herself in the center of the room and then sat down facing the east, where she remained for a time.

Then she turned and faced the south for precisely the same amount of time.

And then she turned and faced north for exactly the same interval.

Moving sunwise, she now faced each of the four cardinal points. That done, she pulled out her right eyetooth, broke a large piece from one of her four bone awls, and inserted it into the gap where the tooth had been, making thereby a great tusk where there had only been a little tooth before. And as she did so she had this to declare:

"He who shall hereafter dream of losing a right eyetooth," she declared. "That man shall in fact loose a brother."

Whereupon she again placed herself in the middle of the lodge and sat facing first east, then south, then the west and finally the north.

But this time the youngest brother observed that as she faced each of the four cardinal points she did so with her mouth wide open. And he observed that after she had looked in each direction for precisely the same length of time, she tore out her left eyetooth and inserted in its place the pointed end of another awl. And as she did so this is what she declared:

"Hereafter he who shall dream of losing a left eyetooth," she declared, "he in fact shall lose a sister."

After he had watched all of the behavior, the young brother the sloppy brother returned to his elders to tell them what he had heard and what he had seen.

"Go back," he was then told. "Continue to watch her. Continue to listen to whatever she says. For we do not yet know what she intends doing."

So he returned to the place where he had posted himself twice before and continued watching. And as he watched he observed that she made two tusks in her lower jaw exactly as she had made the two tusks in her upper jaw.

"He who dreams of loosing the right lower canine tooth shall lose a child," he heard her declare as she inserted a third bone awl in her jaw.

"He who dreams of losing a left lower canine tooth shall lose a parent," he heard her declare as she inserted the final bone awl in her jaw.

And as she worked to convert her canine teeth to tusks, the youngest brother observed while he watched that hair began to grow on her hands. He saw that the hair then spread up her arms and on her legs, until only her breasts remained bare.

When he was what was happening, the youngest brother again rushed back to tell the others what he had seen and what he had heard.

"Go back again," they told him. "Continue watching her and continue listening to her. We still don't know what she intends doing."

So he again returned to the place where he had posted himself three times before and continued watching. And as he watched he saw her snout grow long. He saw her nostrils enlarge. He saw her teeth begin to gnash. He saw that her nails turned into thick black claws which curled into sharp points. He saw that she grew more and more to resemble *shash yishtłizh*, the great brown bear who now roams our forests and who menaces all who see it, merely on account of its size and its strength.[55]

And even while she was being transformed, she continued her restless pacing around and around the room, around and around, never failing to pause to open her mouth, first to the east, then to the south, then to the west, and then to the north.

Observing all this, the youngest brother remained hidden until dawn. Then, afraid that she would discover him in the light of the morning sun, he hastened back to tell his brothers what else he had seen.

"What she has done to transform herself surely reflects the magic that *Mq'ii* the Coyote our brother-in-law has taught her," the eldest brother said. "It is now obvious that she intends doing someone great harm."

No sooner than which they heard the wheezing and snorting that bears customarily make. And soon they saw a she-bear rush past their door, cracking the branches and twigs underfoot as she went.

They watched her amble powerfully down the trail which *Mq'ii* the Coyote had taken the day before when he set out in pursuit of the twelve brothers. Dumbfounded, they watched her until she disappeared into the woods and toward the forbidden canyon.

•   •   •   •

At dusk that day she came back, making her way slowly up the trail from the fatal canyon through the woods and into the clearing that lay outside the brothers' dwelling. She bore wounds all over her body, for she had been fighting those who slew her husband *Mq'ii.* Moving with difficulty, she picked her way back to the hut that *Mq'ii* her husband had made for himself and her on their first night together as man and wife.

Long after it grew dark, light continued to burn in the bridal shelter. And from time to time the youngest brother the sloppy brother would steal over and peer inside to look upon their sister. All night long she walked around the fire, now and then stopping to use her magic to draw arrowheads out of her body, or stopping to lick her wounds. And then she would resume her pacing again. Not without pain, however, for she would frequently moan as she walked or as she stopped to heal herself.[56]

But then in the morning the brothers again heard her, wheezing and snorting as she rushed past the door to their lodge, pounding the earth with her heavy paws as she went.

And they watched her amble down the trail that she had last seen *Mq'ii* the Coyote take in pursuit of the twelve brothers two days earlier. Amazed that she had recovered so quickly, they watched her until she disappeared into the woods in the direction of the forbidden canyon.

•   •   •   •

At dusk she returned as she had the night before, laboring to bring herself up the trail out of the woods, her body rent with slashes and cuts. For she had been battling against those who slew her husband *Mq'ii*. And all night long the fire burned in the bridal chamber that *Mq'ii* her husband had made for them both to enjoy. Again the youngest brother observed her applying the magic that she had learned to heal her wounds, alternately pacing and stopping as she did the night before. Not without anguish, however, for she cried out frequently as she strove to recover.

The next morning the brothers again heard her, wheezing and snorting as she rushed past their door.

Again they watched her amble down the trail that she had last seen *Mq'ii* the Coyote take to follow her brothers. Incredulous that one so badly torn and beaten the night before could display such angry strength by morning, they watched her until she disappeared into the woods in the direction of the forbidden canyon.

•   •   •   •

At dusk she returned as she had the night before and the night before that, slowly dragging herself up the trail out of the woods, swollen and bleeding with the wounds she had obviously received in her battle with the enemies of her husband *Mq'ii*. And all night long the fire burned in the home *Mq'ii* her husband had made for them to dwell in together. And again she was seen applying the magic she had learned from her beloved Coyote to heal her wounds. Not without sorrow, however, for she wept frequently as she strove to heal herself.

And sure enough, next morning the brothers again heard her rushing past their door, wheezing and snorting in angry pursuit of her husband's murderers.

They watched her, sure enough, as she ambled down the trail that she had last seen *Mq'ii* the Coyote take to catch up with her brothers. Alarmed that one so badly hurt and so filled with grief the night before could by morning be so strong and so angry, they watched her until she disappeared into the woods in the direction of the forbidden canyon.

•   •   •   •

That night she returned as she had the night before and the night before that and the night before that, using her last remaining strength to pull herself up the trail and out of the woods, her body fully covered alike with her own blood and with the blood of her slain enemies. But her war was over now. She had conquered the destroyers of her husband *Mq'ii*. Those few she had not killed she managed to put in full flight so that they would remain scattered forever and would not again dare come near their former home.

To escape her fatal blows, the rockbirds fled the canyon entirely, soaring out of sight beyond the plateaus above. They have never been seen by anyone again.

The surviving swallows flew up upon the high cliffs overlooking the canyon floor to escape her wild vengeance. There they now live to this day, nervously flitting from ledge to ledge, fearful of ever returning to the banks of the stream inside lest the great she-bear should find them there and kill them.

The otters hid themselves in the water in fear that they would be crushed in her clutches. There they would be destined to live forever, forever swimming under the surface, coming up only occasionally to take a furtive breath and then submerging again.

The spiders retreated into holes they dug hastily in the ground to secure themselves against her rage. They fashioned trapdoors to enclose themselves safely, and ever since they have remained in the darkness underground.

In such places and under such conditions have all those creatures been obliged to dwell. They have had to live that way ever since that time, it is said.

Sixteen

It is also said that while the she-bear waged her battle of revenge on her husband's enemies, her brothers stayed at home. But on the last of those four days they decided that they had better leave. For they were afraid that their sister would now make trouble for them.

So late in the evening of the fourth day, after the bride of *Mą'ii* the Coyote had made her way back, they split into four separate groups and fled.

Each group fled in a different direction. Three of the brothers headed east. Three more brothers headed south. Another three of them headed west. And two struck their way north. The remaining brother, the youngest brother the sloppy brother, they left behind, ordering him to spy on their sister and to try to learn what she intended doing.

After the eleven oldest brothers had departed, *Níyol* the Strong Wind and *Béésh ashkii* the Knife Boy came to the lodge to assist the young brother the sloppy one.[57]

They did so by digging a deep hole for him under the center of the hogan. And from that hole they dug four tunnels. One branched to the east. One branched to the south. One branched to the west. And one branched to the north. Over the end of each tunnel they put a slab of gypsum to let light shine in from above.

They also assisted him by giving him four weapons. That way he could defend himself if he had to. Or he could strike his enemy if he saw fit to. They gave him *atsiniltł'ish k'aa'* the chain-lightning arrows. They gave him *atsoolaghał k'aa'* the sheet-lightning arrows. They gave him *shábitł'óól k'aa'* the sunbeam arrows. And they gave him *nááts'íílid k'aa'* the rainbow arrows.

They also assisted him by covering his hiding place. To do that they made a roof of four flat stones. They used one white stone. They used a stone that was blue. They used a stone the color of yellow. And they used a stone colored black. Then they covered this roof of stones with earth, carefully tamping it down so that it looked like the natural floor of the lodge.

Finally they assisted him by assigning two guards to stay by the youth's side and to observe everything that should occur. Warn him of any impending danger, they instructed the two guards, lest harm should come. One of the two guards was *Nítch'i* the Wind, whom they posted at the brother's right ear to warn him by day. The other was *Chahałheeł* the Darkness, whom they posted at his left ear to warn him by night.

And after they had finished doing all these things, *Níyol* the Strong Wind and *Béésh ashkii* the Knife Boy bid the youngest brother climb down into the place they had dug inside the lodge. There he would find safety.

•   •   •   •

Morning came and their sister awoke. She had resumed her original shape, and discovering that her brothers were not in their dwelling she set about finding them.

First she poured water on the ground in the manner of divination that *Mq'ii* the Coyote her husband had taught her. So that when it flowed toward the east she knew in which direction to take pursuit. And swiftly she made her way, soon overtaking the three brothers who had fled in that direction.

And by tricking them she killed them. Pretending to bear them no anger, she bid them rest with her, urging them to resume their close kinship.

"Come," she urged them in a soothing, plaintive voice. "Sit a while and relax.

"Face the east so that the early sun may warm you. Meanwhile, I will remove the lice and sand from your hair and comb it as I used to do."

Relieved to find her behaving as she had behaved before Coyote had married her, they gladly did what she bid them and turned their backs to her towards the sun. Whereupon she instantly became a she-bear again and struck them down before they realized the danger.

Then she returned to their lodge to determine the whereabouts of her remaining brothers. Again using the manner of divination that *Mq'ii* the Coyote had taught her, she poured water on the ground. So that when it flowed to the south she knew which direction to take in pursuit. And with uncanny speed she made her way, soon overtaking the three brothers who had fled in that direction.

And by tricking them she slew them. Pretending that her anger had abated, she bid them rest with her, urging them that they should all try once more to live as sister and brothers.

"Come," she urged in a voice tender with affection. "Sit down and relax here.

"Face the east so that the early sun may warm you, and I will remove the lice and sand from your hair and comb it as I used to do."

Happy to find her behaving as she had behaved before Coyote had married her, they gladly did as she suggested and turned their backs to her towards the sun. Whereupon she instantly turned herself into a she-bear again and struck them down before they knew what was happening.

Then she returned to their lodge to learn where her other brothers had gone. Again she poured water on the ground in the manner of divination that *Mą'ii* had taught her. So that when it flowed to the west she knew which way to pursue them. And with magical speed she went along and soon she overtook the three who had fled in that direction.

And by tricking them she destroyed them. Pretending that her bitterness had subsided, she bid them rest with her, urging them that she and they should once again observe the familiar devotion customary among brothers and sisters.

"Come," she urged them in a voice as soft and as loving as it once had been. "Sit down at this very spot and relax.

"Face the east so that the early sun may warm you, and I will remove the lice and sand from your hair and comb it as I used to do."

Delighted to find her behaving as she had behaved before Coyote had married her, they gladly did as she suggested and turned their backs toward her to face the sun. Whereupon she instantly transformed herself into a she-bear again and struck them down before they could escape.

Then she returned to their lodge to find out where the remaining brothers had run. Again she poured water on the ground in the manner of divination that Coyote had taught her. So that when it flowed to the north she knew where to find them. And with the speed of a sorceress she traveled and soon overtook the two who had fled in that direction.

And by tricking them she took their lives. Pretending that she had purged herself of her hatred, she bid them rest with her, urging them to love her again as they had once loved each other and as she was again prepared to love them.

Come," she urged in a voice full of virtuous devotion. "Sit awhile and relax.

"Face the east so that the early sun may warm you, and I will remove the lice and sand from your hair and comb it as I used to do."

Overcome with joy to find her behaving as she had behaved before Coyote had intruded into their lives, they gladly did as she suggested and turned their backs to her towards the sun. Instantly whereupon she became a she-bear again and slew them before they could defend themselves.

•   •   •   •

It now remained for her to find the one surviving brother and kill him, too. So she returned to their dwelling to determine where he had gone. Again she poured water on the ground in the manner that her husband *Mą'ii* the Coyote had taught her. But this time when she did it sank directly into the earth.

Whereupon she stood in dumb amazement not knowing at first what to do or where to go in pursuit. She gazed around and could see nothing but the lodge where she and her brothers had lived and the deserted shelters that her many suitors had built.

She searched those shelters one by one, picking carefully through each of them for some trace of the missing brother. But she did so without success, for she could find no trace of him in any.

At last she approached the main dwelling itself. She moved slowly around the outside of it, inspecting it carefully and looking at the ground for tracks. Then she went inside and made her way around its inner wall, looking behind bundles and under the various provisions stored there.

Around and around she moved, around and around. She poked at the ground and peered into pots and baskets for some sign that might betray the whereabouts of the one she sought. And gradually she made her way toward the center of the lodge. Until at length she reached the fireplace itself which occupied the middle of the room in the manner customary of those ancient, long-ago times.

Here she noticed the tamped earth where *Níyol* the Strong Wind and *Béésh ashkii* the Knife Boy had tried to disguise the underground hiding place of the young brother the sloppy brother. She looked at it and realized at once that someone had recently finished digging there.

Converting her hands to bear's paws, she dug into the ground vigorously until she had uncovered the hole made to hide the youth. She then found the stones that they had placed over the four-way tunnel. And removing them she saw him at last. Whereupon she spoke these words:

"Ah, there you are little brother," spoke she, her voice plaintive and soothing. "I greet you.

"Will you come up here and talk to your sister?"

And so saying she reached down into the hole, extending her index finger to him.

"Come," she begged as sweetly as she could sound.

"Grasp my finger and I will help you up."

But *Niłch'i* the Wind warned him otherwise:

"Do not permit her to take your finger," warned he in a whisper.

"For if you do let her take it she will snatch you and throw you up in the air.

"She will throw you up so hard in fact that you will soar through the roof. And you will land half-dead at her feet and find yourself completely at her mercy. So instead of taking her hand as she suggests, climb up there without her help."

So the young brother the sloppy brother disappeared into the tunnel to the east and climbed out of the hole on that side of the lodge.

Once out he noticed that his sister must have started to run angrily in that direction. For she now stood only several steps away from the hole where he had climbed through from below. And for an instant he saw a vexed look on her face before she could change her expression.

"Here I am," he said.

"I have come up to greet you and to talk to you, just as you asked me to."

By now she was smiling sweetly at him and looked at him with affection. And this is what she said to him:

"Ah, little brother," she said to him.

"How happy I am to see you. How happy I am that we are again together.

"Come," she said sweetly.

"Come inside with me.

"Come with me into the dwelling where you and I grew up as brother and sister.

"Come with me in there so that we may resume our kinship."

And so saying, she took him by the hand and started to lead him into the lodge.

But *Niłch'i* the Wind warned him otherwise.

"Do not permit her to take you inside," warned he.

"There has been sorrow in that place.

"Your eleven brothers who have been slain this very morning once dwelled in there. Who can say where their spirits are at this moment? Who can say that their restless spirits are not inside at this very moment?"

So the brother refused to enter the lodge with his sister. Instead he suggested that they sit outside together and enjoy the sun. And such, we are told, is the origin of the custom now current among the Navajo people who live on the surface of this world never to enter a house wherein death or misfortune has occurred.

"Very well, then," the sister said.

"Let us just sit out here together and enjoy the warm afternoon sun. Sit here toward the west so that it may warm your face. And I will remove the lice and sand from your hair and comb it like I used to do."

But *Niłch'i* the Wind warned him otherwise.

Do not permit her to stand at your back with the sun directly in front of you," he warned.

For it will blind you long enough for her to pounce on you and overcome you before you can defend yourself.

"She killed your brothers that way. And that is the way she now seeks to kill you. So sit facing the north instead. That way you may watch her shadow and anticipate her every move."

So he sat with his face to the north. And she placed herself behind him and untied his *tsiiyééł*, the knot that bound his hair. Then she began to pick the lice and sand out of it, while he studied her shadow out of the corner of his eye.

Before long he observed that her snout was growing longer, that her ears moved, that she bowed slowly forward, and that her mouth was coming close to the side of his head.

"Sister," said he.

"I see that your snout appears to grow longer. I see that your ears seem to twitch. I see that your body bows forward. And I see that your head moves closer and closer to mine.

"What can such behavior mean?"

Whereupon she made no effort to reply. Instead she drew back her mouth. She arched her body away from his. She kept her ears perfectly still. And she pulled her snout in so that it looked like an ordinary nose.

Then she resumed combing his hair.

She combed and she combed. She combed and she combed. And the minutes went slowly by, he all the while studying her shadow out of the corner of his eye.

And before long he noticed that her snout was again growing

longer, that her ears were again moving, that she was again bowing slowly forward, and that her mouth again moved closer and closer to the side of his head.

"Tell me, sister," he then said.

"Why is it that your nose appears to grow longer? Why is it that your ears twitch so? Why is it that your body leans slowly forward? And why is it that your head slowly inclines toward mine?

"What can all that mean?"

But she made no attempt to answer him. Instead she drew back her mouth. She arched her body away from his. She kept her ears perfectly still. And she pulled her snout in so that it looked the way it had always looked before.

Then she resumed combing his hair.

She combed and she combed. She combed and she combed. And the minutes continued to go slowly by, he all the while observing her shadow out of the corner of his eye.

And soon enough, he noticed again that her snout had been gradually growing, again that her ears had gradually begun to move, again that she had been leaning gradually forward, and again that her mouth had gradually gotten closer and closer to the side of his head.

"Tell me, sister," he repeated.

"Tell me why your nose grows little by little. Tell me why your ears gradually start twitching. Tell me why you bend your body closer to mine little by little. And tell me why your mouth moves ever so gradually closer to the side of my head.

"Explain all that to me."

But no answer came. She drew back her mouth. She arched her body away from his. She kept her ears perfectly still. And she pulled her snout in so that it did not seem at all unusual.

Then she resumed combing his hair.

She combed and she combed. She combed and she combed. And thus the minutes went slowly by, he all the while watching her shadow out of the corner of his eye.

And it was not all that long before he saw that the same things were happening again. Once more her snout was long, her ears were twitching, she was bowing close in upon him, and her mouth was close enough for him to feel the warmth of her breath on the back of his neck.

"You must tell me why, sister," he demanded.

"Why does your nose become a snout? Why do your ears now

twitch? Why do you place yourself so close to me? And why do I feel your hot breath on the back of my neck?

"Why all these things?"

But she refused to make any reply whatever. Instead she closed her mouth, pulled her body erect, drew back her ears, and returned her nose to its original shape.

She simply resumed combing his hair while he sat passively, content to wait and watch for her next move.

But *Niłch'i* the Wind warned him otherwise.

"Do not let this happen a fifth time," he whispered.

"For if it does you are doomed.

"She now realizes that you have been observing her shadow. And this time she will move swiftly. If she is able to extend her snout a fifth time she will bite off your head in an instant!

"So instead of waiting and watching as you have been doing, you must now take the initiative.

"Do you see that chattering squirrel over there?

"Under the patch of weeds at his feet are your sister's vital parts, where he stands guarding them for her. Run and pounce on them! Seize them and destroy them before she can stop you!

"Go quickly!"

So the young brother the sloppy brother sprung up from where he sat and raced toward the spot where the squirrel stood.

When his sister saw what he was doing, she tore after him in angry pursuit. And surely would she have overtaken him and killed him except that suddenly a large yucca bush sprouted up between them and got in her way.

Then a cane cactus sprung up just as suddenly, it too blocking her way. So that while she could easily outrun her brother, she now had to go around these two plants. And by the time he had reached the patch of weeds that covered her vital parts.

He heard the lungs breathing under the weeds, and quickly drew *atsiniltł'ish k'aa'* the chain-lightning arrow and shot it into them. At once a bright stream of blood spurted up from the ground where they had lain concealed. And at precisely that instant the she-bear fell to the ground, bright blood also streaming from her side onto the earth where she now lay helpless.

But as he stood watching, the youth now heard *Niłch'i* the Wind again whispering in his ear.

"Take care," he whispered.

"Do you not see how the blood from her body flows toward the stream of blood flowing from her vital parts? And do you not see how the blood from her vital parts flows toward the stream of blood that comes from her body?

"Notice how swiftly they flow toward one another, those two streams of her fresh blood. If they meet, your sister will come to life again. And you will find yourself in greater danger than you have been in yet.

"So with your stone knife make a line in the ground between the two converging streams."

Whereupon the young brother drew *atsoolaghał k'aa'* the sheet-lightening arrow and cut a straight line between the two streams of blood. And whereupon the blood in both streams congealed instantly, ceasing to flow any further. And so it was that the she-bear died.

Then the youth approached the place where her body lay in a heap on the ground.

"You may come back to life," he said to the corpse. "But you shall no longer live as the mischievous *Asdzání shash nádleehé*, the Woman Who Becomes a Bear. You must live as something else, so that you will be useful to your kind and not a creature of disorder.[58]

So saying, he severed the head of the she-bear from its body and then said this to it:

"Let us see if you do better in another life," he said.

"When you again become a living, breathing creature, behave well toward others. Or else I will slay you again."

Whereupon he threw the head against the trunk of a nearby pinyon tree. And it changed instantly into a real bear such as those we see roaming in the mountain forests today.

At once the creature got up on its feet and started to walk away. But after taking several steps it stopped, shaded its eyes with one paw, looked back at the youth, and asked this question:

"But what if someone should attack me first?" it asked.

"What if someone should threaten me?"

"Then you may defend yourself in whatever way you can," replied the youngest brother. "And you may likewise defend your kin. Otherwise do not start a quarrel or a fight.

"Unless you are bothered by someone, live peaceably and be a friend to your people. Go yonder to *Dziłíjiin* the Black Mountain and make your dwelling there."

So the bear turned and walked away. And to this very day many

such bears dwell at that place, descendants of one who was once a
sorceress, able to transform herself back and forth at will.[59]

•   •   •   •

The youth now knelt beside the headless corpse of the she-bear.
And one at a time he cut the nipples from the creature's breasts.
And to them he had this to say:
"Had you belonged to a good woman and not to a witch, it might
have been your destiny to suckle offspring. But you were no good
to your own kind.
"Perhaps you can be of use in some other form."
Upon saying which words, he threw the dismembered nipples up
into the branches of the pinyon tree, which until that time had
been barren of fruit. And they at once turned into edible pine nuts,
which have nourished men ever since.
That done, he sought the homes of his friends and benefactors,
Níyol the Strong Wind and *Béésh ashkii* the Knife Boy. Sadly,
however, for he grieved for his slain brothers.
But the two holy ones led him to the east where three of them lay.
Then they led him to the south. Then they led him to the west.
And then they led him to the north. And at the place where each
group of brothers were killed they restored life to them.
Together the twelve brothers went back to their old dwelling
place where they resolved to resume their lives. They would hunt
again and grow crops. They would become as successful as they
had been before *Mą'ii* the Coyote brought so much disorder into
their lives.
But they built a new home for themselves. They would not
return to the old one, for that was now a *hóyéé' hooghan*, a
death-dwelling to be shunned forever.[60]

•   •   •   •

Níyol the Strong Wind and *Béésh ashkii* the Knife Boy then gave
the youngest brother a name.
"*Leeyaa neeyání* they called him, which means Man Reared
Under the Earth in the language spoken by *Bilagáana* the White
Man.[61] They gave him that name because they had concealed him
in the ground while his brothers fled from their wrathful sister.
After they named him they instructed him to depart and to dwell

at a place called *Adáá' yitsoh,* or Big Point on the Cliff's Edge, which is shaped like a hogan.

So he bid his brothers farewell and asked to be well remembered among them. And he set out for the place designated to be his home. The Navajo people believe that he dwells there to this very day, it is said.

All of these things happened a long, long time ago, it is said.

PART THREE

Slaying the Monsters

ONE

Of a time long, long ago these things too are said.[1]

It is said that the people had been continuing their flight from the monsters who pursued them.

By now they were calling themselves *Ha'aznání dine'é*. In the language of *Bilagáana* the White Man that name means Emergence People. Those are the people destined to become known as the ancestors of the Navajo people who now live on the surface of this world.

In trying to escape the *Binaayee'* they went from place to place and from place to place, thinking themselves safe at each. They would settle and farm the land, planting corn and squash, beans and pumpkins in the spring. And they hoped that in the fall they could harvest what they had planted.

But then those dreaded creatures the *Binaayéé'* would locate them and would again prey upon them. They destroyed and devoured them unrelentingly as hungry wolves gobble sheep who stray.

Thus it was that the last survivors of that unending flight travelled to *Tsé łigaii íí'áhí*. In the language of *Bilagáana* that name means White Standing Rock.

By now there remained only *Áłtsé hastiin* the First Man and *Áłtsé asdzáá* the First Woman along with four other persons. Only an old man had also survived. And only his wife had survived with him. With them only two of their children had survived. One was a young man and the other was a young woman.[2]

Those four were weary and meager. They were frightened and fully without hope. They now wondered what would be the good of clearing yet another patch of land. Surely *Binaayéé'* the Alien Giants would destroy them as they had destroyed everyone else.

171

•   •   •   •

"They are said," said *Áłtsé hastiin* the First Man to *Áłtsé asdzą́ą́*
the First Woman.

"They have no heart for continuing such an existence."

That is what he said. And this is what she replied:

"Truly they are disheartened," she replied.

"And just as truly are they afraid. Indeed, I am afraid for them,
just as I fear for myself and for you."

To which *Áłtsé hastiin* the First Man then had this to say:

"In any case, we must rest here," he said.

"We must try once more to settle. Perhaps the gods will help us
somehow."[3]

And *Áłtsé asdzą́ą́* the First Woman had this to say in reply:

"Do not count on them," she replied.

"We do not yet altogether know what pleases them and what
annoys them. We do not yet know when they will help us and
when they will act against us."

•   •   •   •

So they all settled themselves for the night, scarcely daring to try
again to make a home for themselves, and wondering how soon the
final misfortune would befall all of them.[4]

Indeed, these were not good times.

In the morning, however, *Áłtsé hastiin* the First Man observed
that a dark cloud had covered the top of *Ch'óol'į́'į́* the Giant Spruce
Mountain which stood yonder by some distance.[5] Saying nothing
to others about what he saw, however, he merely joined them in
their work.

On the second morning he looked and noticed that the cloud had
descended to the middle of *Ch'óol'į́'į́* and that it was raining on the
upper half. But he said nothing to anyone else and joined those
who were working.

When daylight brought the third morning, he looked and saw
that the dark cloud had now settled further down the sides of
Ch'óol'į́'į́ so that only the base of the mountain lay uncovered. But
he still mentioned what he observed to no one, choosing instead to
work along with the others.

On the fourth day, however, when he noticed that the dark cloud
had now enveloped *Ch'óol'į́'į́* clear down to its base and that rain

was falling upon it in torrents, he spoke of what he saw to *Áłtsé asdzą́ą́* the First Woman, saying this to her:

"I wonder what is happening," he said to her.

"For four days *Ch'óol'į́'į́* has been covered with a dark cloud. Only the summit was covered at first. But each day the cloud has forced itself lower and lower, so that now even its flanks are entirely hidden.

"Perhaps I had better go there to investigate."

To which she had this reply to offer:

"It is better that you should stay here," she offered.

"There is great danger out there.

Naayéé' the devouring ones will surely set upon you. Surely you will be devoured like so many others have been."

That is what she replied. And this is what he then had to say:

"Do not be afraid," said he.

"Nothing will go wrong. For I will surround myself with song.[6]

"I will sing as I make my way to the mountain.

"I will sing while I am on the mountain.

"And I will sing as I return.

"I will surround myself with song.

"You may be sure that the words of my songs will protect me."[7]

That is what *Áłtsé hastiin* the First Man said to his wife *Áłtsé asdzą́ą́* the First Woman.

●　　●　　●　　●

So it was that *Áłtsé hastiin* the First Man set out for the cloud-covered mountain of giant spruces. On the very next morning he set out, singing as he went.

"I am *Áłtsé hastiin* the First Man," he sang.

"*Áłtsé hastiin* the First Man am I, maker of much of the earth.

"*Áłtsé hastiin* the First Man am I, and I head for *Ch'óol'į́'į́* the Giant Spruce Mountain, following the dark, rainy cloud.

"I follow the lightning and head for the place where it strikes.

"I follow the rainbow and head for the place where it touches the earth.

"I follow the cloud's trail and head for the place where it is thickest.

"I follow the scent of the falling rain and head for the place where the lines of rain are darkest."

For four days he traveled thus, singing as he went.

"I am *Áłtsé hastiin*," he sang, "and I head for Giant Spruce Mountain in pursuit of good fortune.

"In pursuit of good fortune I follow the lightning and draw closer to the place where it strikes.

"In pursuit of good fortune I follow the rainbow and draw closer to the place where it touches the earth.

"In pursuit of good fortune I follow the trail of the cloud and draw closer to the place where it is thickest.

"In pursuit of good fortune I follow the scent of the falling rain and draw closer to the place where the lines of rain are darkest."

On and on he traveled, continuing to sing as he made his way to *Ch'óol'į́'į́* the Giant Spruce Mountain.

"I am First Man and I head for *Ch'óol'į́'į́* in pursuit of old age and happiness," he sang.[8]

"In pursuit of old age and happiness I follow the lightning and approach the place where it strikes.

"In pursuit of old age and happiness I follow the rainbow and approach the place where it touches the earth.

"In pursuit of old age and happiness I follow the dark cloud's trail and approach the place where it is thickest.

"In pursuit of old age and happiness I follow the scent of the rainfall and approach the place where the lines of rain are darkest."

Thus it was that he continued traveling on and on until he reached the foot of the mountain. And thus it was that he continued on and on, making his way up toward the summit. As he made his way he continued singing boldly.

"*Áłtsé hastiin* is who I am," sang he. "And here I am climbing *Ch'óol'į́'į́* in pursuit of long life and happiness for myself and my people."

"Here I am arriving at the place where the lightning strikes, in pursuit of long life and happiness for myself and my people.

"Here I am arriving at the place where the rainbow touches the earth, in pursuit of long life and happiness for myself and my people.

"Here I am where the trail of the dark cloud is thickest, in pursuit of long life and happiness for myself and my people.

"Here I am where the rich, warm rain drenches me, in pursuit of long life and happiness for myself and my people."

So it was that he made his way higher and higher on the mountain called *Ch'óol'į́'į́* because giant spruces grew thick and abundant upon it. And as he climbed he continued to sing with confidence. Even when he reached the very summit he continued to sing.

"Long life and good fortune I attain for my people and for myself," he sang.

"There is long life and good fortune in front of me.

"There is long life and good fortune in back of me.

"There is long life and good fortune above me and below me.

"All around me there is long life and good fortune."

Thus singing as he reached the very point where the peak of *Ch'óol'į́'į́* meets the sky, he heard the cry of an infant.

And at precisely the moment when he first heard that cry lightning was flashing everywhere; so brightly was it flashing that he could not see. Precisely when he first heard the cry the tip of the rainbow showered the peak with intense colors; so intensely did those colors shower him that he could not see. Just when he first heard the infant crying the dark cloud shut out the last bit of remaining daylight; so thick was the cloud's darkness that he could not see. Just at the moment when he heard the crying infant for the first time the rain blinded him; so heavily did it fall that he could not see.

But although he could see nothing he made his way to the spot where it seemed to him that the crying originated.

And as he reached that spot the lightning ceased. The rainbow's intense shroud became a band of pastel softness. The dark cloud evaporated into a sky of blue. The rain stopped and the rays of the morning sun shone upon him.

He looked down at his feet where he had heard the baby crying. But he beheld only a turquoise figure. In it, however, he recognized the likeness of a female. It was no larger than a newborn child, but its body was fully proportioned like a woman's body. Not knowing what else to do, he picked it up and carried it back with him. Back he carried it to *Áłtsé asdzą́ą́* the First Woman and the others.

"Take it," he bid them.

"Keep it and care for it as if it were real.

"Nurse it and nurture it as if it were our very own."[9]

•   •   •   •

Two days later, very early in the morning, they were all awakened by a familiar sound.

"*Wu'hu'hu'hu'*," they heard, and they recognized that sound as the kindly voice of *Haashch'éé̱ti'í* the Talking God. Barely reaching them at first, it was so faint and so far off that they could scarcely make it out.

But they listened nonetheless and they waited, and soon they heard the voice again, nearer and louder than before. *"Wu'hu'hu'hu',"* it repeated, this time more distinctly.

They continued to listen and now heard the voice a third time. *"Wu'hu'hu'hu',"* it repeated, all the nearer now and all the more distinct.

Continuing to listen, they heard it again, even louder than the last time. *"Wu'hu'hu'hu',"* it repeated, so close and so distinct that it seemed directly upon them.

Whereupon they all heard the soft tread of moccasined feet drawing closer, and whereupon they saw *Haashch'éé̱ti'í* standing before them.

As soon as they set eyes on him, they realized that he was directing the survivors to come to the peak of *Ch'óol'í̱'í̱* the Giant Spruce Mountain twelve nights hence.

He did not speak to them. Instead he motioned with his hands and arms, instructing them by such gestures as they could understand to bring the newly found turquoise image with them when they came.

Then he departed in silence, leaving them to consider his instructions and to wonder what ultimately would befall them.

•   •   •   •

Each day thereafter for twelve days the four adults talked about the instructions they were given, carefully marking the passing days.

They wondered if it really was *Haashch'éé̱ti'í* the Talking God whom they had seen. They wondered why he had come. They wondered what would happen on *Ch'óol'í̱'í̱*. And, scarcely daring to hope for as much, they wondered if indeed their luck would change.

Thus it was that twelve days passed. Twelve nights went by, and twelve times did the sun rise and set, until dawn marked the morning following the twelfth of those days. Then they climbed the mountain.

They mounted *Ch'óol'í̱'í̱* by way of the holy trail, which was made visible to them with the first shaft of morning sunlight, it is said.

Two

It is also said that the survivors climbed *Ch'óol'į́'į́* the Giant
Spruce Mountain until they reached a level spot just below the
summit.

There they found *Haashch'éélti'í* the Talking God, along with
Hashch'éoghan the Growling God. They found *Bits'íís łigaii* the
White Body, who had emerged with the people from the fourth
world below, along with *Bits'íís dootł'izh* the Blue Body, who had
likewise emerged with them from that lower world.

They found *Tséghádi'nídínii dine'é* the Image-Bringing People
there.[10] They found *Níłch'i* the Wind there. They found
Chahałheeł the Darkness there, friend of *Níłch'i* the Wind. And
they found the brothers of *Asdzání shash nádleehé*, the Woman
Who Becomes a Bear.

There they also found *Jį́ dine'é* the Daylight People, standing
apart from the others to the east. There they likewise found *Yá
dootł'izh dine'é* the Blue Sky People, standing apart from the
others to the south. There too they found *Litso adinídíín dine'é* the
Yellow Light People standing apart to the west. And so, too, they
found *Chahałheeł dine'é* the Darkness People there, who stood off
to the north.

To the east among *Jį́ dine'é* the Daylight People stood White
Body, bearing in his hand a small female likeness; and the
survivors saw that it resembled the figurine which *Áłtsé hastiin*
the First Man had found and which they now carried with them. It
was precisely the size of theirs, and it bore precisely the same
shape. It differed only in that it was fashioned of white shell
instead of turquoise.

Saying nothing, *Bits'íís łigaii* the White Body stepped forward
and handed his replica to one of the Mirage Stone People. He then
beckoned to the four surviving adults of the People of the
Emergence Place that they should do much the same with theirs.

So the father handed the turquoise image over to another of the
Mirage Stone People. Then, as each member of that last surviving
family watched, *Haashch'éélti'í* the Talking God laid a buckskin
on the ground, carefully arranging it so that its head faced the west.

Upon that same buckskin the Mirage Stone People laid the two
figurines: the one of turquoise and the one of white shell. They
arranged them carefully so that their heads pointed west. They
also laid upon that buckskin two ears of corn: one white and

the other yellow. They arranged them carefully so that they pointed west.

Atop the figurines and the corn *Haashch'ééłti'í* the Talking God placed another buckskin, this time arranging it so that the head pointed to the east. Then he bid the People of the Emergence Place stand at a distance so the *Niłch'i* the Wind could enter. And with those instructions now given, both he and *Hashch'eoghan* the Calling God withdrew from sight someplace to the east.[11]

Whereupon all those who had assembled there backed away, forming a large circle around the two layers of buckskin. In that circle they had left an opening on the easternmost rim so that *Haashch'ééłti'í* the Talking God and *Hashch'éoghan* the Growling God could pass in and out of the circle. And then the Holy People who had gathered began to sing one of the sacred songs of *hózhǫǫjí sin.*

When the singing began the two gods reappeared from their hiding place to the east. Entering the circle of assembled bystanders through the opening that had been left for them, they approached the buckskin pile, raised the topmost cover, bid *Niłch'i* the Wind make his way between the two blankets, and then lowered the top cover as it originally had been and disappeared.

Meanwhile the assembled gods continued singing the sacred song of *hózhǫǫjí sin.* They chanted and they sang; they sang and they chanted. Then the two gods again reappeared from their hiding place in the east. Entering the circle through the opening that had been left for them, they approached the buckskin pile once more, raised the topmost cover as before, as before bid *Niłch'i* the Wind make his magic way between the two blankets, and then lowered the top cover once again and once again disappeared.

And all the while, those assembled there continued singing the sacred song of *hózhǫǫjí sin.* They chanted and they sang; they sang and they chanted. Until the two gods again reappeared from their hiding place in the east. Entering the circle through the opening that had been left for them they approached the buckskin pile once more, raised the topmost cover as before, as before cried out to *Niłch'i* the Wind to breathe life between the two blankets, and then once more lowered the top cover and disappeared.

And all the while, those assembled in that circle continued singing the sacred song of *hózhǫǫjí sin.* They sang and they chanted; they chanted and they sang. Until the two gods reappeared from their hiding place in the east as they had done three times already. Entering the circle through the opening that had been left for them, they approached the buckskin pile as they had done three times already; they raised the topmost cover as they had previously done, and as they had previously done they cried out to *Nílch'i* the Wind.

But instead of asking him to breathe between the two blankets as they had done three times already, they acknowledged this time that he had indeed already done so. And lo! the images and the ears of corn alike were transformed into living creatures shaped like adult women who live on the surface of the earth today.

What had been the figure of turquoise was now *Asdzą́ą́ nádleehé*, or Changing Woman in the language of *Bilagáana* the White Man.[12] What had been the figure of white shell became *Yoołgai asdzą́ą́*, or White Shell Woman as we would call her today.

The white ear of corn became *Naadą́ǫ́lgaii ashkii*, or as he would now be called, White Corn Boy. And the yellow ear of corn became *Naadą́ǫ́ltsoii at'ééd*, or Yellow Corn Girl.[13]

These four objects had been transformed into living creatures by *Nílch'i* the Wind.

It was *Nílch'i* the Wind who gave them life: the very wind that comes from the four directions. The very wind that comes out of our own mouths now as we speak and breathe. The wind that brings spirit into our bodies from everywhere and which, when it ceases to blow inside of us, can make us all speechless so that we die, it is said.

Three

It is also said that after the ceremony which gave life to *Asdzą́ą́ nádleehé* the Changing Woman, and to *Yoołgai asdzą́ą́* the White Shell Woman, *Bits'íís łigaii* the White Body took *Naadą́ǫ́lgaii ashkii* the White Corn Boy and *Naadą́ǫ́ltsoii at'ééd* the Yellow Corn Girl to the very summit of *Ch'óol'į́'į́* the Giant Spruce Mountain.[14]

He took them there so that they could dwell with the gods. The rest of those who had joined the assembly to participate in giving life to the sisters also departed and returned to their various dwelling places.[15]

So that now the two newly created Air-Spirit People were left alone on the mountainside.

And there they stayed for four days and four nights, gazing at the blue sky by day and looking at the stars by night; hearing the wind blow in the air around them and listening to the water ripple on the ground beneath them; saying nothing to one another and awaiting they knew not what.[16]

Until the fifth morning, when *Asdzą́ą́ nádleehé* the Changing Woman spoke at last to her sister *Yoołgai asdzą́ą́* the White Shell Woman, saying this:

"My sister," she said.

"Why should we remain here saying nothing and doing nothing, seeing no one and waiting? Let us go higher and stand where we can see plainly what lies around us, both above and below."

That is what *Asdzą́ą́ nádleehé* the Changing Woman said, and her sister *Yoołgai asdzą́ą́* the White Shell Woman agreed. So together they went high toward the summit of *Ch'óol'į́'į́* and beheld more clearly than before the sky above them, and more broadly than before the vast expanse below.

There they stayed for four more days and for four more nights. They listened to the wind blowing in the air around them. They heard the sound of water as it gathered along the steep sides of the peak, and as it made its way toward a stream that rippled across the rocks and through a long, winding gully. They listened and they waited, they watched and they anticipated, expecting something to happen which they could not quite understand.

Until at last *Asdzą́ą́ nádleehé* the Changing Woman had this to say:

"Oh, it is so lonely here," she said.

"We hear nothing else but the wind and the water. We see nothing else but the blue sky above us and the sun which makes its way from horizon to horizon each day. Nothing but the stream that makes its way from where we stand to the empty space far below.

"As for me, my sister, I harbor a deep curiosity about that sun.

"Could it not be, I wonder, a living creature like ourselves? A creature with a spirit like ours who is waiting just like we wait now?"

That is what *Asdzą́ą́ nádleehé* the Changing Woman had to say; and this is what her sister *Yoołgai asdzą́ą́* replied:

"I, too, am lonely," she replied.

"And I am as curious about that stream of water there as you are about the sun.

"Could it not be, I wonder as I watch it ripple across that rock there, a living creature like us? A creature with a spirit like yours and like my own?

"Perhaps it, too, longs for whatever it is we long for. Perhaps it is as lonely as we are."

To which *Asdzą́ą́ nádleehé* the Changing Woman answered:

"Suppose we undertake to find out," she answered.

"Suppose I stay here and watch the sun as it makes its way from the east to the west.

"Meanwhile, suppose you go down among the rocks there and watch the water as it falls."

So it was that they made up their minds. At dawn the next morning each would do what *Azdzą́ą́ nádleehé* the Changing Woman suggested.

Accordingly, she found a flat, bare rock near the summit of *Ch'óol'į́'í* on whose sides the giant spruces grow to this very day.[17]

She lay upon it, face up, with her feet to the east and her legs spread comfortably apart. That way she could relax as she observed the sun make its path across the sky. That way it could shine its warmth fully upon her.

Meanwhile, *Yoołgai asdzą́ą́* the White Shell Woman took herself down to where the mountain stream fell from shelf to shelf among the rocks.

She found a flat place in a shallow pool and lay upon it, face up, with her feet flush against a stone and her legs spread comfortably apart. That way she could watch the water as it fell. That way it could sprinkle its cool, refreshing moisture fully upon her.

Each morning they repeated this procedure, for four mornings in all. And at sundown on each of those four days they returned to each other, growing more sharply aware of their loneliness and of a peculiar feeling that girls are said to have when the path of childhood becomes the trail of womanhood.

"To speak the truth, my sister," said *Asdzą́ą́ nádleehé* the Changing Woman one evening. "I grow sad for want of company." The sun had set. The air was still and there was no sound anywhere.

"If there were only someone else," replied *Yoołgai asdzą́ą́* the White Shell Woman, "I would be less unhappy."

"Were we ourselves not made somehow?" answered *Asdzą́ą́ nádleehé* the Changing Woman.

"Perhaps there is some way for us to make people, too: people of our own kind who could help us endure these long days and nights of endless silence."

"You are wise, my sister," said White Shell Woman. "Maybe you can find such a way to make others."

• • • •

After four days of such conversation, *Yoołgai asdzą́ą́* the White Shell Woman felt movement deep inside herself.

"My sister," she cried.

"Something strange is moving within me! What can it be?"

"It is a child, my sister," answered *Asdzą́ą́ nádleehé* the Changing Woman.

"It was for that child that you lay under the waterfall.

"I, too, feel movement within me. And that, too, is a child.

"It was for that child that I lay where the sun could shine upon me."

• • • •

And after four more days both women recognized the throes of labor in their bodies.

"My sister," cried *Yoołgai asdzą́ą́* the White Shell Woman. "I think my child is coming. What am I to do?"[18]

"I, too, feel a child coming," answered *Asdzą́ą́ nádleehé* the Changing Woman. "But like you I do not know what to do."

But no sooner had she said so than they heard the kindly call of *Haashch'éélti'í* the Talking God. "*Wu'hu'hu'hu'*," he called in his familiar way, barely audible at first so faint and far off it was.

But they listened nonetheless and they waited patiently, and soon they heard the voice again, nearer and louder than before. "*Wu'hu'hu'hu'*," it repeated, this time more distinctly.

Continuing to listen, they now heard the voice a third time. "*Wu'hu'hu'hu'*," it repeated, all the nearer now and all the more distinct.

And they continued to listen and wait, listen and wait, until they heard the cry again, even louder than the last time. So close and so distinct did it sound that it seemed to be directly upon them.

And in fact they saw him appear. With him he carried what looked like a dragrope of sunbeam. They also saw the god *Tó*

neinilí appear, whose name in the language of *Bilagáana* the White
Man would be Water Sprinkler the Rain God.[19] He carried what
looked like a dragrope of rainbow with him.

Saying nothing, *Haashch'éélti'í* the Talking God gave Changing
Woman one end of the strand of sunbeam and motioned to her to
pull it with each spasm of pain she felt. Likewise saying nothing,
Tó neinilí the Rain God gave one end of the strand of rainbow to
White Shell Woman and silently bid her pull it with each spasm of
labor she was to feel.[20] Which is how it came to pass that Navajo
women who walk the surface of this world to this day pull upon a
dragrope whenever they deliver new life.

Thus a child was born to each of the two sisters.

Changing Woman's child came forth first. *Haashch'éélti'í*
the kindly Talking God took it aside and washed it.[21] Laughing
happily as he did so, he severed the cord that bound it to its
mother. Then it could nourish itself freely, just as eventually it
could live its own free life.

Next came the child of White Shell Woman. And *Tó neinilí* the
Rain God took it aside and washed it.[22] Laughing triumphantly as
he did so, he severed the cord that bound it to its mother, giving it
the freedom thereby to take food into its own mouth, just as
eventually it was to use its own feet and legs to move about.

· · · ·

Meanwhile, many of the other gods had summoned *Áłtsé hastiin*
the First Man and his wife *Áłtse asdzáá* the First Woman to come
and assist the two sisters as they learned the responsibilities of
motherhood.[23]

And *Haashch'éélti'í* the Talking God together with *Tó neinilí*
the Rain God contributed material so that First Man could make
identical baskets for the two babies. From the former he obtained
planks of sunbeam, and with them he fashioned footrests and
backbattens. From the latter he obtained patches of rainbow and
sinews of sheet lightning and zigzag lightning. Out of them he
fashioned hoods, sidestrings, and lacing.[24]

Once the two infants had been carefully placed each in its own
basket, *Haashch'éélti'í* the Talking God covered the one with a
blanket of dark cloud while *Tó neinilí* the Rain God covered the
other with a small counterpane of female rain.

They each called both children *shináli*, which in the language of

Bilagáana means my grandchild. Then they left, promising that at the end of four days they would return, it is said.[25]

Four

It is also said that Talking God and Rain God did come back four days later as they had promised. By that time the two sons had grown to the size of twelve-year-olds.

"*Shinálí,*" said the god *Haashch'ééłti'í* and the god *Tó neinilí,* "we have come to run a race with you.

"We want to find out how able-bodied you are becoming."[26]

So a race was arranged that would take its runners all the way around a nearby mountain. And at the appointed time they started running: the two boys and the two gods *Haashch'ééłti'í* and *Tó neinilí.*

Although it was to be a long, hard race, the twins jumped off to a quick, bold start and set a fast, confident pace at first. But well before they had run halfway around the course they began to flag. Soon the two gods, who were running at a more sensible stride, caught up with them. For a while they ran alongside the youths, taunting them as they all went.

"You think well of yourselves, don't you?" teased the gods.

"Well, let us see what you think about this race by the time we all finish."

And as they spoke, they flailed the lads with sticks of mountain mahogany. For nearly all the rest of the way they alternately mocked the boys and whipped them. Until, a few paces from the finish line, they easily outdistanced them, with *Haashch'ééłti'í* in the lead and *Tó neinilí* the Rain God close behind.[27]

Before they departed, the two gods warned the two boys that they would return in four days to race again. And the two exhausted youths struggled back home, rubbing their sore backs and hobbling on their aching legs.

• • • •

That evening, as they lay trying to fall asleep, *Níłch'i* the Wind came to them and whispered encouragement, saying this to console them.

"Do not be humiliated, little cousins," he said to them.

"While they are certainly more powerful than the two of you, they are not unlimited in their power.

"Before they return to race you a second time, practice as much as you can. Perhaps then you can run a better race than you did today."

So for each of the days remaining until the next contest, the twins did what *Níłch'i* the Wind advised. They ran hard around the course, circling the entire mountain somewhat faster and at something of a steadier pace than before.

Thus, when the gods returned in four days as they had promised they would, they could see at once that the two boys had grown stronger. Their shoulders had acquired breadth and the muscles in their calves were thicker and harder.

Again the twins started quickly and immediately set a fast, confident pace. But at the halfway point, the gods, who had to run a little faster this time, caught up with them. Taking their place alongside the two younger runners, they again beat them with sticks of mountain mahogany for the rest of the way. But this time they did not taunt them.

And again they easily outdistanced them a few paces from the finish line, with *Haashch'ééʼaałtiʼí* in the lead and *Tó neinilí* close behind. And before they departed they again warned that they would come back in four days to race again. Meanwhile, the two boys made their way back home, tired and sore.

· · · ·

That evening as they lay waiting to fall asleep, *Níłch'i* the Wind again came to them and whispered encouragement, saying this to soothe them.

"Do not be dismayed, little brothers," he said to them.

"While those two are still more powerful than the two of you, they are not beyond defeat.

"Before they return to race you again, continue to practice as much as you can. Then you will compete against them proudly whether you win or lose."

So for each of the days remaining until the next race the youths did what *Nítch'i* the Wind advised. They ran swiftly across the course, circling the entire mountain with more speed and with a more consistently even pace than they had maintained before.

Thus, when the gods returned in four days as they had promised they would do, they could observe at once that the two boys had continued to grow stronger. Their chests had become sinewy and their thighs were thick and muscular.

As before, the twins started quickly and immediately set a fast, confident pace. And it was not until the race was three-fourths run that the gods caught up with them. Taking their place alongside the two growing runners, they neither taunted them nor beat them; it was all they could do to stay abreast of them.

And as they all approached the finish line, *Haashch'ééłti'í* the Talking God and *Tó neinilí* the Rain God had to labor mightily to outdistance the youths. As before, they promised that they would come back in four days to run another race. Then they departed and the two boys walked back home.

•   •   •   •

That evening as they fell asleep, *Nítch'i* the Wind again came to them and told them what by now they had come to understand for themselves.

"Do not give up now, brothers," he told them.

"Those who are fully grown can grow no stronger than they are at present. Those who are younger and weaker grow stronger each day.

"Before they return to race you for the last time, practice as much as you can. Then you will show them how able-bodied you have become."

So for each of the days remaining until the final race the youths did what *Nítch'i* the Wind advised. They virtually flew across the course, circling the entire mountain with the speed of tireless deer. Therefore when the gods returned in four days they could see the full strength of manhood in their bodies and limbs. And they could see the realistic confidence of adulthood in their eyes.

Once more, the boys started quickly. And they immediately set a pace they never relinquished. For the entire distance of the race they neither heard the voices of the two gods nor saw them, so fully did they outrun them. The eldest of the two brothers finished first this time, with his younger twin barely a step behind.

When *Haashch'ééłti'í* the Talking God and *Tó neinilí* the Rain God finally crossed the finish line they were pleased and had this to say:

"Well done, *shináłí!* Well done, grandsons!" they each said, laughing and slapping the two youths on the back affectionately.

"You have grown into what we wanted you to become.

"Perhaps now you can well serve those who have nurtured you."

And with those words the two gods departed, saying nothing about running another race. Meanwhile, the two boys returned home. They were as proud and as confident as brothers can feel when the path of boyhood becomes the trail of manhood, it is said.

Five

It is also said that on the night after their final race with the gods, the two boys overheard their mothers whispering to one another.

As they lay on their beds of skins waiting to fall asleep, they recognized concern in the whispering voices of the two women, and they strained to listen.

But they could not make out a word. So they rose from their beds and walked across the floor of their lodge to the place where the women sat.

"Mothers," they said.

"Something seems to be troubling you.

"Tell us what it is."

"It is nothing," replied the two women.

"Return to your beds and go to sleep."

"But we recognize fear in your voices," said the boys. "Tell us what you are discussing."

"It is nothing," repeated their mothers. "Go to sleep and do not worry yourselves."

Then the first of the two youths stepped forward. And looking at his mother *Asdzą́ą́ nádleehé* the Changing Woman with an intensity he had never before displayed, he had this to ask her:

"Mother," he asked her.

"Who is my father?

"And who is the father of my brother here?"

"You have no father," *Asdzą́ą́ nádleehé* the Changing Woman replied.

"Who is my father?" repeated the first son.

"And who is father to my brother here?

"As our parents you should tell us such things, just as you should tell us what it is that worries you so.

"Truly, we are grown up enough to know such things."

That is what the eldest of the two boys repeated. And this is what *Asdzą́ą́ nádleehé* his mother the Changing Woman answered:

"You have no father," she answered quietly.

"And neither does your brother there have a father.

"For all you need know, you are *yátaashki':* nothing but bastards, that's what you are.

"Now I beg you, go to sleep and do not concern yourselves with that which troubles us no matter what it may be."

Then the second of the two youths stepped forward.

He looked at his mother *Yoołgai asdzą́ą́* the White Shell Woman with a seriousness that she had not recognized in him before, having this to ask:

"Mother," he asked.

"Who is my father? And who is father to my brother, who also wishes to know?"

"It is with you as it is with him," replied *Yoołgai asdzą́ą́* the White Shell Woman.

"You have no father."[28]

"But surely someone sired us," persisted the second son.

"As your children we should know of such things, just as we should know what it is that troubles you."

That is how the second of the two boys persisted. And this is what *Yoołgai asdzą́ą́* his mother the White Shell Woman replied:

"You have no father," she replied quietly.

"Nor does your brother have a father.

"The round cactus and the sitting cactus are your fathers for all you need to know.

"Now I implore you, go to sleep and do not concern yourselves with whatever it is that worries us."

•   •   •   •

In the morning the women made bows of juniper wood for their two sons. And as best they could they fashioned arrows for the boys.

"If you consider yourselves grown up, use these and hunt," they said. "But do not wander beyond sight of our dwelling.

"Above all, do not venture to the east."

But in spite of that warning, the twins headed in that very direction.[29]

When they had traveled a good distance, they sighted an animal with brownish fur and a sharp nose. Drawing their arrows and positioning them in their bows, they took aim at the sharp-nosed creature. But before they could shoot he leaped forward and bounded into a canyon, where he disappeared.

When they returned home that evening, they described in detail the animal that had gotten away.

"We have traveled east this day," they said to their mothers.

"There we saw an animal with a dull brownish coat and a pointed snout, which we tried to shoot. But before we could cast an arrow at him he took flight."

"Beware!" replied the women.

"That is Coyote you saw!

"You must never try to follow him. And you must not follow his ways.

"He makes great mischief, and he brings disorder wherever he goes.

"Besides, it would be just like him to spy for *Déélgééd*, the Horned Monster, one of the alien creatures who seek to destroy you and who have been stalking all of our people ever since they arrived in this world."

•   •   •   •

The next day the boys again went hunting. And although their mothers again warned them to stay within sight of their dwelling and to take special care not to venture to the south, they headed precisely in that direction.

When they had traveled a good distance they sighted a large black bird perched on a tree. They again drew their arrows and placed them in their bows, taking aim at the creature with the glistening black feathers. But before they could shoot, it flapped its wings and took flight further southward, where it drifted entirely out of view.

When they returned home that evening, they told all that had happened.

"We have been to the south this day," they said to their mothers.

"There we sighted a great black bird, which we tried to shoot. But before we could spring an arrow at him he spread his wings and flew away."

"Alas!" cried the two women.

"That is Raven you saw!

"He may very well be a spy for *Tsé nináhálééh*, the Monster Bird. He is one of the alien creatures who would surely destroy you if they could find you and who have been stalking all of our people and yours ever since they arrived in this world."

•　•　•　•

The next day the boys again went out to hunt. And although their mothers cautioned them to stay within sight of their dwelling and to take special care not to venture to the west, they headed precisely in that direction.

They traveled quite a distance but the only game they saw was a giant dark bird with a skinny, featherless red head. Seeing it, they drew their arrows and set them carefully in their bows, taking aim at the creature whose neck was scarcely to be distinguished from its head save for the red markings. But before they could shoot, it raised its giant wings and sailed eastward out of sight.

When they returned home that evening they talked about the strange creature they had seen.

"We have traveled west this day," they said to their mothers.

"There we spied a great dark bird whose head was red and bare of feathers and whose neck was exceedingly long. We tried to shoot it but it flew away before we could get off a single arrow."

"Woe alike to the two of you!" lamented both women.

"That was surely Buzzard you saw.

"No doubt he is a spy for *Tsédah hódziiłtáłii* the Monster That Kicks People Down Cliffs. No doubt he would cast you from a high mesa if he could. Then he would feast on your remains. He is one of the alien creatures who have been stalking all of our people and your people ever since they arrived in this world. It is for fear of him and the others that we worry over you two."

•   •   •   •

The next day the boys again went out to find game. And although their mothers admonished them to stay within sight of their dwelling and to take special care not to go north, they headed precisely in that direction.

After they traveled far they sighted a bird with brilliant black plumage roosting on a tree overlooking the edge of a deep canyon. It seemed to be talking to itself, saying, *"A'a'a'i'! a'a'a'i'!"* Seeing it, they drew their arrows and poised them in their bows, aiming at the glistening bird with the piercing voice. But before they could shoot, it fluttered its wings and spread its tail, taking flight deep into the shadows of the canyon.

When they returned home that evening, they again reported the day's events to their mothers, describing the bird they had seen as accurately as they could.

"We have gone far to the north," they said to their mothers.

"We saw a bird there whose voice was not altogether unlike our own and whose tail fanned outwards as it flew. We aimed our bows at it, but it flew away before we could release them."

"Surely you are doomed!" wailed the two women.

"That was certainly Magpie you saw.

"Certainly he spies for *Bináá' yee agháni* the Monster Who Kills with His Eyes. Once he sees you himself he will paralyze you with a mere glance. Then he will peck your bodies to pieces. And bite by bite he will swallow you. He is one of the alien creatures who have been stalking all of our people, who are likewise your own people, ever since they arrived in this world. And now you know what frightens us and troubles us. Now you know why we whisper furtively when we think you cannot hear."

And with that the two women began to weep and sob.

"Alas, alas!" they cried.

"Alas for our children.

"Alas for the hope of our people, who surely now are doomed.

"As for you, our sons, you disappoint us.

"You question us when we ask you not to.

"You go where we tell you not to go.

"By disobeying us you have allowed yourselves to be seen by the enemies of our people, who are also your people.

"Now the spies of the *Naayéé'* from every corner of this world will know you exist. They will tell their chiefs, and soon the monsters will come from all directions to destroy you and devour you, just as they have destroyed so many of your kinsmen and devoured them."

And the two mothers grew hysterical with grief. Their race was doomed once and for all, they believed. All of the work that had been done in this world was now done in vain, they believed.

And their sons could do nothing to console them, it is said.

Six

It is also said that *Asdzáá nádleehé* the Changing Woman and her sister *Yoołgai asdzáá* the White Shell Woman awoke the next morning and tried as best they could to go about their daily affairs. Early in the day they made a corncake and set it on the ashes of the fire to bake.

Then *Yoołgai asdzáá* the White Shell Woman went outside to fetch more wood. But as she was gathering it she spied *Yé'iitsoh*. Big Giant is his name in the language of *Bilagáana* the White Man. He was tallest and most fierce of the *Naayéé'* and chief of all those monsters.[30]

As quickly as she could, White Shell Woman ran back to their lodge to warn her sister and the two boys:

"Quick!" she warned.

"We must hide the boys. For *Yéiitsoh* the Big Giant is here."

Whereupon she and *Asdzáá nádleehé* the Changing Woman covered them with bundles of sticks in the most remote corner of their dwelling. Then they resumed doing their chores as casually as they could.

Yoołgai asdzáá the White Shell Woman placed a kettle of water near the fire. *Asdzáá nádleehé* the Changing Woman took the corncake out of the ashes.

And just then the awesome, large head of *Yé'iitsoh* the Big Giant appeared through the door, which was scarcely wide enough for it to fit. Here is what he had to say:

"That is a fine-looking cake you have made," he said.

"How good it smells.

"And I have come just in time to taste it."

And this is what *Asdzą́ą́ nádleehé* the Changing Woman replied:

"By no means is it for you," replied she.

"Nothing that I make is for your ugly maw."

"Why should I care anyhow?" replied *Yé'iitsoh* the Big Giant.

"I would much prefer to eat boys.

"And you have some of those around here.

"Or so I have been told.

"Show me where they are.

"For I have come all this way to taste them, and I will be disappointed if I do not."

That is what *Yé'iitsoh* the Big Giant had to say to *Asdzą́ą́ nádleehé* the Changing Woman, and this is what she said in return:

"We have no boys left here," returned she.

"All of our boys are gone.

"All of our boys have disappeared into your gullet. Or they have disappeared into the gizzards of your people.

"You have long since eaten all of our children, which you very well know."

"No boys left here?" mocked *Yé'iitsoh*.

"No more children?

"Then tell me who has made all these tracks I see around here."

"Oh, those," answered *Asdzą́ą́ nádleehé*.

"I have made those.

"I made them to pass the long, silent hours.

"I grow lonely here without children and without kinsmen. So I make those tracks to pretend that there are people around me. Then I imagine what we would say to one another and what we would do together.

"I do it with the side of my hand.

"I do it like this.

"See?"

And to show him, she curled her fingers into a loose fist and fashioned imprints that resembled the tracks which *Yé'iitsoh* the Big Giant spoke of.

He looked closely at them, compared them with the tracks he had seen outside, seemed satisfied, and went away without saying more.

• • • •

When he was gone, *Yoołgai asdzą́ą́* the White Shell Woman
went out and climbed a nearby hill to look around. And from where
she stood she observed many of the alien *Naayéé'* striding toward
the lodge. When she saw them, she returned to warn her sister.

"They are coming this way!" she warned.

"All of them are coming!"

"What shall we do?"

Whereupon *Asdzą́ą́ nádleehé* the Changing Woman picked up
four colored hoops and took them outside.[31]

She cast one of them in each of the four directions. To the east
she threw a white one. To the south she threw a blue one. To
the west she threw a yellow one. And to the north she threw a
black one.

Immediately a great gale gathered where she stood and encircled
the dwelling. As it became more intense, it blew outwards in all
four directions. To the east it blew. To the south it blew. To the
west it blew. To the north it blew. So strong did it blow all around
the dwelling that none of the monsters could get through it.

That much accomplished, *Asdzą́ą́ nádleehé* the Changing
Woman went inside.

"For the time being we are safe," she told her sister *Yoołgaii
asdzą́ą́* the White Shell Woman.

"But by this time tomorrow the wind will have stopped. And I
have no more magic hoops.

"What will happen then, I do not know. Surely *Yé'iitsoh* the Big
Giant together with the other *Naayéé'* will converge on us and
devour the boys.

"Who knows?

"Perhaps they will eat us too."

• • • •

Meanwhile, the two boys had heard everything from the place
where they lay hidden.

That night, as they waited to fall asleep, they talked between
themselves.

They were ashamed of what they had done.

By disobeying their mothers, they had disclosed themselves to the enemies of their people, who were also their own enemies. And now the *Naayéé'* were on their way.

Who was to know?

Perhaps they would eat *Asdzą́ą́ nádleehé* the Changing Woman and *Yoołgai asdzą́ą́* the White Shell Woman, when what they really had a taste for was boys.

If the twins were to run away, perhaps their mothers would be in less danger.

So well before dawn of the next morning they got up and stole out of the lodge.[32]

* * * *

When their mothers awoke, they saw that the twins had taken flight.

They went outside to look for them and examined the ground for fresh tracks. But they found only four footprints for each of the two boys, and these pointed toward *Dził ná'oodiłii* the Travelers Circle Mountain.

It seemed that they had taken *Atiin diyinii* the Holy Trail so that they could not be followed. But by taking such a path they could easily arouse the anger of *Haashch'ééh dine'é* the Holy People.

In any case, to try to search for them would be useless. So *Asdzą́ą́ nádleehé* the Changing Woman and *Yoołgaii asdzą́ą́* the White Shell Woman returned to their dwelling, where they would wait in fear and apprehension.

* * * *

Just as the women had surmised, the boys indeed did take the path of the gods. They did so not by design, but in their confusion and in their eagerness to get away. They did so because they sought the easiest trail to cross. And this trail had been made easy for them by many rainbows, sunbeams, bolts of male lightning, and flashes of female lightning.

So that by daybreak they were in plain sight of the summit of *Dził ná'oodiłii*. Once they saw it, however, they could not decide which way to turn. They were already tired. They were cold and they were hungry.

They looked in every direction, seeing nothing but the nearby summit and the more distant peaks which lay across an expanse of mountains and canyons. No sign of life did they see in the distance, no sign of refuge.

Then they looked on the ground just ahead of them. And they noticed a thin, wispy pillar of smoke arising mysteriously from a spot where there was no flame. It was only barely visible, and they might easily have missed it had they not looked carefully.

Slowly approaching it, they soon saw that it came from the smoke hole of an underground chamber. And when they reached it they spied a ladder blackened by smoke projecting through that hole from a place below.[33]

They peered timidly into the hole and saw that the ladder had four rungs. They also saw that it projected from a spot below where an old woman sat peacefully before a small fire.

It was *Na'ashjéii asdzą́ą́* the Spider Woman they saw.[34] And she looked up at them and smiled. As she did, they set foot on the topmost rung of the ladder.

"Enter *shiyáázh* my sons," she said in a voice that rasped and crackled.

"Welcome to my house in the ground.

"Who are you?

"And where do you come from, walking together on *Atiin diyinii* the trail of the rainbow as you do?"

They gave no answer at first. But they lowered themselves down the ladder by the distance of another rung. And then they spoke, saying this to her:

"We have nowhere in particular to go," they said to her.

"We are here because we do not know indeed where we can go."

"Well, you are welcome here *shiyáázh*," she said.

"But you must tell me who you are and where you are going, following *Atiin diyinii* the trail of sunbeams as you do."

The two youths lowered themselves by another rung, giving no answer at first. But then they said this to her:

"We are uncertain as to who we are," they said to her.

"We are not at all sure where we are going. We know only that we are fleeing for our lives."

"You may rest safely here with me, my sons," she said.

"But you must tell me who you are and what it is you are running from, making your way as you do across *Atiin diyinii* the path of the male lightning bolts and the female lightning flashes."

Whereupon they gave no answer at first. But they lowered themselves by yet another rung so that they were now standing on the bottom one. And then they spoke, saying this to her:

"Alas *nihimásání* our grandmother," they said to her.

"We cannot tell you fully who we are.

"We know only that *Asdzą́ą́ nádleehé* the Changing Woman is our mother. And that *Yoołgai asdzą́ą́* the White Shell Woman is our mother.

"They it was who gave birth to us.

"And we are fleeing from *Naayéé'* the Alien Monsters, who pursue us and who will surely destroy us, just as they will destroy our mothers. And just as they have destroyed our kinsmen before us."

That is what the fleeing brothers said to *Na'ashjéii asdzą́ą́* the Spider Woman. And this is what she said to them in answering:

"From me you can learn much, my sons *shiyáázh*," answered she to them.

"I can tell you things that will bring you safety and comfort.

"But before I tell you anything, you must tell me all that you know. You must tell me as fully as you can who you are. You must tell me what you have done. You must tell me what it is you hope to do as you take flight by way of *Atiin diyinii* the Holy Trail."

The two brothers lowered themselves from the bottom rung of the smoke-blackened ladder to the floor of *Na'ashjé'ii asdzą́ą́* the Spider Woman's underground dwelling, giving no answer at first. But finally they said this to her:

"Alas, *nihimásání*," they finally said to her.

"We know that we are *yátaashki'* born without the blessing of marriage. For all else we know, we were sired by the round cactus and the sitting cactus.

"And we are following the Holy Trail because we are fleeing in disgrace. *Naayéé'* the Alien Monsters who pursue us will also destroy our people if they can."

Na'ashjé'ii asdzą́ą́ the Spider Woman then stood up. And she extended her arms to the boys in a gesture full of welcome.

"Enter my underground home," she said.

"I will tell you who your father is.

"And I will tell you about his dwelling.

"I will tell you how you may get there.

"And I will tell you how you may seek his help."

Whereupon the two twins stepped forward, so that they found

themselves in the very center of her chamber. They noticed that
she had many seats around the fire. The first brother, son of
Asdzą́ą́ nádleehé the Changing Woman, placed himself on a seat of
obsidian. The second brother, son of *Yoołgai asdzą́ą́,* placed
himself on a seat of turquoise. Then the old woman fed them. And
while they ate and warmed themselves, she gave them this
information:

"Your father is in reality *Jóhonaa'éí* the Sun," she informed them.

"And his dwelling is far above us all in the sky.

"The way to his house is long and dangerous.

"Many of the alien monsters dwell between this place here and
the place of *Jóhonaa'éí* your father the Sun. And they will block
your passage if they can.

"Furthermore, I cannot promise you that your father will be
happy to see you. Perhaps he will even punish you for coming to him.

"Who knows?

"But if he does punish you, you must endure his blows. You
must try your best.

"Otherwise you and your people are surely doomed."

"Tell us what we must do to reach the dwelling of our father,
Jóhonaa'éí the Sun," said the boys then. And here is what
Na'ashjé'ii asdzą́ą́ replied:

"You will have to cross four dangerous places," replied she.

"You will have to cross past the rocks that crush all travelers.
You will have to cross among the reeds that cut intruders to pieces.
You will have to cross between the cane cactuses that tear
travelers to shreds. And you will have to cross the boiling sands
that burn all passersby to fine ashes.

"Beyond those four points no ordinary creature can pass. But I
shall give you a talisman that will allow you to surpass those who
are ordinary. That way you can subdue your enemies and preserve
your lives."

So saying, she handed the two boys the sacred *naayéé' ats'os,*
which is a hoop fashioned out of life-feathers plucked from
monster eagles.[35]

After which she had this to say:

"Treat this charm carefully," she warned them.

"And use it correctly.

"Otherwise it will be of no use to you and you will surely perish.

"As you face your enemies, stare directly at them without
flinching. Stare at them without showing fear. As you stare at

them, hold the sacred *naayéé' ats'os* in your hand and extend it
towards whatever threatens you. And then repeat this magic song:

'Rub your feet with pollen and rest them.
Rub your hands with pollen and rest them.
Rub your body with pollen and lie at rest.
Rub your head with pollen and put your mind to rest.
Then truly your feet become pollen.

Your hands become pollen.
Your body becomes pollen.
Your head becomes pollen.
Your spirit will then become pollen.
Your voice will then become pollen.
All of you is as pollen is.
And what pollen is, that is what peace is.[36]
The trail ahead is now a beautiful trail.
Long life is ahead; happiness is ahead.' "

That is the song which *Na'ashjé'ii asdzáá* the Spider Woman
taught the fleeing twins. She recited it to them four times. And
four times they repeated it to her exactly as they heard her sing it,
to assure her that they knew it well.

"Now," she said to them.

"You are ready to go on.

"You have the power to seek help for yourselves and for your
people.[37]

"Be on your way, then. And walk in beauty."

And with those words from her the two youths placed the sacred
naayéé' ats'os in a medicine bundle which she had prepared for
them, stood up, thanked her, and departed on their quest.

Since they now knew fully who they were, and since they now had
a distinct purpose in traveling, they set out confidently, it is said.

Seven

It is also said that the two brothers left the underground dwelling
of *Na'ashjé'ii asdzáá* the Spider Woman and continued on their
way. And soon thereafter they came upon *Tsé ahéénídiłii* the
Rocks that Crush.[38]

They had followed the trail she instructed them to take. Doing so they came to a narrow pass between two high cliffs. And it was here that, when anyone approached, the rocks would open wide as if to offer easy passage. But as soon as the traveler was within the cleft, they would close upon that person like clapping hands and crush him.

In reality these rocks were agents of the *Naayéé'* who had devoured so many people. They looked like high cliffs, true enough. But they thought like monsters and they attacked like monsters.

When the twins saw those rocks, they headed slowly toward them as if they intended to pass between. Whereupon the cliffs opened wide to receive them. But within a few steps of those mighty walls, the two youths stopped short! And, unaware that they were being tricked, the cliffs slammed shut to crush their two newest victims.

Thus did the boys deceive the rocks four times, each time stepping forward as the cliffs opened to receive them, and each time halting no more than a small step or two beyond those thunderous masses.

"Who are you and where do you come from?" called the rocks at last, causing the ground beneath the two travelers to vibrate with the din of their angry voices.

"Where are you going?" called they. "And what is it you intend to do when you get there?"

To which the two boys gave this answer:

"We are children of *Jóhonaa'éí* the Sun," they answered.

"We come from *Dził ná'oodiłii*, the unhappy region of Banded Rock Mountain.

"We seek the dwelling of our father. And when we find it we intend to deliver a message to him from *Na'ashjé'ii asdzáá* the Spider Woman."

"Tell us what that message is," the rocks demanded. "Or else we will destroy you yet."

Whereupon the boys took the sacred *naayéé ats'os* from their bundle, held it at arm's length facing the cliff-monsters, stared straight at them, and recited the magic formula that *Na'ashjé'ii asdzáá* the Spider Woman had taught them. Upon their doing which the rocks opened wide and bid the boys walk between them.

"Continue on your way," they said quietly.

"Long life is ahead. Happiness is ahead."
So it was that the two lads travelled onward through Rock-Monster Pass along *Atiin diyinii* the Holy Trail.

•   •   •   •

Soon, however, they came to a broad plain, which seemed to extend farther than anyone could see. Covering it were reeds that bore great leaves upon them, sharp as knives. These were *Lók'aa' adigishí* the Slashing Reeds that *Na'ashjé'ii asdzą́ą́* the Spider Woman had mentioned to them.

It was at this place that, when anyone approached, the reeds would part as if to allow a path for the unwary traveler. But once the victims set foot between them they would slash him to pieces. In reality they were partners to the *Naayéé'* who had devoured so many people. They resembled reeds, sure enough. But they thought like monsters and they devoured flesh the way monsters did.

Coming within view of the Slashing Reeds, the boys continued walking with no sign of hesitation. Meanwhile, the reeds opened up for them, showing a clear passage all the way across the plain. But merely a step or so before they set foot on the pathway that now lay spread before them, the two stopped short! And as they did the reeds rushed together, slashing and swishing like blades of brandished knives.

Thus did the two travelers deceive the reeds four times, each time stepping forward as the pathway opened up, but each time stopping just beyond reach of the bloody grasp of those bushes.

Until the deadly plants called out to them at last:
"Truly, we wish to know who you are and where you come from," they called, slashing the air as they spoke until the space around them hissed.

"And we want to know where you are going," they called. "And what is your business to be once you arrive there?"

To which the two boys made this retort:
"We are children of *Jóhonaa'éí* the Sun," they retorted.

"Our journey began at *Dził ná'oodiłii*, the region of Banded Rock Mountain where many people have suffered harm.

"It will end when we arrive at the dwelling of our father, where we intend to deliver a message to him from *Na'ashjé'ii asdzą́ą́* the Spider Woman."

"And just what is this message that you intend to repeat to him?" asked the reeds. "Tell us at once lest we yet manage to cut you to shreds."

Whereupon the boys took the sacred *naayéé ats'os* from their bundle, held it at arm's length as they faced the reed-monsters, stared at them fearlessly, and repeated the magic formula that *Na'ashjé'ii asdzáá* the Spider Woman had taught them. And the reeds grew limp and opened up a pathway for the boys to cross.

"Pass this way in peace," they quietly said.

"Long life is ahead. Happiness is ahead."

So it was that the two lads traveled on beyond the place of Slashing-Reed Path along *Atiin diyinii* the Holy Trail.

• • • •

But they soon came to an open country covered with cane cactuses. Everywhere they looked they saw them. These were *Hosh dítsahiitsoh* the Giant Awl Cactus that they knew sooner or later they would meet. As soon as anyone tried to walk among them, they would come to life and leap from where they stood and pierce their victims with poisonous thorns.

In reality these cactus were members of the band of *Naayéé* who had devoured so many people. True enough, they had the appearance of cactus. But they thought like monsters and they feasted upon flesh and bone as monsters did.

When the twins arrived within sight of this grove of cane cactus, they continued walking with no sign of flinching or faltering. Meanwhile, the cactus became flaccid, seemingly to make an aisle for them to pass through. But just this side of the spot where that aisle began, the boys stopped short as they had done before. And they watched unharmed as the cactuses charged upon each other instead of pouncing on them.

Thus did the youths trick those spiny plant-creatures four times, each time pretending to enter the grove and each time stopping just beyond reach of the cactus.

"Tell us who you are and where you came from!" scolded the cactuses at last, gnashing and jabbing as they spoke.

"And tell us where you are going and what you seek to accomplish when you get there."

To which the boys scolded in return:

"We are children of *Jóhonaa'éí* the Sun," they scolded.

"We started out at *Dził ná'oodiłii*, the region of Banded Rock Mountain where our people once hoped to raise their crops in peace but cannot do so. And we will reach our destination when we find the dwelling of our father so that we may deliver a message to him from *Na'ashje'aa'ii asdzą́ą́* the Spider Woman.

"You had better make sure that we too know the contents of this message," demanded the cactuses. "Or we will yet pierce you and fill your bodies with our poison."

Whereupon the boys took the sacred *naayéé' ats'os* from their bundle, held it at arm's length as they faced the cactus-monsters, and repeated the magic formula that *Na'ashjé'ii asdzą́ą́* the Spider Woman had taught them. And whereupon the cactuses ceased to move and left open a lane for the boys to pass through.

"Move through here in peace," quietly said they.

Long life is ahead. Happiness is ahead."

So it was that the two lads traveled through the place of Poison Cactus Country along *Atiin diyinii* the Holy Trail.

•   •   •   •

Before long, however, they arrived at a barren land of rolling sand dunes. It was a great desert where hot, whirling piles of sand encroached upon anyone passing through. These were *Séít'áád* the Boiling Dunes that they were forewarned they would eventually meet.

It was at this place where, boiling like water in a heated pot, these dunes burned the wayfarer to a shrivel and covered up the remains. In reality they had been put there by the *Naayéé'* who had devoured so many people. Sure enough, they assumed the shape of sand dunes. But they had the will of monsters and the unrelenting appetite for the flesh and blood of people that monsters had.

Spotting the desert of rising sands, the twins kept right on walking as though they knew of no reason to do otherwise. Meanwhile, the dunes subsided and flattened out for them, appearing to permit them to come ahead. But barely a step or two shy of the desert's edge, they stopped short! And the dunes, which at once began to swirl and boil, merely converged upon one another instead of submerging their victims.

Thus did the two youths trick the heaps of sand four times, each time behaving as though they would step forward and each time halting at the last instant.

"We must know who you are and where you come from,"
insisted the dunes at last, roaring and filling the air with their
furious heat as they spoke.

"And we seek to learn where you are going and what your
purpose is once you get there."

To which the boys roared this answer:

"We are children of *Jóhonaa'éí* the Sun," they roared.

"We set out from *Dził ná'oodiłii*, the region of Banded Rock
Mountain where our unfortunate people once hoped to settle and
dwell peacefully. And we will fulfill our purpose when we reach
the dwelling of our father to deliver a message to him from
Na'ashjé'ii asdzą́ą́ the Spider Woman."

"What could she possibly have to say to him?" asked the dunes.
"You had better tell us, or we will yet burn you up and bury your
remains."

Whereupon the boys took the sacred *naayéé' ats'os* from their
bundle, held it at arm's length as they faced the dunes, stared at
them confidently and chanted the words of the magic formula that
Na'ashjé'ii asdzą́ą́ the Spider woman had taught them. And
whereupon the dunes slowly collapsed so that the desert floor
could easily be crossed.

"Continue on your journey," they responded quietly.

"Long life is ahead. Happiness is ahead."

So it was that the two lads made their way over Burning Sands
Desert and continued along *Atiin diyinii* the Holy Trail.

•   •   •   •

And so it was that they made their way carefully for the rest of
their journey, coming upon one obstacle after another and dealing
with each.

They traversed the stream of the rushing water monsters, and
they crossed the parched barren land of the old age monsters. They
obtained passage across the barrier placed by the daylight
monsters, which rose like a great range of bleached, barren
mountains; and they made their way through the narrow chasm of
the dark-night monsters, which cut so deeply into a canyon that no
light filtered into it. And at each of these the twins devised a way
to trick those who would stand in their way. With each success
their fear lessened, their pace quickened, their courage increased
and their confidence grew.

• • • •

Until finally they came to the house of their father *Jóhonaa'éí* the Sun.

As they drew within sight of the entrance, they saw that the way was guarded by two bears. One of them crouched to the right of the portal and one to the left, facing each other. As the boys approached, the bears looked at them, stook up on their back legs, growled angrily and poised themselves to attack.[39] But the twins withdrew the sacred *naayéé' ats'os* from their bundle, held it at arm's length, faced the menacing bears, and recited the magic formula that *Na'ashjé'ii asdzą́ą́* the Spider Woman had taught them. And at once the two creatures lay back down to rest.

As they drew closer to the entranceway to the dwelling of *Jóhonaa'éí* the Sun, the twins likewise encountered a pair of guardian serpents, a pair of guardian winds and a pair of guardian lightning bolts. But they subdued each of these pairs with the words of the magic formula just as they has subdued the others.

That is how the fleeing twins finally made their way into the house of their father *Jóhonaa'éí* the Sun, it is said.[40]

Eight

It is also said that the Sun's dwelling was made of turquoise and that it was square like a Pueblo house. It stood on the shore of a great body of water.

Entering it, the boys saw a woman sitting against the western wall. And they saw two handsome young men against the southern wall. These they recognized as *Ii'ni łizhinii* the Black Thunder and as *Ii'ni dootł'izhii* the Blue Thunder. Sitting against the northern wall they saw two handsome young women whom they did not recognize.[41]

The older woman and the two younger ones gave the strangers a quick glance and then immediately looked down. The two young men, however, gazed at the twins for some length of time. But no one among them spoke.

Until finally the two boys who had just entered said this:
"We are the twins from *Dził ná'oodiłii*," they said.

"We are born of *Asdzą́ą́ nádleehé* the Changing Woman, and of *Yoołgai asdzą́ą́* the Woman of the White Shells. But we also belong, so we are told, to *Jóhonaa'éí*, our father the Sun. And we have come here to his dwelling by way of *Atiin diyinii* the Holy Trail in search of him.

"For we need his help."

Instead of replying, the women remained silent. Meanwhile, the young men stood up, stared at the twins, came toward them, and without saying a word wrapped them in the four coverings of the sky. They wrapped them in the blanket of red dawn. Then they wrapped them next in the robe of blue daylight. Next they wrapped them in the counterpane of yellow evening. And finally they wrapped them in the black shroud of darkness.[42]

Then the bundle must have been placed by them high on a shelf. For the twins felt themselves being lifted toward the ceiling of the dwelling.

Not knowing what else to do, they lay in the coverings for quite some time. Then, as evening drew near, they heard a rattle that hung over the dwelling's door shake. And from a distance they heard a similar rattle shake with each step someone was making.

"Our father is returning, now that this day has passed," they heard one of the young women say.

Then the twins recognized what must have been the footfalls of *Jóhonaa'éí* the Sun. They heard him as he entered the door. They heard him as he took from his back a bright red disk, for they could feel its heat even under the covers that enshrouded them, just as they could hear it clang. And they heard him as he moved toward the west wall of the chamber, where he hung the disk on a peg. And they heard it shake and ring for some time after he placed it there.

"*Tláa, tláa, tláa, tláa,*" it rang, until at last there was again silence.

When all became quiet, *Jóhonaa'éí* the Sun turned to the three women, looked first at one, then at the next, and then at the next, asking this:

"Who has come here today?" he asked, not without anger in his voice.[43]

But no one answered him.

The older woman looked straight at her husband without saying anything. The younger two averted his stare.

"Two strangers from the surface world below have come here today," demanded *Jóhonaa'éí* "I wish to know who they are! And I wish to know whhere they are!"

But no one answered him.

The elder woman continued to glare silently at him, while the younger two gazed nervously at each other.

"Who are those who have come here today?" repeated *Jóhonaa'éí.* "And where are they?"

But still no answer came.

The elder woman held her silence as she continued to glare at him. The younger two intermittently looked down at their feet and into the eyes of each other.

"From wherever I was as I made my way across the sky this day I could see two young men make their way along *Atiin diyinii* the Holy Trail," said *Jóhonaa'éí,* his anger increasing.

"They entered here shortly after I reached my zenith. Now I wish to know who they are. And I wish to know where they are."

Finally, the eldest of the three women spoke. There was anger, too, in her voice. And this is what she had to say:

"It would be well for you not to declare too much about this incident," she had to say.[44]

"Or else it would be well for you to speak up and explain yourself truthfully.

"For what you say is correct.

"Two young men did indeed come here from the surface world. They came seeking you, making the claim that you are their father.

"Yet you have assured me repeatedly that you go nowhere as you cross the sky each day.

"Many times have you assured me that you keep your distance from all creatures down there.

"Over and over again you have assured me that I am the only woman you see.

"Well then! Whose sons are those?" she demanded, pointing to the bundle on the shelf as the two young men and the two young women seated against the various walls of the dwelling looked at one another and grinned.

Whereupon she seized the pack of coverings that had been placed on the shelf and unfurled them. First the black shroud of darkness unrolled. Then the counterpane of yellow evening came undone. Next the robe of blue sky unfurled. And finally the blanket of red dawn flew open.

And the two boys who had been bundled in the blankets tumbled out onto the floor before the eyes of *Jóhonaa'éí* the Sun.

At once he seized them and threw them against a bank of sharp spikes of white shell that stood along the eastern wall of his dwelling. But the twins bounced back unhurt from them, for they held tightly onto the *naayéé' ats'os* that *Na'ashjé'ii asdzáá* the Spider Woman had given them.

And when he saw that they survived this blow, he seized them again and threw them against a bank of turquoise spikes that stood along the southern wall. But again they held tightly onto the sacred *naayéé' ats'os* that had been given them, bouncing back uninjured.

So that *Jóhonaa'éí* the Sun was left to seize them again and to throw them against spikes of haliotis in the west. From which blow they likewise survived, holding onto the sacred *naayéé' ats'os* as before.

And in desperation but with growing respect for them he picked them up a fourth time and hurled them against spikes of black rock to the north. And when they returned again uninjured, having again held tightly onto their sacred *naayéé' ats'os*, *Jóhonaa'éí* the Sun at last had this to say:

"Indeed," he said.

"I wish it were true that they were children of mine."[45]

•   •   •   •

"Go out," he then said to the two young men in his household.[46]

"Prepare the sweathouse.

"Prepare it well.

"Heat for it four of the hardest boulders you can find: heat a white boulder and a blue boulder. Heat a yellow boulder and a black one."

But *Nílch'i* the Wind, who had hovered close to the twins during their entire journey, heard these instructions. And at once he started digging a hole into the bank against which the sweathouse had been built.[47]

By doing so he managed to create a tunnel to the steam chamber of the sweat lodge. And he managed to conceal the opening with a large, flat stone. He then whispered to the twins what he had done, and he gave them these instructions:

"Do not hide in the hole," he instructed them.

"Do not hide there until you have answered the questions your father asks you."

* * * *

Ordered to do so, the two youths entered the sweat lodge. Then hot boulders were placed inside and the opening of the lodge was sealed with the four sky-coverings.

Outside stood *Jóhonaa'éí* the Sun.

"Is it hot in there?" he called.

"Yes," replied the boys.

"It is very hot in here."[48]

And after answering his question, they crept into the hiding place that *Nítch'i* the Wind had fashioned for them. There they sheltered themselves against the deadly heat.

Until at length they heard *Jóhonaa'éí* the Sun climb the sweat lodge and pour a great quantity of water through the top onto the red-hot stones inside. When it landed on the hot boulders it burst forth with a mighty noise as steam filled the chamber, hissing and boiling. But in time the steam cooled and the twins crept out of their hiding place back into the sweathouse.

Hoping that this time he would get no reply, *Jóhonaa'éí* the Sun stepped forward again and called out to the boys:

"Have you been hot in there?" he called.

"So we have," they replied.

"But at least it is not as hot now as it was a while ago."

Hearing that reply, *Jóhonaa'éí* raised the coverings from the sweat lodge and bid the boys come out. As he watched them emerge apparently no less strong and no less alert than they had been when they entered, he greeted them with a semblance of cheer.

"Truly you must be my children!" he greeted them.

"For you are strong and you endure hardship."

But even as he spoke, he was thinking of other ways to destroy them should it turn out that they were not his sons after all.

•

Jóhonaa'éí the Sun then spread the four sky-blankets on the ground. Upon the blanket of red dawn he placed the robe of blue sky. On the robe of blue sky he placed the counterpane of yellow evening. And over the counterpane of yellow evening he spread the black shroud of darkness. Then he bid the young men sit upon these layers one behind the other, each facing east.

"My daughters," he then commanded.

"Dress these two strangers as my other sons are dressed.

"Adorn them the way your brothers are adorned."

Whereupon the two young women in his household approached the twins, undid the knots in their hair so that it hung loose like the hair of their two brothers, molded their faces and forms in the manner of the acknowledged sons of *Jóhonaa'éí*, and refashioned their clothing to suit the taste of their father.

Then *Jóhonaa'éí* the Sun ordered all of them to march into his dwelling. The twins were the last to enter.

As they were about to proceed inside, however, they heard the whispering voice of *Nítch'i* the Wind again.

"Be careful!" they heard him whisper.

"Look carefully at the ground where you tread."

Doing what they heard him tell them to do, each of them spied *Wóóseek'idii* the Spiny Caterpillar. And they observed that while he made his way slowly across their path along the ground he emitted two small portions of blue spittle.

"Each of you must take one of these," they heard *Nítch'i* the Wind whisper to them.

"Put it in your mouth," they heard him whisper.

"But do not swallow it. For you will need it to survive what you are about to endure. *Jóhonaa'éí* the Sun is now going to command you to smoke. And the tobacco you will be told to smoke is poisoned."

True to *Nítch'i*'s words, *Jóhonaa'éí* the Sun brought forth a turquoise pipe from a shelf high on the eastern wall of his dwelling. And by the time the twins had come in he was holding it up to his bright red shield hanging on the wall.

Soon the pipe began to glow, and when it was fully lit he gave it to the two strangers, bidding them take turns puffing it and passing it back and forth to one another. This they did until its contents were burned to a few ashes.

"What sweet tobacco that is," remarked the two boys.

When their father saw that the pipe was indeed smoked out, and when he saw that no harm had come to the two twins, he spoke more softly to them than he had spoken to them before.

"Truly you are my sons," he said softly.

"Who but my very own children could endure the poison tobacco which you have just smoked? Who but my very own children could taste its sweetness?

"Now you must tell me why you have come here.

"Now you must tell me what it is that you want of me."

That is what *Jóhonaa'éí* the Sun said to his two boys. And this is the reply they gave him:

"Oh, father," they replied.

"We dwell in the place where *Naayéé'* the Alien Monsters stalk our people. Where we dwell those creatures devour flesh like the grazing herds devour grass.

"*Yé'iitsoh* the Big Giant devours our people, and *Déélgééd* the Horned Monster devours them. *Tsé nináhálééh* the Bird Monster feasts upon us, and so does *Bináá' yee agháni*, who kills with his eyes.

"There are other monsters, too. They are all led by the fearsome *Yé'iitsoh*, and they have eaten nearly all of us. Those who have survived so far have lost hope of ever living a long life or a happy life.

"That is why we have fled to this place, *nihizhé'é* our father. We have fled here to seek your help. Give us weapons so that we may resist the monsters. Give us weapons so that we can destroy *Yé'iitsoh* and his followers.[49]

"Otherwise they will destroy us.

"They will destroy all of us."

As they spoke, *Jóhonaa'éí* listened to the two boys intently.

He nodded, as if to indicate that he had sympathy for them.

Then he looked around.

First he looked carefully at the eastern side of his dwelling. Then he looked as carefully at the southern side. Likewise did he look at the side to the west. And finally he looked carefully at the north side.

Nowhere did he see the older woman who also dwelled in his household.

So he leaned forward.

And, speaking very quietly, he had this to say.

"You must realize," he said quietly, "that *Yé'iitsoh* the Big Giant is reputed to be my son also.[50]

"I do not choose to tell you outright that he is, mind you. But I will admit to you that such things are possible.

"In a manner of speaking it could possibly be said that I am his father."

That is what *Jóhonaa'éí* the Sun confided to the two boys.

And for a little while he said nothing else.

He merely sat where he sat, thoughtfully saying nothing more for a moment. But then at last he spoke again, saying this:

"Even so," he said, speaking again.

"Even so, I shall help you.

"I'll give you weapons so that you may resist the monsters. I'll give you equipment that will enable you to make war on them.

"I shall even help you overcome *Yé'iitsoh* himself.

"In fact, I shall strike the first blow against him myself.

"It is fitting that I do that.

"I shall help you, my sons.

"But you must remember this.

"I am the one who shall strike the first blow when you set out to destroy *Yé'iitsoh* the Big Giant.[51]

That, too, is what *Jóhonaa'éí* the Sun said to the twins. After saying which, he took various items of war from pegs where they hung along the walls of his dwelling. And he gave these items to each of his newly arrived sons.

To each he gave a helmet of hard flint scales.

To each he gave a shirt of flint equally as hard.

And to each he gave these weapons.

He gave them *atsiniltľish k'aa'* the chain lightning arrows. He gave them *atsoolaghał k'aa'*, the mighty sheet lightning arrows. He gave them *shábitľóól k'aa'*, the deadly sunbeam arrows. And he gave them *nááts'íílid k'aa'*, the fatal rainbow arrows.[52]

He also gave each of them *béésh doolghasii*, the stone knife with the hard blade. And he also gave each of them *hatsoiiłhał*, the stone knife with the broad blade.

Those are the weapons that he gave to his sons.

Whereupon they accepted these war-gifts from their father. They put on their armor and fastened the weapons they received from him. And streaks of fire and lightning reflected from their every limb and joint once they were dressed for battle.

Indeed, they looked like warriors.

* * * *

The very next morning, *Jóhonaa'éí* the Sun led the boys eastward to the edge of the world. There the sky and the earth meet, and there nothing lies beyond but empty space.

Along the circumference of that rim sixteen poles leaned toward a distant point in the sky where they all converged. Four of those poles were made of white shell. Four were made of turquoise shell. Four were of haliotis shell. And four were of red stone. It was along these various poles that *Jóhonaa'éí* made his way each day, depending upon the season and upon the amount of warmth and daylight he would ration out on a given day.

A deep stream flowed between the travelers and the row of poles. And as they approached the stream, the twins heard the voice of *Nítch'i* the Wind again.

"You are facing yet another test," they heard him whisper.

"For your father wishes to see how you can possibly get across that stream." And with that he blew a great moist breath and formed a bridge of rainbow over which the brothers safely passed.

"And now," *Nítch'i* whispered then, "you must ask him to take you into the sky along the path of the red poles."

So that when *Jóhonaa'éí* the Sun asked them by way of which poles they wanted to climb, they gave this reply:

"Take us up by way of the poles of red stone," they replied.

"For we seek to make war upon our enemies and to spill their blood."

Upon hearing which *Jóhonaa'éí* put on his garment of dawn-cloud and then lifted one son upon each of his two great arms. And together they rose into the heavens, slowly making their way across the brightening blue sky.

Up and up, they journeyed, up and up. Higher and higher they soared above the surface of the earth. Higher and higher. Hour by hour they climbed. Hour by hour. Until at last they came to *Yágháhookáá'* the Sky Hole, which marks the zenith of *Jóhonaa'éí* the Sun's daily flight. There at last they arrived.

That opening is edged with four smooth, shining cliffs which slope steeply downwards. The cliffs are of white shell, of turquoise shell, of haliotis shell, and of red stone. For they are actually the tops of the poles which connect sky above and earth below. Thus it is that the universe is a strong, well-planned dwelling for all who live there, whether they are gods, Air-Spirit People, or Earth-Surface People.

And there on that highest place in all the heavens the travelers rested. *Jóhonaa'éí* sat on the west side of the hole while the twins sat on the east side. And the boys would have slipped and fallen deep to the earth below, in fact, had not *Nítch'i* the Wind blown hard to hold them aloft.

While they sat there, *Jóhonaa'éí* the Sun pointed down through the sky hole.

"You must show me your home down there," he said.

"Indicate to me where in the world below you and your people belong."

The brothers looked down and scanned the landscape far beneath them. But truly they were so high they could distinguish nothing upon the surface of the earth. From the great height where they now stood, all the land seemed flat. The wooded mountains looked like dark spots on the land. The lakes gleamed like flakes of mica shimmering in the distance. The rivers resembled streaks of lightning which neither moved nor vanished. The forests and the plains seemed like tiny patches of cloth.

"Indeed," said the elder of the two brothers.

"I do not recognize the land.

"Everything looks so strange from up here. How different it looks. How remote from what I have grown accustomed to seeing on the ground."[53]

But even as the twin spoke, *Nítch'i* the Wind was whispering into the ear of his brother, instructing him on how to recognize the sacred mountains, the great rivers, the special peaks and the familiar forests.

"There," exclaimed the second youth when *Jóhonaa'éí* asked him in turn to point out the features of the surface world.

"There below is the male water of the San Juan River. There to the east and flowing southward is the female water of the Rio Grande.

"Yonder to the north is the mountain of *dził naajiní* the Sleeping Ute Mountain. Directly beneath this point where we now sit I can see *Tsoodził* the Blue Bead Mountain. And over there to the west is *Dook'o'oosłííd* the Water Cloud Mountain where the snow never melts. And that white spot well north of the San Juan River is *Dibé nitsaa* on whose summit there are mountain sheep.

"Centered between those peaks you can see *Dził ná'oodiłii* the Traveler's Circle Mountain. Our home is very near to that place.

"And down there you can see the limits of the world that our people made after they fled the rising waters inside the earth, long before the monsters were born who have brought fear and disorder into our lives."

Upon hearing what the younger brother had to say, *Jóhonaa'éí* smiled. And he spoke to them both with more affection than they had so far seen him display.

"It is indeed the truth which you speak, my sons," he said affectionately.

"All that you have told me I now know to be true.

"Truly you are my sons. Truly you wish to save your people. Truly you need weapons of war. And I can promise you truly that you will succeed with them.

"I can also promise you that in your war with the *Naayéé'* you will make the final passage from boyhood to full manhood.

"And I can promise you that if you so choose you can become even like the gods."

That is what *Jóhonaa'éí* the Sun said to them. That is what he promised them.

And with that reply he gave them a last, loving smile. Then he spread before them a streak of lightning which he bid them stand upon. And, saying nothing more to them, he shot them down to the top of *Tsoodził* the Blue Bead Mountain, on which *Yé'iitsoh* the Big Giant made his home.

Down they slid.

Down, down, down, down.

They slid all the way down from the top of the sky to the surface of the earth far below, it is said.

Nine

It is also said that they touched the earth at the summit of *Tsoodził* and came down the mountain by way of its south slope. And from its foot they walked to *Tó sido* or Warm Spring as it is called in the language of *Bilagáana* the White Man.

As they passed under a high bluff where a white circle now stands, they heard voices calling to them.

"Where are you going?" the voices called.

"Come here and rest for a while."

Following the sound of those voices to their source, the twins found *Diné diyiní*, the people who preside over the world of spirits. They found *Dinééh diyiní* the Holy Young Man there, along with his son *Tsiłkéí diyiní* the Holy Youth.

There they also found *Ashkii diyiní* the Holy Boy, along with *At'ééd diyiní* the Spirit Girl. These and others the twins found there. And since darkness was now about to fall upon the surface of the earth, the twins passed the night with them.

Before going to sleep the twins learned from them the origin of *Yé'iitsoh* the Big Giant. It seems that one day soon after *Jóhonaa'éí* the Sun was given the day to rule, a young maiden had gone off alone in the direction of the sunrise. And after defecating she used a smooth pebble from the river to cleanse herself.

She placed the warm stone in her genitals and raised her skirt. Curious about such things as young girls often are, she wanted to examine herself. And at just that moment *Jóhonaa'éí* climbed above the horizon and sent a ray into her. Thus it happened that she became pregnant.[54] And when the time came for her to give birth she stole away to do so alone, so ashamed was she, leaving her infant in the brush to die. There it was discovered by some winds from the north, who raised it until it became a full-grown monster.

The Holy People also told the brothers how the other *Naayéé'* were conceived during the separation of the first couple and of the men and women who followed them. They told them how those monsters were born after the great flood that had driven their people from the fourth world to the present world. And they told them how those alien creatures began to prey on the people in this world, destroying them and devouring them.

"We know full well about *Yé'iitsoh* and the other monsters," said *Dinééh diyiní* the Holy Young Man.

"We know that three times each day he shows himself among the mountains as he makes his way between the peaks. When he shows himself for the fourth time, he descends *Tsoodził* the Blue Bead Mountain to *Tó sido* the Warm Spring, where he comes to quench his thirst by drinking from the lake there.

"When he stoops to drink, one hand rests on the slope of his own mountain, while the other leans high on the hills overlooking the other side of the valley. That is how large he is. So large is he that when he stoops to drink his feet stretch as far away as a man can walk between sunrise and noon.

"Yes, we have seen *Yé'iitsoh* the Big Giant, and yes, we know his ways."

That is what *Dinééh diyiní* the Holy Young Man told the two brothers.

•   •   •   •

The brothers awoke next morning at daybreak and made their way to *Tó sido* the Warm Spring, where there was a lake much larger than the one we find at that place today.

Where the valley was most narrow, a high rocky cliff towered above the water. And from that point the lake extended back upstream so that its blue waters were as wide as they were deep.

When the twins arrived at the water's edge, one of them said this to the other:

"Let us try one of our father's weapons," he said.

"Let's see what it can do."

So they shot a lightning arrow at a slab of high rock overhanging the base of *Tsoodził* the Giant Mountain. There it made a great cleft which remains to this very day for anyone wishing to see it.

"Indeed," said the second brother.

"We cannot lose our battle with *Yé'iitsoh* the Big Giant.

"With such weapons as that, we cannot fail."

And they waited for their enemy to appear.

•   •   •   •

They did not wait long before they heard the sound of footsteps.

They heard them faintly at first. So far off were they that the two brothers could not easily identify the source of the sound they heard.

They listened nonetheless and observed that it grew louder as it came nearer. Continuing to listen, they soon recognized that it was the feet of the stalking *Yé'iitsoh* they heard, so loud did it become. It became as loud as the thunder that shakes the canyon walls and rattles among the peaks.

And then, for an instant, they saw the head of *Yé'iitsoh*. For only a second did they see it, when the monster peered over the top of a peak to the east. Then it disappeared.

Soon, however, they saw *Yé'iitsoh* again. But this time they saw his head and his shoulders. For little more than a minute did they see him, when he showed himself from behind a ridge to the south. Then he disappeared again.

But he displayed himself again soon thereafter, this time from his waist up. For several minutes they could see him, as he stood above a hill to the west. But then he disappeared.

A while later, though, he appeared again, visible all the way from his head to his knees. As the twins watched him, he came down from *Tsoodził* to the north, making his way among the foothills, remaining in full sight this time as he came clear down to the water's edge.

With him he bore a basket in which he carried the remains of whatever prey he seized. And he placed it on the ground as he slowly got down on his all fours to drink.

He lowered his head, then, and placed his lips in the water to take a gulp. Four times he did this, and with each drink he took the water diminished. So that by the time he had taken his last swill the lake was nearly drained.

"Hraagh!" he said, drawing his mighty forearm slowly across his mouth.

"I have finished that."

And then he laughed.

His laughter echoed up and down the valley and among the hills, until it sounded to the twins as though it came from all four directions.

At the sight of this huge creature stooping to drink, and at the sound of his laughter, the brothers lost their nerve for a minute. While he stooped to drink his first three gulps they did nothing. But as he took his last drink they made their way slowly to the water's edge to have a closer look at *Yé'iitsoh*.

When they did, he saw their reflection in the water.

Whereupon, having taken his fill at last, and having laughed at the amount he had swallowed, he raised his head, stood upright, turned to have a look at them, and then roared.

"Hraagh!" roared he.

"What a pretty pair we have here.

"Where have I been hunting, that I have not seen their likes before?

"*Yiiniikeetsóóko! Yiiniikeetsóóko!*[55]

"How delicious you look! How very delicious!"

But by now the twins had regained their courage. They were no longer afraid at the sight of *Yé'iitsoh* the Big Giant, for they recalled what their lightning arrow had done to the rock on the mountainside.

"Just throw his words back at him," said the younger brother to the elder.

So they looked straight at him. And together they cried in unison:

"*Yiiniikeetsóóko! Yiiniikeetsóóko!*" they cried.

"What a paltry foe you are! How paltry!"

"So say you?" questioned *Yé'iitsoh*.

"So say you, when you are so small and I am so large?"

"So say you?" repeated the elder of the two brothers.[56]

"So say you, when you are so weak and we have so much power?"

"What?" demanded *Yé'iitsoh* angrily.

"You dare to speak that way to someone who is about to feast on your flesh?"

"What?" mocked the brother.

"You dare to speak that way to those who are about to destroy you?"

"Hraagh!" roared *Yé'iitsoh* then.

"You cannot treat me that way, as small as you are! As delicious as you are about to taste!"

"Hraagh!" mimicked the brother.

"You cannot treat us so! As disorderly as you are! As lifeless as you are about to become!"

As they taunted the monster thus, they suddenly heard the voice of *Nítch'i* the Wind whispering in their ears:

"*Akóóh! Akóóh!*" he whispered.

"Beware! Beware!"

And without another word from him they found themselves standing on the arc of a rainbow. At that very instant *Yé'iitsoh* the Giant hurled a lightning bolt at them. And just then the rainbow on which the brothers stood descended suddenly until it was flat against the ground. So that the lightning bolt passed thundering over their heads.

Likewise he hurled a second lightning bolt. But as he did so, the arc of the rainbow tightened suddenly so that the brothers were standing much higher than they had been at first. So that this lightning bolt passed thundering beneath their feet.

Yé'iitsoh then threw another bolt of lightning. But this time the brothers themselves maneuvered it to one side so that it passed to the left of them. And when he threw yet another one, they maneuvered the rainbow to the other side so that this time it passed to their right.

He then took aim to strike again. But at precisely that moment a more powerful lightning bolt came out of the sky from the direction of where the sun then stood![57] It struck the side of *Yé'iitsoh* the Big Giant's head. With such force did it strike that the heavens shook thunderously and all the earth repeated its echo.

With such force did it strike that *Yé'iitosh* lost his balance momentarily and reeled from side to side. But he did not quite fall. Somehow he managed to remain on his feet.

At that instant, though, the elder of the two brothers hurled a chain-lightning arrow at *Yé'iitsoh* the Giant. And he tottered toward the east at the blow, wavering dizzily. But somehow he managed to straighten himself again and remain standing.

Then the other brother shot an arrow of chain-lightning at him. And again the giant tottered, his knees buckling slightly. But somehow he managed again to straighten himself and remain on his feet.

Now it was the first brother's turn. He fired another shot of lightning. *Yéiitsoh* swayed dizzily and fell to his knees for a moment. But soon he managed to get back up onto his feet.

But only until the second brother fired another shot of lightning, which struck the giant on the chest. He dropped to his knees and wavered there momentarily as he tried to lift himself up again. But he could not. Instead he fell forward, breaking his fall with his hands, resting there like that for an instant. Then he shook his head slowly from side to side as if to keep himself from tumbling forward. But his head swayed like the top of a tall pine tree in the driving wind, and he finally fell face down on the ground, stretching his limbs out flat and straight.

And he moved no more.[58]

As each of the lightning arrows struck *Yé'iitsoh* it sent chips and splinters of his flint armor flying everywhere. And now, as the giant lay dead before their eyes, the elder of the two brothers spied those bits of flint. And of them he had this to say:

"Let us gather those flint flakes," he said.

"Our people can use them for knives. They can use them for arrowheads. They can cut with them and hunt with them."[59]

"Yes they can." replied the other.

"That way we can turn *Yé'iitsoh*'s evil into something good."

•   •   •   •

After they had gathered the chips of flint, the twins approached the body of the fallen giant and cut away his scalp. And as they did so they decided to give each other names.

"Let's see now," pondered the first as he watched his brother carve the pelt away from the head of the fallen *Yé'iitsoh.*

"What shall I call you?"

And he thought as he watched and watched as he thought.

"Aha!" he cried.

"I have a good name for you.

"*Na'idígishí* you shall be called. Henceforth you shall be known as He Who Cuts the Life Out of the Enemy.

"That is what you shall be called."

•   •   •   •

"Now, then," pondered the second brother as he finished taking *Yé'iitsoh*'s scalp.

"What shall you be called?"

And he thought as he recollected how together they had destroyed the giant. He thought as he recollected and he recollected as he thought.

"Aha!" he cried.

"I have a name well suited for you."

"*Naayéé' neizghání* you shall be called. Henceforth you shall be known as Monster Slayer.

"That is the name by which you shall always be known."[60]

•   •   •   •

Next the brothers cut off the head of *Yé'iitsoh* the Big Giant and threw it far into the hills beyond the summit of *Tsoodził* the Giant Mountain. It may be seen to this very day on the eastern slope by anyone who cares to look at it.

But when it landed, blood from the giant's body began to flow down the valley in a torrent. So great was its force that it broke down the rocky wall blocking the waters of the lake.

"Quickly!" warned the voice of *Niłch'i* the Wind.

"Stop that torrent of blood!

"For if it flows toward the dwelling of *Bináá' yee agháni* the Monster Who Kills With His Eyes, *Yé'iitsoh* the Big Giant will come back to life."

Whereupon *Naayéé' neizgháni* the Slayer of Monsters seized *béésh doolghasii* his stone knife with the hard blade that *Jóhonaa'éi* his Father the Sun had given him. With it he drew a line across the valley downstream of the onrushing river of blood. And there it ceased to flow, backing up in the form of a dark red wall.

Higher and higher it piled as though it had been blocked by a towering dam. But when it had piled to a certain height it began to flow in another direction, rushing and roaring toward a lower part of the valley.

Whereupon *Nítch'i* the Wind again warned the brothers:

"Quickly, quickly!" warned he.

"Stop that torrent of blood.

"For if it flows much further it will arrive at the dwelling of *Shash na'ałkaahii* the Stalking Bear Monster. And if it reaches him, *Yé'iitosh* the Big Giant will most surely come back to life."

Hearing which, *Naayéé' neizgháni* the Monster Slayer again drew the *béésh doolghasii* which his father *Jóhonaa'éi* the Sun had given him. Again he drew a line on the ground with its broad blade. And again the blood piled up as if against a high-walled dam and ceased flowing.

There it again stopped as it had done before, once and for all, darkening as it dried and hardening as it darkened. That blood fills the entire valley at the foot of *Tsoodził* to this very day. Whoever cares to go there can see at that spot the high cliffs of hard, black rock first formed by the congealing blood of *Yé'iitsoh* the Big Giant.

●   ●   ●   ●

Next the two brothers gathered the broken arrows of *Yé'iitsoh* and put them in his basket, along with his scalp and along with the chips and splinters of flint from his armor. And they set out for their home near *Dził ná'oodiłíí* the Banded Rock Mountain.

But first they climbed to the summit of *Tsoodził* the Blue Bead Mountain on which they landed after descending from the sky. There they each sang a song in praise of their father, *Jóhonaa'éi* the Sun as he neared the end of his daily journey across the heavens.

And now that darkness was about to fall, they rested for the night, enjoying a peaceful sleep.

• • • •

When day broke they awoke and started for home.

Along the trail they met *Haashch'ééłti'í* the Talking God. And with him they saw *Tó neinilí* the Rain God. And to them the gods had this to say:

"Well done, *nihináli*," they said.

"Well done, our grandsons.

"You are brave and you are strong: you are worthy of the care we have given you; you are worthy of all that we taught you.

"You have served your people well."

And the two gods each sang a song to celebrate the victory of the twins over *Yé'iitsoh* the Big Giant. Those two selfsame songs have been included among those which the Navajo people sing to this very day whenever the victory chant is performed.[61]

• • • •

When the brothers reached sight of the lodge where their mothers dwelled, they took off their suits of armor which they hid in the bushes. They also hid the basket of *Yé'iitsoh* with everything in it.

Their mothers rejoiced to see their sons. They had given them up for lost, fearing that they had been devoured by the *Naayéé'*.

"Where have you been since you left here two days ago?" asked the women.

"Where did you go and what have you done?

"We have given you up for lost.

"Worse still, we were afraid that one of the alien monsters had devoured you."

To which *Naayéé' neizghání* the Monster Slayer had this answer to give:

"We have followed *Atiin diyinii* the Holy Trail as *Na'ashjé'ii asdzą́ą́* the Spider Woman directed us to do.

"We have been to the house of *Jóhonaa'éí nihitaa'* our Father the Sun.

"We have been to *Tsoodził* the Blue Bead Mountain where *Yé'iitsoh* the Big Giant once lived.

"And truly we have destroyed him so that he shall threaten none of us any more."

That is what he said to *Yoołgai asdzą́ą́* the White Shell Woman and to *Asdzą́ą́ nádleehé* the Changing Woman. And this is what the two sisters replied.

"Oh, children! children!" they replied.

"Do not speak that way.

"Do not mention that name lightly.

"Do not mention it either in jest or in defiance.

"For as surely as you do, just as surely will he descend upon us all and devour us."

To which *Naayéé' neizghání* the Monster Slayer made this response:

"If you do not believe us," he responded, "come with us and see what we have brought you."

And the two brothers led the two women to the place where they had hidden the basket containing their relics of war.

They showed their mothers the trophies of their battle with *Yé'iitsoh* the Big Giant. And when the women saw these objects they believed their sons.

Whereupon they rejoiced.

They danced and they sang to celebrate this great victory, it is said.

Ten

It is also said that *Naayéé' neizghání* was not willing to remain with his family. For he wished to fight one of the other monsters. No sooner had he ceased rejoicing over the death of *Yé'iitsoh* than he began to ask the whereabouts of some other *Naayéé'*.

"Mother," he asked *Asdzą́ą́ nádleehé* the Changing Woman.

"Where does *Déélgééd* the Horned Monster dwell?

"I want to continue fighting the monsters.

"And he is the one I want to fight first."[62]

But *Asdzą́ą́ nádleehé* the Changing Woman objected, saying this to her son:

"Oh, my son," she said to him.

"Do not look for *Déélgééd* the Horned Monster.

"You have done enough.

"Be satisfied with what you have already done.

"The land of the *Naayéé'* is a dangerous place, and the alien monsters are hard to kill.

"Well might they be," replied *Naayéé' neizghání* the Monster Slayer.

"And it was also hard for you to labor in childbirth. But you did so all the same."

"Very well, then, my son," said she.

"*Déélgééd* the Horned Monster lives at *Bik'i halzhin*, where the mountains descend upon a broad plain.

"Go there if you must. But keep your wits about you, and remember what your purpose is."

Then the brothers held a council to determine what should be done. They made two sacrificial prayersticks out of *azee' łahdilt'éhé* the alone-by-itself-medicine plant.[63] They made a blue stem and a black stem, each three finger-widths long. To these they attached a sunbeam. And then they laid them in a turquoise dish.

Whereupon *Naayéé' neizghání* the Monster Slayer said this to *Na'ídígishí* Who Cuts the Life Out of the Enemy:

"My brother," said he.

"I shall go alone to fight *Déélgééd*.[64]

"Meanwhile, you stay here and watch the holy cigarettes.

"If a sunbeam should light either one, you will know that I am in danger.

"If that should happen, you must hasten to find me and to help me. Otherwise, know that I am safe and do nothing but wait here and guard the others."[65]

•   •   •   •

By that time the sun had set. Darkness soon fell and they all slept. *Naayéé' neizghání* awoke early the next morning and set out alone to find *Déélgééd* the Horned Monster.

In time he came to the edge of a great plain. And from one of the hills that overlooked it he spied the monster lying at rest some distance away. He paused, thinking about how he might approach *Déélgééd*. Meanwhile, he poised one of his lighting arrows in his hand, ready to throw it if he had to.

While he thus stood there, deep in thought, *Na'azísí* the Gopher came up to him.

"*Yá'át'ééh, shínaaí*," said he.

"I greet you, older brother," he said.

"What brings you to this place?"

"*Yá'át'ééh, sitsilí*, replied *Naayéé' neizghání*.

"I return your greeting, younger brother.

"I am just wandering around this place."

"It is good to see your likes out here," said *Na'azísí* the Gopher.

"But truly I wonder why you are here."

"It is good that you think so," answered *Nayéé' neizghání* the Monster Slayer. "I am just looking around hereabouts."

"We seldom see you folks any more," answered the Gopher. "Which is why I am curious to know what it is that you seek in this place."

"Sad to say," responded Monster Slayer, "few of us remain on the earth. There is someone hearabouts I seek."

"Are you not afraid?" asked *Na'azísí*. "Do you not fear *Déélgééd* the Horned Monster who feeds on your kind?

"There he lies, you know. Down there on that prairie you see below."

"As a matter of fact it is *Déélgééd* I seek," answered *Naayéé' neizghání* the Monster Slayer.

"Now that you mention it, I intend to kill him. But as yet I don't know how to attack."

"In that case I think I can help you," said *Na'azísí* the Gopher.[66]

"I often walk right up to him and he pays me no mind. After all, I am a small, harmless creature.

"But if I do help you, and if you kill him because of that, I would like a piece of his hide to put over my back.

"After all, I am but a small creature who chills all too easily. But with skin like his I could endure the cold weather."

"Truly, my little friend," promised *Naayéé' neizghání*, "you shall have as much of *Déélgééd*'s hide as you like."

"Then watch me carefully." said Gopher. "And I will show you how you can get close to the monster with horns."

Having said which, he disappeared into a hole in the ground.

While *Na'azísí* the Gopher was lost from his sight, *Naayéé' neizghání* the Monster Slayer stared at *Déélgééd* the Horned Monster. And after watching for a while he observed the great creature rise, walk from where he had been resting in each of the four directions, gaze fully from side to side at the end of each walk, and finally lie down again at the very spot where he had first been sleeping.

Déélgééd was, *Naayéé' neizghání* now fully realized, an enormous four-footed beast with horns like those of a deer.

By then, *Na'azísí* the Gopher had returned. And he had this to say:

"Get ready," he said.

"I have dug a tunnel up to *Déélgééd.* All the way up to him I have dug.

"At the end of that tunnel I have bored four passageways for you to hide in. One passage branches to the east. One branches to the south. One stretches to the west. And one extends to the north.

"From the center I have also made a vertical hole up to the surface.[67] And where that hole opens skyward you can strike a blow at *Déélgééd*'s heart. For he rests directly over that opening.

"I have even gnawed the hair away from the flesh where your arrow must pierce him, big brother. 'Why do you chew my hair that way?' he asks me as I gnaw. 'I need something soft and warm,' I answer him, 'so that I can make a bed for my children.'

"It was at that instant that he got up and walked around, as you must have seen him do.

"Maybe he was suspicious for a moment. But when he could see nothing unusual, he came back and lay down again.

"And there he now lies: exactly as you saw him before; exactly as he was when I got him ready for you to attack him; directly over the hole that leads to his heart; directly where he is vulnerable.

"Now, then, big brother. If you do not kill him it will be through no fault of mine."

That is what *Na'azísí* the Gopher said to *Naayéé' neizghání* the Monster Slayer.

Immediately *Naayéé' neizghání* entered the tunnel and crawled to the end. And when he reached the center of the passageway that *Na'azísí* had burrowed for him, he looked up.

Sure enough! he saw the shaft that *Na'azísí* spoke of. Sure enough! he saw the exposed flesh of *Déélgééd.* He saw the creature's large chest palpitate in and out.

And at that moment he let fly one of the chain-lightning arrows given to him by *Jóhónaa'éí hataa'* his Father the Sun. And without waiting to see if the arrow hit its mark he fled into the eastern tunnel.

With a powerful roar, the monster rose, stuck one of his horns into the ground, and tore open the tunnel. But before *Déélgééd* could spot him *Naayéé' neizghání* fled into the south tunnel.

With a grunt, *Déélgééd* ripped at it with one of his sharp horns. But before he could see his assailant, *Naayéé' neizghání* escaped into the tunnel to the west.

With a snort, *Déélgééd* dug into the earth with his horn at that spot. But by that time the slayer of monsters fled into the north tunnel.

Then, with a whimper, *Déélgééd* put his horn into the ground there. But by now he was too weak to dig very far into the earth. And before he had burrowed halfway down he fell and lay motionless.

Afraid that his enemy was not yet dead, *Naayéé' neizghání* the Monster Slayer crept back through the tunnel that *Na'azísí* the Gopher had dug for him to the spot where the two had first met. And there he waited, wondering how he might learn whether the creature still lived.

While he stood there, he noticed a little old man approach him, dressed in tight leggings and a thin shirt. On his head he wore a cap with a feather. This was *Hazéétosh* the Ground Squirrel. And here is what he said to *Naayéé' neizghání* the Monster Slayer.

"*Yá'át'ééh shínaaí*," he said to him.

"I greet you, big brother.

"What brings you to this place?"

Here, then, is what *Naayéé' neizghání* answered:

"*Yá'át'ééh sitsilí*," he answered.

"I return your greeting, little brother.

"I am just looking at something."

"It is good to see the likes of you," replied *Hazéétsoh* the Squirrel.

"But truly I wonder what it is that you are looking at."

"It reassures me to hear your welcoming words," answered *Naayéé' neizghání.* "I need to know something about that which I see."

"We seldom get to greet people like you in these bad times," replied the Squirrel. "Which is why I wonder at seeing you here in plain view."

"Yes, it saddens me that so few of us remain on the surface of this world," responded *Naayéé' neizghání.* And in that regard there is something which I must know."

"Are you not afraid?" asked *Hazéétsoh.* "Don't you fear *Déélgééd* the Horned Monster, who has stalked and destroyed so many of your kind?

"There he dwells, you know: on the plain over yonder."

"As a matter of fact," replied *Naayéé' neizghání*, "I am trying to decide whether I need fear him or not.

"Although I cannot be sure, I may have killed him."

"Then I shall find out for you," said *Hazéétsoh*. "He pays no attention to me, small as I am. So I can walk right up to him.

"I will go over there now, and if he no longer breathes I will climb up on his horns and dance and sing. Just wait here and watch. If you see me on him, you will know what you want to know.

"But indeed, if he is dead and I tell you so, I would like a bit of his blood. For I am an ugly old man. If I decorate my face with blood like *Déélgééd*'s, perhaps I will not look so bad."

"Truly, little brother," replied *Naayéé' neizghání*, "you may have as much of *Déélgééd*'s blood as you like."

"Then watch for me carefully," said *Hazéétsoh*. And he scampered over to where *Déélgééd* lay motionless.

Naayéé' neizghání the Monster Slayer did not have to wait long before he saw the squirrel climb one of the monster's horns and dance upon it. So he approached his slain enemy; and upon doing so he found that *Hazéétsoh* the Squirrel had already streaked his face with the monster's blood. And this is what he said:

"I shall wear these marks for the rest of my days," he said.

"Then, when your people multiply as I know they now shall, they may remember *Déélgééd*'s thirst for blood.

"Let them also remember how a poor old squirrel once helped you achieve your purpose.

"Besides, I look so much younger this way."

So it is that the face of every ground squirrel bears red streaks to this very day. And so it is that good will has always prevailed between Earth Surface People and the squirrels ever since.

Naayéé' neizghání likewise found that *Na'azísí* the Gopher had already started removing *Déélgééd*'s skin. There he was, slowly gnawing at the insides of the giant's forelegs. And when he finished removing the skin he put it upon his own back.

"I shall wear this pelt in the days to come," said he.

"Then, when your people increase as I am now sure they shall, they may remember what sort of hide the terrible horned monster bore.

"They will also remember that Gopher was your ally in your battle against him.

"Besides, I am much warmer dressed this way."

So it is that the back of gophers is thickly covered to this very day. And so it is that there has always been harmony between Earth Surface People and gophers ever since.

After *Na'azísí* had finished dressing himself in his new coat he cut a piece of tissue away from *Déélgééd*'s bowel, which he filled with blood. Then he tied the ends so that the blood would not escape. He also cut a piece out of one of the monster's lungs.

"This act proves that we no longer have to be afraid of *Déélgééd* the Horned Monster," he said. "And we can do what we wish with him now."

And thereupon he gave the two particles to *Naayéé' neizghání* the slayer of alien monsters, saying this to him:

"Carry these trophies back to your people," he said to him.

"Then you can show them that you have indeed destroyed *Déélgééd* the Horned Monster."

That is what *Na'azísí* the Gopher said to *Naayéé' neizghání* the Monster Slayer.

•   •   •   •

When she saw her son return, *Asdzą́ą́ nádleehé* rejoiced to see him. But after she greeted him she had this to ask:

"Where have you been since you left here?" she asked.

"And what have you been doing?

"Indeed, I had given you up for lost. Worse still, we all feared that *Déélgééd* the Horned Monster had feasted upon you."

To which *Naayéé' neizghání* the Monster Slayer gave this reply:

"I have been to *Bik'i halzhin* where that terrible creature once dwelled," he replied.

"I saw the place where he once rested.

"With my own eyes I saw what an enormous four-footed horned beast he was. I saw that he had the jaws of a monster and a monster's appetite.

"But truly did I slay him, so that he shall threaten us no more."

"Oh, my son! my son!" she said.

"Do not speak that way.

"Do not mention that name lightly, either in jest or in defiance.

"For if you do, surely he will descend upon us and devour us all."

"If you do not believe me," replied *Naayéé' neizghání*, "see what I have brought back with me.

"Here is a portion of *Déélgééd's* blood, wrapped in the flesh of
his bowel. And here is a piece of tissue from his lung.

"Now do you believe what I tell you?"

But even before *Asdzą́ą́ nádleehé* the Changing Woman could
answer him he asked her another question. This is what he asked her:

"Tell me, mother," he asked. "Where do *Tsé nináhálééh* the Bird
Monster and his brood dwell?

"For I wish to seek them and destroy them."

"Oh, my son!" she then said.

"Do not ask where the *Tsé nináhálééhké* dwell.

"You have accomplished enough.

"Be satisfied with what you have accomplished already.

"The land of the *Naayéé'* is a dangerous place, and the monsters
are hard to kill."

"So they may be," replied *Naayéé' neizghání* the Monster Slayer.

"And wasn't it also hard with you when you gave birth to me?
But didn't you do so all the same?"

Whereupon *Asdzą́ą́ nádleehé* the Changing Woman replied
this way:

"Very well, then, my son," replied she.

"The Bird Monsters *Tsé nináhálééhké* live at *Tsé bit'a'í* the
Rock with Wings. All told, four of them dwell there. A male dwells
there with his mate. And two young offspring likewise dwell there.

"Go there if you insist. But approach them with caution. For
they are fierce and strong.

"And remember your one true purpose, my son."

•   •   •   •

Naayéé' neizghání the Monster Slayer arose early next morning
and stole away alone to find the Rock Bird Monsters. With him he
took the packet which contained the blood of *Déélgééd* the Horned
Monster.

He made his way to *Tsézhin dits'in* in the *Ch'óshgai* Mountains,
where he climbed and climbed until he arrived at a place where
two giant snakes lay sunning themselves. Fearing nothing, he
walked gingerly along the back of one snake, then he leaped upon
the back of the other, making his way still further.

Neither snake budged as he stepped from the back of one to the
back of the other, so nimble was he. And thus he proceeded out of
the mountains and across to the plain that lay beyond. As for those

snakes, they turned to stone and remain such to this very day, providing a docile bridge over which travelers can descend eastward from the peaks of *Ch'óshgai,* or the White Spruce Mountains as they would be called today by *Bilagáana* the White Man.

On he traveled across the plain, leaving the mountains far behind him. Until he saw *Tsé bit'a'í* the Rock with Wings in the distance. It was a great black rock towering high above the desert plain surrounding it. And it resembeled a bird with outspread wings ready to take flight.

While he walked along in the direction of the rock, *Naayéé' neizghání* heard a tremendous sound overhead. What he heard sounded like the roar of the rushing whirlwind that sends dust flying and makes dunes of sand vanish in one place and reappear somewhere else.

Looking up, he saw a creature with something of an eagle's shape flying toward him from the east. So great was its size that it covered the sun and virtually darkened the whole sky. *Naayéé' neizghání* recognized it as the male *Tsé nináhálééh* that his mother warned him not to seek. And as it swooped over him he barely managed to throw himself flat on the ground. It passed overhead, its talons poised like hooks of flint ready to carry him off, barely missing him.

As the twin got up to gaze at *Tsé nináhálééh,* the Bird Monster banked sharply and made another pass at him this time from the south. Again he heard the onrushing wind stirred up by its wings. Again the sky darkened overhead. Again *Naayéé' neizghání* threw himself upon the ground as the monster swooped in on him, its talons again closing so as to sieze him and carry him away. And again did the winged creature barely miss him and pass swiftly overhead.

Once more the warrior got up to observe *Tsé nináhálééh* in flight. He saw the monster bank sharply and come in at him from the west this time. And once more he heard the onrushing wind of the monster's beating wings as once more the sky darkened. Once more did *Naayéé' neizghání* cast himself prone on the ground as the creature swooped in, its talons this time scraping against his armor as it flew by. Only by a talon's length did the winged monster fail to carry him away as it passed swiftly overhead.

Yet another time did the twin get up to watch the flight of his enemy. He saw the monster bank sharply and fly in at him directly from the north this time, beating at the sky with its wings until the wind howled as it does during a winter storm and darkened everything the way the heavens are darkened on a moonless winter night. And yet once more did *Naayéé' neizghání* throw himself flat against the earth as *Tsé nináhalééh* swooped in on him, arching its talons like an eagle arches his when it seizes a field mouse.

And that was how the creature finally clasped the slayer of monsters, lifted him off the ground, bore him high into the sky, and carried him all the way to the topmost ledges of *Tsé bit'a'í* and beyond.

• • • •

On one side of that towering mesa there sits a broad, level ledge one-fourth of the way down. There the male and female *Tsé nináhálééhké* rear their young, and there the monster bird now let *Naayéé' neizghání* fall.

That is how he customarily killed his victims, so that his offspring could devour them and thrive. And while his prey plummeted downward, *Tsé nináhálééh* the male Monster Bird would alight on the topmost pinnacle of *Tsé bit'a'í* to perch and watch his children eat.

Surely would *Naayéé' neizghání* the Monster Slayer have perished in that fall had he not remembered to bring along with him the sacred *naayéé' ats'os* of life-feathers that *Na'ashjé'ii asdzą́ą́* the Spider Woman had first given him when he and his brother set out. Now as he fell he clasped it tightly and held it over his head. Thus he fell gently like a bird descending and landed the way a bird lands as it glides in upon the earth.

Once his feet were firmly set on the rock beneath him he cut open the packet of *Déélgééd's* bowel, which he had also brought. And he let the blood of the Horned Monster flow over the rock in such a way that from its perch high overhead the *Tsé nináhálééh* would think him dead.

Meanwhile, the two young fledgling bird monsters approached the body of their father's prey to feast on it. But as they were about to peck at him, *Naayéé' neizghání* cried out:

"Shuuh! Shuuh!" he cried out.

"Here! Here! What are you doing?"

Whereupon the young birds flapped their tiny wings and reared back as they called to their father where he stood watching them.

"This thing is not dead," they called to him.

"It speaks to us.

"*Shuuh! Shuuh!* it tells us."

"Pay no heed to what it says," replied their father.

"You hear no more than the air escaping from its body.

"Think nothing of it and eat your fill."

Whereupon he flew off in search of other prey.

When the adult bird was gone, *Naayéé' neizgháni* the Monster Slayer stood up and spoke boldly to the two young, saying this:

"Tell me," he said.

"Tell me at once!

"When will your father come back?

"And where will he perch when he returns?"

"He will come back with the male rain," replied they.[68]

"He will come back when its thunder roars and when its lightning flashes.

"And he will perch on that rock up there, yonder to the right of where we now stand."

Then *Naayéé' neizgháni* the Monster Slayer demanded this of the young *Tsé nináhálééhké:*

"Tell me also," demanded he.

"And tell me quickly!

"When will your mother come back?

"And where will she place herself when she returns?"

"She will return with the female rain," they replied.

"She will come back when its soft moisture falls and when its warm breezes blow.

"And she will perch on that crag up there to the left of where we now stand."

Naayéé' neizgháni did not have to wait long before the male rain began to fall.

Hard drops fell. Thunder rolled. Lightning flashed. The wind blew hard and cold out of the north. And sure enough! The male *Tsé nináhálééh* dropped out of the sky like a lowering black cloud.

He perched on the rock which his young had pointed out, tucking his wings close into his body. And at precisely that instant the warrior hurled one of the mighty sheet-lightning arrows given to him by *Jóhonaa'éí hataa'* his Father the Sun.

At once the monster crumpled forward and fell all the way down to the foot of *Tsé bit'a'í.* Down he fell: down, down, down, down to the earth far below.

After a while rain fell again.

But this time there was neither thunder nor lightning, neither wind nor cold. This time it fell gently. It fell warmly. It came from the south in a soft, easy spray.

And even as the female rain continued to fall there landed upon the ledge the body of a Pueblo woman, coverd with fine clothes and ornamented with ear pendants and with necklaces of beautiful shells and turquoise.

Naayéé' neizghání looked up and saw the female *Tsé nináhálééh* descending towards her perch to the left of where he now stood. She preyed upon women as her mate preyed upon men.

And in a minute she glided down like fine, silent mist and landed on her favorite crag. No sooner had she done so than the warrior hurled another mighty sheet-lightning arrow given to him by his father.

At once the she-bird monster slouched forward and fell all the way down to the foot of *Tsé bit'a'í*. Down she fell: down, down, down, down to the hard ground far below.

"*Aháláane'! Aháláane'!*" cried the young ones when they saw their mother fall.

"Woe to us! Woe to us!"

"Stop your wailing!" ordered *Naayéé' neizghání.*[69]

"I won't kill you.

"If you were fully grown like your parents are I would. For then you would carry off my people like they have been doing.

"But you are young.

"There is time for you to become something else: something useful to my people and to earth-surface people in the days to come, when men and women shall again increase in the land."

Upon saying which, he seized the elder of the two bird-monster children and made this declaration:

"You shall provide feathers for men to use in their ceremonies," he declared.

"You shall provide bones for whistles.

"You shall soar overhead peacefully and thereby make men aware of the vast expanse of sky."

And as he said these things, *Naayéé' neizghání* the Monster Slayer swung the fledgling back and forth four times. As he did so it became a beautiful bird with strong wings.

"*Suk! suk!*" it cried, just as such birds do to this very day.

"*Suk! suk!*" it repeated, as *Naayéé' neizghání* cast it skyward and it became transformed into an eagle. It spread wide its pinions and soared high into the sky and out of sight. Which is how eagles came to exist, and which is why they exist to this very day.

To the second of the two fledgling bird-monsters *Naayéé' neizghání* the Monster Slayer made this declaration:

"As for you," he declared, "you shall provide prophecy for Earth-Surface People who wish to determine their fate.

"Sometimes you shall speak the truth. And sometimes you shall lie.

"It will be for men to decide what is true and what is false from what you say.

"That way they shall learn from you how to tell the difference between wisdom and folly."

And as he said these things, he swung the fledgling back and forth four times. As he did so its head grew large. Its body became round. Its eyes grew big. And it cried.

"*Uwuu! uwuu!*" it cried, just as such birds do to this very day.

"*Uwuu! uwuu!*" it repeated, as *Naayéé' neizghání* the Monster Slayer cast it high into the air, where it assumed the shape of an owl.[70] It spread its wings and circled downward until it found a roost halfway up the side of the cliff, where from then on it could gaze on everything that was to happen on the surface of the world below. Which is how owls came to exist, and which is why they exist to this very day.

• • • •

Now that his work at *Tsé bit'a'í* was done, *Naayéé' neizghání* the Monster Slayer wanted to go back home.

But he realized that he was still high upon that ledge with no way to descend. Nothing but a winged creature could get up there or leave. Meanwhile, the sun was already halfway between the crown of the sky and the western horizon.

As he wondered how he might get down, he observed *Jaa'abaní asdzą́ą́* the Bat Woman walking along the base of the cliff below.[71]

"*Shimásání!*" he cried down to her.

"Little grandmother!

"Come up here and help me down!"

"*T'áadoo. . . .*" she replied, looking up at him and frowning.

"Go away!" she replied with a frown.

And she clambered behind a rock where he could not see her.

But in a moment or two she peered out. And when she again came into view, *Naayéé' neizghání* cried out to her a second time.

"Please grandmother!" he cried out.

"It's getting late and I must get down."

"*T'áadoo shaa....*" she replied.

"Go away! Get out of my sight!"

And she again hid behind the rock where she could not be seen.

But in a little while she peered out as she had done before. And when she came into view again, *Naayéé' neizghání* cried out to her once more.

"Please, grandmother, please!" he cried out.

"Others have helped me. Why can't you?"

"*T'áadoo shaa nánít'íní!*" she answered angrily.

"Go away and don't bother me! I shall have nothing to do with you."

Again she clambered behind the rock where again he could not see her.

Until at length she ventured forward. And when she could be seen *Naayéé' neizghání* cried out to her again.

"Grandmother, please! please!" he cried again.

"Please help me down from this rock before darkness falls altogether.

"*Na'azísí* the Gopher helped me, and I have rewarded him with the hide of *Déélgééd* the Horned Monster. *Hazéétsoh* the Squirrel helped me, and I gave him *Déélgééd*'s blood to streak his face with. You should see how handsome he now looks.

"If you help me, I will reward you, too. Perhaps you would like the feathers of *Tsé nináhálééh* the Bird Monster."

Hearing that, she scurried toward the base of the rock and disappeared momentarily at the foot of the ledge. But soon *Naayéé' neizghání* heard a strange flapping sound. And then he heard her voice again, saying this.

"Shut your eyes," he heard her say.

"Shut your eyes and step back, so that you cannot see me.

"Do not look at me as I take you down.

"For I am an ugly creature. I do not wish to be seen by you or by the likes of you."

He did as he was told, and in a moment *Jaa'abaní asdzą́ą́* the Bat Woman stood beside him.

"Quickly!" she ordered.

"Get into my basket here, and I will lower you."

He looked at the large carrying-basket she bore upon her back. He saw that it hung on strings as thin as the strands of a spider's web.

"Grandmother," he said.

"I am afraid to ride in there."

"Do as I say!" she demanded. "You have nothing to be afraid of."

"But grandmother, I cannot ride in that basket," said he.

"Do as I bid you," she replied. "Show some trust."

"But little grandmother, you are so small and that basket is so large," he said.

"Why do you refuse?" said she. "Are you afraid because I am so ugly and so small?"

"That basket is so large, but the cords that bind it to you are so thin," said he.

"Listen," she said.

"I can carry a whole deer in that basket. Surely I can carry you, too.

"Why do you have no trust for an ugly creature?

"Very well, then.

"Fill the basket with stones and rocks if you are afraid. Then watch me carry them down to the foot of the cliff.

"See for yourself whether I am strong enough to take you down from here."

So he filled her basket with rocks and stones as she suggested. And he watched her as she danced around with the loaded basket on her back. The stones inside bounced and rattled, but the webbing held fast and the basket remained secure.

"Well," she asked then.

"Do I need to fly with it, too, to convince you?"

"No," he said.

"Then get in," replied she.

"But keep your eyes closed.

"I do not wish to have you stare at me as we fly."

At first he did what she told him to do. He placed himself in the basket and held onto the sides as she began flying; and he clenched his eyes shut, feeling himself being gently lowered.

But then he heard the strange noise her wings made as she flapped them. It was a sound unlike any he had heard and it frightened him. So he opened his eyes to look. And the instant he did so he felt himself falling straight down.

"Close your eyes!" scolded *Jaa'abaní asdzą́ą́* the Bat Woman then. "Did you not hear what I said?"

So he obeyed her and felt himself slowly descending once more.

But then the motion of her wings again frightened him. It seemed that they flapped first at one speed and than at another. And they made that strange sound. Again he opened his eyes to watch her in flight. At which instant he again found himself falling freely.

"Do what you are told to do!" nagged *Jaa'abaní asdzą́ą́* the Bat Woman. "Why can't you listen?"

Whereupon he closed his eyes again and again felt himself descending gradually.

But then her flight seemed curiously irregular. For it appeared that they would careen first to one side and then to another. And the sound of her wings continued to frighten him. So fearful did he become that he opened his eyes again to see which way they were going. But upon doing so he realized that they were again dropping rapidly out of the sky, going faster and faster at a dizzying speed.

"So you refuse to obey again?" cried *Jaa'abaní asdzą́ą́* the Bat Woman. "Close your eyes at once, or else you will perish."

Doing as she commanded, he again recognized the secure feeling of slow, gradual descent.

Until presently he became aware of the strange noise of her flapping wings again. Now they sounded as though they were beating against a rock. He imagined that any minute they would crash against the side of the cliff, and he wondered how soon the collision would occur. So he opened his eyes again to see where they were. But he could make out nothing at all, since they were falling freely again, dropping faster and faster, faster and faster, plummeting earthward so quickly that he could scarcely catch his breath.

"If you want to live you will close your eyes again," cried *Jaa'abaní asdzą́ą́*. "You will close them if you want to see your people again. You will close them if you want to destroy any of the other monsters."

So he shut his eyes once again, and once again he felt himself floating slowly groundward. And no matter how irregularly they seemed to be descending, or what kind of noise her wings seemed to be making, he managed to keep from looking. At last he arrived at the bottom of the cliff unhurt, and he stepped out of the basket none the worse off for having ridden in it.

"Now," said *Naayéé' neizghání* the Monster Slayer, "the feather of *Tsé nináhálééh* are yours.

"Help me gather them, then," ordered *Jaa'abaní asdzą́ą́* the Bat Woman.

"For the sooner I change the way I look the better.

"I am tired of bing so ugly. I am tired of being distrusted because of the way I look."

So together they plucked the body of the dead male Bird Monster. As they pulled them out one by one from his hide they placed the feathers in her basket, although *Naayéé' neizghání* insisted on keeping two of the largest ones as his own trophies.

When they were finished, he helped *Jaa'abaní asdzą́ą́* hoist the bundle onto her back and she hurried to depart. But as she started to walk away, *Naayéé' neizghání* cautioned her not to pass through the dry beds of either of the two temporary lakes, one of which was overgrown with weeds and the other of which was overgrown with sunflowers.

"If you walk that way," he warned, "you may not manage to keep those feathers long enough to put them on."

In spite of that warning, though, she headed straight toward the bed of sunflowers, so eager was she to leave his sight and to change the way she looked.

"I repeat," he cried to her as she hurried off. "Do not walk through the sunflowers!"

But she kept right on walking. And as she went something in her basket fluttered slightly.

"Listen to me!" cried *Naayéé' neizghání* again. "Don't walk through the sunflower bed."

But she continued walking in precisely that direction and entered the sunflower patch. And the fluttering in the basket grew louder. Then a strange little bird flew past her ear and into the sky.

"Whatever you do," repeated *Naayéé' neizghání*, "do not go that way."

But she continued to ignore him, heading straight for the center of the sunflower field. And as she walked, more birds fluttered out of her basket: birds of all sizes, birds of all varieties of feathers, birds such as she had never seen before: birds emerging in flocks and filling the air around her head; birds flying in all directions; birds chirping and clattering as they flew until the sky was as full of the sound of them as it was with the sight of their wings.

"Those who wish to be obeyed should also obey!" cried *Naayéé' neizgháni* to her. "Those who want to be listened to should also listen."

Meanwhile, *Jaa'abaní asdzą́ą́* stopped to look around. And to her astonishment she realized that all those birds she saw and heard were swarming out of the basket she was carrying.

She tired to hold them in. She tried to grab them as they came flying out. She reached up and tried to seize one or two of them as they flew. And then she flailed at all of them in an attempt to draw them back into the basket. But try as she might, she managed to recover none of them. Not a single one of them was she able to catch.

Finally she laid her basket on the ground and watched helplessly as the precious feathers of the dead *Tsé nináhálééh* came to life, took wing, left the basket and flew away as birds of all kinds.

They flew away as wrens. They flew away as warblers. They flew away as sparrows. They flew away as titmice. All of them flew away, until the basket of *Jaa'abaní asdzą́ą́* the Bat Woman was completely empty. And there she sat, all alone in the very middle of the sunflower bed, as ugly as she ever was and as ugly as she would always be.

So it was that small birds were created and so it is that they exist to this very day. And so, too, was it that *Jaa'abaní asdzą́ą́* the Bat Woman remained an ugly creature and continues to this very day to be ugly—untrusted by anyone who looks at her and her kind. That is why bats fly only by night and remain hidden during broad daylight, it is said.

Eleven

It is also said that when *Naayéé' neizgháni* the Monster Slayer returned, his brother was relieved to see him. For this is what he said:

"I watched the sacred prayer-stick carefully," he said.

"For every moment of your absence I observed it.

"At midday the black cigarette began to flame and I was

troubled. I knew then that you were in danger, and I considered coming to your rescue.

"Soon, though, the fire burnt out. I thought then that you were out of danger, but I could not be sure."

That is what *Tó bájísh chíní* the Born For Water said to his brother *Naayéé' neizghání* the Monster Slayer. And this is what was said in return:

"That must have been when *Tsé nináhálééh* seized me," returned *Naayéé' neizghání.*

"He caught me and carried me aloft high over the surface of the earth. Then he dropped me on the rocks overlooking *Tsé bit'a'í,* where he left me for dead, thinking that his young could feed on me."

To which he had nothing more to add.

Saying no more, he hung his trophies on the east side of the dwelling, where he sat and rested for a while.

Then he asked his mother where *Tsé dah hódzíítáłii* the kicking monster dwelled.

Again *Asdzą́ą́ nádleehé* the Changing Woman warned her son that the monsters were dangerous and tried to persuade him to stop pursuing them. But again she finally relented and told him that the creature he now sought lived at *Tsé deez'áhí* the Rock Ridge. Surely he could be found there.

● ● ● ●

So *Naayéé' neizghání* the Monster Slayer set out next morning to find *Tsé dah hódzíítáłii* Who Kicks People Off of Cliffs.

This monster lived high on a steep mountainside. A trail passed the place where he would lie among the rocks to warm himself in the sun. But whoever came along he would kick down into the deep precipice below.

Naayéé' neizghání had not gone far among the peaks at *Tsé deez'áhí* when he discovered a well-beaten trail. Following it, he found himself making his way up the wall of a canyon which cut through a mountain. Higher and higher he climbed along this narrow path until the air grew thin and cold. Higher and higher he climbed, until at last he sighted a giant, man-like creature reclining quietly in a recessed place among the rocks.

The monster lay resting as if he were meditating, one leg crossing the other at the knee, its foot dangling idly over the shin of the other leg. Showing no sign of wishing to do harm, it smiled indolently.

Naayéé' neizghání the Monster Slayer proceeded along the path as though he feared no danger. But he watched the giant closely out of the corner of his eye while he continued walking. And when he was about to pass the place where the monster lay resting, it thrust its dangling foot forward with frightening swiftness. Just as swiftly, though, *Naayéé' neizghání* lunged back, barely missing being kicked off the side of the cliff where he walked.

"Why did you kick at me thus?" he demanded of the giant.

"Oh, my grandson, please forgive me," replied the monster.

"I was just resting here, thinking about this and that.

"I only wanted to stretch my leg."

And so saying, he leaned his head back against the rocks, smiled innocently, relaxed, and appeared to close his eyes contentedly.

Four times did *Naayéé' neizghání* thus try to walk past him. And four times did *Tsé dah hódzííłtáłii* kick at him in vain. Four times did the twin ask why the giant creature struck at him that way, and four times did he hear the same reply.

Until at length *Naayéé' neizghání* seized the great stone knife with the broad blade given to him by his Father, *Jóhónaa'éi hataa'* the Sun. With it he slashed the monster's eyes in a swift, deft movement. He struck him again and again! again and again! until he was sure that he had slain that evil creature whose kick was so deadly.

After he had killed the kicking giant, however, *Naayéé' neizghání* the Monster Slayer was surprised to find that its corpse did not fall off the cliff. With his knife he cut under it in several places, but he could not determine what held it so fast to the rock.

Until at last he looked carefully at the head and realized that its long hair grew into the clefted rock like the roots of mountain pinyon. Thereupon he cut and slashed at that hair until the body at last slid forward and tumbled down the steep canyon wall out of sight.

As it fell, *Naayéé' neizghání* could hear voices clamoring far below, like this:

"I want the eyes," clamored one voice. "They are what tastes best."

"The arms are for me!" cried another. "Give me an arm."

"The liver is mine!" demanded another of those shrieking voices.

"No it's not!" shouted another. "The liver is mine! You take a leg."

"Ah," thought he.

"Those must be the monster's children quarreling over their father's remains.

"They would be fighting over me that way had I not dodged his deadly kicks."

He then tried to make his way down the side of the cliff to the place where the voices were coming from. At first he continued following the trail which had led him to *Tsé dah hódzííłtáłii*. But he found that it stopped a short distance beyond the point where he had killed the kicking giant. So he retraced his steps until he saw another trail which led to the bottom of the cliff.

•   •   •   •

When he finally got down there, he set eyes on the offspring of *Tsé dah hódzííłtáłii*, who by now had completely devoured the corpse of their father. All told there were twelve of them, blood smeared on the face of each.

He charged into them, hacking at them with his great stone knife. They tried to get away, but he was too fast for them and too powerful. He managed to kill them all save one, who ran faster than the rest and somehow climbed upon some rocks overlooking the bottom of the canyon.

Naayéé' neizghání pursued him, however, and finally caught him, too. He seized him by the neck with one hand and held him fast. As he did so, he looked at the monster-child and recoiled with disgust. How filthy it looked! What a grotesque face it had!

"You ugly creature," said *Naayéé' neizghání* the Monster Slayer.

"When I saw how fleet-footed you were and how majestically you leaped onto those rocks when you ran from me, I thought you might be a handsome, worthy foe.

"But now that I look at your disgusting face, I cannot so much as bring myself to kill you.

"So I shall let you live.

"Repulsive as you are, perhaps you can somehow ultimately serve the creatures of this world in some perverse way."

So saying, he held the young monster at arm's length, still gripping it by the scruff of the neck, but so that now its face was away from him. And he turned toward the north, saying this:

"Go north," he said.

"Go to *Naatsis'áán*, the distant mountain you see yonder on the horizon.

"It is cold and barren there.

"There the north wind batters the landscape.

"There the nights are longer and the days shorter.

"There you shall have to work hard if you wish to survive. And there you shall wander forever, naked and hungry.

"If you or any of your offspring are ever seen anywhere else, I shall see to it myself that you are killed after all."

And as he spoke, *Naayéé' neizghání* the Monster Slayer shook the hapless creature in his outstretched fist. When he stopped shaking it and let it go, it sprouted long, bony wings and took flight toward the far-off peaks of *Naatsis'áán* as it was told to do.

There it became known as *Jeeshóó'* the Buzzard. To this day his offspring dwell there among the Paiutes, known as the vermin of the desert because they feast upon the flesh of the dead. They are shunned and despised by all other living creatures to this very day.

•   •   •   •

Naayéé' neizghání the Monster Slayer then returned to the place where the children of *Tsé dah hódzííłtáłii* the Monster Who Kicks People Off of Cliffs had fallen upon their father and eaten his remains. Nothing was left of him but a few bones and his scalp. So the twin took as his trophy a lock of hair from that, which he carried back home with him.

•   •   •   •

"Now tell me this," demanded *Naayéé' neizghání* the Monster Slayer of his mother *Asdzáá nádleehé* the Changing Woman.

"Tell me where I may find the dwelling of *Bináá' yee agháni*. I now wish to destroy those people who slay with their eyes."

But as before his mother begged him not to go. As before she warned him that the monsters were powerful and dangerous. As before, however, he insisted, and as before she finally relented and answered him.

"The creatures you seek dwell at *Tséghálzhiní*," she answered.

"At Black Hole Rock you will find them."

Such a place stands to this very day. Although it has changed a little since *Bináá' yee agháni* the Monster That Kills With His Eyes lived there, it still has an opening on one side which resembles a door. And it has another opening on the top that looks like a smoke hole. Anyone who wishes to do so can go there and see it.

So *Naayéé' neizgháni* the Monster Slayer set out for that place. And with him he took a bag of salt in addition to the weapons that his Father *Jóhonaa'éí* the Sun had given him.

When he arrived at *Tséghálzhiní*, he entered the rock house through its doorway and sat down on the north side, just beyond a fire which burned in the center.

In another part of the rock-lodge sat the two elder *Bináá yee agháni*, the male and the female. With them sat their many children.

They all stared at the intruder with their great bulging eyes. And as they did flashes of lightning streamed at him therefrom. But these flashes could do no harm. They merely glanced off his armor, every one of them.

When they realized that they could not kill *Naayéé' neizgháni* the Monster Slayer as easily as they had been able to kill other victims, they stared harder and harder. Harder and harder they stared, until their eyes protruded far from their sockets.

When suddenly *Naayéé' neizgháni* threw a fistful of salt into the fire. And thereupon it hissed and it sputtered; it crackled and then it threw sparks. White-hot salt also flew in every direction, and it struck the eyes of the awesome birds and blinded them. One by one they lowered their heads into their wings to try to kill the pain they now felt in their eyes, and to try to avoid being hit again.

One by one they lowered their heads that way, and as they did so *Naayéé' neizgháni* struck each of them with the great stone knife which his father had given him. That way he killed all but the two youngest of the fearful staring birds.

And to those two he spoke these words:

"Had you grown up here in this place with this evil family of yours," he said to them, "you would have certainly survived as creatures of destruction.

"By what is right and proper, you should be killed.

"But I am going to let you live, although I will change your destiny.

"For I shall make you useful in the days and years to come, when *Nihookáá' dine'é* the Earth Surface People exist in this world."

That is what *Naayéé' neizgháni* said to the two surviving *Bináá' yee agháni* the Monsters Who Killed With Their Eyes.

Then, to the elder of those two survivors, he had this to add:

"You shall become *Tsídiiłtsooí* the Exploring Bird," he added.

"Henceforth you will remain within earshot of the five-fingered Earth Surface People.

"You will tell them what happens beyond the range of their immediate sight. You shall warn them when their enemies are approaching."

And so saying he seized the bird by its legs, held the young creature at arm's length, shook it four times unitl it flapped its wings, and then released it and watched it fly out of the smoke hole.

Next, to the younger of the two surviving young monsters, he made this declaration:

"Henceforth you will dwell close to my people," he declared.

"Likewise you will dwell close to the five-fingered Earth Surface People when they come to exist in this world.

"You will dwell where those who inhabit the surface of this world can hear the sound of your voice.

"It will be your destiny to make things sound beautiful. It will be your fate to make the world a happy place when darkness falls. For you will become *Hoshdódii* the Whippoorwill.

"You will sleep during the day, and you will come out at night to sing. Your song will reassure all who may hear you that *Jóhonaa'éí* the Sun will rise in the morning and bring forth a new day."

And so saying he took the bird by its legs, held the young creature at arm's length, shook it four times until it began working its wings, and then released it and listened as it flew through the smoke hole overhead, already singing sweetly and reassuringly.

•   •   •   •

When *Naayéé' neizghání* the destroyer of enemies reached home with his trophies, which this time included the two eyes of the first *Bináá' yee agháni* he had killed in the rock lodge; and when he told his mother *Asdzáá nádleehé* the Changing Woman what he had accomplished, she took a piece of the lung of *Déélgééd* the slain Horned Monster and placed it in her mouth. Then she began singing this song, dancing as she sang:

> "*Naayéé' neizghání* brings for me:
> A piece of lung he brings for me,
> *Déélgééd*'s lung he brings for me.
> Our people are restored.

"*Tó bájísh chíní* brings for me:
A piece of wing he brings for me.
Nináhálééh he brings for me.
My people are restored.

"Enemy Slayer brings for me:
A lock of monster hair he brings for me.
Monster of the cliffs he brings for me.
His people are restored.

"Monster Slayer brings for me:
Monster eyes he brings for me.
Bináá' yee agháníí he brings for me.
Our people are restored."

That is what *Asdzą́ą́ nádleehé* the Changing Woman sang.

•   •   •   •

But it was not long after she finished her song of rejoicing before
Naayéé' neizgháni the Monster Slayer wanted to know the
whereabouts of yet another alien monster.

"Where shall I find *Shash na'ałkaahii* the Tracking Bear Monster?"
he wanted to know.

Again *Asdzą́ą́ nádleehé* the Changing Woman begged her son
not to go. Again she warned him that the *Naayéé'* were dangerous,
adding that in time one of them would surely kill him. But again
he insisted that he would keep fighting the monsters. Once again
he persuaded her to tell him where to look for the next one.

"*Shash na'ałkaahii* dwells at *Tsé baa hasti'* she said to him
at last.

"You will find him at Reticence Rock, where all too many of
your people have already perished."

So he set out next morning for that very place. And when he
arrived there he walked all the way around the rock, but he saw no
sign of the creature he was looking for. Until at length he looked
up at the top of *Tsé baa hasti'*, where he saw the bear's head
sticking out of a hole. So he climbed up for a closer look.

The den of *Shash na'ałkaahii* was shaped like a cross. It had four
entrances each of which faced one of the four directions. *Naayéé'
neizgháni* looked into the east entrance first. Then he looked into

the south entrance. Then he looked into the entrance to the west. And in none of those did he see a sign of the enemy.

Finally he approached the north entrance. And when he did he spied the head of the watchful bear monster again. But it was instantly withdrawn and disappeared.

Shash na'ałkaahii was obviously heading for the entranceway to the south, reasoned *Naayéé' neizghání.* So he quickly ran around to that side of the den where he lay in wait. And sure enough! in a little while the bear thrust forth his head to look, whereupon the slayer of enemies drew his great stone knife and cut off the head of the hapless Tracking Bear Monster.

He then picked that head up, seized it by a lock of fur on its scalp, held it aloft so that he could stare directly into its eyes, and spoke these words to it:

"In your old life you were an evildoer," he said to it.

"You were intent upon the slaughter of my people.

"Now, however, you shall have a new life. And your shape will change to fit the purpose of that life.

"In the future you will serve my people as surely as you devoured them. And you will serve the five-fingered Earth Surface People when they come to exist in this world as surely as you would have devoured them in your old shape.

"You shall provide the people who dwell in this world with sweet fruit to eat. You shall provide them with warm foam so that they may bathe themselves until they are clean. And you shall provide them with sturdy thread so that they may sew and mend their clothing."

So saying, he cut the head into three pieces, using the broad-bladed stone knife given to him by *Jóhonaa'éí* the Sun.

One of these pieces he threw to the east, where it landed, took root in the ground and became *tsá'ászi' hashk'aan,* the yucca fruit plant which has nourished all people ever since.

The second of these pieces he threw to the west. There it landed, took root in the earth and became *tsá'ászi'ts'óóz,* the yucca soapsuds plant with which the people have cleansed themselves ever since.

And the last of these pieces he threw to the south. It landed there, and there it took root in the earth. And it became *noodah* the mescal fiber plant which ever since then yielded to people the material for making thread.

Now the work of *Naayéé' neizghání* was done at *Tsé baa hasti'* where *Shash na'ałkaahii* the Tracking Bear Monster once dwelled. So he cut off its left forepaw and returned home with his trophy.

• • • •

"You must now tell me where I may find *Tsé naagháii* the Wandering Stone Monster," he then said to his mother soon after he had returned from his latest victory.

"For I wish to destroy him next."

Again she objected, begging him not to go and warning him that all the monsters were dangerous. But again he persuaded her finally to answer his question.

"You will find him in a lake," she said at last. "He dwells there where *Tséłbáí* the Gray Rock juts out of the water."

So he set out next morning for the place she described, approaching the lake from the north while the wind blew out of the south. But he saw no sign of the stone, at least not at first.

At length he went around to the south side of the lake, whereupon the wind shifted and blew hard from the north. Then, suddenly, the stone rose to the surface of the water, poised itself there for a moment as if floating, and suddenly flew toward *Naayéé' neizgháni* as if some giant hand had hurled it.

Raising his lightning arrow, however, *Naayéé' neizgháni* the Monster Slayer held it up so that it blocked the path of the flying stone, knocking a piece off as it struck. And when the stone landed on the ground, he struck another piece off with his knife. *Tsé naagháii* the Wandering Stone now realized that it was matched against a mighty foe. So instead of hurling itself at him again it fled. And the slayer of enemies followed in swift pursuit.

Over the landscape they ran, the stone in flight, *Naayéé' neizgháni* the Monster Slayer close behind. Across the valley they went, and up over the mountains.

Through the canyons fled the moving stone.

In and out among the mesas chased the twin.

Now *Naayéé' neizgháni* is about to overtake *Tsé naagháii* as they reach the bank of a river. But just then the stone hurls itself into the water and disappears.

Now it surfaces again and throws itself onto the opposite bank, with the slayer of enemies leaping across the water and about to overtake the fugitive.

Four times it escapes its pursuer, and on its fourth leap into the water Monster Slayer sees the stone gleaming like fire beneath the surface and stops to gaze at it.

Suddenly the stone spoke thereupon, and these were its words:

"My dear young man," were its words.

"How relentless you are.

"Take pity on me, for I am exhausted.

"Stop chasing me and I shall change my ways.

"I will stop doing harm. I will start doing good.

"I shall keep the water moving from out of its underground places. I shall force it down from the mountaintops in steady streams. I shall make the rivers flow. I shall cause the lakes to remain full.

"If you decide to kill me, however, the living springs within the earth will also die. Your lands will grow barren. Your fields will lie parched. No corn will grow. No melons will ripen on the vine.

Replied *Naayéé' neizgháni* then:

"If you keep your promise, I will let you live," he replied then.

"But if you so much as make one evil threat, I will destroy you after all."

Ever since then, *Tsé naagháii* has kept the promise he made that day, and there has been enough water for people to use. Notice the water where it bubbles from the underground places on the mountainsides. See how it trickles down from the hills. Observe how it rolls through the canyons. Watch the rivers flow and look at the current upon the lakes.

•   •   •   •

Thus it was that *Naayéé' neizgháni* brought no trophy with him when he returned from his exploit with *Tsé naagháii* the Wandering Stone Monster. But he had much to tell about in describing how he had won assurance that there would be water in the land. And together he and his family sang and danced as they discussed his adventures from first to last.

•   •   •   •

It had now been eight days since the brothers had left the house of *Jóhonaa'éí* the Sun. And it had been more days than that since they had first undertaken their quest to rescue their people from the *Naayéé'*.

Now *Naayéé' neizgháni* the Monster Slayer realized that he was

weary. So he decided that he would rest for four days and recover
from his bruises and his wounds. Then he would slay the
remaining monsters, one by one, it is said.

Twelve

It is also said that the four days passed. And four nights went by.
Four times did the sun rise and set, and four times the moon
passed overhead. During that time *Naayéé' neizgháni* the Monster
Slayer rested as well as he could.

But there were still many *Naayéé'* to be killed, and he knew that
he could not remain quietly among his people until he had
destroyed them all.

Yé'iitsoh łigai tséyaa the White Monster Under the Rock
remained to be killed. *Yé' iitsoh łitso tséyaa* the Yellow Monster
Under the Rock had yet to be killed. There was *Yé'iitsoh łizhin
tséyaa* the Black Giant Under the Rock yet to kill. And *Yé
iitsohíbáhí nahasdzáán biyi'* the Brown Giant Hiding in the
Earth remained alive.

Besides these alien creatures there were various animals who
dwelled among some Pueblo ruins. They foraged all over the
countryside and raided the crops which the people tried to grow.
Naayéé' neizgháni knew all too well that there remained much to
do before the world was fit for people to live there.

During that four-day resting period, the brothers talked about
how they might destroy their remaining enemies. Until at last they
resolved to visit the dwelling of their Father *Jóhonaa'éí hataa'* the
Sun again. Again they would seek what help he might give them.

So on the morning following the fourth day they set out together
for the east, where *Atiin diyinii* the Holy Trail would take them
along the path of the rainbow to the mighty sky-dwelling they had
visited once before.[72]

•   •   •   •

They had an easy journey along the way since they encountered
no enemies. But when they arrived at the house of the Sun and

entered, no one there greeted them. No one even as much as
offered them a seat. So they had to place themselves on the floor,
and they were insulted by such a lack of hospitality.

No sooner had they settled themselves than bolts of lightning
began to flash into the dwelling, which annoyed them even more.
Four such bolts darted in through the entrance and struck the
ground directly in front of them. And with each one their anger
increased all the more.

Immediately afer the last of those four flashes, in walked
Jaa'abaní the Bat and *Tó neinilí* the Water Sprinkler, who
immediately had this to say:

"Do not be angry with us," they immediately said.

"And do not be alarmed.

"We fling these lightning bolts only out of happiness.

"We want to play with you. We want to rejoice in your company.
We want to congratulate you. And we want to celebrate your
victories in the world below."

But that explaination did little to placate the brothers. They said
nothing in reply, remaining silent and restrained for having
received no better welcome than that.

At last, however, they heard the voice of *Niłch'i* the Wind, who
whispered silently in their ears. And this is what he said:

"Do not be angry with these two," said he.

"It is as they say. They want to play with you and enjoy your
company. They want to congratulate you and celebrate in
your behalf.

"Once they were allies of the *Naayéé'* and would not have
wanted to see them die. But now they desire to be your friends and
they seek to make the world a better place."

These words calmed the two brothers somewhat and they began
to relax. Then *Jóhonaa'éí* the Sun spoke to them, telling them this:

"You must forgive those who dwell here with me for their
rudeness," he told them.

"They respect no one, and you should learn to ignore them.

"It seems that they do not even respect me.

"Although I may rule the sky by day, here in my own home I am
no one special. Perhaps it is that way with powerful men
everywhere.

"Here are seats for the two of you.

"Here," he said to *Naayéé' neizghání* the Monster Slayer. "Seat
yourself here upon this chair of shell, my son.

"And there," he said to *Tó bájísh chíní* the Child of Water. "Seat yourself upon that turquoise bench there, my son."

But as the two brothers were about to do as their father bid them, *Nítch'i* again whispered a warning.

"Do not sit on those seats he offers you," warned he.

"At least do not sit on them yet.

"For those are the seats of peace. Once you place yourselves in them the weapons *Jóhonaa'éí* has given you will be useless. And with their power gone you will be helpless in any battle you have with the other monsters.

"*Naayéé' neizghání,*" warned *Nítchi,* "you take the seat of red stone over there, which is a warrior's seat.

"And *Tó bájísh chíní,*" he warned, "you remain standing right where you stand now, which is the position of one who intends to continue fighting his enemies."

When *Jóhonaa'éí* the Sun saw the brothers behave contrary to his instructions, he looked at them sternly. And this is what he asked them:

"Why have you come here to see me again?" he asked them.

"We come for no special purpose," answered *Tó bájísh chíní.*

"Surely you have one reason or another for coming," said *Jóhonaa'éí.* Tell me what it is!"

"We merely come to visit," repeated the two brothers. "We simply come to pass the time with you, father."

"There is more to your second visit than that," said *Jóhonaa'éí* the Sun. "There is a purpose to your being here, that much I know. Now tell me what it is you want of me!"

"It is as we say," replied both brothers."We come to pass the time with you. We come to visit you and to enjoy your company."

Now it was *Jóhonaa'éí* who was growing angry.

"I know that you have come for a reason," said he.

"I know that you have a purpose in seeking me again.

"I can see how restless you are. I can see the boldness of your actions. It is obvious to me that you intend to continue waging war on your enemies.

"Now tell me the truth about this second visit of yours."

To which *Naayéé' neizghání* at last replied:

"Father," he replied.

"Many of the *Naayéé'* remain on the surface of the earth.

"And those who do remain continue to increase.

"Even now as we talk here with you they are conceiving and

giving birth to their young. Soon there will be as many as there were before we visited you the last time.

"We want to destroy them all!

"Until each one of them has been destroyed there will be disorder on the surface of the world."

To which *Jóhonaa'éí* made this reply in turn:

"Children," he replied.

"When I helped you before I asked nothing for myself in return, is that not right?"

"That is right," said they.

"But if I am to help you again, this time I must ask for something.

"I have a long way to travel each day.

"Often, especially during the summer when my days are long, my journey through the sky seems endless.

"I yearn for a place to rest. Sometimes I long for something to eat as I labor through the sky away from this dwelling and all the way back around the far side of the world.

"Sometimes I am so tired I fear that I cannot complete the cycle before I am to begin another.

"Sometimes I long for someone who will welcome me and speak a kind word or two before I rest.

"I bid you send your mother to a place in the west!

"Have her make a second home for me halfway around the sky which girdles the world. A home where I might rest and refresh myself before I start the second half of my journey. A home where I can relax with her and enjoy the pleasure of her company."[73]

"That I will surely do, father," said *Naayéé' neizghání* the Monster Slayer.

"If you so wish, I will order her to find a suitable place in the west and to make a home for you."

"No," said *Tó bájísh chíní*.

"You cannot order her to do anything!

"*Asdzą́ą́ nádleehé* the Changing Woman is under nobody's power. We cannot make promises in her behalf.

"She will speak for herself if she is to speak at all. The decisions that concern her are her own decisions to make. For she is her own mistress and no one else's.

"Father, I sympathize with you. What you wish for sounds reasonable. And we will help you if we can.

"But the best that we can promise is that we will tell *Asdzą́ą́*

nádleehé what you desire. Indeed, we will plead your case for
you. But finally it will be her wish and not yours or ours that
will count."

Having heard what his sons replied to his request, *Jóhonaa'éí* the
Sun arose and walked to the center of the chamber where they
all were.

In that chamber there were four curtains which sealed off
passageways to four other compartments. He removed the curtain
covering the passageway to the east, which was black, and took
five hoops therefrom. One of these was black. Another was blue. A
third was yellow. And a fourth was white. The fifth was
multicolored and resplendent with flakes of shining mica.[74]
Attached to each hoop was a knife of the same color as itself..

He also took out four great hailstones colored exactly like the
five hoops and the five accompanying knives. And, giving all of
these items to his sons, he said this to them:

"Take these," he said to them.

"Your mother will know what to do with them.

"Simply tell her to do what must be done. Then your victory
over the remaining monsters is all but assured."

•   •   •   •

With those gifts from *Jóhonaa'éí hataa'* their Father the Sun,
Naayéé' neizghání the Monster Slayer and *Tó bájísh chíní* the
Child of Water set out for home again. And as they made their
way back along *Atiin diyinii* the Holy Trail they beheld a
wonderful vision.

For the gods spread before them the country of the five-fingered
Earth Surface People who would someday be known as the Navajo,
once all the *Naayéé'* were disposed of.

These new people would increase their numbers. They would
learn fully how to plant and to reap. They would learn to husband
their own livestock. And they would learn how to conduct rituals
to maintain order and harmony on the surface of the world.

The two brothers discussed what their father had said to them
during their visits. They discussed what they had seen and done in
his dwelling. They talked about the weapons and the gifts he had
given them. And they talked about the marvelous things that had
occurred to them in their lives.

And with renewed confidence in themselves and in the future

that lay ahead, they sang this song as they traveled the path of the rainbow down the Holy Trail:

> "*Naayéé' neizghání*, he is holy:
> So says our father *Jóhonaa'éí.*
> So says the Sun to each of us,
> Himself a holy man.

> *Tó bájísh chíní*, he is holy:
> So says our kinsman *Tl'éhonaa'éí.*
> So says the Moon of each of us,
> Himself a holy man.

> Child of earthloam he is holy:
> So says our father *Jóhonaa'éí.*
> So says the Sun to each of us,
> Himself a holy man.

> Child of water he is holy,
> So says our kinsman *Tl'éhonaa'éí.*
> So says the Moon of each of us,
> Himself a holy man."

So sang they as they walked along the Holy Trail. And when they reached sight of their home they announced their arrival by singing yet another song:

> "From out of the heavens a voice rings out!
> From the depths of the earth rings out a voice!
> 'Behold the slayer of giants!' proclaims the voice.
> A holy voice. A sacred voice.

> From the depths of the earth a voice rings out!
> 'Behold the Child of the Water!' proclaims the voice.
> From deep within the waters a voice proclaims.
> A holy voice. A sacred voice.

> From the loins of the earth a voice rings out!
> 'Behold the child of the earth!' the voice proclaims.
> From beneath the canyon floors proclaims the voice.
> A holy voice. A sacred voice.

> From beyond the clouds a voice rings out!
> From every direction rings out the voice!
> 'Behold our holy kinsmen!' proclaims the voice.
> A holy voice. A sacred voice."

And when the brothers saw her, they greeted *Asdzą́ą́ nádleehé* the Changing Woman with joy, saying this to her:

"We have been to see our Father *Jóhonaa'éí nihitaa'* the Sun again," they said to her.

"And he gave us these hoops.

"Now show us what to do with them.

"Do with them what must be done.

"Then our victory over the remaining monsters is all but assured."

To which *Asdzą́ą́ nádleehé* the Changing Woman replied:

"I know nothing about hoops," she replied.

"But these are the hoops that our Father *Jóhonaa'éí nihitaa'* the Sun has given us," said *Tó bájísh chíní*. "These are the hailstones and these are the knives he gave us."

"I have no knowledge of hoops," replied she. "I know nothing of hailstones and knives."

"But *Jóhonaa'éí nihitaa'* our Father the Sun bid us give you these hoops. He gave us these hailstones and these knives and bid us give them to you," protested *Naayéé' neizghání*.

"I know nothing of those hoops. Nor do I know anything of whatever else he might have given you," answered she. "And I care nothing for any of his possessions.

"*Jóhonaa'éí* the Sun has no right to make promises to you that I am to keep!"

"But these hoops are talismen from our Father the Sun *Jóhonaa'éí nihitaa'*," protested *Tó bájísh chíní*. "It is likewise with the hailstones and the knives. And inasmuch as you are our mother just as he is our father, surely you must know what he says you know. Surely you can do for us what he says you will do."

Asdzą́ą́ nádleehé the Changing Woman sighed.

She looked wistfully up at the sky where *Jóhonaa'éí* the Sun was slowly making his way. And to her sons she spoke these words:

"Once I felt the warmth of him," she said to them.

"Deep within my body I felt his loving warmth.

"I was lonely then, and I sought his company. It was a lasting partnership that I sought.

"So I rejoiced to feel such warmth deep inside my body.

"But ever since that singular time I have seen *Jóhonaa'éí* only from afar. And I have never felt that warmth inside of me again.

"Since that time he has never come to visit me.

"Since that time he has told me nothing."

That is what *Asdzą́ą́ nádleehé* the Changing Woman said to *Naayéé' neizgháni* the Monster Slayer and to *Tó bájísh chíni* the Child of Water.

She said that to them and nothing more.

She took a deep breath as she lowered her gaze from the sky where *Jóhonaa'éí* the Sun was slowly making his way. Her eyes fell to the ground before her while the two youths stood there asking for her help. And finally she wept.

As she continued to weep and as her silence continued, she reached out to accept from the two boys the hoops they had brought with them from the house in the sky. From them she accepted the knives and the hailstones that they had also brought.

Then she walked to a place east of where they had all been standing. And she set the black hoop up so that it would roll. Then she spat through it with spittle of black hail which was four-cornered. And she nudged the hoop so that it moved.[75]

At once it rolled off to the east and out of sight.

Then she took the blue hoop to a place south of where they had been standing. She set it up so that it too would roll. And she spat through it with spittle of blue hail which was six-cornered. And she nudged that hoop until it moved.

It rolled at once off to the east and out of sight.

Then she carried the yellow hoop to a place west of where they had stood. Likewise she set it up so that it would roll like the others had rolled. She spat through it with spittle of yellow hail that was eight-cornered. And she gave the hoop a gentle shove to get it started.

It rolled off to the west at once and out of sight.

And finally she carried the white hoop to a place north of where the twins stood. In a similar fashion she set it up so that it would roll exactly like the others had been made to roll. She spat through it with pieces of eleven-cornered white hail spittle. And giving the hoop a gentle shove, she started it rolling.

It rolled off to the north and out of sight at once, never to be seen again.

The fifth hoop, which was the resplendently multicolored one, she threw straight up. Up it sailed, skyward out of sight, directly toward the sun's noontime zenith. And once it disappeared she threw the five-colored knives in the same heavenly direction, blowing a powerful breath after them.

Up and up they flew. Up and up, so that they too sailed higher and higher until they were out of sight. It was in the direction of the sun at its highest noontime zenith that they disappeared.

As the hoops rolled out of sight, and as the knives disappeared deep into the sky overhead, clouds gathered from all four directions. From the east came black clouds. From the south blue clouds came. From the west rolled yellow clouds. And from the north there came thick, white, swirling clouds.

Gathering from all four cardinal directions and filling the sky, those clouds converged overhead. And when they did thunder bellowed and rumbled all over the sky.

From the east it crackled. From the south it rolled. From the west it echoed. From the north it rumbled. Overhead it crackled and rolled, echoed and rumbled; the clouds mingled and thickened and the whole world darkened under the weight of a strange orange light. Space around and overhead filled with the terrible sight of that strange orange glow and the sound of the thunder.

As she listened to it, *Asdzą́ą́ nádleehé* the Changing Woman said nothing. She stood and looked up silently at the place overhead where the shimmering hoop and the flying knives had disappeared. There she stood, looking and gazing, gazing and looking.

Meanwhile the earth shook violently under the feet of all of them.

And at long last, still saying nothing to her sons, *Asdzą́ą́ nádleehé* the Changing Woman turned and walked away. She walked alone to the lodge wherein she had labored to give birth to her offspring, it is said.

Thirteen

It is also said that four more days went by. Four more nights passed. But during these days and nights the sun remained hidden and the moon likewise was not seen. Thunder continued crackling in the sky and rolling down from the peaks; it echoed across the plains and rumbled among the canyons without ceasing.

On the morning of the fifth day, the sky cleared and there began a four-day period of good weather. But then the sky grew dark again and something like a thick white cloud descended.

Asdzą́ą́ nádleehé the Changing Woman, who had remained in her lodge with the others, went outside to observe the effects of the weather. Everywhere she looked she saw whirlwinds. So fiercely did they blow that tall trees were uprooted like weeds and giant boulders were tossed around as if they were pebbles.

Who could endure such winds? she reflected. Neither giant nor insect is safe from this force.

"My son, I fear for our very house," she said to *Naayéé' neizghání* the Monster slayer as she came back inside.

"We live high in the mountains where the great winds now blowing can easily destroy this place."

Seeing how fearful she was, *Naayéé' neizghání* went outside to determine how he might protect their home. He observed the thickness of the clouds overhead, and he cut from them a large black square with the broad-bladed stone knife his father had given him.

Thereby he made a thick, protective blanket. With it he covered the dwelling, fastening the cloud-patch to the ground with shafts of rainbow. Next he covered the dwelling with a layer of black fog, which he similarly cut with his knife. This he fastened to the ground with sunbeams.

And for additional safety he cut a second blanket of black cloud and covered the dwelling a third time, securing that layer to the ground with sheet-lightning. And he added a final layer of fog, which he fastened to the ground with chain-lightning. Then he made his way back inside.

At the hour of sunset that evening, they all caught a glimpse of the sun through a patch of blue in the sky. But otherwise thick clouds and dense fog still filled the air. And thereafter for four more days and four more nights the storm continued. Hail such as no one had ever seen lashed the countryside. The air was full of sharp stones driven by the wind, which carried everything before it, so forceful it was. And the people could do nothing but keep refuge in their lodge, where they listened to the storm.

"Surely such weather is our ally," said *Asdzą́ą́ nádleehé* the Changing Woman.

"Not even monsters can survive such a wind and such hail."

•　　•　　•　　•

At last, on the morning following the final full stormy day, the tumult ceased.

Naayéé' neizghání went outside at his mother's bidding to try to determine if the storm was really over. And he discovered that although a heavy cloud still hung over the earth, the air was calm and still. So he removed the four coverings from the lodge and cast them up toward the heavens where they rightfully belonged.

As the first covering ascended, the chain-lightning which he had used to lash it to the ground shot out of it and flashed across the sky. And as the second covering ascended, the sheet-lightning which had fastened it to the ground shot out of it and momentarily filled the sky.

As the third covering rose upward, the sunbeams that had been used to hold it fast to the earth streamed from it and brought light where there had been darkness only an instant before. And as the fourth blanket made its way heavenward, the shafts of rainbow that had moored it to the firmament now adorned the sky.

Never before had such beauty been see by anyone. And such beauty may never be seen again, inasmuch as it has not been seen since then to this day. Everywhere the sky was resplendent with color. Multihued bands of light shimmered alike in the brightness of the sun's light and in the glassy sparkle of drops of clear water. Then a gentle shower of soft, warm rain fell and cleansed the air of all dust. And when the sky again cleared, the bright sun was seen to make its way across the turquoise sky.

Those who had taken shelter now emerged. And they marveled to see what changes the storm had made. Near their house a deep canyon had been formed by the force of the wind blowing away loose soil that once filled an area between two giant walls of rock. The bluffs overlooking the slopes around the dwelling were now stark in naked rockiness. The mountain grass and the soil in which that grass had rooted itself was gone, having been torn away by the wind and washed far downstream in the swollen, rapid rivers.

Solitary pillars of rock now towered above the high desert plain, although they had once been fertile mountains of sandy loam. And the canyon walls, once slopes green with grass and aspen were now sheer, vertical cliffs of red and yellow rock. A new terrain had been hewn, giving the land the shape and character it bears to this very day.

"Surely the *Naayéé'* have all been destroyed by now," said *Asdzą́ą́ nádleehé* the Changing Woman.

"How can anyone have survived such a storm? Great or small, fierce or gentle, those exposed to it must surely have perished."

And everyone agreed with her that the enemy of *Ha'aznání dine'é* the Emergence People must by now have been overcome.

"Not so!" whispered *Nítch'i* the Wind into the ear of *Naayéé' neizghání* the Monster Slayer.

"Some still survive," he whispered.

"For instance *Są́* the Old Age Woman still remains. She looks like a frail creature who can do no harm. But where the fearsome monsters you have already slain can destroy someone in a single blow and swallow them in one easy gulp, *Są́* slowly saps strength with the passing years. She devours life so gradually that from one day to the next you cannot feel yourself being consumed.

"Beware of her."

Whereupon *Naayéé' neizghání* had these words to say to *Asdzą́ą́ nádleehé* the Changing Woman:

"Mother," he said.

"Tell me where I can find the dwelling place of *Są́* the One Who Brings Old Age?"

"Do not speak of her," replied *Asdzą́ą́ nádleehé.*

"But I wish to see for myself whether she has truly been destroyed," answered *Naayéé' neizghání.*

"There is no need for you to seek her," said his mother. "There is no need for you to visit any monster's dwelling place again."

"But I wish to satisfy myself once and for all that she has been destroyed with the others. I wish to determine once and for all that we are truly safe," said her son.

"My son," said she. "You have nothing to fear. Those whose destruction we desired you have destroyed. Otherwise certain things are better left the way they are."

"But I have reason to believe that *Są́* the Aging Monster is alive. I have reason to suspect that even now she is slowly eating away at our strength with the passing days," he said.

"All the same, do not ask of her," said she. "And do not seek to know of any others. Perhaps it is better for all of us in the long run that certain enemies remain.

"I am sorry, my son.

"But this time I will not tell you where to look for those you seek to destroy.

Nevertheless, *Naayéé' neizghání* again heard the whispering voice of *Nítch'i* the Wind.

"*Sạ* lives among the mountains at *Dibé nitsaa* the Place of Mountain Sheep," he whispered.

"That is where you must go if you wish to find her. That is where you can see for yourself what her presence on earth may mean to you and your people."

So *Naayéé' neizgháni* the Monster Slayer resolved that once again he would set out to fight the *Naayéé'*, it is said.

Fourteen

It is also said that he awoke early next morning and set out for the north. And when he arrived at *Dibé nitsaa* after a long journey he saw an old woman.

She walked slowly toward him, leaning on a staff. Her back was bent. Her hair was white. Her face was deeply wrinkled. Her arms and hands were bony. He knew that this must be *Sạ* the One Who Brings Old Age, and he said this to her:

"Old grandmother," he said to her.

"It does not please me to tell you so, but I have come here to kill you."

But she merely smiled when she heard his words, and this is what she replied:

"I do you no harm, grandson," she replied.

"So why would you want to kill a feeble old woman like me?"

"What you say is untrue, "replied *Naayéé' neizgháni.*

"For you will slowly sap my strength with the passing of the years. And with the passing of the years you will likewise sap the strength of the five-fingered Earth Surface People when they come to exist in this world.

"Eventually you will devour everyone just as *Naayéé'* the alien monsters would have done."

That is what *Naayéé' neizgháni* the Monster Slayer said to Sạ the Aging One. And this is what she replied:

"Grandson," she replied.

"I hear that you have performed great deeds.

"I hear that it has been your purpose to make this world a good place for your people. And I hear that you wish to make it a good place for the five-fingered Earth Surface People who are yet to be created.

"Very well, then, grandson.

"But think it over before you kill me.

"For once the people discover that *Sá* will no longer slowly sap their strength with the passing of the years and finally devour them, they will have no incentive to beget offspring.

"The boys will not become fathers when their bodies are ready for fatherhood. The girls will not become mothers when their bodies shape them for motherhood. And when they are all past their prime, worthless old men and wasted old women will live on. So the people will stand still and never increase.

"Is it not better that people die at length and pass their wisdom and their responsibilities to those who are younger?[76]

"Let me live, my grandson.

"Let me live to inspire the people to bring children into the world. Let me live to inspire them to nurture those children. Let me live to inspire them to teach their young and to pass their wisdom on."

"If that is what you will do, I shall indeed spare you," replied *Naayéé' neizgháni*. And he returned to his mother without a trophy.

* * * *

But soon after his return he again heard the voice of *Niłch'i* the Wind:

"*Hak'az asdzáá* the Cold Woman still lives," he whispered into the ear of *Naayéé' neizgháni*.

"Each year she freezes the earth..

"She puts the animals to flight or sends them into hiding.

"She covers the streams with ice. She dries up the leaves on the cottonwoods and the aspens so that they wither and fall to the ground. She kills the plants so that the vines bear no melons and the stalks bear no corn."

"Mother," demanded *Naayéé' neizgháni* then.

"Tell me where I might find the dwelling of *Hak'az asdzáá* the Cold Woman. I have reason to believe that she still lives and that she will soon freeze the earth."

But *Asdzáá nádleehé* the Changing Woman refused to answer

his question, declaring that he had already accomplished enough
and that certain things are better left as they are.

Finally, it was *Nílch'i* the Wind who told him what he wanted
to know.

"*Hak'az asdzą́ą́* the Cold Woman lives high on the summit of
Dibé nitsaa where the mountain sheep are," whispered *Nílch'i*
to him.

"She dwells on the north slope just below the peak where the
snow never melts."

Accordingly, *Naayéé' neizghání* the Monster Slayer awoke early
next morning and set out to kill her. He traveled to *Dibé nitsaa*
and climbed far beyond the timberline, where even scrawny
juniper shrubs fail to grow and where the snow lies white and
frozen all summer long.

There he found a lean old woman sitting alone on the bare white
ground. She wore no clothing whatsoever. She had no food to eat.
She took no warmth from any fire. No roof sheltered her.

Her skin was pale as the snow. She shivered from head to foot.
Her hands trembled and her teeth chattered. Her eyes watered from
the cold as giant snowflakes whirled thickly about her.

Among the snowflakes a multitude of snow buntings played.
These were the couriers she sent out each fall to announce the
coming of the winter storms.

"Grandmother," he said to her.

"I will take no pleasure in telling you so, but I am here to kill
you. Then the five-fingered Earth Surface People will not have to
suffer each year because of you."

"Whatever you wish, grandson," she replied.

"You may kill me or you may let me live. Either way I do not
care, for I am wretched up here where I dwell.

"But if you really care for those who are to inhabit this world in
the future you will mind well the consequences.

"Once I am dead it will always be hot on the earth.

"Once I am dead the land will evntually dry up from exhaustion,
having no season to rest itself each year.

"The springs will cease to flow once all snow melts and the
waters diminish. The aspens and the cedars will have nowhere to
deposit their seeds safely in the ground each autumn. Over the
years the people will perish, since they will have no melons and no
corn to eat."

Listening carefully to her words, *Naayéé' neizghání* paused and reflected on the wisdom they conveyed. And he finally lowered the hand he had raised to strike her.

"If that is the effect you have on the world, in the long run you serve us well, " he replied. And he turned his back on her and started the long journey home without a trophy.

•   •   •   •

He was not back long, however, before he again heard the voice of *Nilch'i* the Wind.

"*Té'é'į dine'é* the Poverty Creatures still live," whispered *Nilch'i* into his ear.

"They will destroy people by gradually using up possessions. They will leave no tools for anyone to use and no clothing to wear."

So when *Naayéé' neizghání* asked his mother to point the way to the dwelling place of *Té'é'į*, and she refused, urging him to leave certain things as they are, *Nilch'i* the Wind informed him that those creatures lived at *Dził dah neeztínii* the Roof Butte Mountain, and he resolved to go there and destroy them.

To which place he traveled early the next day, finding there a tattered old man and a filthy old woman. Their garments were in shreds, and in their house they had no goods. They had no utensils, no provisions, no baskets, no bowls.

"Grandmother. Grandfather," he said.

"It gives me no pleasure to tell you so, but I have come here to kill you. Then people will not suffer the consequences of your wear and tear."

"It is good of you to show such concern for your people, grandson," they replied.

"But stop and think for a minute before you destroy us.

"If we were to die, people would wear the same clothes day after day and year after year.

"If we were to be slain, they would have no reason to replace anything, no cause to improve upon the tools they are accustomed to using.

"But if we go on living and continue slowly to wear out what others use, ingenuity will flourish among them. They will think of better ways to sew and to carve. Garments will become more beautiful. Tools will become stronger and more useful. Designs of all kind will improve."

And hearing what Poverty Man and Poverty Woman said,
Naayéé' neizghání again changed his mind and decided to spare
them. Whereupon he again went home without a trophy.

• • • •

Next he set out to seek *Dichin hastiin* the Hunger Man, again
incited by *Niłch'i* the Wind, who bid him travel to *Tł'oh adaasgaii*
the White Spot of Grass.

When he arrived there he found twelve ravenous creatures who
stuffed themselves with anything that grew. The eldest among
them was a big, corpulent beast who ate nothing but brown cactus.
With first one paw and then another he jammed them into his
mouth, scarcely chewing one before he reached for another.

"There is no pleasure in my telling you so, grandfather," he said
to that creature.

"But I have come here to kill you. Then people will not feel the
pangs of hunger and ultimately starve for want of food."

"I do not blame you for wanting me dead," replied *Dichin
hastiin* the Hunger Man, continuing to chew and swallow as
he talked.

"But if you really want people to thrive and prosper in the days
and years to come, think again.

"If you kill us, people will lose their taste for food.

"If you kill us, they will never know the pleasure of cooking
and eating.

"But if we live, they will continue to plant seeds and harvest
crops. They will care about livestock and they will husband their
domestic animals well. They will remain skilled hunters. They
will cure meat and prepare food enthusiastically."

And having heard these words he chose not to kill *Dichin
hastiin* after all, again returning home without a trophy.

• • • •

"Why is it that you come back again without a trophy?" asked
his mother *Asdzą́ą́ nádleehé* the Changing Woman.

"Can it be that you have lost your desire to fight the *Naayéé*?"

"Some things are better left as they are," he replied.

And so saying, he removed the sheath wherein he carried the

great stone knife that his Father *Jóhonaa'éí hataa'* the Sun had given him.

He now realized that his work was done, it is said.

Fifteen

It is also said the *Níłch'i* the Wind spoke no more of enemies to *Naayéé' neizghání* the Monster Slayer. And therewith the warrior took off his armor.

Off came his battle moccasins.

Off came his leggings.

Off came his war shirt.

Off came his headdress.

All of these articles of war he laid in a pile. And with them he placed the various weapons which *Jóhonaa'éí* had given him.

Then he set out to see the results of what he had accomplished.

•   •   •   •

Four days later he returned to tell his mother *Asdzą́ą́ nádleehé* the Changing Woman what he had found.

"I find that this is now a peaceful world," he told her.

"Everywhere I go I find that I am treated like a kinsman.

"Those whom I meet greet me as one of their own. They call me grandson. They call me son. They call me brother. They call me cousin.

"I have been everywhere, and everywhere I find it is the same.

"I have been to the edge of the waters. I have been to the boundaries of the sky. I have been among the highest peaks. I have been deep into the lowest crags and canyons.

"And wherever I went I found no one who was not my friend and a friend to all of the people."

Happy to find the world the way he described it, he sang this song:

"Now the enemy slayer arrives:
From the house of the dark stone blades he arrives.
From where the stone knives hang he arrives.
And the treasures he has won are yours, oh you gods.

   Now the Child of the Water arrives:
   From the house of the jagged blades he arrives.
   From where the sharp knives hang he arrives.
   And the treasures he has won are yours, oh you gods.

Now the Child of the Earth arrives:
From the heavenly house of blades he arrives.
From where all sorts of knives hang he arrives.
And the treasures he has won are yours, oh you gods.

   Now the son of the gods arrives:
   From the house of the yellow blades he arrives.
   From where the yellow knives hang he arrives.
   And the treasures he has won are yours, oh you gods."

Scarcely had he finished singing when they all heard the sound
of another voice singing.

It came from a place far to the east, but as they listened and
waited, listened and waited, it grew stronger and more distinct
until at last they could make out the words:

"With the Slayer of Alien Monsters I come:
From the house of the dark stone blades I come.
From where the dark stone knives hang I come.
Giver of the sacred hoops I come.
   I come, I come! The dreaded one.

   With the Child of the Water I come:
   From the house of the jagged blades I come.
   From the place of the jagged knives I come.
   Giver of the sacred hoops I come.
      I come, I come! the godly one.

With Child of the Earth I come:
From the heavenly house of blades I come.
Where all sorts of knives are stored I come.
Giver of the sacred hoops I come.
   I come, I come! The holy one.

> With the Grandson of the Gods I come:
> From the house of the yellow blades I come.
> Where the yellow blades are stored I come.
> Bestower of the sacred rites I come.
>   I come, I come! The sacred one."

As the voice drew nearer and the song continued, *Asdzą́ą́ nádleehé* became excited.

"Quickly!" she said to the two youths.

"Dress yourselves.

"It is the voice of your father you hear. *Jóhonaa'éí* the Sun is coming."

Then she left the lodge so that she would not have to listen to the three of them talk about the *Naayéé'*. And she left so that she would not have to face him herself.

•   •   •   •

When *Jóhonaa'éí* the Sun entered he greeted *Naayéé' neizghání* the Monster Slayer and *Tó bájísh chíní* the Water's Child. Then he had this question to ask of the eldest of the two twins:

"My son," he asked, "do you now think that you have slain all the enemies of your people?"

To which *Naayéé' neizghání* made this reply:

"Indeed I have," he replied.

"Those who should die I have killed. And now there is order and harmony in this world.

"I have been among the highest peaks, and I have been through the deepest canyons. I have been to the edge of the waters, and I have been to the boundaries of the sky. And wherever I went I found no one who is not a friend to our people."

"And do you have trophies to show me?" asked *Jóhonaa'éí* the Sun.

"Truly I have, my father," replied the youth.

"I have brought wing-feathers and hair, eyes and innards. From each of my battles I have returned with some part of a monster that could be taken only with its death."

To which *Jóhonaa'éí* the Sun had this to say:

"It is not good that the bodies of the *Naayéé'* should lie where they have fallen.[77]

"I will have then all buried near the corpse of *Yé'iitsoh* the Big Giant."

And therewith he commanded that the various remains should be carried to *Tsoodził* the Blue Bead Mountain in the east, and that they should be buried under the blood of *Yé'iitsoh*, mightiest of the *Naayéé'* and first among them to be slain.

That is why to this very day we do not see them lying all over the landscape. Although sometimes if we look very carefully we can see small parts of them protruding out of the rocks: a finger here, a claw there which *Naayéé neizghání* managed to hack off in one of his battles with them. Some passersby might think of those protrusions as fossils. But we who know the story of how the monsters were destroyed recognize them for what they really are.

As soon as the corpses were disposed of as he wanted them to be, *Jóhonaa'éí* the Sun took the trophies that his sons had given him. And he took the armor and the weapons that he had given his sons. And then he said this to the two of them:

"These trophies I shall carry back with me to my house in the east," he said.

"There I shall keep them, along with the armor and the weapons that I gave you when you first visited me.

"If you should ever need those things again, you may come there and get them."

Then he bid them farewell. As he departed he promised to return in four days. But this time, said he, he would come looking for *Asdzą́ą́ nádleehé* the Changing Woman for whom he would have a message. And he was asking his two sons to bid her meet him at the summit of *Ch'óol'į́'į́* the Giant Spruce Mountain, it is said.

Sixteen

It is also said that four more days passed, and that four more nights went by. Four times the sun rose and set, and four times the moon passed overhead.

And on the morning of the fifth day *Asdzą́ą́ nádleehé* the Changing Woman made her way to the summit of *Ch'óol'į́'į́* the Giant Spruce Mountain and sat down on a rock.

She recognized that spot well. It was where she had lain when

she was all alone and wished for a consort. It was where she had
first felt the warmth of the sun deep within her body.

And as she sat there recollecting, *Jóhonaa'éí* the Sun arrived and
placed himself beside her.

He sought to embrace her.

But she struggled to free herself.

As she did so she said these words to him:

"What do you mean by molesting me so?" she said to him.

"I want no part of you!"

To which he gave her this reply:

"I mean simply that I want you for my own," he replied.

"I mean that I want you to come to the west and make a home
for me there."

"But I wish to do no such thing," replied she.

"By what right do you make such a request of me?"

Said he then:

"Did I not give your sons the weapons they needed to slay
Naayéé' the Alien Monsters? Have I not done a great deal for you
and your people, in truth? In truth, shouldn't you reward me for
what I have done?

Answered she then:

"But I was not the one who asked for those weapons. It was not I
who asked for your help. What you gave you gave of your own free
will. I owe you no reward."

Following her words there was a distance of silence.

Then he tried to embrace her again, offering yet another reason
for allowing himself to do so:

"When our son *Naayéé' neizghání* the Monster Slayer last
visited me, he promised you to me."

And again she struggled to free herself, offering yet another
objection:

"What do I care for promises made by someone else in my
behalf? I make my own promises or else there are no promises to
be made. I speak for myself or else I am not spoken for. I alone
decide what I shall do or else I do nothing."

Hearing which words he sighed, stood up, took four paces apart
from her, and then turned suddenly to face her.

And this is what he said to her:

"Please!" he said to her.

"Come with me to the west and make a home for me.

"I am lonely.

"Each day I labor long and hard alone in the sky. I have no one to talk with. I have no companion for my nights.

"What good is all that I do if I must endure my days and nights all alone? What use is male without female? What use is female without male? What use are we two without one another?"[78]

That is what *Jóhonaa'éí* the Sun said to *Asdzáá nádleehé* the Changing Woman.

She did not answer him at once, leaving another space of silence between his words and her reply.

Then at last she spoke. And this is what she said to him at last:

"You have a beautiful house in the east I am told," she said to him.

"I want just such a house in the west.

"I want it built floating on the shimmering water, away from the shore, so that when the Earth-Surface people multiply they will not bother me with their quarrels.

"And I want all sorts of gems.

"I want white shell. I want blue shell. I want turquoise. I want haliotis. I want soapstone, agate, redstone, jet.

"Such things I want planted around my house so that I may enjoy their beauty.[79]

"Since I wish to live there without my sister and without our sons, I will be lonely while you are gone each day. So I will want animals to keep me company.

Give me elk. Give me buffalo. Give me deer. Give me long-tails. Give me mountain sheep, jackrabbits, prairie dogs, muskrats.[80]

"Provide me with those things and I shall go with you to the west."

That is what *Asdzáá nádleehé* the Changing Woman said to *Jóhonaa'éí* the Sun. And this is how he replied:

"What do you mean by making such demands of me?" he replied.

"Why should I provide you with all of those things?"

This time she answered him quickly. And this is what she said to him:

"I will tell you why," she said to him.

"You are male and I am female.

"You are of the sky and I am of the earth.

"You are constant in your brightness, but I must change with the seasons.

"You move constantly at the very edge of heaven, while I must remain fixed in one place.

"Remember that I willingly let you send your rays into my body. Remember that I gave birth to your son, enduring pain to bring him into the world. Remember that I gave that child growth and protected him from harm. Remember that I taught him to serve his people unselfishly so that he would willingly fight the Alien Monsters.[81]

"Remember, as different as we are, you and I, we are of one spirit. As dissimilar as we are, you and I, we are of equal worth. As unlike as you and I are, there must always be solidarity between the two of us. Unlike each other as you and I are, there can be no harmony in the universe as long as there is no harmony between us.[82]

"If there is to be such harmony, my requests must matter to you. My needs are as important to me as yours are to you. My whims count as much as yours do. My fidelity to you is measured by your loyalty to me. My response to your needs is to reflect the way you respond to mine. There is to be nothing more coming from me to you than there is from you to me. There is to be nothing less."

That is what *Asdzą́ą́ nádleehé* the Changing Woman said to *Jóhonaa'éí* the Sun there on the summit of *Ch'óol'į́'į́* the Giant Spruce Mountain.

At first he gave no reply. He took time to weigh carefully all things that she had said.

Then, slowly, thoughfully, he drew close to her.

Slowly and thoughtfully he placed his arm around her.

And this time she allowed him to do so.

Whereupon he promised her that all the things she wished for she would have. She would have a house in the west on the shimmering water. She would have gems whose beauty she could enjoy. She would have animals to keep her company. All that she wanted she would have.

So it is that she agreed; they would go to a place in the west where they would dwell together in the solid harmony of kinship.

•   •   •   •

When *Asdzą́ą́ nádleehé* the Changing Woman was ready to depart for her new home in the west, *Hadahoniye' dine'é* the Mirage People and *Hadahoneestiin dine'é* the Ground Mist People were instructed to go with her. They were two groups of Holy People assembled to help her drive the animals that would keep her company.

She then bid farewell to her sister *Yoołgai asdzą́ą́* and to their two sons *Naayéé' naizghání* and *Tó bájísh chíní.*

"I have finished with childbearing," she said to them.

"And I have finished rearing children.

"I shall leave now and dwell with your Father *Jóhonaa'éí nitaa'* the Sun.

"You are grown men now, and you have done much for your people and for the five-fingered Earth Surface People who will soon occupy this world. You need parents no longer, so I am no longer necessary here."

And so saying, she left them to go to her new home in the west.[83]

She set forth with gods and animals accompanying her. Together they passed over the mountains at *Béésh łichíí'*, or Red Knife Summit as we would call it in the language of *Bilagáana* the White Man. There the herd trampled down the earth so that they formed a pass. That way the journey back and forth across the mountains would be easier.

They halted in the *Ch'íńlį* valley to celebrate the betrothal of *Asdzą́ą́ nádleehé* the Changing Woman to *Jóhonaa'éí* the Sun. Whereupon her hips widened and her breasts filled out. She grew more beautiful in her womanhood so that she and her husband would flourish in the company of one another.

Thereupon, also, the animals began to increase rapidly.[84] Soon the herd was so large that it trampled a deep pass over the summit of *Dziłíjiin*, or Black Mountain as we would call it in the language of *Bilagáana.* So deep was the pass that its bottom was almost level with the surrounding plain.

There many of the buffalo broke loose from the main herd and drifted eastward to the country of the broad prairie. They never returned to *Asdzą́ą́ nádleehé* the Changing Woman, and for all we know they roam the plains beyond the Great Stone Mountains to this very day.[85]

Likewise the elks increased in numbers until many of them left the main herd and drifted north, never to return. Likewise antelope, deer, and other animals left the herd and drifted off. Ever since then they have populated the mountains and the valleys, the meadows and the plains. They dwell on the land in great numbers, testifying to the affection that was to grow between *Asdzą́ą́ nádleehé* the Changing Woman and *Jóhonaa'éí* the Sun.

The original herd of livestock remained with her, however, and she presides over a household rich with animals to this very day.

•   •   •   •

Four days after they departed from the valley of *Ch'íńlį́*, *Asdzą́ą́ nádleeshé* and her retinue arrived at *Dook'o'oosłííd*, or San Francisco Mountain as we would call it in the language of the White Man.

Here they stopped to perform another ceremony. They laid *Asdzą́ą́ nádleehé* the Changing Woman across the very top of the mountain with her head to the west, because that is where she was to go to dwell with her husband. And they manipulated her body and stretched out her limbs. This ceremony she bid the people perform in the future for all Navajo maidens when the path of childhood becomes the trail of womanhood. Which is why the people perform the ritual of *kinaaldá* to this very day. To this very day they seek to mould the body of a maiden into the perfect form of *Asdzą́ą́ nádleehé* the Changing Woman, wife of *Jóhonaa'éí* the Sun.[86]

What happened on the rest of the journey from *Dook'o'oosłííd*, where the San Francisco Peaks stand, to the great ocean in the west is not known. But it is known that *Asdzą́ą́ nádleehé* finally arrived there to dwell in her floating house beyond the shore. There she lives to this very day. And there *Jóhonaa'éí* the Sun rejoins her each evening when his daily journey across the sky is completed.

Occasionally, however, he does not return. On dark stormy days when the wind blows and the sky is black with overcast clouds, he keeps to his home in the east and sends serpents of lightning to try to brighten the heavens.[87] Often these serpents create great mischief in the absence of harmony between *Jóhonaa'éí* and *Asdzą́ą́ nádleehé*. The whole world suffers when that conjugal solidarity is lost.

•   •   •   •

After *Asdzą́ą́ nádleehé* the Changing Woman had departed to go with her husband *Jóhonaa'éí* the Sun, her son *Naayéé' neizghání* the Monster Slayer and his brother *Tó bájísh chíní* the Water Born went as they were bid by their father to *Tó aheedlí*, where two rivers come together in the valley of the San Juan.[88]

There they made a dwelling for themselves, and there they live to this very day. There we may sometimes see their reflection when, after a summer rain which brings the rainbow, the mist rises from the water as the sky clears. The bright colors shimmer in the moist light and the forms of the monster-slaying twins materialize.

To this very day the Navajo people go there to pray. But they do not pray for rain at that place, and they do not pray for good crops. They do not pray for their livestock to flourish or for success in hunting. They pray only for victory over their enemies at that place. They go there to pray only when they recognize the need to restore order and harmony in the world, it is said.

All of these things happend a long, long time ago, it is said.

PART FOUR

Gathering of the Clans[1]

One

Of a time long, long ago these things too are said.

It is said that before she departed for her home in the west, *Asdzą́ą́ nádleehé* took leave of her sister *Yoołgai asdzą́ą́* the White Shell Woman. In saying good-bye this is what she told her:

"I must leave you now, *shideezhí* my younger sister," she told her.

"But before I go, consider what you want to do now."

And this is what *Yoołgai asdzą́ą́* replied to *Asdzą́ą́ nádleehé* the Changing Woman:

"I shall miss you, *shádí* my older sister," she replied.

"I have thought about what I now want to do.

"More than anything else, I want to go back to *Dibé nitsaa* in the San Juan Mountains. I want to dwell in the place where our people came from."

But you will be lonely there," said *Asdzą́ą́ nádleehé* the Changing Woman.

"Sooner or later you will crave someone to keep you company."

Nevertheless, *Yoołgai aasdzą́ą́* insisted that she wanted nothing more than to return to the place she considered her home. And when *Asdzą́ą́ nádleehé* the Changing Woman left for the west her young sister turned east toward *Dibé nitsaa*.

Naayéé' neizghání the Monster Slayer and *Tó bájísh chíní* the Water Born accompanied her as far as *Tó ahidiiłį* the Place Where Two Waters Join in the valley of the San Juan River where they chose to dwell. And from there she journeyed alone into the mountains.

•   •   •   •

281

Once she was among the slopes and ridges surrounding the summit of *Dibé nitsaa*, she went first of all to a place just east of *Hajíínéí* the Emergence Place. Today that place bears the name *Dził łahdilt'éhé*, which in the language of *Bilagáana* the White Man means Single Mountain. By day she remained on the side of the slope, and at night she climbed to the top to sleep.

The next day she went to a mountain south of the place where the people had emerged called *Dził nidilt'éhé*, which means Two Mountains. While the sun was in the sky she roamed the slopes, and when darkness fell she climbed to the summit to sleep. But she began to feel lonely, and as she lay looking at the stars she began to consider what she would have to do to acquire company.

On the third day she went to a mountain west of the place where the people had emerged called *Dził tált'éhé*, or Three Mountains as it would now be called. There she wandered around while the sun crossed the sky and gave her light; and after the sky became fully dark she made her way to the highest peak to sleep. And as she lay awaiting slumber she began to wish that she had considered her sister's words more carefully. For indeed she had become lonely.

On the fourth day she walked aimlessly around a mountain north of the emergence place called *Dził dįįlt'éhé*, or Four Mountains as people would now call it in English. While the sun gave her light to see she looked absentmindedly at the ruins there. But after darkness fully covered the earth she climbed to the highest point of the mountain to try to sleep. But she could not, for her thoughts dwelled constantly on her loneliness, which hung upon her like pain.

On the morning of the fifth day she came down to the shores of the lake which surrounded *Hajíínéí* the Emergence Place. And there she built a simple brush shelter for herself.

"I may as well stay here," she said to herself.

"What good is it to wander around when I have no one to keep me company?"

And as she sat up late into the night wondering how long she would choose to remain alone where she was, she thought of her sister far to the west.

She thought of the twelve people who had gone with *Asdzą́ą́ nádleehé* the Changing Woman.

She thought about the gods dwelling among the mountains scattered in the distance all around her.

She thought that perhaps she would fare as well by going to live with one or another of them.

But then she wondered if it weren't the company of *Nihookáá' dine'é* the Earth Surface People she longed for.

And thinking such thoughts, she fell at last into a restless, fitful sleep.

●　　●　　●　　●

In the morning she was awakened by a familiar sound.

"*Wu'hu'hu'hu'*," she heard far to the east, so far away that she could scarcely make it out. But she listened nonetheless and patiently waited.

Soon she heard the voice again, nearer and louder than before. "*Wu'hu'hu'hu'*," it repeated, this time somewhat more distinctly.

She continued to listen and wait, listen and wait, and now she heard the voice a third time. "*Wu'hu'hu'hu'*," it repeated, all the nearer now and all the more distinct.

Continuing to listen, she heard it again, even louder than the last time. "*Wu'hu'hu'hu'*," so close now that it seemed directly upon her. Until at last she beheld the kindly face of *Haashch'éélti'í* the Talking God. And this is what she heard him ask her:

"How is it that you managed to survive the destruction of the *Naayeé!*" she heard him ask.

"Where were you while they ravaged the land and devoured the people?"

That is what *Haashch'éélti'í* the Talking God asked her. And this is what she said to him in reply:

"I was at *Dził ná'oodiłii* the Banded Rock Mountain," she said in reply.

"I hid there with my sister.

"But for five nights since the monsters were destroyed I have been all alone in these mountains.

"At first I did not mind the solitude very much.

"But on each day it bothered me more. Until at last I realized how lonely I was.

"Now I long for mortal company. And my longing hangs on my body like pain.

"Tell me *shicheii* my grandfather, where do you come from? Do you, too, dwell there alone? Are you, too, lonely? Or are there others like you where you live?"

Replied *Haashch'ééłti'í* the Talking God, "I come from among the cliffs at *Tséyi'*, where many of the gods dwell.

"And although I am not alone like you are, I understand your loneliness. Indeed, I pity you *sitsói* my grandchild.

"Stay here where you are for four more days. After they pass I shall return. I shall bring your sister *Asdzáá nádleehé* the Changing Woman with me, along with certain others. When I come again, you will understand the purpose of my visit."

Upon saying which, he departed.

• • • •

After *Haashch'ééłti'í* the Talking God left, *Yoołgai asdzáá* the White Shell Woman built a new dwelling for herself.

This one was better than the simple brush shelter she had built before. It was sturdier and more comfortable. It had a window that faced the west and a door which opened to the east.

She swept the floor of it clean. She made a soft bed of grass and leaves in it, it is said.

Two

It is also said that four days passed and four times the night went by. The sun rose and set four times, and four times the moon passed overhead. And at dawn on the fifth day *Yoołgai asdzáá* the White Shell Woman heard the call not of one voice but of two.

Four times she heard those voices. She heard them faintly at first. Then she heard them nearer and louder. Then she heard them still more distinctly. And she finally heard them so clearly that they seemed directly upon her. Until she beheld two gods this time. She beheld *Haashch'ééłti'í* the Talking God and she beheld *Haashch'éoghan* the Growling God.

Since the sky was very dark on this particularly hazy morning she did not at once recognize the others who had arrived with the two gods. Their forms were only faintly visible in the heavy mist.

Those who had come had already positioned themselves east of

the lodge she had built. The Holy People from *Sisnaajiní* the Sierra
Blanca Peak stood furthest east. Those of *Tsoodził* the Blue Bead
Mountain stood furthest south. Those of *Dook'o'oosłííd* the Water
Cloud Mountain stood furthest to the west. And those of *Dibé
nitsaa* the Mountain Sheep Mountain placed themselves at the
northern extreme of the circle they all formed.[2]

Once she saw how they had all placed themselves, *Yoołgai
asdzą́ą́* took a place at the western edge of the formation. But just
as she did, her sister *Asdzą́ą́ nádleehé* spoke to her:

"Do not stand there," she said.

"Stand over there to the east instead. My place is in the west."

Whereupon the younger of the two sisters did as she was told.
And she was ready to observe the ensuing ceremony.

Asdzą́ą́ nádleehé the Changing Woman had brought two sacred
blankets with her. One of these was *diłhił náskad*, or the dark
embroidery as it would be called in the language of *Bilagáana*. The
other was *łigai náskad*, or the white embroidery as the White Man
would call it in his language.

Meanwhile, *Haashch'éełti'í* the Talking God had brought two
sacred buckskins with him. And the divine couple *Naaki naa'aash*
had also come. They walked together and stood arm in arm,
bringing with them two ears of corn. One of those ears was yellow
and the other was white. The female carried both of them in a
turquoise dish.

And now *Haashch'éełti'í* the Talking God carefully laid the
sacred blankets on the ground.

Over one of these he spread one of the sacred buckskins with its
head to the west. From the turquoise dish in which the divine
female partner held the two ears of corn he took the white one and
handed it to *Tséghádi'nídínii ashkii* the Rock Crystal Boy of the
Eastern Mountain. And from the same dish he took the yellow ear
and handed it to *Naadą́łtsoii at'ééd* the Yellow Corn Girl of the
Western Mountain.

These Holy People laid the ears on the buckskin. The yellow one
they laid with its tip pointing toward the west. The white one they
laid with its tip pointing toward the east. Then they backed away.

Then *Haashch'éełti'í* the Talking God stepped forward. He
picked up the ears and placed them carefully against the buckskin
with both tips facing east. But he did not let them actually touch
anything.

And as he held them thus, he uttered his cry.

"*Wu'hu'hu'hu'*," he cried.

Then he nearly laid them down, handling them so that they scarcely touched the buckskin.

And as he held them thus, he uttered the cry of *Haashch'éoghan* the Growling God.

"*Ha wa u'uu*," he cried.

Similarly he pointed the ears to the west, again being careful to allow them barely to touch the buckskin.

And as he held them that way he called out again in his own behalf.

"*Wu'hu'hu'hu'*," he called.

Finally he pointed the ears toward the north, being just as careful as he had been to allow them barely to touch. And holding them that way he called out again in behalf of *Haashch'éoghan* the Growling God.

"*Ha wa u'uu*," he called.

So it was that the two ears were made to face each of the four cardinal directions. The white ear was made to face all four points, and the yellow ear was made to face all four.

And so it now is that the Navajo people never abide in one dwelling like the Pueblo peoples do. Instead they migrate constantly from place to place, from place to place. So, too, is it that the Navajo people never dwell in villages like the Pueblo peoples do. They live in small homes scattered across the land, often at great distances from one another.

Over the ears of corn *Haashch'éélti'í* the Talking God finally laid the other sacred buckskin with its head to the east.

Then *Nítch'i* the Wind entered between the two skins.

Soon thereafter *Haashch'éélti'í* raised the topmost of the two buckskins slightly so that he could peer inside the space between them.

But he quickly lowered it again. Apparently what was to happen had not yet happened.

He waited a few minutes more.

Then he again raised the topmost of the buckskins slightly so that he could again peer in between them.

But he quickly lowered it again, saying nothing.

For a few minutes more he waited.

And once again he raised the top buckskin slightly so that he could again peer in.

Once again he lowered it.

Once again did he raise the top skin and look in.

But this time he did not lower it.

This time he held the two skins apart for a longer while. For this time he saw that the white ear of corn had been changed into a man. And he saw this time that the yellow ear had likewise become a woman.

It was the wind that had given life to these two *Nihookáá' dine'é,* or five-fingered Earth Surface People as *Bilagáana* the White Man would identify them.

It was the very same wind who had similarly breathed life into many *Haashch'ééh dine'é,* or Holy People as *Bilagáana* would call them.

Nítch'i the Wind had entered between the heads of the two buckskins and had made his way through all four legs of both, thus transforming those ears of corn into two mortals.

It is the very same wind that gives those of us who dwell in the world today the breath that we breathe.

The trail of that very same wind can actually be seen in our fingertips to this day.

That very same wind has likewise created our ancestors ever since.

That very same wind continues to blow inside of us until we die.

•　　•　　•　　•

Once *Nítch'i* the Wind gave human life to the white ear of corn and to the yellow ear, *Tséghádi'nídínii ashkii* the Rock Crystal Boy of the Eastern Mountain furnished both the male and the female Earth Surface People with a mind. Then *Naadą́łtsoii at'ééd* the Yellow Corn Girl of the Western Mountain gave them a voice.

And when *Haashch'ééłti'í* the Talking God finally threw off the top buckskin, a dark cloud descended and covered the bodies of the new pair like a blanket.

Whereupon *Yoołgai asdzą́ą́* the White Shell Woman led them into her hogan, rejoicing as she did so. And as she did, the assembled gods all began silently to disperse.

Haashch'ééłti'í the Talking God departed with the others. But before he left he promised her that he would return again in four days.

•　　•　　•　　•

There were no songs sung during this event, and no prayer was uttered. Furthermore, all of it was performed well within the space of a single day.

The dwelling that *Yoołgai asdzą́ą́* the White Shell Woman had built and into which she ushered the first mortal couple still stands. Anyone who wishes to journey to that sacred place may still see it.

However, since it has long since been transformed into a little hill it is not easily recognized. Look at it carefully, lest you mistake it for a small mound of earth.

•   •   •   •

By the time this story was first written down seven subsequent generations of men living to a ripe old age have come and gone. And since that first printed record was made another generation of long-lived Earth Surface People has come and gone.[3]

So you can see now how long ago the Earth Surface People who call themselves the Navajo began their existence as a nation, it is said.

Three

It is also said that *Haashch'ééłti'í* returned four days later as he promised he would. As usual he announced his arrival by crying out four times, faintly at first, then louder and nearer, then more distinctly, and finally so loudly that his presence seemed very near at hand.

When she heard his very first call, *Yoołgai asdzą́ą́* the White Shell Woman bid the young people awaken, saying these words to them:

"Get up *sha'áłchíni* my children," said she during his very first call.

"Get up and make a fire.

"It is *Haashch'ééłti'í* the Talking God you hear. He has come to see us all."

With him he brought another couple. He brought *Hadahoniye' ashkii* the Sky Mirage Boy, and he brought *Hadahoneestiin at'ééd* the Ground Mist Girl. And when he arrived he gave *Yooɫgai asdzą́ą́* the White Shell Woman two ears of corn.

"Grind these," he told her.

"But grind them only one grain at a time."

That was all he said to her. And so saying, he departed.

After he had left, *Yooɫgai asdzą́ą́* the White Shell Woman spoke to the couple who had come with him and who remained behind. And this is what she told them:

"This young man that you see and this young woman with him were made out of corn.

"They cannot marry one another, for they are brother and sister.

Yet they must bring children into this world if there are to be other people like them.

"Surely it is that way with you as well. So perhaps each of you can marry each of them."

Which is how the first mortal couple were married. The young man who had been transformed from an ear of white corn married *Hadahoneestiin at'ééd* the Ground Mist Girl. And the young girl who had been transformed from an ear of yellow corn married *Hadahoniye' ashkii* the Mirage Boy. And soon thereafter each couple bore one boy and one girl.

When these offspring had grown big enough to walk and to run, the entire group moved away from *Hajíínéí* the Emergence Place. They went to *Tsé ɫigaii íí'áhí*, or White Standing Rock as it would be called in the language of *Bilagáana* the White Man.

Once there, the two men took to hunting each day, seeking out rabbits, rats, and other varieties of small game. And it was on such game that they chiefly lived.

From those first people are descended the clan known as *Tséníjíkiní*, or Honeycombed Rock People as they would be called in the language of *Bilagáana*.[4] They are called that because the gods who created the very first couple out of the two ears of corn emerged from the honeycombed recesses of the dark cliff houses of *Tséyi'*. It was from that very place that they brought forth the two ears of corn out of which two breathing, speaking people were made.

•   •   •   •

For thirteen years the Honeycombed Rock People lived at *Tsé ɫigaii íí'áhí* where the white rock stands. There they flourished as they could and increased their numbers. But during that time they saw no sign that any other people existed. Until one night they observed the gleam of a fire far off in the distance.

All night long and all of the next day they searched eagerly for the source of that gleam. But they could not find it.

The next night they saw it again at what seemed to be the very same spot where they had seen it before. And for the rest of the night and for all of the next day they searched again for its source, looking more intensely than they had looked the previous day. But they searched in vain, for they found nothing.

On the third night, when the distant gleam again shone through the darkness, they determined that somehow they would locate it. So they drove a forked stick into the ground. Then one of the men got down on his hands and knees, spread his limbs wide apart, and sighted the fire through the fork of the stick.

The next morning he carefully placed his hands and knees in the impressions he had made the night before. And he assumed the very same position, So doing, he looked through the fork again. His gaze was thus guided to a little wooded hollow on the side of a far-off mountain.

Another of the men then walked to that wooded area at the base of the mountain there in the distance. He entered the hollow, which was so small it could easily be searched in a very short time. But he discovered no trace of anyone having ever been there. He saw no fire. He saw no ashes. He saw no human tracks. He saw no evidence of any kind of human presence.

On the fourth night, all of the adults in the group sighted the fire's distant twinkle through the forked stick. And in the morning when they again looked they agreed that they had all sighted the same little grove on the same side of the same mountain.

"How strange!" declared the man who had ventured over there the day before.

"It is a small place, easily combed from one edge to the next.

"Yet search as I might, I found no sign of life there. I saw no fire. I saw no ashes. I saw no human tracks. I saw no sign whatever of anyone's presence.

"I did not see as much as a drop of water that would reflect a star's ray or a moonbeam."

Then all of the males in the clan, men and boys alike, decided that they would venture to the grove together and explore it again. But between them all they could discover not so much as a trace of human life. Sadly they decided that they might as well turn back.

But just as they were about to leave the grove, one of them heard the voice of *Nít̲ch'i* the Wind whispering in his ear.

"This desert terrain deceives your eyes," whispered *Nít̲ch'i*.

"The light you see at night is one that shines through a narrow cleft in the mountain not easy to find.

"Cross the ridge there on the far side of this wooded area, and you will soon find what it is that you seek."

They did what *Nít̲ch'i* the Wind bid them do. And before they had gone far over the ridge he spoke about, they spied the footprints of adult men. Soon thereafter they found the footprints of grown women. Not long after that they found the footprints of younger people. And then they found the footprints of very small children.

Then, at last, to the surprise of none of them by that time, they came to a small encampment of five-fingered Earth Surface People like themselves.

One party rejoiced as much as the other. They embraced each other and hurled greetings back and forth.

"Where do you come from?" asked members of one band.

"What are your origins?" asked members of the other.

"We come from *Tsé t̲igaii íí'áhí*," cried those in the newly arrived group. "From the Place Where the White Rock Stands we come."

"Our last resting place was at *Tó nidoots'os*, the Place Where the Channel Narrows," cried those in the newly found group. "It is a poor country where we could scarcely find game.

"We survived only on ducks and snakes there.

"We have been here at this place for only a few days, and we fare scarcely any better than we did where we came from.

"Now we live only on ground rats, on prairie dogs, on whatever wild berries our women are able to gather, and on the few seeds our children are able to find."

The new party consisted of but twelve people. There were five men. There were three women. There was one grown girl and one grown boy.[5] And there were two very small children.

"Come with us," cried the menfolk of *Tséníjíkiní* the Honeycombed Rock Clan.

"Perhaps we fare somewhat better than you do, although by not very much.

"But you are welcome to travel the path we travel, to rest where we rest, to hunt where we hunt and to share that which we have."

And so saying, they took the strangers back with them, where *Yoołgai asdzą́ą́* the White Shell Woman welcomed them, saying these words:

"*Ahaláane' sha'áłchíní,*" she said.

"My poor, woebegone children.

"I greet you.

"I welcome you as if you were my own."

The place where the people of *Tséníjíkiní* found the strangers is called *Tsétł'ahnii,* or Rock Corner Place as it would be identified today. Accordingly, they were given the name *Tsétł'ahnii dine'é,* which means Rock Corner People. And from that group the present Navajo clan called by that name descends, it is said.[6]

Four

It is also said that on the morning following the arrival of the newcomers, *Haashch'éélti'í* the Talking God came again to the home of *Yoołgai asdzą́ą́* the White Shell Woman. But he took her aside where no one could hear his words. Nor did she reveal to anyone what he said.

Three days later he came back again. Again they talked where no one could overhear them. And again she was silent about what had been spoken between them.

By that time it had become her custom to sleep with one of the little girls of the clan. This child was a favorite of hers and her constant companion. And shortly after *Haashch'éélti'í* departed following his second of the two most recent visits, *Yoołgai asdzą́ą́* the White Shell Woman had this to say to the child:

"I am going to leave you," she said to her.

"The gods of *Tséyi'* have sent for me.

"But I shall not forget your people any more than I shall forget you *sitsóí* my grandchild.

"I will come often to see them. And I shall watch over them, just as I shall always be watching over you. Their need for me is no longer great. They are growing stronger as a people. They are learning to control the things of this world."

So spoke *Yoołgai asdzą́ą́* the White Shell Woman. And so saying, she disappeared as if she had vanished into the air.

When the people awoke the next morning they searched everywhere for her. But try as they might they could not find her. And they began to wonder if she had not gone to *Tséyi'*, if she might not remain there for a while, and if she might not finally make her way to *Dibé nitsaa* the Place of Mountain Sheep.

Then, four nights after her departure, the young girl had a dream.

In that dream *Yoołgai asdzą́ą́* the White Shell Woman came to her, stood before her, smiled, and then spoke these words:

"*Sitsóí* my grandchild," she spoke.

"It is as your people have supposed.

"I have indeed gone to *Tséyi'*.

"From there I will go to *Dibé nitsaa* the Place of Mountain Sheep, where I will dwell forever in the house of white shell which *Haashch'ééh dine'é* the Holy People have prepared for me.

"I would have gladly taken you there with me. But your parents also love you and they would mourn in your absence. Such is the way of *Nihookáá' dine'é* the five-fingered Earth Surface People. Since they live but for a short time in this world they suffer bitterly over the loss of those they love.

"So I am leaving you behind.

"Do not think that you will never see me again.

"But do not think either that when you do see me I will appear in the form that has grown familiar to you. Instead, look for me in some other form.

"Look for me when it rains.

"You will see me in the gentle showers of the female rain. You will see me there when it falls near your dwelling. You will see me in the moisture that it brings. Perhaps you will even see me in the crops that grow because of that gentle rain."[7]

That is what *Yoołgai asdzą́ą́* said to the young girl in a dream. And that is precisely what the child repeated to the others in the morning when she awoke.

Yoołgai asdzą́ą́ was no longer to be among them in her familiar way, she told them. But she would dwell with them in a new way.

•　•　•　•

While the small assembly of clans was at *Tsé łigaii íí'áhí* Where the White Rock Stands, the men had hunted everywhere for meat. But they could find very little.

Some of them who had been to a place called *Tó dik'ǫzhí* which *Bilagáana* the White Man would call Saline Water in his language. It was a better place to hunt, they thought. There porcupines could be found. Rats could be found. Prairie dogs could be found in abundance. Many kinds of seed-bearing plants grew there. High on the mesas surrounding that place larger game might even be found.

So the people moved there. But they remained for only a few days at that place, for they were not satisfied with the quantity of food they managed to obtain. Instead they decided to move on to *Chá'ałhaashzhéé'*. Today nobody can say what that name means in the language of *Bilagáana* the White Man. There, suggested some of them, they might be able to plant crops of their own.

So they planted some grains of corn, taken from the ears that *Haashch'éełti'í* the Talking God had given to *Yoołgai asdzą́ą́* the White Shell Woman. These were the same ears that she had in turn passed on to them, which they had kept ever since, waiting for the right time to put them to use.

As they had been taught, they removed one grain at a time from the ears. And they planted the grains with great care. Indeed, they discovered what prolific seeds those grains were when placed properly into the ground and when nourished properly by the gentle female rain. For it yielded stalks which grew out of the earth and reached toward the blue sky. Each stalk yielded several ears, and each ear was richly laden with moist kernels.

Furthermore, each grain could be dried and ground, and when ground properly it produced meal. Together the grains of a single stalk produced meal in large portions, and each portion lasted those who ground it for many days.

•　　•　　•　　•

When they had been at *Chá'ałhaashzhéé'* for fourteen years, the people were joined by another group. These newcomers came from the sacred mountain of *Dził ná'oodiłii*. Thus they were called *Dził ná'oodiłnii*, or the Travelers Circle Clan.

And they would be considered holy people. For they had no traditions to recite and they could not account for their origins. Hence it was understood that they must somehow have escaped the ravages of the *Naayéé'*, perhaps by virtue of help from the gods.

At first the people from *Dził ná'oodiłii* the Travelers Circle

Mountain did not camp with the others. Instead they dwelled apart, often sending their children to borrow pots or stones for grinding corn. Eventually, however, they joined the main group and behaved as if they were all one people.

The newcomers dug among old ruins and found pots and stone axes. Soon they were able to cook like the others and build like the others. Soon they could hunt like the others and grow like the others. Soon their homes were the same and their clothes were the same; their tools were the same and their hunting gear was the same. It was only a matter of time before they came to be considered members of the same tribe with the same traditions and the same ways.

• • • •

Seven years after the arrival of the *Dził ná'oodiłnii,* a fourth clan joined the Navajos. These newcomers said that for many years they had been seeking the Travelers Circle Mountain People everywhere, for they had long since discovered traces of them.

Sometimes they would find the trampled bushes where a group had camped. Sometimes they found deserted brush shelters, often with some of the limbs still green. Sometimes they would arrive so soon after the people they sought had left that all of the boughs were still green. And sometimes they could still see footprints on the ground and feel warmth in the embers of burnt-out campfires. Meanwhile, they became more and more eager to encounter people like themselves in such a desolate land. But then all traces of activity would be lost to them, and they wondered if they would ever meet anyone else.

Now they rejoiced to meet the people they had sought for so long a time.

These newcomers camped close to *Dził ná'oodiłnii* the Travelers Circle Mountain People. And soon they discovered that like themselves they bore red arrow-holders which were very similar to their own. No other clan had arrow-holders like these, which led them all to consider themselves kinsmen.

The strangers said that they had just come from a place called *Hashk'ąą hadzohó,* which would be called Yucca Strung Out In a Line. And they said further that they would be content to be called *Hashk'ąą hadzohó dine'é,* the Yucca Strung Out In a Line Clan, it is said.

Five

It is also said that fourteen years after the arrival of the *Hashk'ąą hadzohó dine'é,* the growing Navajo tribe moved on to *Kin nteel* the Broad House Place in the Chaco Canyon and occupied the ruins there. They spent their first night camped in small groups. So they made many fires and attracted the attention of a group of strangers encamped on a distant mountain.

The next day these strangers came down to the valley to see who these people were who were so numerous they needed that many fires. Like *Dził ná'oodiłnii* the Travelers Circle Mountain People who had arrived earlier, these newcomers had no traditions to recite and no origins to account for.

They had recently come from *Nihoobá,* they said, which *Bilagáana* the White Man would call Where the Gray Streak Ends in the language he speaks. Thus the Navajos called them *Nihoobáanii* the Gray Streak Clan and bid them join the tribe, which they gladly did.

These people were the fifth group to join the growing Navajo nation. They arrived in the autumn when the yucca plants were drying. The leaves were turning yellow. They fell from the aspens, curled on the ground, and gave way to the frost. Whereupon the whole tribe moved from the higher elevations down to the banks of the San Juan River.

They settled at a place called *Tsintóbétłoh,* which in the language of *Bilagáana* the White Man means Tree Sweeping Water. It is given that name because there the long branches of a peculiar white tree overhang the stream and sweep the surface as the swift current carries the water down. There is no such tree anywhere else in the land.

Here in this valley they decided they would stay. For here it seemed they could plant seeds and grow crops. So they built warm huts to shelter themselves against the winter weather. And during the remainder of the fall and all winter long, weather permitting, they worked the bottomlands.

They cleared the ground of anything that would hamper growth. They grubbed up roots. They readied the soil for seeds. And they fashioned what tools they could. The older clans camped downstream while the newer ones camped up. They all helped each other as they prepared the soil for planting in the spring.

•

When the tribe had been living for six years at *Tsintóbétłoh*
where the tree's branches swept the swiftly flowing water, a band
joined them from a place called *Tsi'naajin*, which means Dark
Streak of Wood. Hence they were given the name *Tsi'naajinii*, or
Dark Streak of Wood Clan. The people of the Navajo tribe observed
that among this group was a man who spoke majestically to the
others almost every morning and evening, and they all listened
attentively to his words.

At first the Navajos did not grasp the significance of this man's
relationship with the rest of the group. But gradually they learned
that the others relied on his wisdom and had confidence in what he
saw and heard. He was, they discovered, their cheif because of all
that he knew and because of his manner of persuading men and
women alike. By holding council with him all the people in that
group worked effectively together.

Nabiniłt'áhí was that man's name, which in the language of the
White Man means Something Inspired Him to Lecture.

•   •   •   •

While they lived in the valley of the San Juan River they amused
themselves with games. During the day they played *na'azhǫǫsh*
the hoop-and-pole game. And at night they played *késhjéé'* the
moccasin game.

In such a manner did they entertain themselves during those
crude times.

Together these peoples prospered as they forged their various
bands into a single tribe with a single set of ways. At the same
time they continued to live together very simply, just as each
group had lived simply before they began to merge.

As yet they did not have horses. They as yet had no sheep. They
did not as yet have goats. Indeed, they had no domestic animals of
any kind as yet.

Since their methods of hunting were crude as yet, they rarely
succeeded in killing deer or in slaying Rocky Mountain sheep. If
someone managed to secure larger game he did so by lying hidden
in one place for long spells of time, patiently waiting to ambush an
animal who came to graze. Occasionally a hunting party would

surround a fully grown doe or a larger buck and chase it until it
was exhausted. Or there were rare occasions when they could drive
one over a cliff.

In such a manner did they obtain meat during those simple times.

Whenever a man managed to acquire two skins of the larger
animals, he made a cloak of them by tying the forelegs of each
together over his shoulders. The women made cloaks by weaving
two webs of cedar bark and then lashing them together. One hung
in front and the other hung over her shoulders and down her back.
Men and women alike wore sandals made of yucca fiber or of
cedar bark.

They covered their heads with skins of weasels or of rats. The
tails hung down the backs of their necks. Often the headdresses
were decorated with artificial horns colored and fashioned out of
wood. Sometimes they would decorate them with the horns of
female mountain sheep ground thin.

Their blankets they wove out of cedar bark or yucca fiber. Or
when they hunted successfully and had some skins to spare, they
would sew these together.

In such a manner did they clothe themselves during these
early times.

At the front of each house outside the main entrance there stood
a long passageway. Over it they hung two coverings, one at the
outer end and one at the inner. These doors were also woven out of
cedar bark. During the months of winter they brought plenty of
wood inside. Then they closed both curtains and made their homes
warm before going to sleep.

In such a manner did they shelter themselves during these times
of learning.

Their bows were made of plain wood. As yet the Navajo people
had not learned to strengthen the backs of each bow with animal
fiber. Their arrows were made of reeds tipped with wood. As yet
not everyone was able to fashion an arrow entirely of wood.

The bottomland which they farmed was surrounded by high
cliffs. Both upstream and down the valley was hemmed in by
mighty bluffs which jutted down close to the river.

By and by the tribe became too large for everyone to dwell in this
narrow valley. Soon cropland was in short supply for so many
people in so narrow a space. So some of them moved up onto the
headlands to live. These people built storehouses of stone among
the cliffs. Others such as *Tsi'naajinii* the Dark Streak of Wood

People, went downstream beyond the lower peaks to grow their crops. Still others crossed the river and worked the land opposite the bank.

In such a manner did they learn to distribute themselves during those times of growing ability.[8]

•   •   •   •

Eight years after the *Tsi'naajinii* joined the tribe, a few members of one clan spied a few scattered fires on a distant slope north of the river one dark night.

Scouts were sent to see who it was who had camped out there. And soon they brought back word that a party of strangers had stopped at a place called *Ta'neeszah*. In the language of *Bilagáana* that name means a Tangle.

Those wanderers were invited to come and join the Navajo people, which they gladly did. And soon there was another clan added to the tribe. It became known as *Ta'neeszah dine'é* or the Tangle People. These newcomers said that they were descendants of *Hadahoniye' dine'é* the Mirage People. The remains of their old huts can still be seen at a Tangle by anyone who cares to look there.

•   •   •   •

Five years after the *Ta'neeszah dine'é* became a part of the Navajo nation another group joined the tribe. What gods sent them nobody knows. They came from a place originally called *Dziłtł'ah*, a name that means Mountain Cove in the language spoken today. So they were called *Dziłtł'ahnii* the Mountain Cove Clan.

These newcomers had headdresses, bows, arrows, and arrow holders similar to those of the Tangle People. Thus they supposed themselves kinsmen to them. And at once a close affinity grew between the two groups. So close did they become that now the members of the one clan cannot marry those of the other.

Dziłtł'ahnii the Mountain Cove People knew how to make wicker water-bottles, and they knew how to make carrying-baskets. They knew how to make earthen pots, and they knew how to make other useful vessels. Accordingly, they taught these skills to the others.

In such a manner did they add to their domestic arts in those time of increased learning.

•   •   •   •

Five years later another group joined them along the banks and
bluffs of the San Juan River. This was a numerous band which had
come originally from a place called *Tábąąh łigai*, a name that means
White Shore in the language of *Bilagáana*. It is very near to the spot
where the modern city of Santa Fe now stands.

From their old dwelling place these people had long gazed at the
mountains in the distance to the west where the Navajos lived.
They wondered if anyone could possibly live there. And if someone
did indeed dwell at that distant place, they wondered, would they
be at all like themselves? So at length they decided to go there
and see.

They journeyed westward for twelve days until they reached the
mountains. And once among them they traveled for eight more
days until they found the Navajos at last. Now that they were here,
they settled nearby at *Tó nidoots'os* Where the River Narrows.

For twelve years they lived there, subsisting on ducks and fish
instead of farming. During those years they became friendly with
the Navajos, often visiting among them and trading with them.
Even so, they found no evidence of kinship with them, so at first
they chose to live apart.

But one by one and family by family they moved closer to the
San Juan Valley to live. Many of them married into one or another
Navajo clan. Many learned to play Navajo games or to speak the
Navajo language. And many taught their own language to the
Navajos. By and by many of them became fully a part of the Navajo
nation. Until at last they formed a clan of their own called *Tábąąha*,
a name that means the Water's Edge Clan in the language that
Bilagáana the White Man speaks.

They moved closer to the banks and the bluffs of the San Juan
River and settled at a place called *Ha'atiin*, which would be called
Trail Leading Upward in the language of *Bilagáana* the White Man.
Here they found a smooth, sandy plain suitable for growing crops.

The people of *Tábąąha* the Water's Edge Clan also had a chief
whose knowledge and wisdom were useful to everyone. His name
was *Godtsoh*, which would be Big Knee in the language of
Bilagáana. He advised his people to set stakes around the sandy
plain to indicate to all others that they intended to plant there.

These newcomers were good hunters. They were skilled in
making weapons and skilled in putting them to use. They were
skilled in spotting game and skilled in catching it. As a result they

had many buckskins, which meant that they had also acquired skills in curing those skins and in sewing them. From them they made beautiful shirts and comfortable coats. And they gladly taught those skills to the other Navajo clans.

In such a manner did the people add to their ability to hunt and their ability to clothe themselves in those prospering times.

The language that the people of *Tábąąha* the Water's Edge Clan spoke was more like the modern Navajo language spoken today than that which members of the other clans spoke. For at this time their respective languages were not alike. Nor were they like languages spoken today. So less could be understood among them than is understood now.

Godtsoh and the chief of *Tsi'naajinii* the Dark Streak of Wood Clan often visited one another at night. And night after night for year after year they spoke together, the one to the other, for the purpose of uniting their different languages. They contrived to pick out the words in each tongue that seemed most suitable. Very often the words of the *Tábąąha* were considered the plainest and the best. But just as often the words used by the *Tsi'naajinii* were considered plain and good.

In such manner did the clans of the Navajo nation learn to speak together in those times of growing solidarity.

The *Tábąąhá* were good farmers whose crops grew in abundance. In fact, they were better growers than any of their neighbors were. Sometimes they were unable to harvest all that they grew, so skilled were they at working the soil. So sometimes they would let food lie ungathered in the field. They built stone storehouses something like those the Pueblos built among the cliffs. And in these they stored great amounts of corn. Those storehouses stand there to this very day for anyone who wishes to go there and see them, it is said.[9]

Six

It is also said that the *Tábąąhá* remained at *Ha'atiin* where the trail led upward for thirteen years. And during that time something happened which was to have a lasting impact on everyone who lives in that region to this very day.[10]

It seems that the great chief *Godtsoh* the Big Knee had taken twelve wives for himself.Four of these were from *Tsi'naajinii* the Dark Streak of Wood Clan. Four were from *Dziłtł'ahnii* the Mountain Cove Clan. And four were from *Ta'neeszah dine'é* the Tangle Clan.

He got these twelves wives by trading huge quantities of grain for them: grain from the abundant harvests that the *Tábąąhá* were able to reap. But such prolific giving did not impress his wives. Nor did it win their affection. For they were unfaithful to him.

He complained about their behavior to their various kinfolk and to the chiefs of all three clans. Those who heard his complaints disliked what the women were doing, although they did not especially like *Godtsoh*. However, adultery was a threat to the harmony needed in every marriage. So the kinsmen urged the wives to mend their ways. But they still continued to be unfaithful. Until at last the clan chiefs lost their patience with the women and summoned *Godtsoh*. And to him they had this to say:

"It may well be that you have done little to win the affection of your wives," they said to him.

"Nonetheless, what they do creates disorder.

"So you have our permission to punish these unfaithful women."

Whereupon *Godtsoh* the Big Knee cut out the genitals of the next wife who committed adultery in defiance of him. And as a consequence she died.

A second wife was undeterred by what had been done to the first, and she too committed adultery again. Whereupon *Godtsoh* cut the ears away from her head. And as a consequence she, too, died.

All the same, a third wife, undeterred by what had happened to the first and the second, also committed adultery again. Whereupon *Godtsoh* amputated her breasts. As a consequence she died, too.

Even so, a fourth wife was undeterred by what had happened to the other three. She, too, committed adultery again. Whereupon *Godtsoh* cut off her nose. She did not die as a consequence; instead she lived to be marked for the rest of her life as a woman guilty of infidelity.

Henceforth, decided *Godtsoh* the Big Knee, the punishment for adultery would be the removal of a nose. And the other men agreed.

But the remaining wives were not deterred by *Godtsoh*'s decree.

What he decided did not make any of them care for him any the more, and they all continued to sleep with other men. So before long each of the remaining wives was without a nose.

Soon after the twelfth wife lost her nose, they all joined together to contrive against their husband, so great had their hatred of *Godtsoh* and the other men become.

They made no secret of their intent to hurt him, and eventually he was afraid to share his lodge with any of them. By now he was sleeping alone each night no matter how many wives he had.

In spite of what he had done to deserve it, many of the people now felt sorry for the bad luck that had befallen him. So they arranged for a full nine-night ceremony for him. Perhaps then, thought they, the cause of his misfortune would be removed.

During the first eight nights of the chantway the mutilated women stayed by themselves in a hut. Bitterly, thay talked about *Godtsoh* the Big Knee's cruelty to them. And they talked just as bitterly about how quickly the other men gave in to *Godtsoh*. They would get even with their husband, they decided; and they would have their vengeance against all the men of the tribe.

"We will leave the Navajo people," they said to each other.

"We will go elsewhere.

"We are not slaves to be traded for grain.

"We are not game to be hunted and butchered."

Each of the first eight nights of the nine-night ceremony came and went, until it was time for the ninth and last. As custom would have it, a corral was built for the last night's dancing. It was made of a circle of branches such as the Navajo people now fashion to complete the nine-night ceremony of the Mountain Chant to this very day.[11] And on this last night everyone was expected to enter the circle and join the dancing.

When the time came for them to go inside the ring, the nine surviving wives appeared. But each carried a sharp knife in her hand. And as each danced along with all the others around the central fire she brandished her knife. Each looked so menacing that *Godtsoh* was afraid to be seen. So instead of sitting where everyone could look at him, he hid himself in the wall of branches that ringed the area.

Meanwhile the wives continued to dance, making more and more noise as they did. Soon everyone recognized what they were singing while they danced.

"Bééshlá áshiilaa," they sang as they danced.

"Bééshlá áshiilaa! Bééshlá áshiilaa!"

Round and round they danced. Round and round! Round and round! And they kept repeating the words of their angry song:

"The knife has disfigured me," they repeated.

"The knife has disfigured me! The knife has disfigured me!"

As they danced, they poised themselves as if to cut the nose off the face of any man who got in their way. And no man had the courage to stop them.

One by one, everybody withdrew from the circle until only the disfigured wives were left dancing. There they danced, round and round, singing their angry song without interruption, until at last they ran out of the circle themselves and fled into the darkness beyond the reach of the fire's light.

Once out of sight, they began to curse the people. Their voices rang out so that all could hear:

"May the waters drown you!" they cursed.

"May the cold weather freeze you all.

"May the fires burn you!

"May the lightning strike you all."

Over and over they repeated those curses, all the while moving further and further away until at last their voices could no longer be heard. But well after they were gone their words continued to ring in the ears of many of the people.

Some claim that even now, when the north wind blows, they can hear the voices of *Godtsoh* the Big Knee's angry, noseless wives:

"May the waters drown you.

"May the cold weather freeze you!

"May the fires burn you.

"May the lightning strike you all!"

If they listen carefully, anyone who travels in the area round the valley of the San Juan River can hear those voices when the north wind brings a summer storm or a winter blizzard.

For that's where the wives of *Godtsoh* fled: far to the north.

And they dwell there to this very day. Their anger has not subsided, and from time to time they resume their curses upon the Navajo people.

From time to time they turn their noseless faces to the south and repeat their angry cries. When they do, the north wind blows fiercely, bringing cold snow and harsh gales in the winter and torrential rain and fierce lightning in the summer it is said.

Seven

It is also said that soon after that memorable ceremony a group of Utes visited the Navajos.

They came early in the summer when the corn was small, and they remained until early fall when it was ripe and ready for picking. They worked for the Navajos and helped them harvest. And when their stomachs were full and they were able to carry away excess grain to help them get through the winter, they left, except for one family, which included an older man and an older woman, their two young daughters and their one young son.

At first they intended to stay for only a short time after their kinsmen left. But somehow they remained. One day passed and then another; one month went by and then the next; one season came and went and then another; one year lapsed and then the next. Always intending to leave soon, they postponed their departure for one or another reason. At last they ended up staying with the Navajo people until they died.

In particular they became friends with those of *Tábąąhá* the Water's Edge Clan. Eventually they learned the language of those people, and by the time of their death they had come to regard them as relatives.

One of their two daughters, meanwhile, whose name was *Ts'ah yisk'id*, which means Sage Brush Hill in the language of the White Man, had married a *Tábąąhá*. She then gave birth often and became the mother of many children, finally dying herself at a ripe old age as a respected Navajo woman. From her descends the clan called *Ts'ah yisk'idnii* the Sage Brush Hill People. That clan is so closely related to the Water's Edge Clan that no member of one is allowed to marry any member of the other.

•　　•　　•　　•

Soon after the departure of the Utes, the Navajos were joined by still another band. These people came from *Tábąąh łigai*, the White Shore, like another clan who had managed to arrive earlier. They too, had gazed at the western mountains which they could see in the distance. They too, wondered if anyone might possibly live there. They, too, had wondered whether those who might live there would be people like themselves. So at length they, too, decided to travel there and see. They spoke a language that was like the language the *Tábąąhá* spoke, and when it was decided that they would join the Navajo nation they were considered part of that growing clan.

• • • •

Some years later a large band came from the country south of the San Juan Valley, where the people of the Apache tribe are said to have lived at that time.

These newcomers revealed that they had not come merely to visit. They had left the land of the Apaches forever, and they now wanted to become Navajos. They had all belonged to the same group among their former people, and they called themselves *Tsézhin ndii aaí*, a name that becomes Black Rock Standing Like a Wall Clan in the language that *Bilagáana* the White Man speaks. Thus they were admitted into the growing Navajo nation as a new clan, although they kept their old name.[12]

From the very start they showed a desire to associate closely with *Tábąąhá* the Water's Edge Clan. So by now they are closely related to them. No member of the one may marry any member of the other.

• • • •

At about that time there was a great famine in the pueblo of Zuni.[13] So people from there came to the San Juan Valley to dwell among the Navajos lest they starve. First they lived among the *Tábąąhá*, and although they had womenfolk with them they did not yet become a new clan. The Zuni clan was to be created later.

Famine prevailed among the other pueblos, too. And from an old settlement called *Tł'ógí*, not far from where the present pueblo of Zia now stands, there came a band of starving people begging to be included among the Navajo tribe. They were gladly accepted as *Tł'ógí dine'é*, the *Tł'ógí* Village Clan. They, too, became especially friendly with the *Tábąąhá*.

• • • •

The next group to join the Navajo nation was a band of seven adults with their various children who came from a place called *Tó'áhání*. In the language of *Bilagáana* the White Man that name means Near the Water. At first they stayed with *Dziłtł'ahnii* the

Mountain Recess People. But soon they declared their intention to become a part of the tribe as a separate clan, whereupon they were given the name *Tó'áhání dine'é*, the Clan From the Place Near the Water.

•　　•　　•　　•

Those who were to join the growing Navajo nation next comprised a group of people who arrived from a place called *Táchii'* which means Red Extends into the Water. From their traditions it became apparent that they were not a newly created people. Somehow they had escaped the destruction of the *Naayéé'*, although no one among them could say exactly how. For that reason they were also considered holy people.

Since there were so many of them, they were divided into two clans. Half of them became *Táchii'nii*, the Red Extends into the Water Clan. The second half of them became *K'ai' dine'é*, the Willow People.

At first they were content to be considered people of two separate clans. But in the days and months and seasons and years that have come and gone since that time, the two clans remained so close that they are now regarded as one. Sometimes they are together called *K'ai' dine'é* the Willow People. And sometimes they are together called *Táchii'nii* the Red Extends into the Water Clan.

•　　•　　•　　•

Earlier the Navajos had been a small and a weak people. But now they found themselves numerous and strong. Some among them, especially the younger men, began to observe their increased numbers and their added strength. And now and then they talked of making war, it is said.

Eight

It is also said that as the days and months and seasons and years followed one upon the other, people began to talk about the great pueblos along the Rio Grande.

Some spoke of stories those people told and of the many things
they knew. Some suggested that they could tell the Navajos how it
happened that certain clans had escaped the terrible *Naayéé'*. And
some thought that the people of the great pueblos might tell of
their own deliverance from the alien monsters.

So great was the curiosity about these people that a restless
young warrior assembled a party to raid the pueblo called *Kinłichíí*,
which means Red House in today's language.[14]

They returned several days later with a group of captives from
that place. Among them was a young girl whom the warrior himself
had captured. She became his wife and in time gave birth often. So
it was that she also became the mother of many children and
finally died at a ripe old age as a respected Navajo woman. From
her descends the clan known as *Kin łichíí'nii*, which means Red
House Clan in the language spoken by *Bilagáana* today.

The members of the Red House Clan are closely related to
Tsi'naajinii the Black Horizontal Forest People, since that is the
clan of the warrior who led the raid. Which is why no member of
the one clan may marry any member of the other.

At first the captives taken from the great pueblo of *Kinłichíí'* the
Red House were treated as slaves. But their descendants
participated fully in the life of the Navajo people and eventually
became free. By marrying among them they alike increased their
own numbers and the numbers of the tribe. From them there grew
another clan called *Tł'iziłání*. Today that would be called the Many
Goats Clan. Like the people of the Red House Clan, they are closely
related to *Tsi'naajinii* the Black Horizontal Forest People.

•   •   •   •

Next came a band of Apaches from the south. Among this group
there were members representing two clans of that tribe. One was
Deeshchíí'nii, who in the language spoken by *Bilagáana* would be
called Start of the Red Streak People. The other was *Tł'aashchí'i*,
who in the language spoken by the White Man would be called Red
Bottom People. Both groups were quickly adopted into the Navajo
tribe as two separate clans. But they have always been considered
close relatives to one another, so that no member of the one people
may marry any member of the other.

•   •   •   •

Soon after the arrival of the Apaches another group of Utes came into the Navajo region. They camped at a place called *Tsé' yik'ání,* which means Rock Hogback, not far from *Ha' atiin* Where the Trail Leads Upward. These newcomers had good weapons of all sorts. They also had two kinds of shields. One type was perfectly round, while another had a crescent cut out of the top.

At first they lived apart from the Navajos, for they were unruly and rude. But by and by they learned to conduct themselves acceptably and they gradually merged into the Navajo nation. They formed the *Nóóda'í dine'é* Clan, which means Ute People in the language that *Bilagáana* the White Man speaks.

• • • •

Not long after the people of *Nóóda'í dine'é* the Ute Clan became fully accepted as Navajo people, they assembled a war party and led a raid on a Mexican settlement, where a strange race had established themselves at the site of the modern city of Socorro. This place was far to the south in the valley of the river called the Rio Grande.

They captured a Spanish woman, brought her back with them, made her a slave, and then married her to one of the young men. Accordingly, she gave birth often, thus becoming the mother of many children and finally dying at a ripe old age as a respected Navajo woman. Her children were considered free, and from among them the *Naakaii dine'é* came into existence. In the language of *Bilagáana* that name means People Who Move About, although nowadays they are also called the Mexican Clan. Their members cannot marry members of the *Nóóda'í dine'é* the Ute Clan.

• • • •

While the young warriors were making such raids among the Spanish settlements, old *Godtsoh* the Big Knee, chief of *Tábąąhá* the Water's Edge People, was vainly trying to restore the health and good fortune he had enjoyed in his earlier years. Although he had become famous and respected long ago, now he was feeble with age.

During those long-ago times the people often conducted a great winter ceremony called *Naachid.*[15] For it was still believed then that the gods could be persuaded to give an aging man back his youth. Such a ceremony lasted all winter long; it was begun with the harvest and lasted until planting time next spring.

The Navajo people have long ceased to conduct *Naachid*, for they came to understand that one generation of five-fingered Earth Surface People must graciously give way to the next. But at the time we now speak of the rites of that ceremony were practiced at the sacred place of *Tó aheedlį* Where the Rivers Merged and where *Naayéé' neizghání* the Enemy Slayer and *Tó bájísh chíní* the One Born for Water now dwelled.

One night during that winter season long ago, while the rites of *Naachid* were being conducted, some strangers appeared from the direction of the river. They had heard that a ceremony was being conducted for so great a chief as *Godtsoh*, and they wished to attend. They remained for its duration and stayed on to help with the planting. Eventually they were adopted into the tribe, forming the clan known as *Tó aheedlįinii*. In the language of the White Man that name means Where the Waters Join Clan. They formed a close alliance with *Nóóda'í dine'é* the Ute Clan and *Naakaii dine'é* the Mexican Clan.

•　　•　　•　　•

Later during the same winter another group of Apaches came from the country in the south, also wishing to witness the rites of *Naachid*. At first they chose to remain apart from the Navajos, camping at a place near the San Juan River.

One evening one of the women of *Tábąąhá* the Water's Edge People visited the camp of the Apache visitors and stayed all night there. Soon thereafter it was discovered that she had attached herself to an Apache youth. And when the visitors left she stole away with him.

For a long time her people did not know what had happened to her. But many years after she had disappeared some of her kinsmen learned where she was. And they journeyed to the country of the Apaches to persuade her to return to her people. Although she was an old woman by that time, it still pleased her to do so.

With her came her husband and a family of three daughters. These girls were beautiful maidens by then with light skin and fair hair. Their grandmother, who admired them when she saw them for the first time, desired that they should become the founders of a new clan. Soon they were married, and as they raised families of their own their offspring became known as *Litso dine'é*. That name means Yellow People in the language of *Bilagáana* the White Man. The father of those three women lived to a ripe old age and finally died as a respected Navajo.

•　•　•　•

On yet another night while the rites of *Naachid* were being conducted for the feeble old chief, *Godtsoh* the Big Knee, two strange men entered the land of the Navajos. They looked tired and hungry. And on their faces they wore signs of weariness and sadness. It was obvious that they had been traveling long and far.

Nobody could recall having ever seen their likes before. But to everyone's surprise they spoke a language much like the language of the Navajo people. And they rejoiced to find themselves among the Navajos, who, they said over and over again, were precisely the people they sought.

When asked who they were, they replied that they were two scouts dispatched by a large group of wanderers. All of them had long ago left a land far to the west bordering a great expanse of water that reached farther than any man's eye could see. All of them, insisted the two weary strangers, were kinsmen to the Navajos and now wished to be united with them. To do so, they had traveled for a long time across mountains and desert.

The story of this large group of kindred people who had come so far is well worth hearing. For these people would indeed join the Navajos. And together their two peoples would eventually become a great nation, it is said.

Nine

It is also said that four mountains surrounded the new home of *Asdzáá nádleehé* the Changing Woman where she had gone to dwell in the west.[16] Those mountains were positioned exactly like the mountains around *Hajíínéí* the Emergence Place. One stood to the east. One stood to the south. One stood to the west. And one stood to the north.

When she first arrived at that floating house on the shimmering water, *Asdzáá nádleehé* would dance among the four mountains.

She danced on the eastern mountain to create clouds. She danced on the mountain to the south to obtain adornments such as jewels and clothing. She danced on the mountain to the west to bring forth all varieties of plants. And she danced on the northern mountain to summon corn and animals.[17]

She would begin these dancing journeys on the eastern mountain. Then she would make her way to the mountain to the south. From there she would go to the mountain which stood to the west. And finally she would move on to the mountain standing to the north. Thus would she follow the path of *Jóhonaa'éí* the Sun as he observed the changing seasons.

Except that when she finished her dance on the northern mountain, she did not pass directly from there to her starting place in the east. Never would she dare complete a circle in the sky.[18] Instead she would carefully retrace her path back through the mountain to the west. Then she would return to the mountain to the south. And finally she would return to the eastern mountain where her journey began.

But even with her dancing, *Asdzáá nádleehé* the Changing Woman had begun to feel lonely soon after arriving at her western home. For she had no companions where she now lived.

Those who had accompanied her to that place did not choose to stay with her. So she found herself each day adrift in all that solitude. And it seemed that each daily interval between the departure of her husband in the morning and his arrival in the evening grew longer and longer, longer and longer.

•   •   •   •

Perhaps *Nihookáá dine'é* the Earth Surface People might keep her company, she reasoned one day, just as they had provided company for her sister *Yoołgai asdzáá* the White Shell Woman.[19]

So on that very day, after she had completed one of her dancing journeys around the four mountains, she returned to the one which stood to the east. There she sat down on its eastern slope. And there she rubbed an outer layer of skin from under her left arm with her right hand.

This she held in her palm for a short while as it was transformed into four humans: two fully grown males and two adult females.

From these two five-fingered Earth Surface couples would descend a clan, although no name was yet given it. As we shall see, though, eventually it would bear the name *Honágháahnii,* a name which in the language of *Bilagáana* the White Man means He Walks Around One Clan. But that was not to happen for quite some time.

Next she rubbed an outer layer of skin from under her right arm with her left hand.

This she held in her palm for a short while as it, too, changed into four Earth Surface People: two adult males and two fully grown females.

From these two human couples would descend another clan, although they did not receive a name at first. In good time, as we shall see, they would come to be known as *Kin yaa'áanii,* a name which in the language of *Bilagáana* means Towering House People. But much would happen first.

In the same fashion did she rub an outer layer of her skin from under her left breast with her right hand.

This she held in her palm for a short while until it, too, changed into four humans: two fully grown males and two adult females.

From these two Earth Surface couples with five fingers would descend yet another clan, although they would also go unnamed at first. At the proper time they would earn the name *Tó dích'íí'nii,* a name which in the language of the White Man means Bitter Water Clan. But there were other things that would take place beforehand.

Similarly she rubbed an outer layer of skin from under her right breast with her left hand.

This tissue she then held in her palm for a short while until it became four Earth Surface People like those who daily walk around in this world today: two adult men and two fully grown women.

From these two five-fingered Earth Surface couples another clan was to descend, although they were not yet named. When the proper time was to come, they would earn the name *Bit'qhnii* which means Within His Cover People in the language of the White Man. But first they would have to endure great hardship.

Likewise she rubbed a coating of her own skin from a spot on her chest midway between her two breasts.

This skin she held in her hand until it changed into four humans like those we recognize in the world to this very day: two were fully grown men and two were adult women.

From these two human couples still another clan would descend. They, too, did not receive a name at first. At the appropriate time, however, they would win the name *Hashtł'ishnii*. In today's language that name means Mud Clan. But many things lay ahead of them before that would happen.

And finally she rubbed a layer of her own skin from a place on her back between the two shoulder blades.

This skin she rubbed in her hand until it became four Earth Surface People like ourselves who come into the world as infants, grow into mature adults, age, and finally depart from this life: two of them were adult men, and two were fully grown women.

From these couples a sixth clan would eventually descend. Unnamed at first, they would untimately gain the name *Bit'anii*, a name which means Close to Her Body Clan.[20] But they would have to see much and suffer a great deal before that was to happen.

To these twelve original couples she had this to say:

"I have created you to dwell near me," she said.

"I have created you so that I can see you and enjoy your companionship.

"But I must also tell you that to the east of this place my sister dwells. She had also caused Earth Surface People to exist.

"So you have kinsmen.

"Some day you may wish to go where they dwell. Or else your descendants may choose to go there some day.

"If that happens, I will understand."

Thereupon she took them from her floating home between the mountains to the mainland that extended eastward from the water's edge. And she placed them on the land to live.

There they lived for thirty years, during which time they married and had children who in turn gave birth to children of their own.

•　•　•　•

At the end of that thirty-year period those who remained of the original twelve couples called their offspring together and spoke to them. By this time they had become known as *Dine'é naakits'áadah,* which in the language of the White Man means People of the Twelve.

This is what they said to their children and to their grandchildren:

"We have grown old," they said to them.

"Two of us have already died. Already, one of our younger brothers whom we loved has died. And an elder sister who cared for us and who attended to our needs has died.

"As for us, we have no homes of our own. And we do not know where we might go.

"We have come here to have you look out over the water where your grandmother *Asdzáá nádleehé* dwells. But we have also gathered you here to tell you something that she told us many years ago.

"To the east of this place the sister of *Asdzáá nádleehé* had also caused people to exist.

"It is our understanding that they are people like us and like yourselves.

"So you have kinsmen somewhere.

"And unlike us you are young enough and strong enough to go where they live and to make homes for yourselves with them."

Eager to verify what they had told their children and their grandchildren, the surviving *Dine'é naakits'áadah* called out to *Asdzáá nádleehé* the Changing Woman. And upon their doing so a gentle rain fell, following which a rainbow filled the sky. One end of its arch touched the spot where they all stood. And the other extended all the way to the place where her house stood on the sea in the middle of the four mountains.

Seeing which, they all crossed that rainbow bridge. And there *Asdzáá nádleehé* greeted them all, especially the *Diné naakits'áadah.* She embraced each one of the remaining ten, and she told each one of her pleasure in seeing them. When she saw that two of them had died, she replaced them with two others, fashioning them out of sacred turquoise.

"My children," she said to them.

"I know why you have come.

"For thirty years you have lived as it was intended that you should.

"During those years you married and had children. In turn, those children have married and given birth to children of their own.

And their children shall likewise bear children, as their own children shall. That is the way it will be forever on the surface of this world.

"As for you, however, you are old and have nowhere to go.

"Perhaps you can stay here and dwell with me.

"So saying, she opened four doors to show them four rooms that led in four different directions from the central chamber of her house. In those four rooms the *Dine'é naakits'áadah* saw all sorts of treasure.

They saw white shell. They saw blue shell. They saw turquoise. They saw haliotis. They saw soapstone, agate, redstone, jet. The likes of such things they had never before seen. And as they looked at all they saw, *Asdzą́ą́ nádleehé* the Changing Woman resumed speaking to them, saying this:

"My children," she said.

"I know what your descendants are thinking.

"I know that they wish to leave their country by the shore and travel east to join their kinfolk beyond the mountains.

"Let them do so.

"Let them go, while you remain here with me.

"Then these treasures which you see will be yours. This home will be yours. The mountains that you see around you will be yours. The sky overhead will be yours."

So it was that the *Dine'é naakits'áadah* agreed to stay with *Asdzą́ą́ nádleehé* the Changing Woman. Meanwhile, their descendants returned to the mainland, excited by what they had heard about the people who lived across the desert and over the mountains to the east. Each one had a different version of the story to tell. Some spoke about how those people lived. Some talked about what they ate. Some talked about the crops they grew. Some mentioned the names of various clans.

For twelve days they could talk of nothing else. For twelve days they could think of nothing else.

"There are not that many of us here where we live," declared some of them.

"Perhaps we would fare better where there are many others," declared some.

On and on they talked, until by the end of those twelve days they were sure that they wanted to migrate east. They resolved that they would make their homes with the grandchildren of their grandmother's sister, *Yoołgai asdzą́ą́* the White Shell Woman. They resolved that once united with them they would all be as one people. And now that they had decided to go, they resolved that in fourteen days they would leave.

•   •   •   •

Before their departure, *Asdzą́ą́ nádleehé* the Changing Woman came to see them off. *Dine'é naakits'áadah* the People of the Twelve also came to see them.

"My grandchildren," said Changing Woman to them.

"It is a long, dangerous journey that you have resolved to take.

"You will need protection along the way.

"So I will give you five of my pets to guard you.

"I am giving you *Bįįh* the Gentle Deer. I am giving you *Dahsání* the Upright Porcupine. I am giving you *Náshdóítsoh* the Mighty Puma. I am giving you *Shash* the Fearless Bear. And I am giving you *Tł'iistsoh* the Great Snake.[21]

"Take good care of those creatures. Behave well towards them and they will not desert you. Speak no evil in the presence of *Shash* the Bear or *Tł'iish* the Snake, for they might very well do the evil things you mention. *Bįįh* the Deer and *Dahsání* the Porcupine are less mischievous. In their presence you may say what you will."

In addition to the five pets, she gave the people five magic wands. To those who would eventually become the clan called *Honágháahnii* she gave a wand of turquoise. To those whose clan was later to be called *Kin yaa'áanii* she gave a wand of white shell. To those who were to become the clan called *Tó dích'íí'nii* she gave a wand of haliotis shell. To those who were to become the clan now called *Bit'anii* she gave a wand of black stone. And to those who were to become the clan called *Hashtł'ishnii* she gave a wand of red stone.

"These," said she, "I give you for added protection.

"With them you will increase the likelihood of your safekeeping. But even then I shall be watching you myself as you travel."

Thus the day of their departure came. And thus did they bid farewell to their parents, *Dine'é naakits'áadah*, the People of the Twelve. Thus, too, they said good-bye to their grandmother, *Asdzą́ą́ nádleehé* the Changing Woman. And thus their journey began. It was to be a long migration and a hard one, it is said.[22]

Ten

It is also said that after twelve days of marching the children of the *Dine'é naakits'áadah* crossed a high ridge overlooking an endless, barren plain.

There they spotted some dark objects moving around in the distance. What these objects were they could not determine. But they suspected that they were people like themselves.

They kept on moving, but they did not head toward the dark, moving objects which they saw in the distance. Instead they made their way carefully among the foothills that bordered the wide plain, using brush and timber for cover as they went. And as they continued, they could see the objects more plainly. They were indeed human beings. So the migrants remained among the foothills, and at night they camped in the woods.

In spite of their precautions, however, they had been observed by the plains people. And at night two of them visited the camp of the travelers. They were *K'iiłtsoiidine'é*, People of the Big Rabbit Bush. Their tribe was large; the plain where they lived was extensive; and in their gardens they grew ripening watermelons and maturing corn. The travelers from the west were welcome to camp among them, they added.

So the migrants decided to rest for a while. And on their second night two more young men of the *K'iiłtsoiidine'é* visited the camp. One of these took a fancy to a maiden among them, and before many days had passed he asked for her in marriage. At first her people refused. But when he begged for her again and again, and when she said that she wanted to become his wife, her people consented.

For as long as the people remained there among the *K'iiłtsoiidine'é* he stayed with her in the camp. Except that for the last two nights of their sojourn in that place she stayed with his people. And when the travelers were ready to move on, they implored the young husband to join them. But he insisted that his wife should remain in the valley with him and with his people, who had given the wanderers an abundance of produce in exchange for her.

They argued for a long time over who would go or who would stay. Finally the young woman's relatives prevailed and the young man of the *K'iiłtsoiidine'é* agreed to join them.

Meanwhile, four other young men from that tribe had likewise fallen in love with maidens among the wanderers. They, too, asked to have them as wives. And the migrants were willing to allow their daughters to marry these outsiders, but they would not leave them behind. So the enamored young men agreed to join the travelers. Their tribesmen had tried to persuade the migrants to dwell with them forever, but they were determined to finish their long trek and to join their kinsmen in the east. So they moved on, it is said.

Eleven

It is also said that they broke camp early one morning and traveled all day.[23]

That night a great wind arose. And *Shash* the Fearless Bear grew restive. He ran around the camp all night long, uneasy and watchful. Noticing how he stirred, the men looked out over the plain and observed some of the *K'iiłtsoiidine'é* lurking among the brush and shrubs just beyond camp. But when the bear snarled and growled they disappeared. Next morning the people discovered that the men of the *K'iiłtsoiidine'é* who had joined them by marriage were now gone. Perhaps they were somehow in league with their kinsmen outside.

The second day the wanderers journeyed as far as they could and did not make camp until after darkness fell. And again they observed *Shash* the Fearless Bear grow restless. Around and around he ran, uneasy and watchful all night long. Not until after day broke and the people were all awake and stirring did he lie down. Not until then did he sleep, while preparations were being made for another day's march.

On the third day they traveled as far as they could and again did not make camp until after darkness fell. And once again they observed *Shash* the Fearless Bear grow restless. All night long he ran from one side of camp to the other, visibly uneasy and visibly watchful.

"Why are you so restless, our pet?" asked one of the men to him.

"What is it that makes you pace and snarl so?"

Shash the Bear gave no reply but a grunt. But then he made a motion with his nose in the direction of the land of the *K'iiłtsoiidine'é*. And then he continued to circle around the camp. Not until after daybreak did he lie down and sleep himself, while the people made ready for the day's march ahead.

Again they traveled as far as they could, continuing until not a thread of daylight was left in the sky and only then making camp. They were more cautious than ever this night, camping close together as an extra measure of safety.

All during the night many of them were aware of the restlessness of *Shash* the Bear. But this time instead of moving uneasily and watchfully around the camp he sat on a neighboring hill where he could watch over the sleepers. And all night long he snarled and growled as he sat. Only after day broke did he fall asleep while the people prepared for another day's march.

Before they set out, however, someone suggested that they take a close look around.

"Let us see if we can discover what it is that has troubled our bear," came the suggestion.

So they sent two scouts out to the east and two to the west, bidding each pair circle round the camp and return from the opposite direction.

Those who had gone to the east came back having found nothing. But those who ventured to the west returned saying that they had seen a strange array of footprints. It was as though a group of men had encroached silently upon the camp, were suddenly startled, and had then turned to flee. But instead of leading away from camp in the direction whence they came, their prints simply vanished.

Whereupon several others reported having been awakened at night by the sound of *Shash* the Bear. They heard him growling and snarling, they said. Some even claimed to have heard the cries of frightened men and the sound of an attacking beast. Or at least they claimed to have dreamed of hearing such cries and such a sound. Everyone then turned to look at the bear, who merely seemed less restless now than he had seemed for several days. There he lay, sleeping more soundly now than he had slept since they all left the valley of the *K'iiłtsoiidine'é*.

•   •   •   •

They traveled on for four more days. And for four days after that they traveled. During the second four days' march they went without water. And by now the children were crying with thirst. Some of the older men and women complained that they could go no further with nothing to drink.

On this the fifth day of the second part of that long stretch beyond the wide plain where the *K'iiłtsoiidine'é* lived, they stopped at noon and held a council, which began when one among them asked this question:

"How shall we get water?" he asked.

"We can go no further without it."

To which another among them gave this reply:

"Let us try the power of our magic wands," she replied.

"Surely it was for such an emergency that our grandmother *Asdzą́ą́ nádleehé* the Changing Woman gave them to us."

Whereupon a man of the clan which had taken possession of the turquoise wand thrust it into the ground right where he stood.

He worked it back and forth and round and round to make a good-sized hole. Back and forth he worked it. Round and round he turned it. Deeper and deeper went the wand; wider and wider grew the hole.

And as the hole went deeper and grew wider, moisture began to build around the opening in the earth. Then water began to accumulate in that opening until it finally bubbled forth like a spring.

Unable to contain her thirst, an elderly woman from another clan threw herself upon the newly made pool and filled her mouth with handfuls of water. Then suddenly she cried out:

"It is bitter water," she cried out. But she did not cry out in dismay. It was a happy cry she gave.

"You have brought forth bitter water," she cried happily. "But it slakes my thirst, and I thank you for it."

Others then did as she had done. They threw themselves upon the newly made spring and drank by handfuls.

"Bitter water," they cried. "Bitter water.

"But what does it matter how bitter it is? You have saved us by bringing it forth, and we thank you for it."

"Let the name of your clan be People of the Bitter Water," cried one of the elders who had quenched his thirst. And all the others agreed. That is how the *Tó dích'íí'nii* Clan gets its name, for that is what Bitter Water People is called in the language of *Diné* the Navajo, it is said.

Twelve

It is also said that after the thirsty travelers had all taken their fill they cooked their food and ate it. Then, seeing a mountain far to the east, one of them pointed to it and made this suggestion:

"Let us try to reach the slope of that mountain before nightfall," he suggested.

So they pushed on toward the mountain and arrived there while daylight still filled the sky. As they drew close to it they noticed moccasin tracks, so they knew there had to be people like themselves near at hand.

At the base of the mountain they saw a cluster of cottonwood trees. Thinking that there might be a spring nearby, they headed straight for the wooded grove and entered. And suddenly they found themselves among a strange people who lived there.

The strangers greeted the newcomers warmly. They embraced them and expressed their pleasure at seeing people so much like themselves. They bid the travelers tell who they were, where they were coming from, what their purpose was in traveling so far, and where they were headed.

The wanderers told their story briefly; and the strangers replied that according to their own traditions they were created right there among those cottonwoods, where they had always lived.

"This place is called *Mạ'iitó*," said one of them. Which is what Coyote Spring is named in the language of *Diné* the Navajo.

"And we are *Mạ'ii dine'é* the Coyote People," he continued.

Ever since that first meeting, however, the Navajos have chosen to call them *Mạ'iitó dine'é*, the Coyote Spring People.

For four days the migrating group tarried among the Coyote Spring People. During that stay they all talked and sang together. And they exchanged stories as if they were all one people. Until at length the travelers from the west persuaded their friends to join them in their journey to the east. This the *Mạ'iitó dine'é* gladly consented to do, encouraged by the prospect of becoming part of a mighty nation.

• • • •

On the following day they all broke camp and set out together to find the people in the east that they had heard of. Before they started, however, the Coyote Spring People warned that the spring here in the cottonwoods was the only water within two days march in any direction.

"Do not be afraid," replied one of the migrants.

"We have resources. We can get water when we need it."

All day long they traveled across arid ground in relentless heat. They went as far as they could and made a dry camp as darkness fell. And on the next morning they resumed their march, having to start out with no water to fortify themselves against the day's journey under the hot sun.

By noon, many of the elderly and some of the children began to complain of thirst. So they halted and decided to try the magic of another of the five wands that *Asdzą́ą́ nádleehé* the Changing Woman had given them.

This time a man of the clan which had taken possession of the white-shell wand seized it and thrust it into the ground where he stood.

He worked it round and round and back and forth until he had made a good-sized hole. Round and round he turned it. Back and forth he worked it. The hole grew wider and wider; the wand went deeper and deeper. Then moisture began to accumulate at the surface as the hole widened and deepened. Water began to build in the opening, until it finally bubbled forth like a spring.

"Watch out," cried a mother from another clan.

"That water is muddy.

"Surely it will make the children sick!"

But an older woman from yet another clan whose thirst was great threw herself upon the spring. And she filled her mouth with handfuls of the muddy water.

"Maybe this water is muddy," she said.

"But it quenches my thirst and I am thankful for it."

And when the others saw that no harm had befallen her, they too threw themselves upon the spring and drank.

"What does it matter if this water is muddy?" they said.

"It relieves our thirst and we are thankful for it."

"Then let the name of your people be the Muddy Water Clan,"
said one of the elders who had quenched his thirst. And everyone
else agreed. Which is how the *Hashtł'ishnii* got its name,
inasmuch as that is what the Mud Clan is called in the language of
Diné the Navajo.

• • • •

Having drunk their fill, the people then moved on, heading
farther east across the hot desert until darkness fell. Again they
camped at a place where there was no water, and they rested for
the night as best they could. And again they started out the next
morning for another day's long march in the heat of the sun.

Until by noon they were all thirsty, with the young children
crying and the older, more feeble folk moaning. So they halted and
decided once more to rely on one of the five magic wands that
Asdzą́ą́ nádleehé had given them.

This time someone from the clan to whom the haliotis wand had
been given dug a well, working it back and forth and round and
round until moisture began to build as the hole grew wider
and deeper. Soon water mounted in the opening and a spring
bubbled forth.

When the spring thus appeared, one woman whose thirst was so
great that she could not restrain herself threw herself upon it to
drink. Then she cried out, but not in dismay:

"It is alkaline," she cried.

"There is a salty taste to it.

"But it is refreshing just the same, and I am happy to have it."

Whereupon others drank it also. And after so doing they declared
that those whose clan had taken possession of the haliotis wand
would be known as *Tó dík'ǫzhi*, which is how the Alkaline Water
Clan got its name. For that is what those people are called in *Diné
bizaad* the language of the Navajos.

• • • •

Having thus quenched their thirst, the people resumed
traveling, bearing east across hot, dry country and camping once
again in a dry place. And once again they started out on the
following day without water.

Until once again by noon they halted, when the cries of the
young and the complaints of the old permitted them to continue

no longer. And this time someone whose clan bore the black stone wand dug a well. A stream of fine, clear water bubbled forth, and all drank heartily except for one youth and a maiden whose people had carried the wand.

"Why is it?" asked an elder of a different clan.

"Instead of drinking like the others, you two just stand there."

But neither one of the two answered. Both merely stood there silently, the girl with her arms folded under her dress close to her body. Which is why her clan now bears the name *Bit'anii*, which is how the Close to Her Body Clan got its name. For that is what those people are called in *Diné bizaad* the language of the Navajos.

●   ●   ●   ●

Travel was again resumed, with the people pursuing their eastward course across the desert. They slept at yet another place where there was no water, and they departed on the morning of the following day with nothing more to drink. At noon they struck another well, using the magic of the red stone wand which *Asdzą́ą́ nadleehé* the Changing Woman had provided. But as the people filled their vessels and drank what they wished, no outcries or declarations were made. So the migrants continued without naming the clan to whom the red wand had been given.

●   ●   ●   ●

Following that day they camped for two nights without water. And at noon on the second day thereafter they reached a wide canyon wherein they found a spring. So they gave that place the name *Halgaitó*, which is what Spring on the Flatland is called in *Diné bizaad* the language of the Navajos. And they decided that they would travel no farther that day. Instead they would spend the afternoon and the night where there was plenty to drink, it is said.

Thirteen

It is also said that once they departed from *Halgaitó*, they traveled for twenty-five days more. Each day they managed to find enough water to meet their needs, although they were now less successful at getting food. For summer had given way to autumn and there was less to be found. Still, they moved on steadily until they arrived at a small river just to the west of *Dook'o'oosłííd* the San Francisco Peak, which *Áłtsé hastiin* had fashioned to mark the western boundary of the fifth world.

There they stopped for five nights and five days to hunt. One man, but only one, was able to kill a deer. *Baa' yinił'íní* was his name, which means Looks on at Battle in the language of *Bilagáana*. He cut it into small pieces and distributed it so that each person had a taste.

They finally left the small river and moved across to the east side of the mountain. There, beside a little peak, they stopped at a spring that nobody bothered to name.

They spent several days at that place. Around their camp they built a stone wall to protect themselves from the bite of the wind, which now began to blow steadily from the north. That wall still stands for anyone wishing to go there to see it.

Náshdóítsoh the Mighty Puma that *Asdzą́ą́ nádleehé* the Changing Woman had given them was kept by the clan called *Bit'anii* which had borne the black stone wand. And while the people were camped at the nameless spring they bid him go hunt for them. He managed to kill a deer, which was then cooked and cut into small pieces and distributed so that everyone could have at least a taste. Otherwise they survived on small game like squirrels and rats plus whatever seeds they were able to gather. They were not yet familiar with the techniques of hunting and tracking game.

Shash the Fearless Bear also helped the people find meat by occasionally killing a rabbit. *Bįįh* the Gentle Deer provided no game, but he was a companion to them and could find enough to feed himself. *Tł'iistsoh* the Great Snake and *Dahsání* the Upright Porcupine, however, were more of a nuisance. Not only did they contribute no game or companionship; they had to be carried along and fed. So while the migrants traveled from the spring near *Dook'o'oos'ałííd* the San Francisco Peak to *Bidahóóchii'* the Red Streak Mountain, and while they traveled from there to *Tsídii yilyá* the Black Rock Made with a Bird, they gave more and more thought to what they might do with those two.

Finally they held a council and decided to turn *Tł'iistsoh* the Great Snake and *Dahsání* the Porcupine loose among the rocks

and pines at Navajo Mountain, or *Naatsis'áán* as it is called in
Diné bizaad the language of the Navajo.[24] Eventually those
two creatures grew comfortable in that region. They settled in
and soon multiplied, which explains why there are so many
snakes and porcupines east of the San Francisco Peaks to this
very day.

●   ●   ●   ●

Next the weary travelers marched to a place now called
Aghaałą́, or Lots of Fur as *Bilagáana* the White Man would call it,
which lies close to the present dwelling places of the Hopis. They
camped among the peaks there and again tried their hand at
hunting. Some of them noticed that while their deer foraged for his
own food other deer would appear. So several of the men took to
wearing deer masks for decoys while they hunted.

Those who did succeed in killing many deer. And none too soon,
for it was growing colder each day and the people needed warm
clothing. So after butchering the deer which the hunters killed,
after cooking it, and after eating it, they used the hides for outer
garments.

They dressed many skins as quickly as they could. And as they
worked the wind blew quantities of hair against a rock, where it
soon lay in a great pile. Seeing what was happening, one member of
Honágháahnii, which would eventually earn the name He Walks
Around One Clan, proposed that they call the spot *Aghaałą́*, which
is why it bears such a name to this very day.

From *Aghaałą́*, the migrants went to *Tséhootsooi biyázhi*, or
Little Yellow Rock Place as *Bilagáana* would call it. And from
there they moved on to *Yootsoh*, or Big Bead as it would be called
in the White Man's language. Along the way they camped more
and more often, spending less and less time traveling from one day
to the next. For they were growing wearier and wearier. Sometimes
they would tarry for a night and then move on as best they could.
But there were now many times when they elected to linger for a
full day, or even for two or three.

It was now very late in the autumn. Each night frost covered the
land. Each morning when they awoke the ground was frozen. Some
of the travelers began to fear that winter would be upon them
before they could reach their destination. Others protested that if

they moved faster they might find their kinsmen all the sooner.
Some feared that they were lost. Others began to wonder if they
really had relatives in this part of the world after all.

Moving more and more slowly with greater and greater difficulty
they reached Big Bead. There they found moccasin tracks, but
these were evidently not fresh. It had been some time since anyone
else had been there.

"Even so," said a member of one clan.

"Perhaps these are the footprints of the people we seek."

"But if they are," answered a member of another, "many days
have passed since they have been this way."

"We had better stop here and bide out the winter," said
someone else.

"But we want to bring our journey to an end," said yet another.

"We are tired! Many of the elders are afraid that they will not
live to see their kinsmen."

"But if they are so tired," said still another, "how can we ask
them to go on? The elders in our group complain that they cannot
possibly continue. Our children weep with exhaustion."

So it was that different views now prevailed about what should
be done. Some argued against traveling during the winter. Others
feared waiting in one place until spring. Even within the separate
clans there were those who wanted to stop and those who wanted
to continue. The division among the travelers was deep and serious.

So, too, was it that the party which feared waiting out the winter
at Big Bead decided to go on, while the party which feared pressing
on elected to stay until spring. Within each clan there was strong
contention on both sides. Those who left did so without saying
good-bye to those who stayed behind. Those who stayed refused to
bid farewell to those who left.

•   •   •   •

But before too many days passed, the ones who stayed began to
regret their anger. One by one they realized their sorrow. One by
one they feared for those who had gone on. One by one they
admitted to each other that they missed their tribesmen. So they
held a council and decided to send two messengers out to seek the
others and to beg them to return.

Days passed, however, with one sun rising and setting and one moon following the last. But neither of the two scouts returned. Neither was ever to be seen again. So two additional couriers were dispatched with the same instructions and the same message.

The second two went out, but they never managed to find the first two. In searching, they located the place where the runaways had apparently separated into two smaller bands, perhaps arguing about which way to go.

The scouts followed each set of footprints as far as they could. From one of the two lost bands the Jicarilla Apaches are believed to have descended, and ever since then the Navajos have visited that tribe often. It is believed that the other lost band vanished during the ensuing winter. Perhaps they wandered off course far to the north where it is believed that their descendants now live. They are spoken of from time to time by the Navajos to this very day, who call them *Diné nááhódlóonii*, which is what the White Man would call the Other Navajo People in the language he speaks.

• • • •

The second pair of scouts continued searching for as long as they dared, hoping to find some trace of at least one of the two lost groups. Perhaps, thought they as they continued looking, they might at least be able to find a straggler or two.

They would look for a sign of the one group and then give up and look for a sign of the other. On and on they looked as the weather grew worse. One night they thought they spied a small cluster of campfires. But they could not be sure. A heavy snow was falling; the fires were at a great distance; the wind howled fiercely; and the two men were very tired. Neither had enough strength to go on. They never did find out if they had seen any fires that night.

At last they gave up hope of ever finding their lost tribesmen. They even feared that they were lost themselves. In desperation they decided to take refuge from the wind and the cold in whatever valley they could find. And in doing so, it seems, they made their way to the San Juan River, where by chance they came upon the long-sought people of the Navajo nation.

In fact, those two hapless messengers were the very two bedraggled, exhausted strangers who had stumbled into the camp of *Godtsoh* during the rites of *Naachid*. It was they who told their kinsmen all about the immigrants from the west, it is said.[25]

Fourteen

It is also said that when spring came the people who had stayed at Big Bead resumed their journey, assured that they were within easy distance of their destination. But before long some members of *Tó dích'íí'nii* the Bitter Water Clan grew tired. Many of their children had swollen knees and blistered feet. Many of their elders were stiff and sore. Some men and women who might otherwise have traveled easily were weak after a long winter of meager rations.

"We will have to stop at this tree," declared one member of the clan.

"Let the others go on if they wish. But we have traveled as far as we can. We will make our home right here. After all, we are now close to the place where our kinsmen live."

Thus it was that part of the clan stayed behind to dwell where that lone tree stood. They were to become the people called *Tsin sikaadnii,* or the Clumped Tree Clan. To this day they remain close relatives of *Tó dích'íí'nii* the Bitter Water People, and no member of the one clan may marry any member of the other.

At a place called *Bįįh bitooh,* or Deer Spring as *Bilagáana* the White Man would call it, another group from the Bitter Water Clan also had to stop. Even after the long winter's rest their children were lame from the walking they had done the previous summer. And their elderly were simply too weak to go any farther. So they remained at a spring which they claimed relieved their aches and pains.

One member of that group had taken care of the deer that *Asdzą́ą́ nádleehé* the Changing Woman had given them. And now at this place where they elected to stop they bid their pet continue with the others all the way to the valley of the San Juan.

But he refused to leave those who had cared for him during the long migration. Instead he remained among them, and great numbers of his offspring dwell in that area to this very day. The clan which descended from that group has ever since been called *Bįįh bitoodnii,* or the Deer Spring People as they would now be called. What finally became of *Bįįh* the Gentle Deer is not known. But the people of the Deer Spring Clan have paid special reverence to his memory ever since then.

Meanwhile, the rest of the migrants continued on their way. And soon after leaving Deer Spring they arrived at *Ha'atiin*, where Trails Lead Upward and where the people of *Tábąąhá* had their farms. *Godtsoh* the Big Knee was still alive when the migrants arrived from the west. But he was very old by now and very feeble. Scarcely anyone obeyed him or took him seriously.

When the people of *Tábąąhá* the Water's Edge Clan met the people of *Hashtł'ishnii* the Mud Clan, they rejoiced to see each other. They recited stories to one another about their ways and their traditions. And they recognized many likenesses between them. Their languages were similar. Their names had much the same meanings. Their headdresses were alike. They adorned themselves similarly.

For that reason the *Tábąąhá* invited the *Hashtł'ishnii* to make their homes nearby. To this day they are as closely related as two different clans can be, and members of the one are not permitted to marry members of the other.

It was very much the same with other clans among the Navajos and their various counterparts from the west. Those among certain clans from the San Juan Valley found closely related groups among the migrants. And all spring long and well into summer there was rejoicing and singing, storytelling and dancing. So, it seems, the days and months passed and the newcomers recovered from the injuries and afflictions of their long journey. Soon they were participating fully in the life of their kinsmen as though they had all been of one single tribe from the very beginning of life in this world.

* * * *

Of the five pets which the immigrants had brought with them from the ocean home of their grandmother *Asdzą́ą́ nádleehé* the Changing Woman, *Shash* the Fearless Bear was the last to leave. They had grown fond of him, for he had protected them and he had provided food for them and company for them during many hard days and many long months. But they knew that he could not be happy living among five-fingered Earth Surface People forever. So they held a council and decided to turn him loose.

"Our dear, beloved pet," they said to him sadly.

"You have served us well.

"For many hard days and many long months you have kept us company and provided food for us. You have protected us and guarded us. We are grateful to you now and we will always be grateful.

"But we are safe among our kinsmen now, and we no longer need you.

"If you could dwell among us that would make us happy. But we are of one kind and you are of another.

"In the forest and among the buttes of *Ch'óshgai* the White Spruce Mountain there are others of your species. You have as much right to live with your kinsmen there as we have to abide among our own people here."

Hearing those words, *Shash* the Fearless Bear glanced kindly at all of those who had traveled such a long distance with him. Then he turned and made his way toward the White Spruce Mountain. And his offspring live in great numbers there to this day.

● ● ● ●

Of the people from the west there was as yet one unnamed clan. This was the clan to which *Asdzą́ą́ nádleehé* the Changing Woman had given the red stone wand.

These people did not choose to stay on the banks of the San Juan River very long before they moved to a place farther south.

One day while two of their numbers were hunting, they came to a place called *Tsé nahabiił*, or Rock Ready to Fall, as it is thought to mean in English. There, underneath a cluster of high, overhanging rocks, they found fresh footprints left by people who apparently had nothing on their feet.

They followed these tracks for a short distance, and while doing so they observed a man watching them from a rocky pinnacle high overhead. As soon as he realized he had been spotted he disappeared. But the hunters pursued him to the far side of the rock where they had first spotted him.

"Why do you run from us?" asked one of the hunters.

"We mean you no harm," assured the other.

Hearing those words, the stranger stopped and permitted them to catch up with him. Whereupon they realized that he understood their language. So they addressed him in the manner in which they address their own kinsmen.

"Where do you live, brother?" asked one.

"In a canyon high on the mount up there," answered he.

"Are there people like yourself there, brother?" asked the other hunter.

"There is a whole group of us," he replied.

"What do you live on?" the hunters asked.

"We live mostly on seeds," he answered. "But when luck is with us we manage to catch a wood rat or two. And when there is rain enough we can grow a few crops."

Said the hunters then:

"We have many things to teach you.

"We can show you how to hunt. And we can tell you how to get corn to grow in dry soil. We can show you how to make moccasins, and we can tell you how to cure skins to make clothing.

"Brother, tell your people to come to this spot later in the day. Meanwhile, we will return to our camp and bring our own people back here with us."

So the hunters returned to their home, where their kinsmen were preparing a meal of rabbit and seed mush. As they all ate, the two told the others about the barefoot stranger they had found and about the conversation they had had with him.

After the meal, they all climbed the mountain to the place where the pair of hunters had found the stranger. And there they encountered him along with the rest of his people. The two parties camped together that night, exchanging stories and telling each other about their ways and their traditions.

The strangers reported that they had been created at the place where they all now sat. Seven years ago, they said, they had been placed there. Now they lived nearby at *Naadą́ą́' bił atiin*, or Corn Pass as *Bilagáana* the White Man would call it. But they returned here often to harvest fruit from the cactus and the yucca that grew in abundance nearby.

They called themselves *Tsédine'é*, which means Rock People in the language of *Bilagáana* the White Man. But to them the nameless ones gave the clan the title *Tsé nahabiłnii*, which means Rock Ready to Fall People, for that is where the hunters first discovered one of them. And once the new people were given that

name they were accepted as a Navajo clan, as indeed they now
consider themselves to be, it is said.

Fifteen

It is also said that the clanspeople of *Tsé nahabiłnii* led their
newly found kinsmen to some corn and pumpkins they had stored
at a place a short distance away. Then they suggested that together
the two groups should prepare for a journey. They knew of some
Apaches to the south whom they might all visit. For among them
were clans with names similar to those of the Navajo clans.

So they all went to the place where the corn and pumpkins were
hidden and made corncakes to eat on the way. Then they departed.
At length they arrived at a village far to the south called
Tsoohaanaa, which has no known meaning in the language of the
White Man. There they were immediately accepted as friends and
kinsmen. Indeed, the Apaches treated them so well that the
visitors resolved to remain for a while.

Three years passed before the *Tsé nahabiłnii* decided to return
north to join the Navajos along the San Juan Valley. The clan with
no name, however, remained for four additional years. Toward the
end of the fourth year, though, they began to talk of leaving.

Their Apache friends tried to persuade them to stay, but with no
success. And when they had their goods all packed and were ready
to begin their journey back up north, an old woman sitting on the
ground who had been observing them got up slowly and slowly
began circling them.

Around and around them she walked, around and around, coming
back to the place where she first began her circular movement.
Four times all told she made such a circle. Then, finally returning
to the spot where she had first been sitting, she faced them and
said these words to them:

"You came to live with us without a name," she said to them.

"And for seven years you have dwelt among us without a name.

"Without a name you have been our good friends. Without a
name you have exchanged stories with our own people.

"Well, you should not leave us unnamed.

"That is why I have walked around you.

"From now on you shall be known as *Honágháahnii* the He Walks Around One Clan. Henceforth you shall no longer be nameless."

So it was that those without a name were given one. And it is that name which has been theirs ever since.

• • • •

When the *Hoágháahnii* returned to the region of the San Juan Valley they found that their friends of *Tsé nahabiłnii* the Rock Ready to Fall Clan had long been settled among the other Navajo clans. They had formed close relationships with *Táchii'nii* Among the Red Waters People; with *Deeshchíí'nii* the Start of the Red Streak People; with *Kin łichíí'nii* the Red House People; and with *Tsi'naajinii* the Black Horizontal Forest People. To this very day, those five clans are like one large clan, so that no member of any one of them can marry any member of any of the others.

Likewise, before many more years passed the people of *Honágháahnii* the He Walks Around One Clan established close ties with the people of *Tł'ízíłání* the Many Goats Clan, with the people of *Dziłtł'ahnii* the Mountain Cove Clan; and with the people of *Tó'áhání* the Place Near the Water Clan; and with the people of *Nihoobáanii* the Gray Horizontal Streak Clan. So closely related are those five clans to this very day that every member of each one of them is forbidden to marry any other member of any of them.

So it was that the newer clans were accepted among the older ones. And that is how members of the various clans both new and old became bonded into a single Navajo tribe, it is said.

Sixteen

It is also said that about the time the *Honágháahnii* had returned to the San Juan Valley, a group of *Tábąąhá* had gone to *Aghaałą́* for a while.

One day during their stay at that place they sent two children to a nearby spring for water. The couple did as they were instructed, leaving the camp with two wicker bottles. But they returned with four.

"And where did you get these two extra bottles?" they were asked.

"We came upon two little girls at the spring," replied the children. "And we took the two bottles from them."

"What?" scolded their parents.

"Why did you do such a thing? And who are the two girls?"

"We don't know," replied the two.

"All we know is that they were strangers. We have never seen them before. They were dirty and badly dressed. They looked like no-account people."

At once the adults set out to find the girls and to return their property to them. And they did not go very far before they saw the two walking toward the *Tábqqhá* camp.

"Pray tell us who you are," asked the grown-ups.

"We belong to a band of wanderers encamped on that mountain over there," replied the little girls.

"Our people have fared poorly at hunting, and we have had little to eat. Many of them are tired. Many others are sick and sore. So they sent us to the spring to fetch water."

To which the adults of the *Tábqqhá* replied:

"First we shall name you.

"We shall call your people *Tó baazhní'ázhí* the Two Came to Water Clan.

"Then we shall make amends for the rude way our children have treated you. Come with us and rest. Let us feed you and care for you. Let us provide your people with the food and the help they need.[26]

"We will send several of our young men to the place where your people are camped. They will take plenty of food and water with them. And they will invite each of your kinsmen to come and live with us when they are strong enough to travel again."

When they arrived among *Tábqqhá* the Water's Edge People, the wanderers were welcomed as friends and kinsmen and were told that henceforth they would have a name. Under the name they were given they joined the Navajo nation as a flourishing clan. They would quickly establish a close bond with the people of *Tábqqhá*, and to this day members of the one group may not marry members of the other.

• • • •

Not long after the people of *Tó baazhní'ázhí* the Two Came to
Water Clan arrived at the valley of the San Juan, a group of Apaches
joined the growing Navajo nation. They too were quickly adopted
by the *Tábąąhá* and became members of that clan. At about the
same time a band of Paiutes came and were likewise adopted. They
too are members of that clan to this very day, although it is still
understood that they are of a different origin and they retain some
of their own traditions. And somewhat later yet another party of
Apaches came to the San Juan Valley and was adopted into the
Tábąąhá clan.

• • • •

Some years passed before another addition was made to the
Navajo tribe. This occurred when a party of Zunis arrived and were
also taken in by the *Tábąąhá*.

Soon thereafter came another band of Zunis, who combined with
those who had preceded them. Eventually they formed a separate
clan called *Naasht'ézhí dine'é*. That is what the Navajos had
formerly called all Zunis. It means Black Horizontal Striped People
in the language of *Bilagáana* the White Man. Those newcomers
had left the Zuni villages because food was scarce there.

Shortly after the second group of Zunis arrived, still another
people came, this time from the west. They bore painted faces, and
they are supposed once to have been part of the tribe now called
Mojaves who live along the banks of the lower Colorado River.
They brought with them the name *Dilzhę́'é*. In the language of
Bilagáana the White Man that name means Bird-voice People.
They have kept that name to this day.

• • • •

Shortly thereafter a raiding party was organized among several
different clans. Their purpose was to attack a pueblo called *Séí bee
hooghan*, which in the language of *Bilagáana* means House
of Sand.

There they captured two maidens and brought them back as
slaves. Near their former home there had been a salt lake. So their

many descendants among the Navajo came to form the clan known to this day as *Áshįįhí,* which in the language of the White Man means Salt Clan. And since the captives were taken by members of *Tséníjíkiní* the Honeycombed Rock People, those two groups are closely related to one another to this day. No member of the one clan may marry any member of the other.

•   •   •   •

Next a raiding party was organized among members of several clans to attack the people of Jemez Pueblo. On this raid a member of *Tł'aashchí'í* the Red Bottom Clan captured a Jemez maiden whom he sold to a member of *Nóóda'í dine'é* the Ute Clan. And inasmuch as she ultimately had many descendants she became ancestor to the clan now called *Mą'ii deeshgiizhnii.* That name means Coyote Pass People in the language of *Bilagáana* the White Man.

•   •   •   •

Not long after the Navajos attacked *Séí bee hooghan* the Sand House Pueblo there was a famine at that village. So some of the people who lived there abandoned their homes to join the Navajo nation. They claimed to come from a clan there known as *Tábąąhá,* and learning that they had counterparts along the San Juan Valley they asked to join the Navajo clan bearing the same name.

•   •   •   •

Next came a party of seven people from a distant place called *Tséyaanaato,* or Horizontal Water under the Cliffs. They had come, they said, to pay a short visit and to get to know the Navajos. But as the days and the months and the seasons and the years passed, they delayed their departure and ultimately remained. Their descendants have been known as *Tséyaanaadoohnii,* or Horizontal Water Under the Cliffs People. But that clan did not flourish as the other clans did and it is now extinct.

•   •   •   •

The people from the west whom *Asdzą́ą́ nádleehé* the Changing
Woman created out of the skin from under her right arm, to whom
she had the wand of the white shell, to whom the others had
originally given the name *Hashtł'ishnii*, or Mud Clan, and who had
arrived at the San Juan Valley after the long migration, eventually
made their homes near a high stone house built by an earlier
people that overlooked the river. Consequently they became
known as *Kiyaa'áanii*, which the White Man would call Standing
House Clan in his language.

•   •   •   •

And when *Bit'anii* the Close to Her Body Clan was encamped at
a place called *Tótsoh*, which in his language the White Man would
call Big Water, a man and a woman appeared mysteriously out of
the lake there. From this mysterious couple is descended a people
now called *Tótsohnii*. Of course, their name in the language that
Bilagáana the White Man speaks would be Big Water People. They
became affiliated with the people of *Bit'anii* the Close to Her Body
Clan. So close are they to this day that no member of the one can
marry any member of the other.

•   •   •   •

The *Tótsohnii* were the last to join the Navajo nation as a
distinct clan. Henceforth the people were to increase their
numbers and their strength from within.

But their existence as a tribe was secure. They flourish here on
the surface of the fifth world to this very day, it is said.

•   •   •   •

Those are the things that happened a long, long time ago, it
is said.

NOTES

Introduction

1. Or else those biases might themselves have intensified the racism; it is a complicated matter. Pearce calls the strong, deep-seated prejudice of Europeans against tribal peoples *savagism*. Turner traces that proclivity back beyond its recorded Old Testament roots and follows its development through the conquest of the New World.

2. What astonishes me now, as I recall that experience, is that the question I was raising so innocently had already been explored and was continuing to receive scholarly attention. Serious investigations of what we can call Native American poetry go back quite far. Exactly how far is an open question, depending to some degree on what we consider disinterested objectivity or valid scholarship. Early collectors like Schoolcraft now seem somewhat patronizing to the traditions they explored, perhaps because they distorted what they put into print to accommodate contemporary taste and prejudices. The influence of Schoolcraft's Rousseauistic sentimentality has in fact carried well into the twentieth century. See, for example, Canfield; and see Cronyn. As the nineteenth century drew to a close, however, some investigators became more open-minded and objective. Among the best of the nineteenth-century anthologizer is Brinton. Other scholars, led largely by Franz Boas, began investigating Indian material more rigorously. See Andrews for a bibliography of his writings. Step by step and item by item, such pioneer anthropologists were making it easier for successive scholars to identify aspects of native cultures that are specifically poetic. Unfortunately, their work was more or less ignored by most literary critics, whose attention was fixed on Old World influences throughout the first half of the present century. In a fairly haphazard fashion I began to come across some interesting and provocative publications that were overlooked by mainstream literary scholars. By no means were they all necessarily adequate or well translated; but to varying degrees they succeeded in transmitting some notion that there was such a thing as Native American

poetry and that it was worth investigating. Frances Densmore explored
the close relationship between poetry and music in preliterate cultures, for
example. Alice Fletcher compiled an early anthology that reflected the
new objectivity fostered by pioneer ethnographers. Paul Radin (1915)
attempted to link Native American mythology with poetic theory. Nellie
Barnes studied some of the features of North American tribal poetry in the
manner of early formalist critics. Mary Austin (1931) was one of the first
to argue that Native American poetry represented an integral part of
American literary tradition. The works of such writers, I was to discover,
represented no more than a sampling of the kind of material abundantly
available but virtually unaccounted for in most literary curricula or
graduate programs. Much of that material is listed in the bibliographies of
two serviceable (though inadequate) anthologies still easy to find: Astrov,
pp. 345–58; and Day, pp. 185–98. For a later and more comprehensive
bibliography, see Marken.

3. Had I examined them more carefully as a direct extension of the
spoken or singing voice, the works of quite a few traditional English poets
could have helped me reduce the distance between oral and written
performance. This is especially true of certain Renaissance poets. Only
recently, however, have scholars—at least in the twentieth
century—become aware of the relationship between music and poetry or
oral performance and print. See Welsh, especially chapter 8, pp. 190–242.
For a demonstration of how a particular set of lyrics can combine
sophisticated verse with artful music, see Mark W. Booth's discussion of
Thomas Campion's "I Care Not For These Ladies," pp. 75–96.

4. For a representative list of earlier anthologies, see Marken,
pp. 11–17.

5. Robert Young summarizes the theme more elaborately. In a personal
correspondence he writes the following: "Preparation of the Fifth World
and the coming of man are explained in the Creation (or Origin) Myth as
events that were predestined, and which took place in conformity with a
cosmic plan developed in the First World through magic and intelligence.
The sequence of events is evolutionary, thereafter, with the creation of the
essences of female and male, the power of reproduction, the prototypes of
the animate beings that would be necessary to man, the mountains into
which the perfect prototypes could be instilled and preserved, the 'essence'
of rain (clouds over the mountains) and the 'essence' of harmony and peace
as the necessary concomitant of reproduction and immortality of the
human species *(bik'eh hózhóón/tsi'ah naagháii)*—the stars, the moon, the
sun were created in the course of events and, when all was ready, the
ultimate goal of the cosmic plan, man, was created. The Creation Myth
carries this pervasive theme from the beginning." Witherspoon (1977)
likewise explores the philosophical dimensions implicit in the theme of
the creation story. See especially chapter 1, pp. 13–46.

6. I subsequently went through Matthews's papers and field notes at the Wheelwright Museum in Santa Fe, where they are on deposit, and I still have no sure sense of the way he actually proceeded. Among his effects I found copious notations on the language, including makeshift word lists in various notebooks and on numerous note cards, as well as handwritten glosses of Navajo songs which he transcribed—all indicating that he could translate Navajo into English quite well by the end of his career. It became obvious to me that he took great pains to render songs and prayers accurately, and those translations are still highly regarded. But I found no transcriptions in the Navajo script he employed of any portion of the creation story. In fact, among his field notes and notebooks there was no full-length, handwritten manuscript version of what ultimately appears as the printed version of "The Navaho Origin Legend," which is the title he gave his translation of the narrative. In his introduction he suggests that the cycle is based on a version which he "selected" because it was the most complete. But I was able to locate no manuscript copy of that particular account nor any set of notes that matches it. Only two fragments among the papers seem at all related to what appears in the book. One is an unbound set of small, unlined pages that summarizes part of the story and that obviously provided the basis for an account of the narrative he had published earlier. The other is a set of entries in a bound, lined notebook that seems to have some bearing on parts of the story he actually recorded in *Navaho Legends*. However, there are some discrepancies between what that notebook contains and what eventually found its way into print in the final volume. In addition, there is another notebook account, recited to him by Old Torlino, which he refers to as "Version A" in his introduction and in the notes, but which bears very little resemblance to what appears in the 1897 publication. See note 19, p. 354 below. There is no full-length biography of Matthews that I am aware of. For what I know about him I have relied on the Wheelwright Museum papers and on Poor. Also, I have used three brief sketches: *American Anthropologist*, 7 (1905), pp. 514–23; *Journal of American Folklore*, 18 (1905), pp. 245–47; and Link (1960).

7. Gummere applies the term mainly to the traditional ballad in England and on the Continent; see p. 194. But he also acknowledges its importance in "savage" poetry; see pp. 252–56. Barnes discusses it more thoroughly and more particularly as an important element in Native American poetic style.

8. The episode in which First Woman creates genitals appears in Goddard, pp. 138–39. For the seduction scene, see pp. 134–36 below. See also n. 42, p. 376. See also Haile: 1932a, pp. 17–19; and see Reichard: n.d., pp. 19–21, and Haile: 1981b, p.210. For a thorough discussion of male-female relationships in the broad context of the Navajo kinship system, see Witherspoon (1975).

9. For a detailed discussion of some of these effects, see Toelken and Scott. For a brief, nontechnical discussion of the Navajo language, see Kluckhohn and Leighton, chapter 8, pp. 182–214. For a brief but somewhat more technical discussion, see Witherspoon (1977), chapters 2 and 3, pp. 47–150. Young and Morgan (1943) provide a concise grammar. They describe the language more thoroughly in 1980.

10. The text I am quoting from appears in Matthews (1907), pp. 54–55.

11. Reichard (1944b), provides a remarkably thorough poetic analysis of Navajo prayers. If a more comprehensive study of Navajo poetics were to be assembled, it could very well be done according to the principles she applies in this valuable work.

12. See Hatcher; see, also, Reichard (1977); and see McGreevy.

13. See also Tedlock (1972b). See, too, Hymes (1965, 1975a, both reprinted in 1981), pp. 35–64, 79–141.

14. My reasons for rejecting Tedlock's translations as a model also more or less apply to translations such as those by Hymes and Toelken—much as I admire what they have done. The difference between a longer narrative which deals explicitly with creation and a shorter narrative which does not is, I think, significant. Tedlock himself explores that difference somewhat when he makes the distinction between two kinds of Zuni narrative: the *chimiky'ana'kowa*, which "belongs to a period when the world was 'soft,' " and "is regarded as literally true," and the *telapnaawe*, which is "set in a world which had already hardened" and which is "regarded as fiction" (1972, p. 222). There are other differences, too, which might very well dictate whether an English translation should be rendered in the kind of patterned prose I finally elected to use in developing my text, or in the more deliberately crafted, rich poetic texture Tedlock employs and Hymes and Toelken/Scott more or less emulate. These differences should probably bear upon the choice of how an English translation should be typeset. A *telapnaawe* can be recited only during the winter storytelling season when snakes are hibernating. It is, says Tedlock, "clearly identified as such as the formulaic frame which encloses it" (ibid.). In other words, it is apt to be more stylized in the way it is written down. Personally, I do not think a longer narrative could bear such a deliberately formal arrangement. That would be something like trying to write a novel in ballad stanzas or to produce a play where the characters all speak in sonnets. In any case, the question of how Native American narratives should be transformed into print is an extremely complicated one, and I do not presume to have the last word on it here by any means. The complexity of the issue is well presented by Hymes (1981) and by Tedlock (1972b). See, also, Ramsey. For background on the whole question of defining the place and function of oral written tradition in the broader context of literary study, see Bascomb (1953), Taylor, and Utley. See, also, Bascomb (1954). In suggesting that preliterate

narratives might be classified as either *chimiky'ana'kowa* or *telapnaawe*, of course, I am simplifying beyond the established way of classifying oral narratives. For an explanation of the more conventional distinction between myth, legend and tale, see Brunvand, pp. 79–128. The bibliographical notes, pp. 99–102 and pp. 124–28, are especially helpful to the newcomer to this question. See, also, Dorson, pp. 147–66.

15. Various portions of a number of the Haile-Reichard manuscripts had been published by the time I discovered the originals. Several others have been published since. Few, however, have been duplicated as originally transcribed and translated, even allowing that the subsequent development of a standard Navajo orthography necessitated a routine change in the original script. None of these published versions has been treated as poetry. See Haile (1943a, 1943b, 1978, 1979, 1981a, 1981b); Luckert (1975, 1979); and Wyman (1957, 1962, 1965, 1970, 1975).

16. Other versions and fragments of the Navajo creation story exist in print in various places. For an annotated bibliographical guide to those texts, see Spencer (1947), pp. 12–30. Subsequently published versions include King, Oakes and Campbell; Link (1956); Fishler; O'Bryan; Newcomb; Yazzie; Haile (1981a, 1981b). See, also, Wyman (1970), a monumental volume which contains a set of corollary tales which demonstrate, among other things, the philosophical underpinning of the Navajo creation cycle. The material there also provides a broad framework of tradition for the entire narrative.

17. This bias is a far more complex matter than I at first suspected. The forces that seem to account for it combine to create a major cultural watershed. See Eisenstein. See also Turner, especially pp. 31–47. Likewise, see Pearce; and see Zolla.

18. For a specific set of examples, see Duran. The bibliography, pp. 478–84, is especially valuable. See, also, Zolla, pp. 148–72, 229–76, for a broad summary of how tribal poetry has been received and treated in North America.

19. Even the conception of "folk," with its implicit hierarchy of a dominant culture and a subordinate subculture, should be reexamined, as Ginzburg suggests and then illustrates. Nowadays there is less rectitude about what is appropriate to literary study; perhaps the intellectual climate is right for rethinking the relationship between oral and alphabetical transmission of traditions. See Park, who touches upon some of the issues that concern me here.

20. Consider this statement, for example, and compare it with the description of how *Dook'o'oosłííd* (the San Francisco Peaks) was created, p. 88 below. "This peak was made by the holy people in the beginning. At that time when it was made it was made only by the holy people, not by the white people nor any Indians, it was made just by the holy people and this thing here, this San Francisco Peak is prayers, is a prayer and it is

sitting there with prayers and it has white shell beads and turquoise and Apache teardrops and abalone and that is what is sitting there with and also plants of life, sitting there with life" (Deposition of Frank Goldtooth, Sr., No. 26761, Wilson vs. Coconino County Board of Supervisors, Tuba City, Arizona, Dec. 20, 1972, In the Superior Court of the State of Arizona, Coconino County, p. 33).

21. See Aberle (1967), for example. The argument applies to other tribes as well. See Dorris.

22. It is hazardous to generalize so glibly about the broad cultural matrix in which the Navajo creation story functions. Nor is it easy to summarize the intricate relationship between that particular narrative cycle and the tradition it defines. Navajo culture is no simple affair. Like any so-called primitive culture, it is the product of an expansive world view all too easily overlooked or oversimplified by outsiders like ourselves. For a good introduction to the Navajo world view and to some of the ways it is linked to Navajo art, see Witherspoon (1977). For one study that demonstrates well how Navajo poetry and Navajo culture are linked, see Luckert (1975). And see Revard. On p. 90 he makes an assertion that bears repeating here. Speaking of Charles Eastman, a Santee Sioux who eventually received a Dartmouth education, he says that by listening to and repeating "the legends of his ancestors and his race" as a child, Eastman received "a schooling, but without having school and home, or school and family, or school and tribe, separated into different buildings and different systems run by different people, as schools are with us." Obviously, the close symbiotic relationship being spoken of here between poetry and culture is not unique to the Navajos.

23. The meaning of the word "literature" is actually less stable and less precise than we might suppose. See Williams, pp. 150–54.

24. I do not mean to suggest that such a discovery is my own. Austin (1931) tried to advance that assertion a half-century ago. It is convincingly displayed more recently by Quasha and Rothenberg.

Part One

1. Navajo storytellers frequently add the verbal phrase "It is said" (jiní: one says, he says, they say) when they recite narrative. According to Matthews (1902), p. 311, n. 26, variants are sometimes used "for melodious repetition." One Navajo informant I consulted told me that the term is actually the third person distributive plural (three or more) form of

the verb *dajini,* often compressed in oral narrative to two syllables *(jiní)* or to one *(djin)* so that rhythm can be maintained. The expression immediately places the narrative in the past, and the distributive plural implies that many others have formerly told the story, which establishes its authority.

2. I have seen the phrase *Nílch'i dine'é* translated as "mist people" (O'Bryan [1956], p. 2), and as "air people" (Witherspoon [1977], p. 58). Literally the expression means "wind people." I have chosen to avoid that translation, however, so as not to confuse the *níílchi dine'é* with a supernatural character who is later identified as *Nílch'i łigai,* the White Wind, who breathes animating life into First Man and First Woman, pp. 49–50 below; or with *Nílch'i* the Wind, a tutelary god who helps the monster-slaying twins, *Naayéé' neizghání* and *Tó bájísh chíní,* throughout their various exploits in Part Three below. See note 30, p. 372, below, There is a close relationship between the god *Nílch'i* and *Nílch'i dine'é* it seems to me, and to call them wind people or air people would be accurate enough. But I choose to translate the term as "Air-Spirit People" to keep them distinct as a group from the more highly deified winds and to underscore something typical in Navajo mythology: the objects and forces of nature are frequently seen as possessing an animus or life-force that corresponds roughly with our concept of the soul. See Haile (1943a).

In using the English verb *move around* here, I follow Matthews's example. I assume that he selects it to reflect the Navajo continuitive imperfective third person plural *naakai:* they are walking around, moving around, going back and forth, etc. Having that verb and form in mind, I picture these creatures performing the continuous activity of going about their daily business.

3. The symbolic value of colors basic to Navajo ceremonialism is clearly identified early in the narrative. Generally, the four colors represent the four sectors of the sky. White, a male color, stands for dawn; blue, a female color, stands for broad daylight; yellow, also female, is the evening twilight; and black, a male color, is the darkness of night. See Reichard (1950), pp. 187ff., for a full description of what the colors symbolize. Also see her summary, p. 206. Hatcher, pp. 121–33, explains how the meanings traditionally associated with the four standard colors continue to apply today, at least in reference to Navajo art. The four colors identified here anticipate the creation of the sacred mountains marking the four cardinal points in the fifth world in Part Two, Chapter 4, below, p. 86. Also see Wyman (1970), p. 369, in Frank Mitchell's *Blessingway* version of the making of day and night. It becomes obvious that there is a clear association between colors and the cosmic view of reality thoroughly integrated into the Navajo world view. See, too, Witherspoon (1977), pp. 145–46.

4. Even though Matthews does not actually mention the stream

flowing to the north in his text proper, he does suggest in a note that there could very well have been such a stream. See Matthews (1897), p. 216, note 19. I posit the existence of that stream here because so much within the narrative implicitly supports its being there. Likewise, so much of what is known about Navajo design and symbolism suggest that it should be there. For example, as the story progresses notice how the image of the four cardinal directions emanating from a central point is related to the image of the circle. See Reichard (1950), pp. 161–70. The sense of symmetrical, orderly design permeates religious and even secular life in Navajo culture. McAllester, for instance (1954), p. 16, notes that " . . . when the drumhead is tied down, the [medicine man] sings five songs. With the first four he beats the drum near the rim on the north, east, south and west sides respectively. For the fifth song he beats the drum in the center."

5. See Wyman (1965), p. 19, for a statement on the importance of insects in Navajo thought. For a more impressionistic response to the place of insects in the Navajo world view, but nevertheless a usefully suggestive one, see Moon, p. 17.

6. I refer again to the sense of design expressed throughout the opening passage. Hatcher discusses one aspect of that design and concludes that "rhythm in [Navajo] drypainting . . . takes the form of small variations in the repetition of the principal figures or design units" (p. 75). And, of course, we see such a pattern of repetition "with small variations" in the progression from unit to unit here, too, expressed verbally instead of graphically. Mills, describing the procedure for undertaking a sandpainting, reports that "Navajos begin near the center and work outward" (p. 42), suggesting that the ceremonial procedure replicates the process of emergence as it is being described here. The statement implies centrality of the Navajo creation story to the overall culture.

Something that Matthews observed in an untitled, unpublished pencil manuscript (n.d.c.) suggests that the symmetrical variation represented here is by no means mere decoration or meaningless design. It appears to indicate a tradition of careful observation transformed into a stylized art, not only among Navajos but among other tribes as well. "It has been well shown," Matthews writes in a discussion that focuses initially on the sun and its attendant deity, "that the Hero God of the American aborigines is but a myth of the light of day and that it is not confined to the Western Continent, but has its counterparts throughout the world and among all races of men. He is a light god but not the Sun God for the morning light appears before the Sun and to the savage mind is not identical with the sun although associated with it. In some form of the myth he is the child of the sun, in others the creation of it."

As Matthews continues discussing this mythic percursor to the sun, his argument becomes germane to the function of the four "chiefs" in the scheme that materializes in this early part of the narrative. "As the daylight begins in the east," Matthews proceeds, "he is commonly represented as born in the east; but the particular quarter in which he is born is not always specific. He is often represented as one of four brothers (as in Peru in the days of the Incas), the others being now considered gods of the other cardinal points" (n.d.c., pp. 1–2). Here, then, we can see the relationship between the relatively simplistic deification of light in contrast with a countervailing deification of darkness. The duality is then broken down into a four-way relationship as the observation of the day-night cycle gives way over time to an observed cycle of four seasons. León-Portilla talks about such an expanded cycle in his discussion of Aztec cosmology, where he identifies a four-way rivalry between four deities vying over the course of the year for the center of the cosmos. This perpetual contention governs the seasonal behavior of the earth as it is seen by people who must plant and hunt and celebrate holidays (pp. 32–36). Numerous graphic configurations among the various artifacts of Native Americans express such a relationship. Why shouldn't verbal expressions as well record an equally clear, sophisticated understanding of time and of closely related cosmic forces?

Hence the number four functions again and again as a multiple of two, with constant references to various pairs—and pairs of pairs—always seeking and ultimately defining balance as a dynamic relationship linking opposites and aligning them. See note 15, pp. 352–53, below, especially the statement on pairing, p. 353. Cardinal direction is associated with seasons. And beneath the abstraction of stylized design there is always expressed a clear awareness of time as it is seen in the daily cycles of the sun's movement, of the monthly phases of the moon, of the yearly patterns of two solstices and two equinoxes. Concomitantly, there are various ways of expressing a related awareness of times for planting and harvesting, for hunting certain game, and the like. So that what at first seems like an innocent element of balance or symmetry in an abstract Native American design turns out, if the speculations above are correct, to be art in the highest sense of transforming awareness into an ordered pattern.

7. Generally, Matthews underplays references to sexuality, not an uncommon tendency among nineteenth-century ethnographers. See note 15, pp. 386–87, below. Still, as I have suggested in the introduction, sexual behavior has a manifestly important function in this narrative and in other Navajo narratives. Sexual excesses are often responsible for cosmic disharmony or for social disorder in Navajo tradition. See pp. 00ff., for example, where the men and the women quarrel and separate. See, too, pp. 94–97, where the autoeroticism of the women leads to the creation of monsters. Or see pp. 134ff., where the sexual contact between Changing Bear Maiden and Coyote leads to a disruptive chain of events.

The matter of harmony between the genders and its centrality in Navajo culture is discussed elsewhere, especially in note 82, pp. 404–6.

Among the existing versions of this episode, reasons for the squabbling that occurs vary, but it inevitably reverts to sexual behavior. In Wyman's version of the emergence (1965), for instance, the insect people make war on each other (p. 107), which eventually leads to adultery (p. 113). The lone exception to the pattern of improper sexual behavior leading to social disarray that I know of occurs in Wheelwright's version, where the quarrel is between *Begochidi* and *Haashch'ééshzhini,* or Black God the son of fire, who complains that the former gets to make the rules. Black God then "floods" the first world with fire, forcing the insect people to escape to the second world with *Begochidi*'s help. Wheelwright's version is, like Fishler's, one that reflects Christian influence. Both were compiled in the twentieth century and show attrition either because the informants had been Christianized or because they were sensitive to the Christian beliefs of those to whom they dictated. Reichard (1944a), p. 19, speculates that Mary Wheelwright herself might have been responsible for some of the Christian accretions in her version.

8. Throughout the earlier portions of the narrative especially, we see statements like this one where characters are unable to control circumstances which they should be able to control. The result is social conflict or the absence of *k'é* or solidarity, as it is discussed in note 82, p. 404 below. These uncontrollable circumstances include such things as actions that should have otherwise been performed or prevented; tabooed relationships with supernaturals, with certain lower forms of life, or with members of one's family or clan; certain emotions that should have been curbed, and so forth. Contrast the lack of control identified here with the harmonious bonding that is achieved throughout Part Four. See, also, note 6, p. 410 below. In general, control is a highly important motif throughout the narrative, just as it is a prized attribute in Navajo society. First Man's problem (p. 59) when he quarrels with First Woman is that he loses control. He *lets* her remarks anger him. Witherspoon, who argues that the motif of control permeates all aspects of Navajo culture, explains how it can be seen at work in the fabric of the language. See 1977, pp. 71–73, for example, where he demonstrates that actions performed by one noun of higher status upon a noun of lower status must be appropriately recorded as active or passive.

9. See Spencer (1947), pp. 70–81, for an explanation of "chiefs and councils." See especially p. 70: "Activities concerning order within the group, measures for the welfare of the group, or relations with other groups are regulated by 'chiefs,' by councils of the people, or by a combination of both. Usually the unit of political organization over which a chief has control is not specified, although sometimes this unit seems to be the clan." One of the developments we can observe in the ensuing narrative is

the evolution of a less autocratic polity than what we find in this passage. See, for example, the statement on egalitarian relationships, note 26, pp. 415–16, below.

10. Here we have the first indication of the theme of emergence, common to many Native American cultures. For a full guide to literature on the emergence theme in Navajo tradition, see Wyman (1965), pp. 65–102. For a more general study of the emergence theme in North America, see Wheeler-Voegelin and Moore. For one attempt (but only one) to find universal meaning in this theme, see Luckert (1976), p. 163. Elsewhere (1979, pp. 146–47), Luckert links the theme of emergence with birth, healing, and perhaps rebirth. For an overall grasp of the significance of the emergence theme in Navajo narratives, it is useful to consider a statement by Wyman (1962), p. 27. In discussing one of the prayers that are part of a Windway ceremony, he says, "This is one of the prayers which describe a supernatural, usually Talking God, descending to the underworlds to find the patient's spiritual self in the 'home of things evil in kind,' and leading him back to safety, retracing his steps past direful guards, such as red snakes, red wind, red coyote, until the patient is returned to his fields and his hogan." Thus a set of underworlds which are described in the Navajo creation story acquire a perspective as the loci of a flawed collective past which must be, in effect, subliminally relived and corrected. See note 11, below.

11. See Mills, pp. 188–89: "Unable to call in good from the outside and unable to drive out evil, the Navajoes had to so move themselves to a new world—an uncontaminated life-space where the process began again, culminating with emergence into the present world. Emergence can hardly be called flight because it is a venturing into the next concentric space, more extensive and dangerous than the last."

Such a perception helps us to understand the importance of creating a sandpainting, which is in effect a duplication of the creation process as it is described in this narrative. The sandpainting, an essential part of a Navajo healing ceremony, thus helps the patient to "emerge" from the locus of his illness back into the world which, dangerous as it is, can be kept orderly and controlled. To a large extent this control is maintained by participation in activities we would consider artistic, such as music, weaving, and storytelling.

12. For a reference to early contact between ancestral Navajos and Pueblo peoples, see Young, p. 6. Spencer (1947), pp. 86–92, summarizes the way the Pueblos are dealt with in various printed accounts of the Navajo creation. She also compares the so-called mythological accounts with historical and ethnological data. Haile (1938), p. 17, indicates that the origin of the Pueblo peoples "is usually passed over in silence in Navajo legends and is accepted as an accomplished fact." The conventionally held notion is that the Pueblos are long-time dwellers in the Southwest while

the Athabascan Navajos are recent migrants to that region. But that is a view which calls for further scrutiny. See Forbes, pp. xi–xxiii.

13. The concept of Holy People is well summarized by Wyman (1970), p. 312, n. 219. The "pantheon" of Navajo gods is not easy to master, since in some versions of the creation story their names change from the lower worlds to the upper ones, and since in some of the chantway narratives a god can be a member of a type all of whose other members bear the same name. Some storytellers say either that a deity such as *Haashch'ééłti'í* can travel with the speed of light, or that he has counterparts with the same name who can materialize wherever they are needed or see fit to appear. In either case, the Holy People have important roles to play among the corpus of printed Navajo ceremonial and creation literature. Each supernatural, it seems, has a certain set of traits. Often these can lead to some interesting speculation. For instance, in Wyman (1962), *Bits'íís łizhin* kidnaps a child inexplicably and grows angry when some of the other gods come to fetch it. He finally demands offerings in exchange for it, including a dark bow, a fawnskin, a tobacco pouch with the figure of the sun placed on one side and the figure of the moon on the other, a pipe of jet, a piece of rock crystal for lighting the pipe, and a special cigarette (p. 92). Associated with fire and with the center of the earth, he suggests some ancient sacrificial demand that has been linked with an archaic Olmec tradition that the volcanic inner earth extracted heavy penalty from fearful people. Consult Luckert (1976), pp. 41–63, 65–90. Haile (1938), p. 35, indicates that the origins of *Bits'íís łizhin* are unknown. He goes back as far as the origin of the first world itself, Navajos seem to believe. Perhaps the account provided by Wyman the possibility that human sacrifice should be replaced with a surrogate offering. If so, we have a Native American analogue to the Biblical account of Abraham and Isaac. See note 16, pp. 365–66; note 18, pp. 366–67; and note 59, p. 398, below.

14. Reichard (1950), p. 530, explains that "mythologically buckskin is an emblem of life; ritualistically it is a life symbol." On the overall use of the buckskin, see Luckert (1975), p. 109. Hill (1938), pp. 132–34, describes the way sacred buckskins are obtained. Also see Matthews (1902), p. 54.

15. Written accounts of the origin of First Man and First Woman vary fairly widely. In Wheelwright, p. 39, for example, First Man's mother is "Night," and his father is "the blue above the place where the Sun has set." First Woman's mother is the daybreak, while her father is "the yellow light after the sun has set." In O'Bryan, pp. 1–2, First Man and First Woman are created in the first world at the beginning of the narrative. First Man is created "at the place where the Black Cloud and the White Cloud meet." With him is created "the white corn, perfect in shape." First Woman has created where "Blue Cloud" and "Yellow Cloud" come together. With her appears "the yellow corn . . . also perfect." O'Bryan identifies her informant as Sandoval, *Hastiin tlo'tsehee* (Old Man Buffalo

Grass), whose version seems to have reflected some mild Christian accretions. Even among Matthews's old field notes there is variation in the accounts of how the first couple came into being. In an unpublished item titled "Notes on Navajo Cosmogony," (Wheelwright Museum Papers, Box III, Folder 1, Item #193, p. 20), he records that First Man and First Woman were among the original inhabitants of the first world, which differs quite obviously from what we find here. On what Matthews finally records in *Navaho Legends*, Reichard (1950), p. 27, writes: "From this account we may conclude that First Man and First Woman not only *had* corn in the early worlds but also *were* corn and came to symbolize transformation into human form." See, too, Hill (1938), p. 26, p. 53.

Notice the motif of pairing here. This is one of the major motifs in the story. Reichard (1950), pp. 248–49, observes that this episode provides the first real example of pairing; significantly, it occurs with the creation of the "first pair," the effects of whose divisive quarrel are not fully resolved until the reconciliation of *Jóhonaa'éí* the Sun and *Asdzą́ą́ nádleehé* the Changing Woman. By then, however, the monsters who are indirectly created as the result of the cleavage between them have already done their damage. We see pairing at work also in Wyman (1970), pp. 393–96. Even the twin goals of "Long-Life" and "Happiness" reflect the extent of pairing in Navajo culture. See Wyman (1970), pp. 397–98. And see Witherspoon (1977), p. 17, p. 202. See also, note 7, p. 343 above; note 9, p. 385 below; note 13, p. 386 below; and most especially, see note 82, pp. 404–6.

Matthews recognizes an incipient understanding of evolutionary principles in this portion of the narrative and elsewhere in Navajo lore. In 1886a, pp. 9–10, he writes: "With a strange suggestion of the existence of a primeval Darwin we find in the [Navajo creation story] the animals assuming more and more the human character, until the lower worlds which were once peopled only by flying animals are later inhabited by creatures who are spoken of as men." What he expresses here is repeated in 1886b.

16. See Reichard (1950), p. 149: " . . . the transformation of corn ears into human beings indicates an obvious association between wind and breath, and cross references establish whorls . . . as elements of the associative group; hence the explanation that breath enters the body at the place were there are whorls. Since down is easily set in motion by the winds or breath, down feathers and motion are further extensions of the group." Hence the significance of the enchanted hoop of feathers *(naayéé' ats'os)*, p. 198 below. See, too, note 35, p. 392 below. Likewise, we get a clear sense of the significance of the various winds in Wyman (1962), where they function to warn and to chastise, to trap the errant hero, and to deliver him. They are sometimes supplicants, sometimes benign messengers, sometimes tutelaries who keep the hero mindful of his purpose. See, too,

Joseph Campbell's statement in King, Oakes and Campbell, p. 76. We also begin to understand the pervasive role of *Niłch'i* the Wind, who rides on the folds of the hero's ear and whispers advice to him. Likewise, we appreciate the close association between him and some of the Holy People. It is an incarnation of the wind's power that gives humans in particular their inner integrity. For a thorough study of the wind as a deity in Navajo storytelling and a force in Navajo thought, see McNeley. See especially pp. 7–13, where the role of the wind in the context of this passage is discussed.

17. For a survey of the various accounts of what First Man and First Woman do after they are created, see Reichard (1950), pp. 433ff. Haile (1938), p. 17, questions the possibility that the couple themselves had children.

18. Frequently the various heroes and heroines of the chantway myths visit the dwelling places of the gods, where they are taught healing and blessing rites. For an elaborate discussion of that pattern, see Spencer (1957), pp. 100–218. Perhaps the most detailed printed account of such a visit is found in Wyman (1970), pp. 219ff.

19. It is not uncharacteristic for First Woman to make such decisions herself. See Matthews (1902), p. 17, where he describes the woman's overall position in Navajo culture as "one of much independence and power." Among the supernaturals, he writes, "the female is potent and conspicuous. Spencer (1947), pp. 31–39, surveys the way marriage is treated in various published accounts of the creation. See also Changing Woman's assertion, p. 275 below. (And see note 82, pp. 404–6 below.) This paragraph, the paragraph preceding, and the two that follow are my own additions. The passage seems to belong to the overall narrative, although it is one that Matthews might have bowdlerized had he heard it. My source is Goddard, pp. 139–40.

20. References to the hermaphrodites are catalogued in Spencer (1947), pp. 98–101. According to Wyman (1965), the original *nádleeh* are credited with the invention of pottery, wicker water-bottles, grinding stones, and other domestic utensils and procedures. Haile (1932b), p. 92, note 6, defines hermaphrodites as men "performing a woman's labor." They are not without status in the Navajo creation cycle and seem to have no particular stigma to overcome. Later in Haile's account of the quarrel between the sexes they exercise a great deal of authority. Before First Man and First Woman work out a reconciliation, they must get the hermaphrodites to agree. Furthermore, Haile's informant refers to them as *asdzáni-ada'iłíinii*, which translates as wife-venerable uncle. See Hill (1935), pp. 273–79. Also see Hill (1937). On their skill and status, see note 29, p. 357 below.

21. This passage accounts for the "stalking way" of hunting deer, according to Hill (1938), p. 123. See, also, p. 96, where he explains the ritual nature of hunting. Also, a statement appears on p. 111 that should not be overlooked, brief as it is. One of his informants told him, Hill

reports while describing the process of skinning and butchering a deer during a ritual hunt, "The Talking God instructed the people in this way of butchering when he told them how to skin the game for their own use." The statement attests to the very direct relationship between narrative and everyday life in Navajo culture. It also suggests how that relationship may matter in other preliterate cultures where the collective memory serves to store information. Listening to a story such as this one, then, is by no means mere entertainment. It is an act of sharing knowledge wherein art and learning cannot be separated. The Navajo hunter tradition, examined by Luckert (1975), is clearly evident here, which suggests to me that this is an especially old segment of the story. The technique of hunting with a disguise is described in Matthews (1887), pp. 391–92.

22. The origin of the male penis and the female vagina is not described in Matthews. The source is Goddard, pp. 138–39.

23. Reichard (1950), p. 79, sees Coyote as an "exponent of irresponsibility" and "an uncontrolled aspect of either Sun himself or his child." She calls him a "child of Sky" who "represents lust on earth, matching Sun's promiscuity as a celestial being" and who "observes no rules." According to Wheelwright, pp. 55–56, his mother is the light of dawn and he is the bringer of fire in the fourth world. Newcomb, pp. 138–50, gives a detailed and well-told account of Coyote's fire-bringing exploits. Hill (1938), p. 72, reports that some Navajos attribute to Coyote "control of the rain." To this day Navajos of all ages take great delight in heaping scorn upon Coyote for his misadventures, yet they maintain a sturdy reverence for him. It is all too easy to overgeneralize in making statements about Coyote, and all too easy for non-Native Americans to oversimplify his role. Yet he is one of the most important characters in the narrative and perhaps the singlemost important personage in the full assembly of Navajo characters. See note 3, pp. 360–61; and note 35, pp. 373–74; along with note 52, p. 379 below. It is not enough to call him simply amoral or self-serving, even though he sometimes indulges in amoral or self-serving escapades. Ultimately, I see him as the figurehead of individualistic impulses in a tribal culture where selfhood is frequently subordinated to the needs of the group and often repressed. That impulse is sometimes good, sometimes bad. But more important than evaluating it as a positive force or a negative one is acknowledging its strength and its frequent appeal. A useful analogue to the Navajo Coyote figure is the Winnebago Trickster whose exploits and attributes are described and whose behavior is analyzed by Radin (1956).

24. On Coyote's appearance, see Fishler, p. 23: "Coyote at this time was not like he is now. He was the same physically except he only had hair underneath his arms, on his lips (like a mustache), head and pubic area." Haile (1932a), p. 6, provides one account of how he gets his luxurious coat, which he will lose in a later episode, pp. 147–48 below.

25. In a print-oriented culture like ours, it is easy to overlook the importance of naming. First Man and First Woman assert their leadership as creators by speaking out and naming places and things, which is something like mapping an entire culture. See Witherspoon (1977), p. 131; and see Revard, especially p. 85. Haile (1981b), p. 8, presents a version of the emergence that seems to represent a much older set of traditions. We find that the earlier worlds are associated with speech. That account seems to be one that refers primarily to migration, perhaps of the early Athabascan forerunners to the Navajo tribe. Analogously, the earlier worlds are barren places and the initial migrations seem like attempts to find (or to create by naming objects and places in) a fuller, more variegated world. In this passage we see First Man likewise filling the fifth world by naming things in it. Having named the mountains, he can now identify the deities occupying them, which in turn gives them sacred meaning.

26. Other tasks performed by the women are mentioned in Matthews (1883), pp. 207–24. Additional details about the division of labor are found in Haile (1932b), p. 3. Spencer (1947), pp. 21–31, provides a more thorough breakdown of the division of labor. Generally, the women till the soil, carry water, weave, cook, make clothing and care for children. Men generally hunt, clear the fields, help with tilling, and "guide and assist" the women in their labors.

27. Here is where First Man loses control. See note 8, p. 343 above. For a guide to various accounts of the separation that have found their way into print, see Wyman (1965), pp. 80–84. Note the wide array of explanations, with adultery or sexual conflict being named most frequently. The reasons for the quarrel are ultimately less important than the fact that it occurs to begin with. The overriding theme here, which permeates the whole narrative, is the lack of solidarity between male and female, which is simply a particularization of the theme of social disharmony needing to be resolved. That need will be articulated by Changing Woman, p. 275 below. See, also, note 82, pp. 404–6.

The forms of *jóósh* (vagina) used here are explained thus: *Jóósh* = the indefinite noun, vagina which is a part of any woman's anatomy; *shijóózh* = my vagina (first person singular possessive); *nijóózh* = your vagina (second person singular possessive); *nihijóózh* = the vaginas that are part of the anatomy of all of you (second person distributive plural). For a discussion of possessive pronoun prefixes, see Young and Morgan (1980), pp. 24–30.

28. See Haile (1932b), p. 5, for one list of those living in the fourth world at the time of the quarrel: "Now of these inhabitants it seems, there were the wolf people, the blue fox people, yellow fox people, badger people, wildcat people, spotted wildcat people, bear people, locust people, white locust people, owl people, turtledove people, piñonero people, swift people, eagle people, you see that many people dwelt there."

29. We get a better sense of the skill and status of the hermaphrodites than Matthews provides in Haile (1932b), p. 14, where one of them says: " 'I myself (can) plant. I myself make millstones. . . . I myself make baking stones. I make pots myself and earthen bowls, guards I plant myself. I (can) make water jugs . . . and stirring sticks and brooms. . . . Liquid corn mush,' he mentioned, 'stiff corn mush, and baked on stone (paper bread), and dumplings I can make,' he said, 'three-eared (gruel in cornhusks) I make, and many beads. . . .'" Also see Reichard (1950), p. 140.

30. To outsiders, Navajos seem aloof, undemonstrative, and anything but emotional. However, strong feelings and emotional outbursts are not in the least uncommon in Navajo narratives. The feelings displayed by these men are corroborated in other versions. Haile's informant, Curly Toaxedlini, in 1932b, for example, recites (p. 16): "Without feeling backward about it they wept, some did, that had great love for one-another." Some of the women also weep openly.

Incidentally, in translating the phrasing of his informant, Haile preserves the passive form and writes that the wailing of the women "was heard," alertly repeating the nuance that the incident is recited from the point of view of the men. It is my impression after consulting the untranslated text that Curly Toaxedlini was an excellent storyteller. He was aware of the contrasting effects of employing the passive voice as opposed to the active; he could choose concrete details economically, creating graphic, vivid effects with a minimum number of words; his dramatic passages capture the humor and pathos so often combined in a Navajo narrative; and when he wanted to he could sustain suspense over long passages. Often his recitation appears to have been marked by a rhythm unique to him among all of the transcriptions in Navajo of performances by various others that I have seen. Although in places Haile's translations are too literal to be easily read and appreciated in English, they sometimes succeed in transmitting a sense of the style employed by a Navajo storyteller. A preliterate performer can indeed put his own individualistic mark on what he says just as readily as a conventional novelist or poet in our own literate culture can develop his own particular style. For one analysis of such a style, see Toelken and Scott.

31. O'Bryan, p. 8, provides an explicit account of the sexual frustrations of the men and women. In Haile (1932b, pp. 19–22, reprinted in 1981a, pp. 23–27), Curly Toaxedlini is also more explicit, and I have based what appears on pp. 63–69 here upon his version since Matthews scarcely alludes to the thwarted sex of the men and the women. Evidence found among his unpublished papers indicates that he knew of such episodes. He acknowledges, (n.d.a., p. 22) for instance that during the separation "the men used hot liver" for the purpose of masturbation. He also aroused a small controversy when he decided not to include an explicit and vivid

description of sexual buffoonery in his account of the tenth dance of the *Mountain Chant* (1887), p. 441. Obviously, he shared the extreme prudishness of the times, and he was apparently not without a certain idiosyncratic priggishness of his own. (See Poor, p. 36, and pp. 124–26.) His tacit decision to delete sexual and scatological episodes demonstrates how, in the act of converting performance to print, those who control the technology of book or manuscript making have the power to force mutations on the original. The broad humor obvious in Curly Toaxedlini's version is not to be overlooked. In fact, humor of all kinds plays an important part in Navajo art and life. See Hill (1937), especially pp. 7–28.

32. In an editorial note in Haile (1981a), p. 23, Luckert suggests that this episode reflects how, "in early agricultural history the men had to recapture their traditional role as providers. They literally had to wrest agriculture away from the women." The separation, then, indicates that since he and the men eventually plant and grow more successfully than the women, First Man's image of himself as a provider will be virtually restored.

33. In Haile (1981b), p. 96, the women must bathe because "they were filthy, ragged and haggard sights, and the smell coming from them reminded strongly of coyote urine and other disagreeable odors." See Matthews (1902), p. 43, concerning the process of drying with corn meal, which "in this case" is "a substitute for towels—articles of which the Navahoes know very little." He describes the ceremonial procedure of drying along with the everyday process. The passage thus suggests that verbal artifacts like this one can serve to provide information about preliterate peoples which conventionally gathered archaeological material cannot always supply.

34. In Haile (1981a), p. 33, the joy of both the men and the women is clearly expressed: "My! how the people tumbled about (in each other's embrace)! saying 'my dear' to one another, and what a weeping went up. . . . 'My dear husband' [First Woman] said as she embraced the old man." Other versions reflect a fuller capitulation of the women to the men that what is suggested here. See Fishler, p. 26, for instance; or Wheelwright, p. 48, where the women accept an ultimatum that they are to remain in a submissive role. I cannot altogether endorse such accounts in light of the way female characters behave elsewhere in the narrative as Matthews writes it, or in light of what Witherspoon (1975), pp. 3–29, says about marriage and the status of Navajo women.

35. According to Matthews (1902), p. 309, *Tééhooɫtsódii* is associated chiefly with terrestrial waters to the east, possibly including the remote Atlantic Ocean. Eventually he is assumed to dwell in every permanent spring and river. See note 19, p. 388 below. See also Reichard (1950), pp. 490–91. Newcomb, pp. 57–65, includes an entertaining version of an encounter with him.

36. This young man will be made the sun-bearer. Hence, he is to become the emergent form of *Jóhonaa'éí* the Sun. See p. 90ff. below.

37. There is a variant account of this episode in Newcomb, pp. 23–56. With its emphasis on the behavior of the individual animal people, the retelling is an example of how the prototype can be converted to "folk tales" for children. See, too, Fishler, p. 28, where the reed is described in greater detail, suggesting how an informant can give particulars when he so chooses. In Matthews (1883), p. 209, the reed is used twice, once to provide access to the fourth world from the third, and again to provide escape from the fourth world to the fifth. In Haile (1981b), pp. 114–15, the use of the reed is described in a slightly different context.

38. Matthews identifies the loons as "grebes" in an unpublished manuscript (n.d.a) in which the arrow is inserted "into his mouth" and drawn "out of his anus." Then "he put another into his anus and drew it out of his mouth." In turn the locust "thrust an arrow from side to side through his heart in one direction and drew it out at the other side and thrust another arrow similarly thro [*sic*] in the other direction." Such a variation from this account to the version published in *Navaho Legends* suggests two things. First of all, it indicates the possibility that he wanted the slightly more "tasteful" account to appear in book form; second it suggests that he had options to work with in selecting details that he would eventually include in his published text of the Navajo creation story. Other field notes in his unpublished papers confirm that possibility. Apparently he accumulated different accounts of various episodes.

39. Haile (1942), p. 411, suggests that it does not matter to Navajos whether these people were "plants, animals [or] other beings." They are still considered ancestors who emerged from an inner world. Young, p. 2, writes that he is "tempted to view the migration of beings from the first to the present world on a horizontal rather than a vertical plane, interpreting the First or Black Worlds as the Arctic north, the second group as the northern plains and the last division as the Rocky Mountain area—with [*Hajíínéí*], the place of emergence, as the point at which the earliest ancestors of the Navajo entered the region of their original occupancy in the Southwest." The possibility is a fascinating one, especially in the more stark account of the emergence from world to world in Haile's early unpublished manuscript version (1908), pp. 1–4, where the movement is described more explicitly from one barren geographical location to another. The cycle of emergence in that account is through twelve worlds rather than five, with First Man functioning primarily as a creator of rocks, hills, the sun, and so on. It may be well and good to see the image of emergence as something like an extended metaphor for migration into the Southwest by a tribe of Athabascan migrants; but we must be careful not to reduce the artistry of the story to facts of history as we like to reckon them in accounting for our own recorded past. The poetic imagination is

manifestly at work in a *chimiky'ana'kowa*, and the narrative should be seen primarily as art and only secondarily as historic data.

Part Two

1. Chapters 1–6 narrate the creation of the fifth world. Implicit in the passage is a philosophical depth that is deceptively easy to overlook. See, for instance, note 5, p. 341 above. The suggestion, of course, is that peoples like the Navajos have the same capacity for abstract thought that is found in Western traditions. The reader is advised to consult a work like Kirk and Raven. And see Wyman (1970), pp. 343ff.

2. See Franciscan Fathers, pp. 478–89, on the Navajo pastime of gambling. As with many other activities which we would consider completely secular, gambling and game-playing have religious implications among the Navajo and are often rooted in mythology. See Aberle (1942). Spencer (1947), pp. 93–97, summarizes the place of games in Navajo society.

3. A statement by Witherspoon (1977), pp. 131–32, helps put Coyote's behavior here and in subsequent passages in a broad perspective: "The polar positions of random, unordered things and patterned, ordered things seem to be associated with the terms *hózhǫ* and *hochxo*, the former of which describes a beautiful, harmonious, and orderly environment and the latter of which describes an ugly, disharmonious and disorderly environment. Both order and disorder are first conceived in the thought, and then projected on the world through speech and action."

Coyote is the prototype of one who conceives disorder in his thought and projects it on the world through what he says and does. Even when he argues in behalf of orderliness, he conceives of disorder. Reichard (1950), p. 183, points out that "order, the foundation of Navaho ritual, is reversed in his character." See p. 93 above, where Coyote strews stars helter-skelter across the heavens. In some ways I see him as an analogue to Satan in Milton's *Paradise Lost*. While there are some differences—e.g., Satan is more willfully an evildoer, and he deliberately defines himself as God's nemesis and as man's—the similarity seems to be that both are proponents of disorder in a universe where others are trying to establish and maintain order. Coyote's ceremonial name is *Áłtsé hashké*, which means First Scolder. That seems an appropriate name in a passage like this one, where he scolds others for accusing him and acquits himself by identifying the long-term benefits of his disorderly behavior. Frequently he shows in the ceremonial narratives a capacity to see with a certain clarity and wisdom, even though what he observes is spoken as rationalization for his impulsive, self-serving acts and ideas. For example, see a statement he makes in Wyman (1970), p. 346, after arguing that seeds should not be planted in orderly rows but should be broadcast helter-skelter. If they are seeded in rows, he argues, and one stalk should die, there would be an unsightly gap. In a footnote on that page, Wyman calls Coyote "the wise philosopher in this instance." That statement seems fully appropriate, and as we continue with the passage we find ourselves admiring Coyote's reasoning and his ability to speak in terms of relationships. See also, note 20, p. 368 below.

According to Fishler's informant, Frank Goldtooth, Coyote starts out as a god. It is his appetite for self-gratification that reduces him to the dissolute, sorry figure we eventually see in this cycle. See, too, Luckert (1979), especially pp. 6–11, where Coyote's origins as "a divine person" or a god are explained. Also see W. W. Hill and Dorothy W. Hill.

4. See pp. 264–65 below.

5. If placed in a broader framework, this incident can suggest how extensively Pueblo traditions have been incorporated into Navajo lore. A statement by Luckert (1979), p. 18, illustrates this point. The Coyoteway ceremonial, he writes, "originated in . . . the place where Navajo-Apachean hunter shamans first seem to have come in contact with the Pueblo Indian four-directional four-level cosmology and with the anthropogony of emergence. Courageous shamans that they were, a few of them ventured down into the hole of emergence from where, according to the new world view, all life and power originates. Coyote and fox tutelaries have been showing their fellow hunters the right way all along—by digging burrows for themselves and by living in the 'underworld.' Now, at last in the light of the Pueblo myth of emergence, could the pioneering efforts and hints of the Coyote people be fully understood."

The various treatments of the first death are surveyed in Spencer (1947), pp. 108–11. For a supplementary view of the incident, see Haile (1942), especially p. 416. The more recently published version in O'Bryan has something of an Orpheus-like ring to it. Fishler's informant, pp. 31–32, suggests an awareness that Coyote is associated with the origin of death. See Haile (1943b), pp. 87–92, for a general discussion of Navajo eschatology. For an expression of what death means among the Navajos even now, see Mills, p. 13.

6. Newcomb, pp. 33–41, tells in a version intended for children how seeds were brought into the fifth world by Turkey. Perhaps Turkey's bravery in tarrying to bring seeds out of the soon-to-be-flooded underworld can be associated with the "courageous shamans" who venture down into the hole of emergence as described by Luckert (1979), p. 18, and mentioned in note 5 above.

7. For a succinct comment on the sacred mountains, see Wyman (1970), pp. 16–20. Also see the chart in Reichard (1950), pp. 20–22, which arranges the details regarding those mountains in a convenient graphic scheme.

Observe what First Man and First Woman are doing. They are actively creating, performing tasks that we who have absorbed the Old Testament tradition would attribute to God. Their creativity implies an active spiritual effort, or perhaps even what we might call a cerebral conceptual effort. The spiritual or mental effort is every bit as important as the geography of what they assemble, for it indicates how thoroughly the narrative reflects both observation and thought on the part of those who were instrumental in the composition of the creation cycle. See Witherspoon (1977), p. 181, for a statement as to why "creativity implies activity and transformation." And see Tedlock (1981), for a useful statement about the relationship between poetic language and conceptions of creation.

As the narrative progresses all the way to its conclusion, however, bear in mind that First Man and First Woman do not give shape and form to the fifth world all by themselves. They need help and cooperation. They need participation from and consultation with others. They even need dynamic opposition like that which they get from Coyote. And of course what they shape and form is based upon what had been created before they themselves came into being. This widely distributed creative power can be called "shared power," a concept well explained by Allen. First Man and First Woman merely serve to orchestrate this power during one phase of the entire creation. See note 24, p. 388 below. In Wyman (1970), pp. 111–12, First Man functions as a very confident, very mature participant in the process. He knows what he is doing; he speaks and acts with authority, although he is seldom autocratic. He shows characteristics common to a Navajo "chief," who generally earns his position by his actions and deeds rather than by formal decree or inheritance. See Witherspoon (1977), p. 29, for a generalization that summarizes the more intellectual dimensions of First Man's and First Woman's creativity: "What [those two] and the others brought into being by their thoughts were the inner forms of all the natural phenomena that would be prominent in the structure and operation of this world." Luckert (1975), p. 161, denies the relationship implied or asserted by Haile and Witherspoon between the presence of "inner forms" in such things as animals and inanimate objects such as rocks and mountains, on the one hand, and the concept of the soul as commonly employed in Western tradition, on the other. He tends to see the animating force within nonhuman entities as a more neutral sort of animus devoid of any implicit moral spiritualism. Whether we wish to consider "inner forms" in terms of a soul-like existence, or in terms of a more "primitive" sort of animism, their existence as an essential part of the Navajo conception of the creation represents a belief system which manifests poetic sophistication beyond what the usual literate person expects of preliterate verbal artifacts. Religious belief, however, seems to me as much the product of a people's imagination as it is of some nonspecific credulousness. In fact, I would say that imagination and religious belief go hand in hand, which is plain enough to see here. Like the pleasure dome in Coleridge's "Kubla Khan," the cosmos that emerges from a shared account of the creation stands as a tangible manifestation of the poetic imagination.

As a particular example, consider what Wyman (1970), pp. 10–16, says about the *hoghan*, the traditional home of individual families. It seems very much as if First Man is, by analogy, making the world his home. And in placing "inner forms" in the individual mountains, he is investing the earth itself with the same spirits who will either dwell in or visit individual homes. Everything, then, has a kind of indwelling spiritual essence, including the mountains, the sun, the moon, the four directions, etc. See, for example, the account of the investiture on p. 357 in Wyman (1970). The implication is that the deity placed in the mountains gives things a purpose. Hence, the animism in nature simply makes things work. The world, then becomes another functional work of art. Haile (1938), p. 251, note 13, says that the Navajo word which he renders in English as the familiar term "inner forms" used by the scholastics literally means "It lies within." He elaborates considerably on his conception of inner forms in (1943b), pp. 69–77. The belief in an indwelling life-form still seems to prevail among Navajos today. See Mills, p. 12. There Mills writes that when he showed a Navajo woman from the Rimrock area a professional Indian painting of a bear standing under a rainbow, "she interpreted the rainbow as a mountain and was perplexed as to how the bear would get out." See p. 54, too, where Mills discusses the sandpaintings of one medicine man. And see, for example, what the informant CAB reports in McNeley, p. 21, which is one of a number of statements indicating not only a prevailing belief in inner forms, but also a relationship between them and the various winds.

If Matthews did not have what we might today regard as a fully developed understanding of the concept of "inner forms" or "animus," he at least had a solid appreciation of what the concept meant to the Navajos while he worked among them. He also had a wholesome respect for what they believed. In an unpublished paper, "The Gods of the Navahos" (1886a), p. 26, he records that ". . . the resident deities of [the sacred mountains] seem to receive more honor than any other place gods, but the presiding genii of other mountains rock and canons [sic] are not neglected by the devout." Perhaps we get the sharpest sense of those spirits in the story of the Stricken Twins in the narrative literature associated with the *Night Chant*, in Matthews's monumental edition of the ceremony (1902), pp. 212–65. Seeking extrication from misfortunes that have befallen them, the two brothers enter deeper and deeper into a great rock, moving from chamber to chamber, until they eventually find themselves in the company of the Holy People in the innermost one.

Thus, as they appear in the various narratives, the "inner forms" occupy rocks, hills, mountains, and even the sun and the moon; and we find them presented not as spiritual essences but as real characters, or at least as characters as real as Ariel and Puck are in Shakespeare or as Dracula and Frankenstein are in Hollywood films. Each one is a palpable animus, seen in terms of flesh and blood, as fully material and corporeal as real people or real animals. They walk, talk, eat, exhibit the emotions of anger and jealousy. And they have their ultimate origins in the tribal imagination as it finds manifestation in the story of creation.

8. *Sisnaajiní,* sometimes confused with *Dził naajiní,* has variously been identified as Sierra Blanca Peak, Sleeping Ute Mountain, Wheeler Peak, Black Belted Mountain, or Dark Horizontal Ridge. Its exact location is uncertain, just as there is uncertainty over the exact location of several of the others. See Wyman (1970), pp. 17–20; Reichard (1950), pp. 19–25, 452–53; Van Valkenburg (1974), p. 21.

9. The origins of these two deities and of some of the others associated with the sacred mountains are given in Wyman (1970), p. 395.

10. See Wyman (1970), p. 16. According to him, the Navajo name for *Tsoodził* (Tongue Mountain) "is derived from the fact that in the Blessingway myth it is the tongue of the inner form of the earth." See note 25, where Wyman indicates that Matthews misinterpreted its name. See Van Valkenburgh (1974), p. 57.

11. *Dibé nitsaa* in the north is one of the sacred peaks whose identity and location are uncertain. See Wyman (1970), pp. 17–20. See, also, Haile (1938), p. 42. See Van Valkenburgh (1974), p. 136.

12. In version II of the *Blessingway* narrative, Wyman (1970), p. 357, only two central mountains are identified. They are *Dził ná'oodiłii,* which is more literally translated there as "Mountain-around-which-moving-was-done," and *Ch'óol'í'í,* sometimes translated as Spruce Hill, sometimes as Giant Spruce Mountain, and sometimes not translated at all. According to this account, originally narrated to Father Berard Haile by Frank Mitchell, the central mountains appear to have had a special significance. For they would be the focal point for Talking God *(Haashch'ééłti'í)* and for Growling God *(Hashch'éoghan),* erroneously identified by Matthews as House God in English. Both, as the narrative eventually demonstrates, become helpfully involved in the affairs of the people who populate the fifth world, and both are identified as powerful deities among Navajos today. Perhaps it is not inaccurate to say that their role in human affairs is "central." And it may appear that First Man and First Woman intended that to be the case. Also see Van Valkenburg (1974), p. 29, p. 31.

13. As best I have been able to determine from conversations with several Navajos, "mirage stone" is quartz crystal. Looking through it creates distortions such as occur when objects are viewed through a prism. The quartz is considered a highly sacred rock and is used in making sacrifices, preparing sacred buckskin, presenting offerings to the gods, etc. See the passing references in Franciscan Fathers, pp. 346–421, where the stone is referred to as rock crystal. See, too, Frank Goldtooth's remark to Fishler, p. 24, that "nowadays when there is a mirage, it goes up into the sky where it turns into clouds. The clouds then let the water out as rain and then the water turns into a mirage once more."

14. In his research, Mills, p. 168, reports that he found that the four mountains marking the outer limits of the Navajo world remain important even when many people lose sight of their precise meaning in traditional lore. The creation of the sacred mountains that mark the limits of the Navajo world is an initial act of establishing order and control in a universe that had been all too disorderly and all too difficult to control. In the estimation of many Navajos today, then, it would seem that the world beyond the limit set by the sacred mountains remains disorderly and chaotic. See, for example, Reichard (1944b), p. 16, for a statement about the prevailing uncertainty among Navajos today toward the outside world, "which is subject to many more uncontrolled factors than the home ground where all is familiar and reasonably certain."

15. For an example of the kind of discussion or debate there might have been, see Wyman (1970), pp. 369ff. Since the power to create was shared widely by those who occupied the soft, growing world, creation was a matter of wide discussion.

16. For some other accounts of the creation of the sun, see Goddard, pp. 134–36. See also, Wheelwright, pp. 65–66. Most other versions account in one way or another for the establishment of the sun with its "inner form" placed in it. For a guide to the various accounts, consult Wyman (1965), pp. 88–89. For a more purely philosophical rendering of this series of events, see Wyman (1970), pp. 366ff. Notice that the placing of the sun in the sky becomes synonymous with the naming of the months. It seems that Native Americans have had a sophisticated comprehension of what time is, and of the relationship between time and space. For a provocative introduction to the idea of Native American conceptions of time and space, see Aveni. It would be worthwhile to compare the Navajo treatment of the placing of the sun with Aztec conceptions of the sun, especially in light of the implicit suggestion in this narrative that the sun demands the regular tribute of human life. See, for example, the reproduction of Tonatihuhco, the sun-glyph, in Ross, p. 51. See, too, Durán, p. 78, which describes the contention among four gods concerning whose "land" the sun should rise over. And see the description, p. 186, describing the feast of the sun and the rite of sacrifice to the sun god. In conjunction with such

items, consider the assertion of "Turquoise Boy" in Goddard, p. 135, when he is asked to enter the sun as its inner form: "Then [First Man] asked Turquoise Boy who was to step inside (the sun), where he was from. 'I am from the east side of Pelado Peak,' replied Turquoise Boy. 'Step inside,' he told him. 'Put the flute made of large reed with twelve holes under your shirt. Let the Mirage People step in with you. By means of them you will pass unseen.' 'All right,' he replied. 'But whenever I pass by I shall be paid by a person's death. Not only your people here, but wherever they move they must pay it.'" See also note 18, p. 366 below.

17. While it varies in some slight ways, Matthews's account of the origin of the sun is not inconsistent with other accounts and descriptions which have found their way into print in English. The only version I know of from which this one differs is Frank Goldtooth's in Fishler, p. 19, where the sun is created at the behest of a character referred to as Supreme Sacred Wind, who sounds somewhat like the Old Testament God. Poor, pp. 18–19, suggests that Matthews initially brought a westernized conception of Indian deities to the Fort Wingate area, which is easy to suppose. But by the time he prepared his manuscript for the *Night Chant*, he had gained a secure understanding of *Jóhonaa'éí* and the other Navajo supernaturals. See, for example, Matthews 1886b, 1902, p. 30.

18. See Wyman (1970), pp. 386–87, where there is a passage explaining who is to live with the sun, why he is to be fearful, etc. Notice, too, the passage describing the resplendent rise of *Jóhonaa'éí*, p. 390. For a fuller explanation of why the dead are placed in the keeping of the sun and the moon, see p. 392, fn. 287.

Matthews himself apparently recorded an account wherein the sun exacts the daily payment of human life for his work. In an unpublished paper, "Notes on Navaho Cosmology," (n.d.a.), p. 27, he writes, "So when the sun got far enough away and everything was fixed the sun rose on 5th day and reached the meridian but there he stopped and all wondered why he did not set. So the Coyote who knew more than any else [sic] said the sun needs pay for his work and his pay for a days [sic] work is a life and he will not set again until someone dies, so he staid [sic] in the zenith until one died and then he sets. So ever since some one must die or the sun would not go round. And the same thing happened with the moon, and the Coyote explained as before, but with the moon it is some member of the other tribes or some animal among them who might pay the debt by dying at night." In Haile (1981b), p. 140, the Sun Carrier sings, ". . . every time I make my journey east and west, one of the Earth People shall die. That is my pay." See also Wyman (1970), p. 380, where it appears to be Coyote, the "inventor" of death, who gives the sun the idea of demanding tribute. Remember, too, that the sun is to become primarily a war god; in Part Three, below, his twin sons go to him to ask for his help in their attempt to conduct a successful battle against the monsters. Which again is in

keeping with the classical Aztec conception of the sun deity. And see
Wheelwright, p. 68, where the sun says, "I am glad when a person dies as
that is what keeps me moving, and I am glad to keep moving." Or see
O'Bryan, pp. 18–19, where the sun insists, "Everything is right so far, but I
will not travel for nothing. I will travel if I am paid with the lives of the
people of the earth, all the human beings, the animals which have four
legs, the birds and insects of the air, the fishes and all the people of the
under-water."

Again, I reiterate my curiosity about the extent to which the episode and
the various treatments it seems to receive by different storytellers touch
upon the matter of human sacrifice such as that practiced by the Aztecs.
We also see oblique but identifiable references to the practice in Wyman
(1962), pp. 86–98, where he presents the *Windways* narrative. A child is
seized by the snake people, carried underground by them, and recovered by
the surface-people only after a tribute is paid to Black God *cum* Fire God
for it. Its capture and subsequent rescue, which suggest what Luckert
(1976), p. 44, calls "the greater-than-human reality of the volcanic Earth
Serpent" endemic to ancient Olmec belief systems, mark the child as a
"chosen one." But at the same time the motif of his rescue—a deliberate
act on the part of some determined individuals—suggests that Navajo
culture may be one where human sacrifice underwent a process of
repudiation. Or perhaps Navajo culture has absorbed from some other
culture the verbal remnants of such a repudiation. One idea that seems to
emerge from a reading of the *Windways* narrative is that the gods can be
placated with surrogate offerings of jewels and tobacco instead of human
tribute. See Wyman (1962), p. 102.

19. In *Navajo Legends* (1897), p. 223, note 70, Matthews quotes one
version of this episode. "Many of the Indians tell that the world was
originally small and was increased in size," he writes. "The following is
the version of *Náltsos Nigéhani* (B): 'The mountains that bounded the
world were not so far apart then as they are now; hence the world was
smaller, and when the sun went over the earth he came nearer to the
surface than he does now. So the first day the sun went on his journey it
was intolerably hot; the people were almost burned to death, and they
prayed to the four winds that each one would pull his mountain away
from the centre of the earth, and thus widen the borders of the world. It
was done as they desired, and the seas that bounded the land receded
before the mountains. But on the second day, although the weather was
milder, it was still too hot, and again were the mountains and seas
removed. All this occurred again on the third day; but on the fourth day
they found the weather pleasant, and they prayed no more for the earth to
be changed.'"

Compare that note with this passage from Matthews's unpublished
paper, "Notes on Navaho Cosmology," p. 27: "The sun began to shine but

they found it too hot the first day as the world was small & they begged the colored winds each to pull his mountain further back and make the world bigger, and they did so & the seas receded before the mountains, & the same heat recurred and the same they [sic] done, and the sun of course had to go farther away each day in consequence of the increasing size of the earth, and of course on the 4th day they got things so that the weather was pleasant and there they stopped."

The pair of quotes raises some interesting questions. It suggests either that Matthews wrote as quickly as he could while taking notes, then reworked the prose carefully later, or that he got a number of versions and then synthesized them. This contrast raises the question of how he acquired these notes. Did his informant narrate in Navajo while Matthews translated immediately and wrote in English? Did the informant narrate in English? Did Matthews make Navajo transcriptions that may have gotten lost or destroyed, and did he translate later at his leisure? The third possibility seems the least likely. Nor is it very likely that Matthews wrote in English what was recited in Navajo, although I would not rule out that possibility. My doubt arises from my own experience with Navajo; I simply find it difficult to imagine that any non-native-speaker could master Navajo well enough in a few years to be able to listen to it and translate it into English script extemporaneously. The various possibilities of how oral material may be gathered in one language and translated-transcribed in another are worth considering. See Hymes (1975a), p. 19.

20. See Wyman (1970), pp. 372–74, where Coyote argues against the simple dichotomy between day, when traveling can be done, and night, when it is too dark for anyone to travel and all should sleep. In effect, he reasons, the cosmos should now be adjusted and refined so that those creatures who prefer to be active at night can at least have some light. So he proposes the scheme of months, with its cycle of moon phases and circulating stars.

21. Matthews's version comes no closer to an account of a calendrical system than what we find here, which might suggest that the narrative he was able to retrieve in the eastern part of Navajo country where he did his work antedates the introduction of agriculture into Navajo life. Or at least this portion of it does. I find very little reference to any sort of calendar among his papers. For a fairly precise description of the Navajo calendar, see Hill (1938), pp. 14–18. Accounts of how the monthly calendar was established appear scattered throughout the ceremonial literature compiled since the publication of *Navaho Legends*. In addition to Wyman (1970), pp. 369–77, see Goddard, p. 134. There is a fairly detailed account of the making of a calendrical system in Haile (1932b), although in an introductory note he suggests that the actual naming of the months is more closely related to a series of separate coyote tales than to the overall story of the creation; see p. v, vi. There is also an explicit reference to the

establishment of months in Haile (1981b), p. 129. In her version of the
narrative, Yazzie, pp. 20–21, says nothing about how the months were
perceived or named. That volume, she told me, reflects a consensus among
Navajo singers and storytellers, which indicates that there was no
strong drift of agreement that the account should be included. Ultimately,
it is possible that Matthews himself arrived at that conclusion.

22. On Coyote's penchant for creating disorder, see note 3, pp. 360–61
above. According to Haile (1947), where the details of Navajo astronomy
are summarized, little information about the stars is shared by those
medicine men who know it; see p. 4.

23. Reichard (1950), pp. 70–75, provides a good overall summary of how
the monsters fit into the Navajo belief system. "The monsters," she
writes, "are essentially evil, the result of abnormal sexual indulgence in a
lower world or of blood shed at their birth and not ritualistically disposed
of because they were not acknowledged by their mothers." See, too,
Wyman (1970), p. 403, where the monsters are associated with failure to
keep things holy. And when we read what Witherspoon (1975), pp. 15–22
says about the traditional conception of motherhood, we discover that
those women who give birth to the monstrous infants compound their
own transgressions by failing to acknowledge and to nurture them. In
Fishler, p. 38, Frank Goldtooth explains that monsters came into being
because "women had been running around having intercourse with
petrified wood, cactus plants, and men. . . ." Contrast the birth of the
monster slaying twins, pp. 182–83 below. And see note 20, p. 388 below.

24. When I first began reading the various printed narratives from
Navajo tradition and from other Native American traditions, I had no easy
time distinguishing sharply between characters who were physically and
essentially human and those who were not. Gradually, however, I learned
that the distinction is not necessarily to be made in terms that have
become conventional in Anglo-European tradition. The relationship
between human and non-human as it applies in Navajo storytelling and
ceremonial tradition is well explained by Luckert (1975), pp. 133ff., where
he introduces the useful term, "prehuman flux" and explains how it may
be understood. That term, he says, "refers to man's primeval kinship with
all creatures of the living world and to the essential continuity among
them all." In the soft world of "prehuman mythical times all living
beings existed in a state of flux—their external forms were
interchangeable." The world of animate beings included "all that moves
about in air and sky, on earth, below the earth, and in the sea." Even the
gods were part of that animate world and participated in a panoply of
living things bound to no one particular shape.

25. This passage bears a close resemblance to a description by Matthews
(1899), of a trip he took into Canyon de Chelly in the spring of 1892. So it
suggests the possibility that in assembling his own version of the creation

story and in synthesizing what he picked up from his informants in doing so, he was not reluctant to depend on his own direct impressions as well. See also, Young, pp. 5–6, who speaks of "large population centers in the Kayenta, Chaco Canyon, Mesa Verde and La Plata localities" which "were abandoned in the twelfth and thirteenth centuries." Apparently these "prehistoric Pueblo peoples" moved out of "their former areas of occupancy," leaving "a vacuum into a portion of which the ancestral Navajos apparently moved." These "ancient fortified cities," Young adds, "figure prominently in Navajo legends as the homes of supernatural beings or the scenes of mythological events; but they were already unoccupied at the time the early Navajo arrived." See Hester, too.

26. Obviously, this episode is an accretion that comes into the overall creation cycle fairly late, especially because of its reference to the Mexicans (see p. 112 below). The value of the story of Nááhwiiłbįįhí the Gambler to the whole narrative might be that here for the first time Talking God and Growling God become directly involved in the affairs of the Earth Surface People. Or perhaps its place in the overall fabric of the story is more subtle. In Wyman (1965), pp. 119–20, we learn that killing, which occurred in the lower worlds continues even in the fifth world, even though it is infrequently spoken of. The Gambler's antisocial behavior can be taken as an extension of that sort of destructiveness. A Hopi tale contains some striking parallels, as indeed there are bound to be resemblances linking the Navajo creation cycle with various Pueblo narratives. See the story of Tsorwukiqulö in Malotki, pp. 151–208. There, the Gambler, Hasookata, is a far more sinister figure than the Navajo Nááhwiiłbįįhí. He, too, however, is finally tricked by benign spirits, who manage to destroy him. The important thing to notice in the Hopi story is that while gaming itself is not regarded as a bad activity, it can lead to the sort of excess that prudent individuals would do well to avoid. Furthermore, excessive or inordinate winning seems to represent grossly antisocial behavior just as excessive losing may also be socially harmful. So it is quite logical that the gambler who becomes a relentless winner would finally be associated with the Europeans, whose initial incursion from Mexico in the middle and late sixteenth century brought the kind of greed and forced bondage that Nááhwiiłbįįhí suggests by his behavior. See Aberle (1942), for a statement on the relationship between gambling and mythology in Navajo culture. Forbes discusses the impact of the Spaniards on the tribes of the Southwest; see note 34, p. 373 below.

27. Matthews (1902), p. 9, describes Haashch'ééłti'í as "a god of dawn and of the eastern sky. He is also a god of animals of the chase, although he is not supposed to have created them." He is closely associated with Hashch'éoghan, who is more or less his equal in importance. Compare his role in this narrative with that in the story of the Stricken Twins in the Night Chant, pp. 212–65, where Haashch'ééłti'í secretly courts a young

virgin who then gives birth to twin sons. In some ways his relationship with them in that narrative resembles the relationship that will be established between *Jóhonaa'éí* the Sun and the monster-slaying twins in Part Three below. For an account of the origin of Talking God and Growling God, see Wyman (1970), pp. 357–58; and, for a somewhat different version, see pp. 495ff. Talking God is also referred to as *Yeibicheii* or Grandfather God. See, also, Reichard (1950), pp. 476–80. On Talking God's call, see p. 260, where we are told that his approach is "heralded a long way off by a faint trace of his cry, which becomes regularly louder as it is repeated nearer and nearer. At the fourth cry," he appears.

28. The young husband will become a prototype of the "culture hero," described by Luckert (1976), pp. 72–73, as aptly as it is anywhere in the context of Navajo narrative and ceremonial literature. In that passage, he says that the culture hero begins the process of civilizing a group by struggling "against traditional greater-than-human reality configurations." By mediating "between the people and the sources of power," he "becomes awe-inspiring himself." The people are thus challenged to trust him "and to accept his revised definitions of human possibilities and limitations. Also see pp. 109–10, for a discussion of the culture hero in relation to the practice of sacrifice. The young husband in this passage, of course, is not a strong example of the culture hero. Rather, his exploits serve here as something of a precursor to the exploits of *Leeyaa neeyání*, or Reared In the Earth, who overcomes the evil caused by Coyote in chapters 11–16 below, and to the more spectacular exploits of *Naayéé' neizghání* the Monster Slayer, who is the more active and aggressive of the enemy-slaying twins in Part Three. Largely of the trickster, nonwarrior variety of culture hero, the young husband here is seen as a direct extension of the will of the supernaturals and exercises no purpose of his own choosing. In O'Bryan, pp. 48–62, there is a version of this series of episodes in which the Gambler and the young husband are both identified as offspring of the Sun. The Gambler is conceived so that he might win a beautiful piece of turquoise coveted by *Jóhonaa'éí;* and the young husband is conceived by him to serve as an instrument of revenge when the first son refuses to give the turquoise to his father after winning it.

Jewels are traditionally favored by the gods. Hence, they have special value among Earth Surface People as "offerings." See Reichard (1950), p. 306, who speaks of an offering as something "tendered to compel assent before support is granted." She is referring to the fact that getting help from the supernaturals is to a Navajo not so much a one-sided supplication as it is a transaction. The offering places the deity under an obligation to bring about the kind of control required by the offerer. See, too, Reichard (1944b). Thus the Gambler interlude here illustrates how highly jewels can be valued by the Holy People. See below, too, p. 274, where Changing

Woman, in making her demands upon the Sun, insists that she should
have various jewels. Goddard, pp. 140–46, provides an account of
Náάhwííłbííhí the Gambler where the young husband is explicitly linked
with Naayéé' neizghání the Monster Slayer.

29. Hashch'éoghan is discussed in Reichard (1950), pp. 502–5. His origin
is described in Wyman (1970), p. 497.

30. Nítch'i the Wind makes an innocuous appearance here, but his
importance increases steadily throughout the remainder of Part Two and
well into Part Three. See note 2, p. 347 above. Luckert (1976), p. 73,
explains that because the culture hero must know how to placate angry
divinities "he needs a strong guardian spirit who will defend his cause and
the cause of his fellow hunters against all other greater-than-human odds."
See Witherspoon (1977), p. 29, for a suggestion that Nítch'i provides a
common denominator for understanding conceptions of "inner forms"
mentioned above, p. 363. See also McNeley, especially pp. 1–13. And see
Reichard (1950), pp. 497–500. I am tempted to match some of what Nítch'i
seems to represent with such terms familiar to western culture as spirit,
inspiration, a priori knowledge, insight, inscape, imagination, and wit. It
is also tempting to match his role with the role of the gods in Homeric
tradition or in certain elements of post-Homeric literature. Juxtapose the
part he plays in episodes to follow with the way Pallas Athene instructs
Odysseus or the way Virgil guides Dante in the Commedia, for instance.

31. The games are described in greater detail in O'Bryan pp. 56–70. Also
see, Franciscan Fathers, pp. 478–89.

32. A curse like this, it is believed among Navajos, can have serious
consequences. See Witherspoon (1977), p. 9. Also see Reichard (1950), p.
275. "The power of the word is as strong for evil as for good," she writes,
"an inverse wish being a curse." See below, p. 145; p. 304. See, too,
Franciscan Fathers, pp. 444–46.

33. Begochídí figures more prominently in other versions of the Navajo
creation story than in this one. In some accounts, he reflects European or
Christian influence. He has been variously identified as a trickster, a
divine creator, a supreme deity much like the God of Judeo-Christian
tradition, and the father of the alien monsters. He is discussed in Reichard
(1950), pp. 386–90; Sandner, p. 38; Wheelwright, p. 39; Luckert (1975), pp.
176–77; Fishler, pp. 2–3; Hill (1938), p. 99, etc. The impression I have is
that he is a deity that enters the Navajo pantheon of supernaturals fairly
late, reflecting Christian and European influence in one way or another.
Matthews says very little about Begochídí. He inserts a fairly brief
footnote on him in Navaho Legends, p. 226, n. 78, where he acknowledges
that he has obtained vague descriptions of him and says that no discussion
of him has been recorded. Professor Jerrold E. Levy of the University of
Arizona shared with me the opinion during a conversation (4/10/79) that
Matthews had overlooked the importance of Begochídí. In subsequent

correspondence (6/18/79), however, Dr. Levy added that while *Begochídí* is important, he is important "perhaps only to a few ceremonialists." He is not necessarily "a central deity of 'old' Navajo belief." But he is "the patron deity of the *Kloogi diné* in the myth of Mothway, and Frank Goldtooth knew Mothway. Perhaps *Begochídí* was added to the pantheon rather later and intruded himself into the underworld sections of the myth in a strange way."

There seem to be few entries regarding *Begochídí* among the Matthews papers deposited in the Wheelwright Museum, which confirms that he did not pay as much attention to that supernatural as he paid to certain other gods. In notebook no. 707, for instance, where most of what Matthews does say about him is concentrated, we find these remarks: "*[Begochídí]* and *[Jóhonaa'éí]* made all the animals while they were sitting together in the same room—*[Begochídí]* in the north, *[Jóhonaa'éí]* in the south. While the former was making a horse, the latter was making an antelope and this is why the antelope is so much like the horse. . . ." (p. 17). "The name *[Begochídí]* signifies, 'He tried to Catch It.' He got his name while he was out hunting. An incident story is told to account for this" (p. 79). I have been unable to locate such a story.

34. This theme is common to many of the ceremonial narratives. Matthews writes in *Navaho Legends,* p. 53: "The story of the Great Shell of *[Kin nteel]* . . . conveys a moral often found in Navajo tales, which is, that we must not despise the poor and humble. They may be favored by the gods and prove themselves, tomorrow, more potent than those who yesterday despised and mocked them." That theme seems especially apt for explaining who the Mexicans (i.e., Hispanic Europeans) are. In Fishler, p. 106, Frank Goldtooth reports, "The descendants of *[Nááhwíílbįįhí]* are thought to be Spanish." According to Forbes, p. 57, the first recorded contact between Navajos and Spaniards occurred in 1582, which suggests that this episode as Matthews recorded it is no older than 400 years. That does not mean, however, that no other part of the creation story can be older than that. Some portions are likely to go back as far as the earliest Athabascan contact with the Pueblos, which in all probability had long since taken place when the Spaniards first arrived. See Young, pp. 18–19; and see Van Valkenburgh (1938), p. 207.

35. The Coyote cycle seems endless. Matthews himself repeats additional episodes throughout his notes. On p. 31, in notebook 674, for example, where there is a great deal of material that he seems to have digested and incorporated into what ultimately became *Navaho Legends,* I find an episode which he titles "The Beaver and the Coyote," and another which bears the title, "Coyote and the Horned Frog." It would be helpful to know what actually governed his choice in determining what to include in his published account of Coyote's exploits. But it seems to me that the material he selected fits fairly well in the overall scheme of his finished

edition. We see Coyote indulge himself, behave impulsively, make a
mockery of the male-female relationship, practice witchcraft, and teach it
to the woman he ultimately seduces and tricks into marrying him. By
displaying characteristics that should be shunned, he illustrates the kind
of disharmony the five-fingered Earth Surface People must learn to avoid as
they organize into clans in Part IV. See what Luckert (1975), p. 189, says
about Coyote (i.e., Slim-Trotter, "poor cousin" to the more burly wolf of
Athabascan lore). Also see the Jungian perspective on Coyote presented by
Moon, pp. 38–45. And see the redoubtable Paul Radin. For a representative
of Coyote tales from the Navajo cycle, see Hill and Hill. The narratives
included by Luckert in *Coyoteway* (1979) are supplemented by two
unpublished manuscript versions that overlap considerably with what
Matthews incorporated into *Navaho Legends* (1897). They are Haile
(1932a) and Reichard (n.d.).

36. Here, apparently, is one instance of many where Coyote violates
custom. See Hill (1938), p. 97: "With the exception of deer (in rare cases
rabbits also) fire was never used in hunting to drive game."

37. Notice that Coyote completes the circle here. Contrast this
movement with Changing Woman's cycle of movement, p. 312 below,
where she deliberately avoids making a complete circle. See also, note 75,
p. 402 below, where Changing Woman uses the circular hoops to control
the directional winds. See what Mills, pp. 151–52, says about open and
closed circles in Navajo art. Hill (1938), p. 75, states that in a rain
ceremony the medicine man carefully avoids completing a circle around
the ceremonial hogan as he moves clockwise. Reichard (1944b), p. 16,
explains the aversion to complete circles in the making of rugs and
sandpaintings: "The Navajo believe that when anything has gone wrong,
either for them as a tribe or for one of them as an individual, they or he is
involved in a circle of confusion or bafflement with evils. When this
happens no good power can come in to aid in rescue and there is no way
for the evils to get out. This idea is repeatedly symbolized in the properties
of the ritual and in ritualistic acts." So when Coyote completes the circle
in this passage, or when he completes it on p. 144 below, he may also be
identifying himself with the powers of evil, which aligns him with the
practice of witchcraft. Remember, however, that good and evil are not
taken as two entirely separate forces in Navajo thought. Rather, they are
seen, so to speak, as opposite sides of the same coin. Anything that
summons or symbolizes evil can also be made to summon or symbolize
good when dealt with properly. See, for example, how Changing Woman
uses the colored hoops to protect herself from the monsters on p. 194
below, or how she uses the hoops relayed to her by Jóhonaa'éí the Sun to
exorcise evil from the world, p. 259 below. See, too, Reichard (1950), pp.
564–65, 649–57; and see Franciscan Fathers, pp. 415–17.

38. It frequently occurs that Coyote is unwelcome. See, for example,

Matthews (1902), p. 201, where he is driven away by an assembly of holy people. "You have no right here and no interest in our ceremonies," they tell him. "You must not return again." Reason for the reluctance to let Coyote participate in activities is provided in Haile (1932a), p. 25, where he wants to join "the swift people" and "the spider people" in a game they are playing. They tell him: " . . . get away from here Coyote, first scolder! Don't make it uncomfortable for us! Don't make this place unsacred!" The discomfort they show is very real, apparently, and it actually tells something about the Navajo sense of obligation, especially to kin and clansmen, which is well known for creating conflicts among individuals. We see the source of that discomfort elsewhere in the same manuscript (p. 6) when Coyote asks the spider people for a robe. He repeats his request four times; for the first three he is refused, but then, after the fourth, one of them finally says, to the rest, "You may as well let him have it, his evil spell is to be feared."

39. See Matthews (1902), pp. 6–7: "In this and other healing ceremonies . . . it is important that a life element, or what appears to the Indian mind to be such, should be preserved as much as possible. . . . If you kill the bird that has entered the pollen, your pollen will be dead medicine, they say. In procuring sacred buckskin, they do not choose to flay the deer alive, but think that if they do not wound it, and close the exit of its breath with pollen, a certain vital element remains even though the animal dies; one of its souls may depart, but not all." It seems, then, that Coyote has the capacity to protect that life-force or set of other souls entirely on his own, which helps to explain why he is sacred while at the same time being evil. See note 46, pp. 377–78.

40. In Haile's unpublished version (1932a) of the episode which begins here, narrated by Curly Toaxedlini, the maiden is identified as *Ch'ikééh na'azíli* the Tingling Maiden. Hence the cycle of two Coyote exploits with women is reduced to a single one. In Haile (1981b), p. 111, the maiden is identified as mother of one of the monsters whose birth is described on pp. 94–97 above.

Whitherspoon (1977), p. 77, makes a statement that may help identify the significance of the episode: "Beings and entities in the Navajo world are categorized and ranked according to a scale based on who can control whom. Beings of lower intelligence cannot control or act upon beings of higher intelligence, unless the beings of higher intelligence unwittingly or inadvertently yield to the control of beings of lower intelligence." The maiden never should have submitted to Coyote to begin with. By doing so, she creates evil and disorder. However, Reichard (1950), p. 139, hints that she has some magic powers of her own to begin with.

41. According to Frank Goldtooth in Fishler, p. 35, the first sweat lodge was made by First Man during the building of the fifth world "to cure disease and for the purification of the people." Matthews (1902), pp.

50–53, discusses the sweat lodge at some length. Among other things, he says that one name for the structure in this particular incident is *ch'ahałyeeł biyázhi* or little darkness, which helps to explain why Gray Giant cannot see what is actually happening. Luckert (1975), pp. 142–46, discusses the sweat lodge in a traditional framework. See also, Franciscan Fathers, pp. 340–43. I am told by Ethelou Yazzie of Bird Spring, Arizona, that stories are exchanged in the sweat lodge.

42. See Luckert (1975), p. 140: "Marriage with animals signifies marriage with gods in the still divine world of prehuman flux. Even after human beings and the ordinary animals had been fixed to permanent shapes, the gods have retained the ability to appear in animal form. Intermarriages with animals under the condition of prehuman flux are therefore sacred events. Inasfar as in these stories the offspring are mentioned, it means the beginnings of new families and tribes. . . . Thus, before becoming too analytical and too critical, the Western reader is advised to peruse the ancient Greek stories about Father Zeus and the manifestations by which he had affairs with women of the human kind. American Indian mythology is not any less noble than that of ancient Greece."

The passage which begins here and continues through the paragraph on p. 136 ending, ". . . discussing it with her brothers," is based upon a corresponding passage in Reichard (n.d.), pp. 19–21. The episode is handled similarly by Curly Toaxedlini in Haile (1932a), pp. 17–19. The close similarity between these two unpublished versions of Coyote's seduction of the maiden leads me to believe that the incident should be incorporated into this text. It provides explicit emphasis on the erotic aspects of Coyote's behavior, which seems appropriate to any trickster cycle.

43. In Reichard (n.d.), Red Mustache merely has him running crazily around, although he has him urinate inside the lodge beforehand. I choose to insert this detail to place greater explicit emphasis on Coyote's disruptive trickster qualities. Notice that he reverses the traditional clockwise movement when he makes a circle. Also, by urinating to the north of the dwelling he violates a taboo. See Wyman and Bailey. See also Wyman and Kluckhohn (1940), p. 19: "Some singers warn their patients not to urinate or defecate to the north during the course of a chant."

44. In *Navaho Legends*, p. 94, Matthews has one of the brothers say simply, "It smells as if some animal has been in the woodpile." But in their respective transcriptions, both Haile (1932a) and Reichard (n.d.) identify the odor as that of Coyote's urine. In fact, Haile, p. 20, records the older brother's outright anger when he perceives the smell.

45. The youngest brother will witness sexual excess and will learn of some of the magic to be practiced by Coyote and his new wife. Luckert (1975), p. 49, indicates that the youngest brother is traditionally called "sloppy." Curly Toaxedlini, in Haile (1932a), p. 30, refers to him thus. Haile adds, p. 63, n. 8, that "Sloppy" is "a nickname for the youngest of

the family, probably because this youngest brother was ugly and covered with running pus of the eye and a running (snotty) nose." Often such a character acquires traits associated with those marking the culture hero in religious narrative or the epic hero in literary narrative. We also see in the youngest a semblance of the scapegoat early in the narrative, just as we see in him as the story progresses the precursor to the warrior and the shaper of a new reality. He is a familiar figure indeed in Navajo narrative and in the narratives of other tribes, at first suffering such misfortunes as privation, humiliation, the lack of an identifiable parent, and the like. See, for instance, the account of the visionary in Matthews (1902). Consider this passage, pp. 169–70: "All the time that the singing was going on the youngest brother . . . had lain beside his grandmother, seeming to be asleep. Now the others bade him get up and try to learn [the songs], and told him that if he tried, perhaps he could learn first. But his grandmother said: 'No, he is stupid. His elder brothers have better minds than he. If they cannot learn the songs how can he learn them?' For all that, she caught him by the ear, made him rise, and bade him help in the singing. . . ." Also see p. 312, n. 38. In this particular episode, it actually turns out that the brother is mastering the songs unbeknownst to members of his family. In other cases, the youngest really is less capable or less crafty to begin with. But he acquires wisdom or ability swiftly at some point during the action of the story, sometimes with the help of the gods. If he is not a "sloppy" younger brother with sores and a runny nose, he is despised because he is homeless or poor or both. See, for instance, the Slim Curly account of the "Scrap Picker Boy" in Haile (1978), pp. 1–12. Such a protagonist invites comparison with epic heroes in traditional western literature or with the protagonists of the more modern genre of the *Bildungsroman*.

46. The role reversal implicit here suggests that an exchange of magic powers has transpired, and that the chief magic power being exchanged is that of witchcraft. In this case, the transaction is obvious. If Coyote has not yet transmitted all of his evil power to the maiden, he soon will. And she will accept them when he does. For a parallel exchange, see Haile (1938), p. 143, where a man's daughter tells a suitor, who asks her how it is that her father knows every move they make and has full control over all that happens, that the old man possesses a medicine bag containing " . . . parts of an enemy's fetus . . . , the enemy's leg tendons, the enemy's rain mask. . . ." She then promises the young man that she will make a duplicate and exchange it with the original, giving the genuine one to him and the worthless one to her father. After she makes the exchange, the young suitor manages to reverse the relationship between himself and his "father-in-law," so that he gains the magical upper hand over the older man in exactly the same way that the elder had used sorcery to have the upper hand over the younger one.

In that case, the medicine bundle serves to make manifest just the kind of magic power we can equate with the indestructible "life-force" displayed first by Coyote and then by his new wife. To the Navajos such bundles have very real power. They are used by medicine men to this day. Obviously, there are those which contain good magic as well as those that contain evil magic and hence can be used for witchcraft. Certain esoteric knowledge is needed to make them work, and it is such knowledge that is now to be passed by Coyote to the woman he has seduced. I see this passage as one more element in the pattern of positive and negative relationships between male and female so pervasive throughout the Navajo creation story.

47. Implicit here is the possibility that the woman possessed power of her own which she did not share with Coyote. See Reichard (1950), p. 139: "The Navajo believe that all secrets, even those of sorcery, are divulged during sexual intercourse."

48. See note 37, p. 374 above. Here again we see Coyote invite evil by completing a circle. And it may be that in bidding him go around the sheep the eldest brother is prompting him to do so and thus to bring disorder upon himself.

49. See p. 109 above; see also n. 32, p. 372. In Haile (1932a), the eldest does not utter the curse. Instead he says, "Surely nothing is sacred to you wherever you go First Scolder."

50. According to Curly Toaxedlini, in Haile (1932a), p. 24; p. 41, n. 7, Coyote violates a taboo when he stops and takes the meat from his back: " . . . (Carrying) must be done without sitting down, until (one reached) the hogan. Then only it should be opened and upon opening it there it would increase very much."

51. See Luckert (1979), p. 225, for an example of how details of the creation story predicate ceremonial practice. At a certain point during the Coyoteway ceremony the patient is ritualistically identified with the stricken Coyote. He, along with those participants who are inside the ceremonial hogan with him, must strip to the shirt or breech cloth. "Then, as flames shoot up toward the smoke hole . . . the leader sings a song about the 'fur of the patient.' " The patient hence becomes the archetypal trickster, creator of his own misfortune. It is fundamental to Navajo religion that the ailing individual has brought his illness upon himself by some mistake or transgression. The essence of the healing ceremony thus becomes an act of forgiveness. The patient's family undergoes a great deal of trouble and expense to bring about his cure, as if to say, "We know you did something wrong—something that Coyote himself might have done, perhaps. But we don't care. We want you to get well." Even Coyote himself is revered as someone whose life and well-being is worth saving. "Coyote has been the first sufferer," says Luckert (1979), p. 97, which may or may not be true depending upon how suffering is to be defined. But he

certainly is the first to endure physical pain in the story. It might even be said that one of his functions in the narrative is to explain the existence of physical discomfort. And as the first victim of that sort of thing, he arouses a measure of pity no matter how badly he behaves. In that respect, we can relate him at least to a certain extent to the tragic hero in western literary tradition.

52. The death of Coyote has deep implications, not easily understood but well worth pondering. On every occasion of my mentioning this passage to Navajos, I got the same response, whether from a young person fully assimilated into the Anglo world, or from a traditional old-timer dwelling on the mythical past: Coyote really didn't die then. Or, if he did, he would come back to life again. More than any other character he represents the impulse for survival, endurance, perpetuation. He is ultimately seen as the force that transcends any predisposition to be destructive, foolish, antisocial, counter-creative. See Luckert (1979), pp. 185–88. In Luckert's account of the Coyoteway ceremonial, the shaman presiding over the ritual adheres to a version of the story wherein Coyote, instead of being killed, is merely "shot full with the Bird People's feathery arrows" and becomes sick. He then escapes to "the rim of Narrow Canyon" where "his kinsmen restored him" (p. 48). Thus we have a not uncharacteristic departure from the main line of the creation story. It seems to me that one explanation for the variation is this. As the absolute basis for the Navajo belief system, the creation myth provides the foundation for all chantway narratives, just as each chantway provides the full etiological basis for every single segment of the healing process. It seems reasonable to assume that the medicine man who is treating the patient will want to adjust the narrative (or his conception of how the story progresses) in whatever way he thinks he should to provide the best, most effective therapy. So the story can be reworked to apply to a particular healing ceremony conducted by a particular practitioner the way the Coyoteway myth is reworked in Luckert's account. And when it thus becomes something of a self-contained story in its own right to be reinstated as ritual drama, this episode could undergo a change wherein Coyote is wounded rather than killed, and then is carefully treated and cured by allies or kin. That is the Coyote with whom, in this instance, the patient is to identify.

53. The etiological element is prominent throughout the entire narrative, and here is one more incident explaining the cause of a particular set of features in the world. But Washington Matthews provides, for such lore, a useful perspective. In an unpublished manuscript titled "Natural Naturalists," reprinted in Poor, pp. 131–39, Matthews says: "Everywhere in Indian folk-lore and in Indian song the lower animals are characters of the greatest interest, and wherever they appear they always present themselves in proper shape. True, they speak in the language of

man and exhibit the possession of human reason, but apart from this their
words and actions do no violence to the facts of natural history; on the
contrary the Indian tales and songs show a close and discriminating study
of nature on the part of the authors. The subject of a large part of the
Indian myths is the distinctive attributes and peculiarities of animals and
the imaginary causation of these attributes. On one occasion, in order that
he might reach home ere the sun rose the wood-rat had to run so far and so
fast that he blistered the soles of his feet and this accounts for the
callosites we see on the feet of the rat now." The point he is making is
that the Indians not only saw fit to name everything they encountered, but
also saw well and attempted to explain what they saw. Such storytelling,
whether in print or in performance, reflects human curiosity, human
observation, the exclusively human impulse both to explain and to
contemplate. It is an activity whose origins in human evolution should be
sought just as eagerly as archaeologists seek fossils and artifacts and whose
practice, once it is better understood as a basic human activity, can add
much to what little we know about the advent of human culture.

54. In Haile (1932a), p. 27, she openly accuses the brothers of killing
Coyote: "Where did he go who accompanied you? Ye must have killed
him. . . . The fact is ye hate him, ye despise him, I know it!"

55. Her transformation provides a good illustration of what Luckert
(1975, pp. 133–65) means when he explains the concept of "prehuman flux."

56. In Haile (1932a), pp. 27–28, Curly Toaxedlini explains that she heals
herself by applying the powers Coyote had taught her. "This whole
(knowledge) was placed in her and she had mastered it all," he says.

57. In Haile (1932a), pp. 29–30, the eldest brother is the tutelary, not the
two holy people mentioned here. He assists the sloppy brother much as
the two deities do here, but he does so before he takes flight from the
angry she-bear sister. It may be that since this version is a much more
recent one than Matthews's, the informant could be responding to less
constraint to attribute certain actions to the gods. I believe that the Haile
version has undergone some attrition since the brothers there seem to
hunt with guns. We are told, for example (p. 23), that they "brought both
[of the mountain sheep flushed out by Coyote] down with a shot. . . ."

58. The act of neutralizing evil or of converting it to something useful
becomes an established pattern in the conquest passages in Part Three
below, pp. 220ff. See also note 59, p. 398 below.

59. While more fearsome than other animals, the bear also seems to be
considered more pliable to the Navajos than Coyote does. See Hill (1938),
p. 38, where one informant is quoted as saying, "A bear will always listen
to a prayer if you say it. You can go out in the field where he had been and
pray. If he continues to come back it is all right to kill him." Also see p.

157: "When a bear attacked, a man was permitted to kill it in self-defense."

60. See Wyman (1970), p. 10; see also Haile (1942), p. 412, for a more complete etiological account of the death-dwelling. Hill (1938), explains the land on which there was such a hogan was never used for farming purposes. Rather, crops were planted around the small areas on which a hogan in which someone died once stood. The aversion to death remains especially strong to this day.

61. The name *Leeyaa neeyáni*, or Reared in the Earth, has great significance when considered in the broad context of Navajo-Pueblo narrative tradition. See, for instance, Wyman (1962), which I consider an essentially ancient ceremonial narrative because of its obvious allusions to kiva culture. When they go down into the netherworld domain of the snake people, those who rescue the child who "was chosen" are told by one snake, p. 96, that the purloined youngster grew up "in a dark mirage . . . within a dark hoop . . . by means of collected water." Then, three other snakes provide similar information, after which the boy is revealed to them and allowed to climb back up to the surface of the earth. The interior of the earth thus becomes the locus for the reenactment of the emergence. That—in a broad sense fairly well-defined in Part One and the first section of Part Two of the creation story—summarizes the kind of evolving maturity and creativity illustrated in the behavior of First Man and First Woman, which helps to explain the role of the culture hero. He is a destroyer of enemies and a creator of agricultural goods; but before that he is "born" (or "reborn") out of the earth's interior. Haile (1932a), p. iv, acknowledges the close association made in the Navajo mind between *Leeya neeyáni* and *Naayéé' neizghání* the Monster Slayer prominent in Part Three below, which furthers the argument that the episode involving Coyote and Changing-Bear-Maiden is a fully integrated part of the overall narrative.

Part Three

1. In Part Three of the narrative, where the monsters are killed, the action of the story reaches a climax, at least on one level. But it remains a stylized action, where movement is expressed in terms of design. The useful point of reference is the Navajo sandpainting, with its peculiar

expressions of movement, proportion, and relationships. And as this portion of the narrative begins, it is helpful to consider a statement by Hatcher, p. 171: "Just as symmetry does not employ the opposition of the bilateral form, so the movement which is conveyed by the figures is not that of opposed or conflicting actions. The anthropomorphic figures are not in violent action. The movement is a collective one. All move in the same direction at the same rate like celestial bodies. This is very striking when one comes to consider the myths which the paintings illustrate. Illustrations in the European tradition would center on the battles of Monster Slayer with much use of conflicting movement in the form of opposed diagonals and active lines full of wiggly curves such as can be seen in the numerous representations of St. George and the Dragon. But the drypaintings, both in content and in form, glorify not the conflict but the order achieved as a result of it." Similarly, descriptions of the exploits of the twins against the monsters who occupy the fifth world convey little sense of struggle in the way that medieval and renaissance narratives in Western tradition convey conflict. The monsters and the twins do not fight each other. The former are simply slain by the latter in what seems almost to resemble a choreographed movement.

2. Witherspoon (1975), p. 15, says that by this time "the people had lost the ability to reproduce," which explains the significance of this particular configuration of survivors. The elderly pair are beyond the age of reproduction, while the two children are siblings and cannot defy the strong incest taboo.

3. The discovery of Changing Woman and White Shell Woman is one of the great Navajo mysteries. See Reichard (1950), pp. 26ff. Haile (1947) indicates that the answers to questions about the two goddesses remain concealed in esoteric knowledge carefully guarded by a small group of medicine men.

4. In rewriting this section (pp. 172–76), I have used material in Goddard, pp. 59ff.

5. One explanation for the dark cloud appears in Wyman (1970), p. 140. First Man placed it there himself by holding up his medicine bundle in the direction of the mountain (Gobernador Knob). According to note 122, "the inner forms of the earth, the young man and the young woman . . . were contained in First Man's magic bundle with its jewelled corn." In version II of Blessingway it is further implied that First Man is actually the "first cause" of the creation of Changing Woman. One thing that emerges from the Blessingway mythology is First Man's enthusiasm for this mission and for the idea of raising the infant he will find on the shrouded mountain. In the second version of the narrative there is only one baby, not two, which places some uncertainty on the relationship between Changing Woman and White Shell Woman. See, too, Wyman (1970), pp. 509–15. There are other differences between what is recorded in Haile's accounts of the

Blessingway narratives and what is said here in the Matthews version and what Goddard records. Something that we generally neglect to consider when we read the surviving manuscript accounts of works like *Beowulf* or the Homeric epics is the extent to which the storyteller whose words have been written down could have been speculating on the mysteries of his own tradition. Or we neglect to consider to what extent the scribe is deliberately, casually, or inadvertently interpreting by arbitrarily making a choice among divergent accounts. Unfortunately, the printed remains of an oral tradition long since disappeared may totally obscure the fact that a given storyteller may not be merely an entertainer, but an interpreter: an intellectual whose choice of what to say represents deep thought and careful reflection upon such mysteries as the origin of culture heroes, the relationship between gods and mortals, the meanings of symbols and the implications of things which take place in the narrative he recites. It is conceivable that some early preliterate performer of Beowulf's defeat of Grendel's mother knew exactly how it came to pass that he was able to slay her. It is also conceivable that some early teller of some segment of the Arthurian cycle would have objected to the ultimate association of the holy grail with Christian iconography.

6. Within the mythological framework of the narrative, perhaps we can see First Man as the prototype of the Navajo chanter or medicine man. See Reichard (1950), p. xliii. Also see note 37, p. 393 below. In describing the singer-shaman who orchestrates and leads the healing ceremony, she is in effect describing First Man, who by now is a seasoned, mature leader. He is distinguished "from the youth untrained in ceremonial lore," she writes, "in that he has knowledge and, in acquiring it, has accepted responsibility for the welfare of his fellow men." It is worth observing that the shamanic act is in many instances seen as a vicarious quest wherein the chanter-healer departs from his own body and ventures to a world apart where only spirits dwell. At the very least, the act of singing, praying, chanting, and reciting is one involving a certain kind of psychic transportation. Consider this description of the medicine man in the act of singing in Luckert (1979), p. 34: "On the rapturous wings of traditional songs the leader [of the ceremonial] is transported into another space—the real world where underworld and surface-world have blended into one. With his rattle he maintains an ecstatic rhythm—restructuring the neutral flow of past, present and future into the externally returning heartbeats of sacred time." The photograph of the man Luckert is describing (p. 38) is worth looking at; the expression on his face suggests that he is indeed experiencing a transportation to another world or another time.

7. It surprises me to a certain extent that there has been little done in the field of literary study by way of investigating the aesthetics of song and prayer. Lyric poetry, for instance, is seldom considered in conjunction with musicology. And prayer is even more seldom considered as poetry in

its own right or in conjunction with the study of religion. Yet prayer and song lyrics both bear a direct relationship with what we conventionally call poetry. Perhaps we neglect this dimension of poetry because over the years we have been conditioned to "read" poetry and to isolate it from the broader context of performance wherein we would have to reckon more directly with the sound of the human voice and the immediate impact upon the listening audience. One admirable exception in recent literary scholarship is Welsh. See, also, Mark W. Booth. Otherwise, ethnographers seem to have led the way in investigating the relationships between poetry and music and between poetry and prayer. Reichard, for instance, has a number of things to say about Navajo prayer and song that might suggest how much we stand to gain by giving more thought to such matters. See 1950, for instance, pp. 279–300, where she discusses song at length. And in 1944b, pp. 35–49, she analyzes the structure of selected Navajo prayers, directing our attention to the strong poetic element at work in a significant corpus of Navajo prayers. Sandner, pp. 61–67, discusses songs from the refreshing perspective of a nonspecialist discovering them for the first time but carefully analyzing his own reaction to hearing them. For a statement about how a given set of songs is intergrated into a particular ceremony in Navajo culture, see McAllester. And see Matthews (1894), pp. 185–94, where he transcribes Navajo lyrics and translates them into English and expresses doubt that their metrics can be reproduced in that language. All told, the place of song in the Navajo creation cycle is secure and suggests that the relationship between music and poetry is a stronger, more instructive one than literary scholars in general have realized.

8. See Witherspoon (1977), p. 17. *Old age* or *long life* is the English translation of *sq'ah naagháii; bik'eh hózhǫ́* is what has been rendered here as *happiness*. That term could just as easily be translated as *good fortune*, but the oversimplifying translations do little justice to the actual meanings of these very important terms. In addition to what Witherspoon has to say about them, consider the possibility discussed by Haile (1947), pp. 17–22, that *sq'ah naagháii* and *bik'eh hózhǫ́* are twin female deities ensconced in the heavens among the stars. Also see the suggestion in note 9, p. 385 below, that *Asdzą́ą́ nádleehé* the Changing Woman is the child of *Sá'ah naagháii ashkii* or Long Life Boy and *Bik'eh hózhǫ at'ééd* or Happiness Girl. Or consider what Reichard (1944b), p. 33, says where she indicates that in its most abstract sense *sq'ah naagháii* means moving from the helplessness of infancy to the full attainment of a ripe old age; and analogously moving from helpless illness to fully restored health. The term also indicates movement toward one's destiny, or "man's final identification with all that is good." See, too, Haile (1943b). *Bik'eh hózhǫ́*, which may be a term that identifies the highest ideal in the Navajo world view, suggests a state of functioning according to absolute beauty. But beauty in this sense does not merely suggest a set of aesthetic standards; it

also suggests the presence of harmony among all the elements in the cosmos. The two terms, when fully understood, amply demonstrate the wrongness of the allegation that preliterate peoples have no grasp of abstractions or ideals. More germane to this section of the narrative, however, is the fact that First Man acknowledges that he is in pursuit of such ideals as he ventures toward the shrouded mountain. See Wyman (1970), pp. 28–30. See also McAllester, p. 67: "If one asks what a particular song is for, or what music in general is for, the most frequent response will be, 'to bring happiness and long life.' " It would seem, then, that there never is very much distance separating the concertedly identifiable function of First Man's particular song here and songs in general. But then, too, it is never easy to isolate any work of art in Navajo culture from its perceived function.

9. There are variants to this episode, chief of which is the version in which First Man finds an actual infant. According to Wyman (1970), p. 47, Changing Woman "was the child of Long Life Boy *[Są'ah naagháii ashkii]* and Happiness Girl *[Bik'eh hózhǫ at'ééd]*, the inner forms of the Earth or of Earth and Sky." According to what Matthews has recorded in his unpublished "Notes on Navajo Cosmology" (n.d.a), p. 31, side 1, it is First Woman who ventures out. And she finds an infant rather than a figurine. (It is worth noticing that the entire episode is reduced to a single sentence in that version, and he amplifies it only slightly in 1883, p. 215, which suggests again that he may have taken down the barest outline in his notes and filled it out later when he actually prepared the manuscript for *Navaho Legends.*) See, too, Witherspoon (1977), p. 202, where we learn that *są'ah naagháii* is equated with the static male and *Bik'eh hózhǫ* is equated with the active female. Hence, Changing Woman can be seen as the "child" of two basic Navajo ideals. Notice how the concept of pairing is again applied, to say nothing about what is implied about the pairing of a male inner form with the female or about how male or female are aligned with cosmic features which between them represent the attainment of a certain measure of control. See the discussion of pairing, p. 353 above.

10. See Wyman (1970), p. 147. Many of those who attend this gathering are the various inner forms, made manifest to the survivors.

11. In traditional Navajo ceremonial activity, the gods generally do not appear only once. They—or more properly speaking those who impersonate them in the chantways—appear, disappear, and then reappear a fixed number of times.

12. Here we encounter what is probably the most revered of all Navajo deities. Of her Matthews (1886a), p. 14, says, "She embodies the attributes of various queens of heaven, of various wives of the highest deities which appear in a hundred mythologies. She has, however, none of the low jealousy and petty spite of her sister Juno, she reminds one more of the Scandanavian Frigga. . . . [Her] name signifies the woman who changes or rejuvenates, and it is said of her that she never remains in one state, but

that she grows to be an old woman, and in the course of time, at will, she becomes a young girl again, and so passes on through an endless cycle of lives, changing but never dying. . . . We see her as none other than our own mother nature, the goddess of the changing year, with its youth of Spring, its middle age of Summer, its senility of Autumn, growing old only to become young again." See also 1902, pp. 31–32, where Matthews discusses her and White Shell Woman further. And see Whitherspoon (1977), p. 91; and Wyman (1970), pp. 72, 469, 514. In the only passage I know of containing any description of her, some of her features are mentioned in Haile (1981b), p. 156.

13. See note 15, pp. 352–53 above. In her statement on pairing (1950, pp. 248–49), Reichard writes that it "is an artifice that lends force to the power of repetition and recapitulation, and it is also a means of elaboration, of obtaining balance, symmetry, and contrast. . . ." An outstanding example of what she discusses is the relationship between White Shell Woman and Changing Woman and their two sons, the "active, impulsive" Monster Slayer and his "gentle, pacific, steady foil" Born for Water. Once we begin to think about it, we can see how frequently this sort of pairing occurs in Western literature. We find Roland and Ganelon in *Chanson de Roland*; Hector and Achilles in the *Iliad*; Prince Hal and Hotspur in *Henry IV*, Part One; Huck Finn and Tom Sawyer; and so on. By establishing two selves for each character, so to speak, the narrative tradition can account for the duality within an individual that mirrors the dualities without—earth/sky, male/female, life/death, and so forth. In O'Bryan, pp. 2, 14, even Coyote has a "double"—the "Great-Coyote-Who-Was-Formed-In-the-Water," who is the one who helps with the creation of the fifth world, whereas Ma̜'ii is the trickster, the evildoer, the mischief-maker, the bringer of disorder. See also, Franciscan Fathers, p. 140, p. 175, p. 351. And see note 60, pp. 398–99 below.

14. In other accounts, notably Wyman (1970), and Haile (1938), p. 85, First Man and First Woman function more explicitly as nurturing parents than they do here. See, too, O'Bryan, pp. 71–77. In *Blessingway*, pp. 437–45, Wyman includes a dramatic interlude wherein Changing Woman's adopted parents object to her decision to go away and live with the sun. See note 23, p. 388 below.

15. For a variant of the "virgin birth" see Wyman (1970), pp. 195–98, 419, 517. Chief differences are that there is only one mother, Changing Woman, who is to be in charge of "all giving birth [reproduction], vegetation and everything which exists on the surface of the earth. . . ." Also, First Man is much more directly instrumental in the procreation of the twins. He has ordered the Sun to visit her and have intercourse with her. There is still further variation in Version II. See p. 404. And we see yet another account in Haile (1938), p. 87. A comprehensive guide to the

various accounts of the conception, birth, nurturance, and coming of age of the twins appears in Spencer (1947), pp. 54–60.

The highly simplified and seemingly bowdlerized version of the birth of the twins found in Hasteen Klah's version, in Wheelwright, pp. 77–78, indicates what seems to have been a problem from the time of the earliest English transcriptions of the Navajo creation story until well into the twentieth century. There appears to have been an aversion among whites to the relatively blunt Navajo allusions to sexuality. Bear in mind that even an objective observer like Matthews was writing under the circumstances of that general set of restraints we now call Victorianism. But he was at least willing to use euphemisms for sexual acts and sexual allusions. In the early part of the twentieth century, however, the tendency to repress such elements seems to have grown stronger. My impression is that Hasteen Klah is responsible for the mutations we find in Wheelwright's bland account, for he appears to have been a somewhat anglicized Indian. Although he was himself a medicine man, it is not at all inconceivable that he felt no uneasiness at bringing Christian overtones into his traditional material. After all, the Navajos have had a history of adapting with ease, somehow retaining their own beliefs and practices as they accepted certain ideas from outside. Another possibility is that he was responding to Ms. Wheelwright's own sensibilities and handed her a version of the narrative he considered acceptable to her. Another possibility, suggested to me by people who knew Mary Wheelwright, is that she bowdlerized Klah's version herself. But that account is still useful because it helps us to see what elements and episodes have resisted the incursions of European culture over the years.

16. Reichard (1950), p. xxxix, writes that "loneliness has become a mythical and religious symbol," and that "from loneliness stem some of the greatest powers the Navajo conceive. The co-operation that extends from the individual, on the one hand to family and all residential relationships, and on the other to clan members, father's clan relatives, clan-group members, and finally, to strangers, seem to be due to the fight against loneliness." Witherspoon (1977), p. 202, identifies the dichotomy of male (static) and female (active) and observes that it is the active, restless female whose impulses are to create.

17. There are versions where only Changing Woman has intercourse, and where she has it with sun and water alike. See Reichard (1950), p. 29, for a set of references to other texts.

18. See the version of the birth of the twins in Wyman (1970), pp. 528ff., which includes an account of their whole "childhood." See, too, Witherspoon (1975), p. 15, for a statement identifying motherhood in terms of lifegiving and sustenance and of the symbols representing those forces.

19. See Matthews (1902), p. 29: "Water-Sprinkler is the literal translation of the name to *Tó neinilí*—the rain-god—the Navajo Tlaloc. We speak of him in the singular although there are thought to be many gods of this name. It seems that the home of the most important rain-god is at *[Tséyi']* yet one is represented as dwelling at each place where there is a community of celestial waters, of precipitated waters. The ocean, rivers, and lakes seem more under the control of *[Tééhooltsódii* the Water Monster]."

20. See Reichard (1950), p. 30: "The function of sun and water in generation and the Navaho belief that two fathers are responsible for twins explain the agreement about the fatherhood of The Twins or War Gods."

21. Contrast this detail with the birth of the monsters, pp. 94–97 above, where there is no such cleansing. See, too, note 23, p. 369.

22. Reichard (1950), p. 249, repeats what Matthews says about the difference between the two brothers when she identifies the son of White Shell Woman as "the gentle, pacific, steady foil to the active, impulsive Monster Slayer." See note 13, p. 386 above.

23. This is the last we see of First Man and First Woman in the Matthews version. In Wyman (1970), Version II, they remain active participants in the action until after the twins return from their second journey to the sun (pp. 252–256 above). Then they tell Changing Woman in effect that she is in charge (Wyman, p. 432). But there is to be a conflict between them and her in that version (p. 437ff.), for they are opposed to her "marriage" to the sun and to her removal to the west. Nor do First Man and First Woman maintain an altogether positive image such as the one they acquire here. In his earlier published outline version of the story, Matthews (1883), p. 224, records this statement: "But First Man and First Woman were angry because they were banished to the east [while Changing Woman went to the west], and before they left they swore undying hatred and enmity to our people. And for this reason all evils come from the east, small-pox and other diseases, war and the white intruder."

24. Creation in Native American traditions is a joint effort, not the result of a single deity. See note 7, pp. 362–64 above. Just as a number of gods collectively make the fifth world and the things in it, so a number of them participate in the creation and subsequent nurturance of the monster-slaying twins. Creation is a matter of "shared power," which helps to explain why there is no absolute, all-prevailing deity as there is in our own monotheistic tradition. See Allen, p. 146.

25. Frank Goldtooth, in Fishler, p. 38, gives one explanation for intervening against the monsters in such a roundabout way: "All of the gods got together to form [the mother of the twins] for they themselves individually had insufficient power to rid the earth of its evil. Had the gods tried to destroy the evil alone, they would have been destroyed themselves."

The two offspring are commonly regarded as twins although they have not by all accounts been sired by the same father or conceived by the same mother. "These gods are twins," says Matthews (n.d.b), p. 1, "according to Indian custom. Although according to one way of speaking they are only cousins." Reichard (1975), p. 25, refers to the "Navajo belief" that "two men are concerned in procreation if a woman bears twins." For a brief but pointed discussion of the modern Navajo attitude toward twins, largely fostered by the influence of the Navajo creation story, see Levy. See, too, Spencer (1957), pp. 69–73, for a discussion of sibling relationships in the chantway narratives.

26. Here begins the process by which the boys prepare for the task ahead of them. See Reichard (1950), pp. 90–91: "The healthy, right-minded Navajo possesses strength, endurance, fortitude; he abhors weakness. In former times boys trained incessantly, exposing themselves to cold, heat, hunger, and thirst, and undergoing rigorous tests for endurance." See, too, Fishler, pp. 44–45. And see Spencer (1947), p. 59. See also, Dyk, pp. 8–9; and Hill (1936), p. 7.

27. Such cruel teasing and practical joking is not out of keeping with the character of a tutelary god. Nor is Talking God without a sense of humor, any more than any other Navajo supernatural would be. We find Talking God having fun at the expense of one of his beneficiaries even when the danger seems greatest. See Matthews (1902), pp. 398–99, for example.

28. Likewise in the story of the stricken twins in Matthews (1902), p. 214, the mother of the boys refuses to reveal the identity of their father to them when they ask.

29. Disobedience and defiance of authority are common in all of the ceremonial narratives. See Spencer (1957), pp. 66–69.

30. *Yé'iitsoh*, of course, invites comparison with the various monsters and demons in Western tradition, from the furies encountered in Hesiod and creatures like Scylla, Glaucus, and the Cyclops in Homer, to the giants and dragons of European folk and literary narratives. Within that broad category of fascinating beings we might also include the various mutants and aberrations common to horror movies, science fiction films, and other electronic narratives. Perhaps we should even consider adding such protagonists and antagonists of gangster films as Little Caesar and Duke Mantee. Physically they resemble humans somewhat more closely than do the likes of Grendel or Swift's Yahoos. But they manifest psychic and social distortions commensurate with the physical distortions of monsters common to narratives of the preelectronic and prerealistic periods.

The monsters we encounter in Native American narratives sometimes provide added understanding of the broad phenomenon of demonology. Frequently they are described in terms of rampant individualism occurring in sharp dissonance with the collective values of tribal society. As such they are seen not only as antisocial agents but as agents that openly threaten the survival of an entire group. Thus Native American demonology might serve as a useful ancillary to the demonology found in works more familiar to us, especially where we wish to read those works from a social perspective. Consider, for instance, this description of the giant, Seven-Macaws, in Nelson's translation of the *Popol Vuh*, p. 40, where destructiveness is seen in terms of vanity: "But amid this serenity, there was a giant called Seven-Macaws who was swollen with pride. 'I am sun and moon! I am the light!' he bragged. 'My splendor knows no shore. My eyes are made of bright silver, my teeth are perfect stone. They shine like the face of the sky. My shiny nose is as beautiful as the moon. When I walk before my silver throne, the face of the earth is lighted. I *am* the sun and moon for my human servants!' "

In such a passage, we find that self-serving vanity is as threatening in its way as *Yé'iitsoh*'s voracious appetite. And the origins of such monsters, which are generally described quite explicitly, help us to understand their role as ultimate threats to the societies where they function disruptively. Given his creation, for instance, as the result of wasteful, autoerotic expenditure of primal sexual energy, Big Giant seems to engender the abject, total waste of life that nearly destroys everyone. Consequently, he adds a dimension to my own understanding of the universal presence of evil creatures in narrative traditions everywhere. For more on this, see Zolbrod (1979).

31. See note 37, p. 374 above, and note 35, p. 392 below. See, too, pp. 259–60 below. Notice how hoops and circles become progressively more important. See Wyman (1962), p. 127, where hoops are used to help restore the hero when he has been transformed into a snake. Thus people learn to exercise control, which is repeated as part of the ceremonial procedure in healing.

32. Here we have the primary example in the story of the exile-quest, a highly significant motif in all Navajo ceremonial literature, just as it is significant in the narrative traditions of other cultures. See Spencer (1957), pp. 18–40, for a succinct guide to the way the quest is implied in the various chantway narratives. The quest that the twins are to undertake is anticipated in earlier parts of the narrative. We glimpse it, for instance, in the journey of First Man when he ventures to the cloud-covered mountain, pp. 173–75 above. We see it to some degree when the youngest of the twelve brothers is sent outside to spy on Coyote and their sister, p. 139. We see a hint of it when the young bridegroom is summoned by the gods to attend the meeting where they contrive to stop the gambler, p. 102. We even see something of an elemental example of the exile-quest in Part One, p. 38 where a man and a woman in the first world seek out *Tééhoołtsódii* the Water Monster to protest in behalf of those who have aroused the displeasure of the gods. Coyote's wanderings suggest the quest to a certain

extent, with the important qualification that he always sets out on a mission that is self-serving and self-indulgent, making him something of an evil or destructive counterpart to the hero and something more like one of the chaos-producing monsters. Insofar as the exile-quest brings about a separation, we even see a mild foreshadowing of the motif in the separation of the sexes early in the story. And we see an interesting variation of that motif in what Wyman (1962), p. 43, calls "impecunious wandering." Frequently in Navajo narrative, individuals and groups find themselves roaming aimlessly in the desert, subsisting on small game and wild plants, sometimes as punishment for wanton slaughter of game, sometimes for inadvertent transgressions and the like. Such a theme, says Wyman, points to "the time before the agriculture when the Navajos (or their Athabascan ancestors) were hunters and gatherers," which sharpens to a degree the conception of the soft world and the transition from soft to hard.

The motif of the quest, to be complete and fully developed, usually culminates in some kind of intervention by the gods and in an ultimate act of service to members of the protagonist's social group: a function, incidentally, that appears to get relatively little attention in standard attempts to define the epic as a literary form. The character who is aided by deities has for one reason or another or for one purpose or another departed into exile or in search of something. This departure and the ultimate service that eventually results is the heart of the various Navajo chantway myths. That is, in every case it serves to promote the ideal of *sạ'ah naagháii, bik'eh hózhó*—long life and happiness discussed in note 8, pp. 384–85 above. In fact, it does so quite directly, since in every case it provides the "plot" or narrative structure that gives linear form to the healing ceremony. See Wyman (1970), p. 474.

33. The image of the ladder sticking out of the ground is a familiar one in the narrative of Southwest tribes. It generally leads to a lower chamber where a benign tutelary resides, or to a netherworld dwelling where an angry god, awaiting an offering, responds favorably. It occurs frequently in traditional Navajo narratives, apparently, and it seems to reflect Pueblo influence. See, for instance, Luckert (1979), pp. 18–19, 199, 205. See, too, Wyman (1962), p. 98. The suggestion made there is that the underground chamber where the responsive spirit resides is in keeping with the idea of emergence so fully a part of Native American narrative traditions. Notice, too, that few underground encounters in western literature or folklore are as positive as this one. Luckert (1976), p. 192, makes the interesting suggestions that the protruding ladder "is obviously related to *kiva* architecture and to the mythic flood caused by the water serpent," and further that "this myth can be traced all the way to the Olmec strata of Middle American Civilization."

34. In Fishler, pp. 45–46, it is Spider Man, not Spider Woman, who helps

the twins, possibly because of the somewhat atypically male orientation of Frank Goldtooth's version. See, for example, his account of the reconciliation between the sexes, p. 26: "First Woman went to First Man and begged him to let the women rejoin the men. They were hungry, without clothes, and were lonely for companionship. First Man said, 'Very well, all will be forgiven and you can go back to your men. But I shall make a law: The male shall rule and whatever the chiefs say, that must be done.' "

35. Here we see the hoop again, with its applied association with the now-familiar circle and its implied association with air and the wind. See note 37, p. 374 above. Hence the significance of the feathers that make up the *naayéé'ats'os*. The more common symbols in traditional Navajo culture represent an interlocking set of cross-references that combine to form a holistic, all-encompassing pattern. So there is actually a direct relationship established here between the control the twins are to gain with possession of the sacred hoop and the power to control endowed in First Man and First Woman when they are transformed out of two ears of corn. The basis of that shared control is manifested in speech: in the things that are said to create and to harness unchecked forces. See Reichard (1950), p. 49: " . . . a comparison of many myths yields associations ultimately valid. For instance, the transformation of corn ears into human beings indicates an obvious association between wind and breath, and cross references establish whorls—through whirlwinds—as elements of the associative group; hence the explanation that breath enters the body at the places where there are whorls. Since down is easily set in motion by wind or breath, down feathers and motion are further extensions of the group."

Speech, too, extends that group, as we have seen already by the songs of First Man as he makes his way to the mountaintop where he finds the female likeness, and as we shall see with the recitations of the twins when they use the sacred hoop to pacify the destructive forces they meet along the holy trail. Speech becomes an additional unit in the interlocking set of elements to a large extent because it is considered an extension of the power of the wind. See what Witherspoon (1977), pp. 30–31, says about the Navajo conception of speech as the result of an initial investment of "wind soul" acquired at birth. That statement helps us to understand that when the brothers use the *nayéé' ats'os* to control the alien forces, they are applying the same kind of power that is applied when they are prompted and instructed by *Niłch'i* the Wind. Thus, much of the unity found within the narrative is attributable in part to the way these various symbols are linked. See n. 16, pp. 353–54 above. See, too, McNeley.

36. It is not easy to explain the significance of pollen in any aspect of Navajo life and culture, but especially in the narratives. The lightest of all tangible substances perceived by the Navajos in their world view, pollen suggests perhaps the force and pervasiveness of light and spirit. It

represents simultaneously the power of wind and air invested in living creatures and the invisible animating force everywhere in the cosmos. Consider, to begin with, this summarizing statement by Reichard (1950), p. 582, who writes, "Pollen clears the trail so that a person may walk safely." Then she goes on to catalog how it functions for the benefit of gods and heroes alike in the various ceremonial narratives. It also functions to assure safe passage out of and back into the known world for contemporary Navajos who maintain their belief in the old traditions. It was explained to me more than once how Navajos from the Tuba City area will carry pollen with them as they leave the reservation.

37. See Reichard (1950), p. 149, for a statement which links the shamanistic medicine man who orchestrates a ceremony with the questing hero in any one of the myriad ceremonial narratives: "He who would control the various supernaturals must start with the aid of mentors, who give him foreknowledge; he must be willing to put forth effort and to profit by it; he must submit to tests which require great courage; and eventually, as a human being, he must identify himself with divinity." See note 6, p. 383 above.

38. See Reichard (1950), pp 71–72, for a discussion of these "dangers conceived as deities," which she calls "mythological motives common to many North American Tribes." For another version of the journey with added details that supplement this passage, see Wyman (1970), pp. 535–39. For some characteristic illustrations of the episode, see King, Oakes, and Campbell, plates II, III, and VIII The variation found in Wheelwright, pp. 95–97, may also supplement what appears here, since there the eldest of the two brothers transforms the monsters into less formidable natural objects which he instructs to become useful. Hence we find the familiar conversion of evil into good. It is a conversion that becomes increasingly important in this version, too. And, of course, the power of speech is a major catalyst in the process.

39. In Wyman (1970), pp. 386–87, there is an account of who these "guardians" are and how they were placed to guard the dwelling of the sun from intruders.

40. See Reichard (1950), p. 150. The incidents describing the coming of the twins to the home of their father "is an elaborate test of judgment and worth which does not end until the evils have been destroyed and their powers brought back to man." By undergoing such a test the hero acquires that power. See note 32, pp. 390–91 above.

41. Sun has a family, and there is nothing untoward in that fact. See Witherspoon (1975), pp. 3–66. See also Wyman (1970), p. 160, n. 136, where Sun's wife is possibly identified as Dawn Woman. Or, according to Haile (1938), she could be the daughter of Dawn Woman. Likewise, Reichard (1950), p. 495 repeats the suggestion occurring elsewhere that she could actually be White Shell Woman. In any case, she is likely to be

quarrelsome. For a full description of Sun's home, see Wyman (1970), p. 387. See also, p. 392, n. 288: "The home of the Sun, adorned with dangerous things, is the final authority for ceremonials other than Blessingway, especially war rites. It is the home, rather than the Sun itself, which gives such rites their power to remove evil. . . ."

42. The blankets are the accoutrements of the Sun, given to him by First Man when he was assigned to rule the sky. See Wyman (1970), p. 386. "Common people shall not visit you without reason," he is told. "There will be a means which causes fear to spread from you. You will live there accompanied by dark cloud, blue cloud, yellow cloud, white cloud, and varicolored cloud."

43. *Jóhonaa'éí* is established as a rather fearsome god, with many regal trappings and with a lot of power. See, for instance, Wyman (1970), p. 386. And see Fishler, pp. 47–48, where he enters his dwelling with "lightning and arrow points all over his body" and with "lightning coming out of his fingers, feet, head and body." In Haile (1938), the Twins are told repeatedly (e.g., by Spider Woman, p. 97; by a field rat, p. 99), "Your father has no mercy." In that version of their journey to the sun, in fact, the twins are wrapped in the blanket by the Sun's children explicitly to hide them from their merciless father. See Witherspoon (1975), p. 33, for a statement about the influence this conception of the angry sun has had in Navajo culture right up to the present.

44. Sun's wife shows anger here and perhaps a trace of hurt feelings. In Haile (1938), p. 101, she responds with more of an attitude of restrained sarcasm, e.g., "Which persons would venture here [where you are such a tyrant]? And yet those that come positively stated that their father lived here! This seems strange, since a certain person is in the habit of boasting that he does nothing wrong on his journeys." Reichard (1950), p. 133, says about Sun's philanderings, " . . . the whole pattern of Sun's character is built upon deceit. He mates with girls without the knowledge of their parents or of his sky wife. He causes them to lead sneaking lives and to tell untruths." In a conversation with me in the fall of 1978, Harry Bilagody, Jr., of Tuba City, Arizona, acknowledged his agreement with Reichard's statement, yet he expressed no outright disapproval of *Jóhonaa'éí*'s behavior. He added that this episode marks the beginning of jealousy, agreeing in that regard with what Frank Goldtooth is quoted by Fishler, p. 47, as having recited: "At last the Twins entered the house and there they found an old woman. She said, 'What are you doing here? You don't belong here!' The boys said, 'We are looking for our father. He is around here somewhere.' The woman became very angry and said she had thought she was the only woman the sun had. It was at this time that jealousy first started. If this had not happened there would be no jealousy today. This is also the reason the Navajo believe it is all right to have more than one wife." Even so, the Sun's polygyny should not be placed in the

same perspective it would have in western societies. His having more than one wife is in itself not the catalyst that brings disharmony in this scene. Rather, the disharmony is more the result of his flagrant deceit. He has promised his wife one thing, but his behavior reveals he has done otherwise. See Reichard (1928), pp. 58–73, where it is explained that stability in a marriage is important but that monogyny is not necessarily the key factor in maintaining that stability. See, too, Haile (1978), pp. 156–58.

45. In Fishler, p. 48, the Sun seems more ambivalent in his attitude toward the boys: "Finally, in the white cloud he found the boys. He said, 'I hope it has come true,' i.e., that these were his boys. 'I will see if they are my children.' He thought that he would try to kill them and see if they were really his sons. The Sun did not want them and he hoped to prove them not to be his sons."

46. For a comprehensive account of the tests he gives to his sons, see Wyman (1970), pp. 541–46.

47. According to Frank Goldtooth in Fishler, p. 50, it is the moon who helps the twins, not the wind. That is the only account I know of where the moon functions as a tutelary god.

48. In discussing this passage with me, Harry Bilagody, Jr., and his younger brother, Jesse, both fairly traditional Navajos from the conservative Tuba City area on the western edge of the reservation, described their first visit to a sweat lodge. They were about five and four respectively at the time. It was their father's wish that they enter the lodge, heated very much as this one was, with the men who customarily used it. They recalled—with good humor and laughter—the shock of being in so dark a place, the suddenness with which the interior filled up with steam, and their inability to stay inside more than a few minutes. "It's like a test for a small boy to go inside," reported Jesse. Thus the mythic reality of the Navajo creation story is quite close at certain points to the real world of contemporary Navajo life.

49. In O'Bryan, p. 81, the twins appeal to the sun's self-interest in asking for help: "Father, if they eat all the people on earth, and themselves last, for whom will you travel? What will you receive as a gift for the price of your journey?" Witherspoon (1975), p. 32–33, explains that "the relationship of a father to his children is one of affection, discipline, instruction, and economic assistance . . . complementary to the mother-child bond, although . . . not as close, intense, and permanent." But there is also a negative side which makes for ambivalence in the relationship as it is traditionally defined in Navajo chantway narratives. After all, in consenting to help these two of his children, *Jóhonaa'éí* is participating in the destruction of a third of his offspring. See Spencer (1947), pp. 39–43.

50. The fact that *Jóhonaa'éí* is also the father of *Yé'iitsoh* tells something about the relationship between gods and demons in Navajo

tradition. Again, Matthews is helpful. In "Gods of the Navahos" (1886a), pp. 18–19, he writes, "To us it may seem that the difference between a god and a devil is a very wide one, but it was not thus with our remote ancestors and it is not thus with the lower races of the present day. It is more than probable that the antithetic words divine and devilish come from the same root. Demon, according to our lexicographers, may mean a good as well as a bad spirit, and it once meant only the former. Lucifer was erst a member of the heavenly court and even Milton tells us that when expelled he looked 'not less than Archangel fallen.'. . . Then we need not be surprised if the Navajos merely divide the gods into the friendly and the unfriendly, the ordinary gods and the 'strange gods,' as our decalogue calls them. The latter being the equivalent of our devils." He apparently gives considerable thought to the matter of the deified culture hero in general and to the way such a personage reflects what we ourselves would be tempted to reduce in our discussions to the simple abstractions of good and evil. "The hero god of the American aborigines," he adds, "is often described as one of two brothers, commonly twins and the other twin is regarded as a myth of the light, of darkness and its associated moisture. In some of the tales the two brothers are represented as friendly, the one assisting the other in good deeds. . . . On the other hand they are sometimes represented as inimical to one another and as having contests in which one is slain by the other." Here Matthews, who had a penchant for applying his ideas broadly once he acquired a good grasp of them, seems aware of some of the universal traits linking heroes of all great literatures.

Frank Goldtooth identifies the mother of Big Giant in Fishler, p. 54, this way: "The Giant was a half-brother to the boys. His father was the sun and his mother was a whore, Loose Running Woman. . . ." Haile (1938), p. 79, presents this account of the conception of Big Giant: "Early one day soon after Jóhonaa'éí was placed in the sky to rule it, a maiden had gone off alone in the direction of the sunrise. And after defecating she used a smooth pebble from the river to cleanse herself. She placed the warm stone in her genitals and raised her skirt so as to examine herself. And just at this moment Jóhonaa'éí climbed above the horizon and sent a ray into her." Elsewhere, Sun says of Big Giant, "Above all others I have loved him" (p. 109). An abbreviated account of the origin of Yé'iitsoh is given to Matthews by his informant Jake (see Matthews n.d.a.), p. 30, side 1. Reichard (1950), p. 76, explains the belief that the Sun is Big Giant's father this way: "During the period when the sexes were separated, normal practices were impossible—the men had little influence on the future; the women may have conceived as a result of self-abuse because the quill feather, elk antler, stone, and cactus were manifestations of Sun, to whom generation is ultimately ascribed."

51. See p. 428 below. And see Reichard (1950), p. 248: "So much importance is attached, in both myth and practice, to beginning an event or to the first time an act takes place as to make initiation a major symbol. The success of a first attack in raiding is an omen of the final outcome." In Haile (1938), p. 107, the impression is given that the Sun only *lends* the weapons to the twins, and that he does so cautiously, wanting to be sure that he maintains control over them. That seems to be why he insists on being the first one to shoot. Later he says that he wants to strike the first blow so that he won't feel quite so bad when *Yé'iitsoh* is destroyed.

52. Reichard (1950), p. 154, mentions "zigzag lightning, flash lightning, sunstreamer and rainbow" in reference to another version of this episode. See, too, pp. 512–14, for a discussion of arrows.

53. See Reichard (1950), p. 152: "One of the most difficult of the hero's tests, a formal requirement of his instruction, was to name every holy place on the earth as he looked upon the panorama from a great height." See, too, Reichard (1944b), p. 26, where it is explained why the shamanistic hero must have a precise command of geography.

54. See note 50, pp. 395–96 above.

55. This expression is used by Matthews in *Navaho Legends*, p. 115. In note 124, p. 234, he states, "No etymology has been discovered for this expression. It is believed to be the equivalent of the '*Fee Fa Fum!*' of the giants in our nursery tales." None of the Navajos I consulted could recognize any meaning, and few were willing to offer a modern Navajo equivalent. One suggestion was that of Dr. William Morgan, of Fort Defiance, who said that it would be appropriate to have the giant say, "*Yaadi lá nizhóní dó'*—What pretty little things!" Matthews (n.d.a.), p. 34b, has the giant say, "Here are two nice little boys. What will I do with them?" And the boys reply, "Here is a fine big monster. What will we do with him?" In 1883, p. 212, he varies this exchange slightly. But because he sees fit to repeat the nonsensical Navajo expression in his more definitive version of the story in *Navaho Legends*, I assume that the additional knowledge he acquired after publishing the earlier account gave him reason to favor it. So I decided merely to convert his orthography to the modern spelling and otherwise keep the phrase he finally chose.

56. The elder brother, who is soon to earn the name *Naayéé' neizghání*, should do most of the talking, since he is brash, restless, and impulsive. In fact, we see him emerge in the various narratives in which he appears as the more daring and bellicose of the two. His ultimate image is that of a war god, and that is how traditional Navajos still regard him. See, for instance, how he behaves in Haile (1938), p. 151, as he summons the menfolk to participate in a raid of revenge against Taos Pueblo.

57. See note 51, p. 397 above.

58. Various treatments among printed versions of the war against the

monsters are identified and summarized in Spencer (1947), pp. 81–86. One of the noticeable differences between what is found in Matthews and what is narrated in most of the others is that *Naayéé' neizghání* suffers no great reversals or setbacks here, whereas in other accounts he does. In Newcomb and Reichard, p. 30, he becomes weak from combat; in Haile (1938), p. 123, he is more nearly threatened with defeat.

59. See p. 166 above. The central idea of converting evil to good is identified here and appears to be another motif that binds Navajo tradition to other Native American traditions in general and to Mesoamerican traditions more particularly. See Luckert (1975), pp. 46–47. See also p. 109, p. 146. Perhaps we have in the image of the slain, man-eating giant something that signifies a repudiation of the idea of human sacrifice. When we are told, as on p. 91 above, and in note 18, p. 366, that the sun demands a life each day, we have a framework for understanding why he can be considered a father to *Yé'iitsoh*, the voracious consumer of living beings. See note 13, p. 352 above.

60. What Matthews says about the two brothers (n.d.b.) is worth repeating in part: "*Naayéé' neizghání* signifies Slayer of the Alien Gods. We may otherwise say 'Slayer of Giants' or 'Slayer of Demons.' Jack the Giant Killer is the nursery-tale counterpart of this deity." Monster Slayer is, says Matthews, "the elder and more potent of the two. His mother was the elder and more important goddess." Between them, the two brothers signify "night and day, light and darkness, heat and moisture." One of them is destined to go "abroad in the day-time to fight his enemies" and to destroy "the monsters inimical to his race." The other, "whose father was the water-fall" remains at home to guard the lodge while the brother goes to war." One is more aggressive, the other "gentler" and a "humble companion." Matthews then adds that as we study the two brothers we "find in them through all the myths, rites and songs in which they appear a pair which have their counterparts all over the world in the myths of different races, high and low in the scale of culture. . . . Our rude Navajo War-Gods, clad in buck-skin, and adorned with paint and feathers, have not only for their kinsmen the Atutish and Mahash of the Hidatsa, the Iosheka and Tawiskara of the Iroquois, the Ahaiyata and Matsilema of the Suni. But perhaps Castor and Pollux and the Asvinau of India are their brethren. There are some who would even place in this category Romulus and Remus, and others who would dare to include Cain and Abel." Also see Matthews's discussion of the similarity between the twins and their counterparts in other Old and New World narratives (1902), p. 20. See pp. 19, 22–23, for additional discussions of both brothers. See, too, note 15, pp. 352–53 above. And see note 61, p. 381 above for references to the association between Monster Slayer and Reared in the Earth. See Haile (1938), pp. 36, 53, 56, where some engaging questions are raised about the twins and are by no means conclusively resolved. See also, note 50, pp. 395–96 above, for a

discussion of pairing. As for the naming and renaming of the two brothers, see Young and Morgan, "The Sobriquet," p. 812, where it is explained that in Navajo Society a descriptive name is commonly bestowed based on certain kinds of distinguishing features, which, I assume, could also include some outstanding deed or achievement.

61. Reichard (1928), p. 113, expresses surprise that Matthews makes no reference to the *anądji* or war dance ceremony. According to her it is a "common and important ceremony." It would have been appropriate for the ceremony to be held when the twins returned to their people after defeating Big Giant, and she says about the occasion that it should have been obvious to Matthews. See p. 117, also.

62. From this point on, *Naayéé' neizgháni* begins to develop an identity and character of his own. He becomes, says Matthews (1886a), p. 17, "distinctly an Indian war-god, and the god of an especially shrewd and crafty tribe. . . . Like the bully Thor he is the terror of evil spirits but unlike Thor, the evil spirits never outwit him. He too has the thunder-bolts for weapons, but he has no unlimited supply of them. He must husband them, even as an Indian husbands his well-made arrows. His chief weapon is a great stone knife; but he depends not so much on his weapons, as on his presence of mind, his craftiness, his power of dissimulation. He is no coward, no vacillator, once sped on his journey he never returns unsuccessful; but in accomplishing his purpose he exhibits more the character of the cunning Ulysses than of the bold Hercules."

63. See Matthews (1902), pp. 36–40, for a detailed discussion of prayersticks. He also describes them and explains their overall function in *The Mountain Chant* (1887), pp. 451–55. There we learn that prayersticks can indeed have the dual purpose of serving as offerings and sacrifices on the one hand and of conveying messages on the other. On p. 452, he includes a good sketch. Also see Wyman and Kluckhohn (1940), pp. 26–28. See, too, Reichard (1950), pp. 254–55, 303–13, 675–79. Notice the presence of feathers (air) and pollen (light) on some prayersticks. The pair of prayersticks being used here might be "talking prayersticks," pp. 308–9, or "warning prayersticks," p. 311. See Wyman (1970), p. 104, for a description of prayersticks used in a Blessingway ceremony. Prayersticks remain an essential element in ceremonials to this day. See Franciscan Fathers, pp. 396–98; Wyman (1965), p. 53; and Luckert (1979), pp. 139–44. Luckert includes photographs of prayersticks used in 1974 in a performance of the Coyoteway ceremony; see pp. 140, 141, 143, 144.

64. In Haile (1938), p. 113, both twins go to fight *Déélgééd*.

65. See Mills, p. 190: ". . . older brother is identified with courage and heroism while younger brother, the stay at home, receives and domesticates the new power."

66. The belief "that wild animals are helpers of human beings" is well established in traditional lore. See Reichard (1950), p. 142. Also see

Matthews (1887), pp. 399–401. It is probably rooted in the hunter tradition and in the concept of "prehuman flux." See note 24, p. 369 above. Wild animals are more highly respected than domestic ones. See Haile (1938), for instance, pp. 115–16; Wheelwright, pp. 56–57; and Mills, p. 55.

67. According to Reichard (1950), pp. 161–70, in a discussion of the cardinal points, the vertical passageway in the center represents a fifth direction.

68. Matthews (1902), p. 6, explains the broad distinction between male and female when applied to "two things which are nearly alike or otherwise comparable." It is common, he says, "to speak of or symbolize the one which is the coarser, rougher, stronger, or more violent as the male, and that which is the finer, weaker, or more gentle as the female. Thus: a shower accompanied by thunder and lightning is called . . . he-rain, while a shower without electric display is called . . . she-rain; the turbulent San Juan river is called . . . Male Water, while the more placid Rio Grande is known as . . . Female Water." According to Frank Goldtooth, in Fishler, p. 59, male rain is "the rain that falls in the summer and is the rain that makes noise in the summer time." Female rain is usually "the rain that falls in the fall. Female rain can also be in the summer time and it is after a big rain which is followed by a little rain with no thunder noise. This rain is very soft." Hence, when Changing Woman calls for harmony and solidarity between herself and the Sun, pp. 274–75 below, she is proclaiming the need for what ultimately suggest a total cosmic ecology, given the way individual elements are linked to one sex or the other. See note 15, pp. 352–53 above. Also see note 82, pp. 404–6 below.

69. Here again, *Naayéé' neizghání* converts something evil to something beneficial. See above, pp. 220ff., 166, and 398, n. 59.

70. For an example of the owl's prophetic features as they occur in Navajo ceremonial narrative, see Matthews (1887), p. 389, p. 396. See, too, Reichard (1950), pp. 455–56. See also the role of the owl in pp. 64–67 above.

71. Haile (1938), p. 38, affirms that Bat Woman is seemingly bashful but fundamentally impatient and full of contempt. She appears "to be ashamed because nature forced her to use her parts in scaling walls." See, too, pp. 117–23, especially p. 121, where she is obviously self-conscious and Monster Slayer is just as obviously aware of her strange appearance. Also see Frank Goldtooth's explanation for her peculiar behavior in Fishler, p. 61. I like this episode because a believable human complexity emerges. The passage seems to illustrate how traditional storytelling in a mythic framework can convey a psychological dimension.

72. The purpose of the second visit varies considerably. In Wyman (1970), pp. 423–26, for instance, the second journey is undertaken to acquire horses from the sun, which is obviously a more modern version. Matthews records (n.d.a), p. 40, side 2 how the twins return for an additional visit because their father has instructed them explicitly to give

back the weapons after they have destroyed the monsters. See also, note 51, p. 397 above.

73. In "Notes on Navaho Cosmology," (Matthews n.d.a), p. 41, side 1, *Jóhonaa'éí* tells his two sons, "Take her to the far west and build her a lodge there where I may behold her every night after my labor." Originally Matthews had written down, "*Where I may rest with,*" and then replaced that phrase with "behold." Likewise he crossed out "day" and replaced it with "night." Then, after making that change, he adds: "And as I do not want to look at the faces of her parents [continues *Jóhonaa'éí*] build for them a lodge in the far east beyond where I live. . . ."

Here we have an interesting example of how a storyteller can exercise options about the length of his narrative, just as the scribe who may put that narrative in writing also makes choices. For we see in the abbreviated version of the creation story that Matthews recorded in his unpublished set of notes (n.d.a) a brief summation of much of what is presented at length in *Navaho Legends:* ". . . and the boys did so and ever since that time it has been a custom with the Navajo man to shun the presence of his wife's mother." By inserting an etiological summary, Matthews's informant Jake short-circuits both of the two lengthier alternative series of episodes that I consider to be the most comprehensive. On the one hand, he manages to curtail the story by leaving out the part that follows here, in which the twins return to Changing Woman with hoops that will enable her to summon winds and destroy the remaining monsters, and in which she has her dramatic encounter with *Jóhonaa'éí.* On the other hand, Jake does not recite an episode repeated by Wyman (1970), p. 437, but not included in *Navaho Legends.* There First Man and First Woman oppose Changing Woman's departure to live with the Sun, which is one of the most dramatic episodes in the entire emergence cycle as I know it from a variety of sources. I wish Matthews had included it, and I was tempted to add it. However, I found no evidence that Matthews had ever heard it, and I was afraid that it may have been too modernized.

All of this leads me to wonder all the more about how a scribe makes choices, for at this juncture we see as sharply as we can see anywhere one of the basic differences between oral narrative and narrative presented through the medium of print or through one of the electronic media. For a live storyteller's performance is governed not only by what he knows but by what he may say as he improvises. He can choose to lengthen or shorten his performance on the spot. He may make one choice or one set of choices on one occasion and an entirely different set of choices on another, depending upon a great number of variables that range from the composition of his audience to the way he feels about its response to him to the time of year. In seeking information about various parts of this cycle I have talked with Navajo storytellers who advised me that they did not feel free to tell me certain things because I was an outsider or because it

was not the proper time of year. I have had similar experiences with
Seneca and Pueblo informants. Print, of course, like video and audio tape,
is a much less pliable medium. Once it is composed it gives options only
to the reader, who hears nothing except an imaginary voice which he
reconstructs in his own mind as his eyes follow the linear pattern of
alphabetical symbols on the page in front of him. She or he can simply
read on, avidly or casually as the case may be. Or he or she can skip an
entire passage altogether. But the context of that choice is by no means a
dynamic social one unless we take print to represent the apex of a whole
set of social circumstances gradually applied from infancy on. And what
gives the medium of print even less flexibility as a storytelling medium is
that when it does finally become the means of storing and transmitting a
narrative the performer's options are gradually lost from sight. They may
be subordinated to the biases of the scribe who records the narrative
alphabetically and to the biases of his entire society inasmuch as he
reflects them. Hence, Matthews's readers may fail to see the extent to
which Jóhonaa'éí is motivated by sexual desire in asking to have Asdzą́ą́
nádleehé join him in the west.

74. Reichard (1950), p. 203, describes multicolored or variegated as "the
summary of all colors. Literally, it means 'projecting-in-every direction.' "
Its place is precisely fixed in a complex pattern of color symbolism, which
Reichard outlines in chapter 12, pp. 187–213. See, too, note 3, p. 347
above.

75. Compare the way Changing Woman uses the hoops here with the
way Coyote completes a circle on p. 144 above or earlier on p. 118. It
becomes obvious that the hoops function principally to control the various
winds to bring about a desired result. See, for example, Wyman (1962), pp.
142–55, for an illustration that the Navajo belief system does not establish
good and evil as polar opposites. Rather, they are applications of the same
primary force. That force is simply made positive or negative by the
correct manipulation or the proper control. See, too, Reichard (1944b), p.
16: "A method for exorcising evil is to narrow down the territory within
which evils may work. Especially true is this if evils are indefinite, such as
ghosts, sorcery, strangers or unknown mistakes. Exorcism therefore is
undertaken either from a limited space, the circle of confusion, outward
toward limitless space or from unbounded space to a controlled circle of
protection." In effect, then, the evil represented and/or performed by the
remaining monsters is "funneled" into the hoops and transformed into the
exorcising storms. Space in all four cardinal directions is then "cleansed"
by the transformation, whose locus is the narrow space defined by the
hoops. We now understand, too, why the feather hoops or naayéé' ats'os
were so effective in helping the twins calm the alien forces they
encountered on the way to the home of their father. See note 37, p. 374 above.

76. See Witherspoon (1977), p. 25: "The goal of Navajo life in this world is to live to maturity in the condition described as *hózhǫ́*, and to die of old age. . . ." See also note 8, p. 384 above. See, too, p. 288. Consider that the succession of generations indicated in that passage would not have been possible if *Naayéé' neizghání* had killed *Sǫ́*. Also observe the other "monsters" in this section that he finally elects not to kill. Then notice the acquisition of various skills and crafts identified in Part Four, such as planting, animal husbandry, crafts, etc. These, too, would not have developed if Monster Slayer had killed the creatures he pursues here. Hence the somewhat subtle but very tight unity of the entire story that Matthews finally printed in *Navaho Legends*.

77. Disposing properly of the dead enemy is, in Navajo tradition, given great importance. See Haile (1938), p. 179, for example. And see note 103, p. 255. Also see McAllester, pp. 8–9. Part III of the *Enemy Way* recorded by Father Berard Haile (i.e., pp. 177–218) is to a great extent an account of the "cleaning up" process made necessary by the destruction of the monsters. That process is actually being acknowledged here by *Jóhonaa'éí*. That is a major part of the Enemy Way, one of the most common of the ceremonials still observed by the Navajo people today. The story of the war against the monsters more or less defines the mythical dimensions of contact with aliens or outsiders and defines the Enemy Way ritual practice alluded to by McAllester.

78. Here I have embellished considerably by adding to the dialogue between Changing Woman and the Sun. But the rationale for doing so is provided by Reichard (1950), p. 29, who writes: "The ritualistic teachings stress male and female as a basic form of symbolism; the notion is that only by pairing can any entity be complete." She also says (1928), p. 52, "Socially, the position of the Navajo woman is high. She has a voice in all family affairs and many times her decision on a matter is final since she may have control of the family pursestrings according to the relative wealth of herself and her husband. It should not be inferred however that wealth is the main cause of the woman's high prestige. For she is held in general regard and the feeling of the family for her opinion is something which one finds difficult to describe." See, too, Witherspoon (1975), pp. 23–28. In Navajo society, which is matrilineal and matrilocal, the woman has always had authority and status. It seems to me that such a fact is reflected throughout the creation cycle and could easily be put in sharp relief here.

79. See Reichard (1950), pp. 208–13, for a discussion of the significance of precious stones in Navajo tradition. See also, Wyman (1970), p. 110, n. 91. First Man's medicine bundle contained "the customary four jewels, each carried to represent an ear of corn with an invisible cob, i.e., with the kernels covering the end of the cob. The bundle also contained the

materials for the inner forms. . . ." It looks as though Changing Woman, in demanding these jewels, is demanding creative powers equal to the powers First Man had in creating the contours of the Fifth World. See, too, pp. 34–35.

80. The fact that no domestic animals are named here suggests to me that at least this part of the performance reflected by Matthews is an old version, antedating the arrival of the Spaniards, who introduced domestic livestock.

81. See Witherspoon (1977), p. 196: "In the west there is a tendency to think of the father and mother as making an equal contribution to the procreation of a child. They are treated as equal parents and relatives on both sides are thought of as equal in their relationship to the child. The Navajo view is one in which the male provides the semen or seed necessary for conception but it is the mother who conceives the child in her womb, who nurtures it in her womb prenatally, who through pain and suffering gives it birth and even after birth it is the mother who primarily nurtures and sustains the life and well being of the child." See also p. 85, where that sense of the mother's role is reflected in Navajo syntax.

82. See Witherspoon (1977), p. 82, where he speaks of "the ideas of *k'é*" or "solidarity," i.e., love, kindness, cooperation. See, too, his assertion that solidarity is the essence of kinship systems (1975), pp. 11–14, 37ff. A clear understanding of how *k'é* or solidarity permeates the overall tribal structure through the relationships among families and clans emerges from a thorough reading of the whole book. In saying what she does to *Jóhonaa'éí*, perhaps *Asdzą́ą́ nádleehé* is talking as much about *k'é* as about *hózhǫ́*. "In simple terms," writes Witherspoon, p. 50, "the fact that one being is a male and another a female permits them to marry and experience sexual intercourse—the primary affinal bond." Moreover, he says, p. 24, "In Navajo society, a woman bestows sexual favors on a man in exchange for something of economic value." See, too, Wyman (1970), p. 432, where Changing Woman enjoys a major share of power and leadership through her relationship with the Sun.

The ideals of *k'é* or solidarity are closely associated with kinship in Navajo culture. The solidarity being discussed here is the solidarity of kinship, which is what I take Changing Woman to be demanding. And that kinship will broaden as the story progresses in Part Four, leading to necessary forms of harmony and hence social order. See below, note 1, pp. 407–9; note 6, p. 410; and note 26, pp. 415–16. When she asserts that she is equal to him in status, in having needs, and in deserving to see them fully met, Changing Woman seems to affirm an important point that we find in many aspects of Navajo culture. To begin with, Witherspoon says (1975), p. 116, "the account of the disastrous effects of the separation in Navajo mythology serves as a reminder that marriage is, however, necessary for satisfactory social existence and cannot be totally disregarded either by men or women. . . ." Moving to a more abstract plane of reasoning and delving into theoretical aesthetics, consider Hatcher's observation, pp. 57–58, that "design units" in Navajo drypaintings are almost always of equal size. "This is especially noticeable in the anthromorphic figures. Even where, according to the myth and symbols, one of the deities is more powerful than the others, he is portrayed as the same size in the layout. This fact offers considerable support to the idea that spatial relationships in this form have something to do with an egalitarian orientation." Notice, likewise, that males are not larger than females in drypaintings where the two are standing side by side. The focal point of the egalitarianism Hatcher is speaking of may actually be upon the relationship between men and women in which neither predominates. And that relationship, as it is now being defined by Changing Woman, is a central theme in the Navajo creation story. Until it can be established, five-fingered Earth Surface People cannot exist in the fifth world. Establishing that relationship is what the overall story is all about!

As I see it, then, there is and must be full balance between male and female. In their failure to achieve that balance, First Man and First Woman were responsible for the existence of the monsters, who represented the ultimate threat to ongoing life. Changing Woman now wants that ideal balance established once and for all on a totally cosmic plane wherein sky and earth achieve *k'é*. But that balance is not so much static and immutable as it is precarious and dynamic, always threatened but always reasserting its own equilibrium. Consider, for instance, the dramatic interlude recorded by Matthews with other material to be included in the *Mountain Chant* but later expurgated. It is reprinted in Poor, pp. 121–26. See, too, what Mills says about the harmony evident in drypainting, p. 51: "The dominant quality is not oneness, rest, and peace, but duality, tension, and power that is carefully, perhaps too carefully, expressed." And, of course, this precarious but necessary balance to be achieved between Changing Woman and the Sun is analogous to the harmony or balance that is to be achieved between the Earth Surface People and the gods, between man and animals, and between all of the disparate elements of the cosmos. This point, I think, is a good entree for the reader steeped in Western tradition who would like to explore Navaho aesthetics in particular and Native American aesthetics more generally. Likewise, readers who wish to explore the broad set of relationships between artistic principles and the principles that distinguish one culture from another might also do well to begin here. See the excellent discussion of formal artistic traits in Mills, pp. 131–62, where his statements regarding structure (p. 141), repetition (p. 143), and balance (p. 144) are especially revealing in light of Changing Woman's assertiveness in this passage.

However, the definition of the relationship between male and female is not necessarily cut and dried. Indeed, few matters are in the Navajo world! See Fishler, p. 85, for instance, where we are told that the Sun has many wives, that he only intends to see the mother of the twins once a week, and that she refuses to go with him and must be coerced by one of the gods.

83. For an elaboration of her departure to the west and of her role there, see Wyman (1970), pp. 187ff. In version II she goes because she wants to, not because Sun asks her to, although later it is revealed that the twins had already talked with their father about her doing so. But First Woman resists that decision and she and Changing Woman quarrel. See pp. 437–39, 440–41, where the opposition of First Man and First Woman becomes especially strong. Because she is unreconciled to Changing Woman's departure, and because First Man sides with his partner, they create fever and death; see p. 441.

84. Changing Woman is traditionally associated with animals, especially with the creation of domesticated animals. See Wyman (1970), pp. 244ff.

85. See Hill (1938), p. 167. Although "buffalo did not inhabit the Navajo territory," they are referred to "in the mythology and chant legends. One legend tells of four buffalo who took one of the culture heroes on a trip. As they passed through Lukachukai, one male and one female urinated. This was given as the origin of the two springs at that locality: one male spring from the male buffalo, one female spring from the female buffalo."

The "mythical" element Hill refers to could easily be an accretion of Pueblo origin. I am inclined to think that the Pueblos acquired an awareness of buffalo from an early Athabascan source, quite possibly as early as the time of busy mutual trade and commerce prior to the Spanish incursion as it is described by Forbes, pp. 3–40. On February 10, 1979, I visited the Hopi village of Shungopovi to see a buffalo dance in the company of a man from Santo Domingo Pueblo well steeped in the traditions of the closely related Keres-speaking groups. He informed me that the dance we were watching narrated the story of a Hopi maiden who had been carried off to the eastern plains by a group of buffalo people. The dance, in which the two male dancers wore buffalo hides and bore buffalo heads high on their shoulders, clearly indicated the awe in which buffalo have been held. It is easy to imagine that mention of those creatures would have stirred the imagination of the sedentary Hopi villagers who listened to descriptions of them and purchased their hides from the itinerant Apachean traders who went back and forth each year between the Great Plains and the Colorado Plateau.

86. Reichard (1950), p. 258, cites a passage from Haile (1938), pp. 87–88, which mentions "Changing Woman's nubility rite." Consult Frisbie, which is "the definitive study." See also, Wyman (1970), p.9; Franciscan Fathers, pp. 345, 446; and Reichard (1928), pp. 135–39. In Fishler, p. 40, the

rite is administered to White Shell Woman while she is being nurtured by First Man and First Woman prior to the birth of the twins.

87. Luckert (1976) theorizes that the symbol of the snake permeates Mesoamerican cultures and the cultures which fell directly or indirectly under their influence. See especially pp. 13–63. Also see Mills, p. 163: "When I showed photographs of a ring and a bracelet made in the shape of a snake, the older women at Jeff Luna's place [at Rimrock, Arizona] protested. 'What kind of fellow is he, going around showing those pictures to people?' They told me that some people refuse to say the word snake because there is an enmity between the snake and the Navajos." Also see Hill (1936), p. 15, where the pre-attack ceremony is described: "At dawn, the morning of the attack, the leader put on a pair of moccasins with the big snake painted on the sides, tied his good luck amulet to his cap, and went a short distance from the camp. . . . The warriors prepared themselves for the attack by painting on their bodies snakes, bear traces, or human hands. . . . the snakes were believed to give the man power and make him feared as the snake was feared. . . ."

88. Matthews identifies this place (1902), p. 20, simply as "the junction of two rivers somewhere in the San Juan Valley." The name, according to William Morgan of Fort Defiance, means "where the waters join." According to version I in Wyman (1970), p. 220, they stayed at this place only for a short time. Then they went to their mother's home in the west to live with her and to guard the medicine bundle of First Man which had been used to give her life. Also see version II, p. 468 and note 357, for a possible explanation for the visions referred to.

Part Four

1. Here, perhaps, what is commonly called Navajo mythology intersects with history as we in the western world tend to perceive it. The matter of how history is served by oral traditions among preliterate peoples remains controversial. For one contribution to that controversy pertinent to the cultures of the Colorado Plateau and the upper Rio Grande watershed, see Eggan. The bibliography on pp. 52–53 should serve as a good introduction to what Eggan, p. 34, calls "the question of the extent to which the memory of actual events is retained in oral tradition. . . ." Matthews (1890) offers some suggestions about how

historical data might be harvested from oral traditions. On p. 107 he
comes very close to suggesting a methodology for establishing historical
accuracy closely linked with glottochronology. To get a feel for the issue
from a Native American point of view, consult a series of articles
appearing in *The Indian Historian,* including Sobosan, Roesler, Cook, and
Ortiz. I am not prepared myself to comment on the matter of how Native
American history should be reconstructed beyond insisting that it deserves
attention. But I would assert that Part Four of the Navajo creation story as
Matthews prints it or as it is printed here should be prefaced with the
statement about the uncertain history of the Navajo people in preliterate
times. Presently there can be no agreement about when they arrived in the
Southwest some time prior to 1541." Aberle uses "a securely dated,
than this remark by Aberle (1963), pp. 1–7: "The Navajos arrived in the
Southwest some time prior to 1541," Aberle uses "a securely dated,
definitely Navaho archeological site" to back his date. He confidently
assumes that "the ancestral Apacheans were not agricultural when they
left southern Canada," and "that the ancestors of the Navajo took on
agriculture from the Pueblo Indians" soon after the Spanish Conquest. Not
long thereafter they acquired horses, and by the early 18th century they
had sheep. See, also, Forbes; see Young.

It strikes me that Matthews's version as it appears in *Navaho Legends* is
amassed from early oral narratives that reflect very little European
influence and relatively little awareness that Old World cultures existed.
Given the fact that with the exception of the Gambler interlude in Part
Two there is scarcely any mention of horses and sheep, my guess is that
this is, all told, an old cycle. Since it was narrated to Matthews in the late
nineteenth century when the Navajos had scarcely been pacified and when
few if any of them were likely to have been literate, it is a conservative
version. Whatever oral narrative can or cannot tell us about the past as
literate historians like to reckon it, this account might ultimately be seen
to suggest the way history and prehistory intersect. It speaks primarily
about the formation of clans in Navajo culture, which probably took place
in the early dawn of history as we understand it in our print-oriented way.
And it is likely to reflect the strong Pueblo influence upon those Apachean
groups that finally become identified as Navajos.

All told, Part Four functions as the culmination of the whole story
because it defines the advent of a distinct Navajo identity. It describes the
transition from a condition of prehuman flux to that of five-fingered
Earth Surface People. The surface world has ultimately been made
habitable by the destruction of the monsters. In traditional terms it can be
considered a hardened world, with its shapes and contours well-defined. A
corollary to the deeds of the various culture heroes, and particularly to the
exploits of *Naayéé' neizghání,* is the manifest readiness of one band of
people to assimilate another, to organize in clan groups, to set appropriate

limits on which clans may intermarry, and to institutionalize agricultural and domestic procedures. That readiness is all the more pronounced now that Changing Woman has asserted her equality and the need for solidarity between men and women. More subtly, Part Four introduces an issue which has a parallel in Christian culture. For it should be noted that this fifth world in which a society coalesces would not have been the locus of such a coalition without the "original sin" of the male-female discord described in Part One. Hence, we have what might be considered a Native American version of the familiar concept of *felix culpa* in which the original transgression of Adam and Eve is ultimately responsible for the advent of Christ. See Lovejoy.

2. See Reichard (1950), p. 535, for a discussion of this sort of ceremonial circle.

3. Perhaps this passage provides a clue as to the age of the narrative. See Reichard (1950), p. 243: "A large and unexplainable number is the reference to 102 years as the age of man—probably the ideal of a long life span. Matthews was also told that 'seven times old age has killed,' meaning that seven full generations of Navajo had existed up to the time he collected the legends." See Matthews (1890), p. 90. Also see Van Valkenburgh (1938), p. 3. And see Witherspoon (1977), p. 139, along with Wyman (1970), p. 139.

4. See Matthews (1890), p. 104: "There is little doubt that in the majority of cases the names of Navajo gentes, which are not the names of the tribes, are simply designation of localities." He discusses names in general on pp. 102–5. For a broad survey of how clans and clan groups are detailed in Navajo mythology, see Spencer (1947), pp. 60–70. See, too, Franciscan Fathers, pp. 424–36. The clan and kinship systems of the Navajo are, as one might guess, quite complex. Reichard (1928), pp. 11–35, deals comprehensively with the Navajo clan and kinship system. A more recent introduction to Navajo kinship is Witherspoon (1975). Another set of narratives relating the origins of the various clans can be found in Sapir and Hoijer, pp. 80–97. Also see Yazzie, pp. 74–82. As for the names of the various clans and the number of them, there can probably be no definitive statement. Matthews himself sensed the degree to which accounts could vary. In his introduction to *Navaho Legends*, p. 29, he writes: "Lists of the Navajo gentes have been obtained from various sources. . . . But no two lists are quite alike; they differ with regard to small or extinct gentes, and one list may supply a name which another has omitted."

5. See Reichard (1950), pp. 246–47: "I think odd numbers are appropriate here because the people were setting out into uncertain and foreign territory. On the other hand, when Changing Woman's own power, which is firmly, definitely divine, is referred to, the numbers are two and four." Thus odd numbers are related to uncertainty, disorder, the unforeseen, etc. Even numbers are usually associated with the opposite.

6. Contrast this passage with what happens in Part One, above, where no such solidarity is established between the emerging Air-Spirit People and the occupants of the second and third worlds. Here, however, a series of events begins wherein groups or clans are added to the growing Navajo tribe. Notice the bonding that takes place among the groups—bonding that is expressed by such statements as White Shell Woman's declaration that these newcomers are her children (i.e., *shi:* my + *álchini:* children); as the assurance to the newcomers that they are welcome to share game and goods; as statements in subsequent passages that marriage will link certain clans with certain other clans in a network of relationships; as expressions that members of the disparate clans can wage war together against a common enemy. See Reichard (1928), p. 30: "The main function [of Navajo clans] is to regulate marriage and in doing so indirectly to affiliate clans." Also see pp. 60–69, where the link between marriage and clan relationships is explained in greater detail. That discussion helps explain why the coalition of the various clans is a logical extension of the narrative and hence an organic part of the story. Also see Witherspoon (1975), p. 64, for a statement about the differences and similarities of kinship and nonkinship "forms of solidarity."

7. This passage provides an example of the familiar motif of the departing tutelary *cum* god. See Wyman (1970), p. 50: "The Holy People announced that after their departure from that ceremonial they would never be seen in person again and warned the people that dire consequences would follow if anyone should claim that he had seen a holy one. They said, however, that their presences would be made manifest in the sound of the wind, the feather of an eagle, in various small birds, or in the growth of corn." What Wyman says about the Holy People in general, we can say about White Shell Woman here. And what applies to her could certainly apply to all of the Holy People in the Navajo creation story, including Monster Slayer, Born-for-Water, and so on. In fact, the manifest presence of the gods is an essential part of the belief invested in the whole Navajo ceremonial system. Under certain conditions of well-defined need, they can be coaxed to approach. But their presence—or the claim that they have been seen—is not an issue to be taken lightly. In a conversation with me a young Navajo artist with whom I discussed the prospects of getting illustrations for this volume insisted that anyone who agreed to paint or draw pictures would have to be careful: he or she could not make likenesses of the gods.

Throughout the pages of the ceremonial literature there are numerous accounts of the departure of gods similar to the one we find here. In the *Night Chant* (Matthews 1902), p. 212, for instance, where *Sho,* the visionary hero who has returned to his people long enough to teach them agricultural methods, bids goodbye: " 'Younger brother, I shall now leave you forever; you will never see me again; but when the summer comes you will watch for the storms and when you see the he-rain you will say, "There is my brother," for I shall be in the storm you behold.' As he spoke he disappeared and has never since been seen except in the thunder showers in the summer." See, too, Luckert (1979), p. 197, where a leader tells his followers before departing to live with the Holy People, "I am doing this for you and the people to come. In the future I will be with you always and will appear in different forms." It is interesting, too, that he has had dreams very much as the favorite child here has (p. 196). Dreaming appears to be a not uncommon way for certain individuals in the Navajo narratives to maintain contact with the gods. See Wyman (1970), pp. 426–432.

8. It is tempting to try to date the narrative—or at least this portion of it—on the basis of a passage such as this one. According to Hill (1940), depositions were sent by Don Joachin Codallos y Rabal, governor of New Mexico, to the viceroy and governor of New Spain. Dispatched in 1744, these statements dealt with a series of forays into Navajo territory from 1706 to 1743. They may be the first documents composed by Europeans describing the Athabascan people who were by then already being called the Navajo. They indicate, as Hill puts it in his summary, that by the early part of the eighteenth century the Navajos were active farmers growing maize, beans, pumpkins and watermelons (p. 396), which suggests that this portion of the creation story might very well overlap with history as it is documented by Anglo-Europeans. The conventional belief is that the great influx of Pueblo ideas and practices into Navajo life took place during and after the revolt against the Spanish in the decade of 1680. At that time, occupants of the various pueblos frequently took refuge with the more isolated Navajos to escape the effects of Spanish rule. The Navajos possessed horses and sheep and were making blankets by the time the Spaniards began exploring their territory. But these items are not mentioned here, which leads me to be somewhat wary of the conclusion that what is being recited here reflects events which took place as recently as the 1700s. Thus I suggest that this part of the story predates the Spanish incursion. Perhaps, too, the Pueblos were influencing the Navajos before they sought refuge among them against the Spanish invaders. Readers of Cabeza DeVaca's account of his long journey across the southern tier of North America (Covey 1961) will easily notice that intertribal commerce was common. Contact between Pueblos and Navajos is very likely to have occurred before any Spaniards arrived in the Southwest.

9. The agriculture that these people introduced is likely to have resembled that described by Hill (1938). In that report we see how closely the daily life of Navajo farmers was tied to ceremonial and religious life. The impression I get from reading works like Forbes, Young, and the various reports of Hill and from conversations I have had with other scholars and with informants, is that this contact between the Puebloan

Tábąąhá and the Athabascan Navajos probably occurred during the Spanish counteroffensive that followed the revolt of 1680 (See Forbes, pp. 225–50). At that time many of the tribes of what is now Arizona, New Mexico, West Texas, and some of the border areas of present-day Mexico more or less united to drive the Spanish out of their Rio Grande enclaves upstream of El Paso and out of the high desert regions to the west. Once the Spanish returned, it is generally believed, many of the Rio Grande Pueblo peoples sought refuge among the Navajos who populated the remote mountainous and desert country northwest of Santa Fe. But perhaps we should look for evidence that this contact occurred earlier, since this version of the Navajo creation story indicates no Spanish influence having as yet altered the life of the newly arrived *Tábąąhá*. There is no hint of conquest by outsiders in what Matthews records in this portion of the narrative, no mention of sheep or horses, no reference to silver, and not so much as an oblique allusion to Christianity. No hint is given of any oppression having taken place at the hands of foreign intruders who were obviously hated. Such omissions indicate at least a possibility that the story Matthews harvested in the 1880s may be older than we can tell, just as pueblo-Navajo contact may reach farther back than is known for certain.

10. See Reichard (1950), pp. 105–6: "Some evils, fortunately few, the residue of unbelievable cruelty, refused to submit to any kind of control." *Godtsoh*'s behavior represents such evil. Brief incidents like this, explains Reichard, "explain in microcosm the attack on evil with the purpose of forcing it to yield to good." It may function here to demonstrate how members of other clans became united in their unwillingness fully to sanction the behavior of the chief. Once again, the incident is not without its humorous dimension in spite of its grim implications. There is a parallel account in Haile (1938), pp. 78–81. The difference between the two versions suggests that an individual storyteller or informant could take liberty with his material and even that he could put his own imagination to work in his own idiosyncratic way. We must bear in mind, too, the likelihood that Matthews's informants were dealing with an unprecedented situation: probably no white man had ever asked them to recite before. They may have had no fixed atitudes about having narratives put into print, in contrast with Navajos today, some of whom object to such a practice. In 1971, for instance, one Navajo leader expressed to me a belief which he said was shared by many. "When all of our stories are written down," he told me, "the world will come to an end." What Matthews was told might have been recited less hesitantly and with less of an inclination to hold back than may occur today. The entire matter of delivery could have been different. What remains constant among the two versions, though, is the emphasis on adultery and its consequences. Also, there is a suggestion in both that for whatever justification the chief

thought he had in punishing the women so seriously, it was generally believed that he reacted too harshly. On p. 138, Reichard summarizes the Navajo attitude toward adultery. While it is mentioned casually and with little reticence, it is not condoned. It reflects just as negatively upon a man when his wife has an affair with someone else as it does on her.

11. See Matthews (1887), p. 386, where the brush circle is described and discussed. The fire in the center of the ring is mentioned on p. 429. The circle is discussed again on pp. 431, 432. The cycle of the corral dances is described on p. 432. A detailed sketch appears on p. 444. The dance cycle includes all kinds of spectacular things, from playacting to burlesque to teasing spectators. The suppressed part of the report is reprinted in Poor, appendix 7, pp. 121–26.

This episode evokes the question of how narrative and ritual are related. Kluckhohn (1942) explores the issue thoroughly. While subsequent research has engendered some points of disagreement, the best detailed introduction to the Navajo chants and to ceremonial practice remains a pair of reports coauthored by Wymen and Kluckhohn (1938, 1940). There is a brief summary of chants and the procedure associated with them in the introductory material in Wyman (1957). A good popularized account of ceremonial practice appears in Sandner, pp. 41–92. Ceremonial literature has become quite extensive. I recommend the bibliography in Sandner as a good starting place for anyone who wants to survey it.

12. Reichard (1928), p. 19, discusses the assimilation of non-Navajo groups into the tribal unit.

13. Starvation is a grim reality whose affliction is frequently and effectively recorded in narrative traditions among Native American tribes. See, for example, Tedlock (1978), pp. 33–64.

14. See Wyman (1970), p. 452, especially note 339, where mention is made of a "tendency of the clans to increase their numbers by capture." See, too, Spencer (1947), p. 84, for a summary of some of the warrior customs and traditions of the Navajos. The image of the hostile Indian, of course, has become so thoroughly integrated into the American frontier tradition that it is now impossible to view the matter objectively. The Navajos and Apaches alike have acquired a reputation for being especially fierce and warlike. Van Valkenburgh (1938), p. 5, for instance, although generally sympathetic in his treatment, provides an example of how some historians emphasize the warfare of the early Navajos in pre- and post-conquest times. Anyone who wishes to try to acquire a balanced sense of just how aggressive or nonaggressive the Navajos—or any other Athabascan people—were, would do well to begin by reading Forbes. His evidence suggests that the Athabascans of the Southwest, rather than being warlike, were more inclined to trade and carry on fairly heavy commerce with the sedentary Pueblos, who relied on them for hides to be used for blankets and clothing. The Apaches and Navajos seem to have

cultivated their aggressive ways only as a reaction to Spanish oppression and atrocities. And, judging from the evidence that Forbes musters, both groups were slower than the Pueblos to resist the Spaniards and much more restrained in their collective decision to carry on a policy of reprisal. The Navajos in particular appear to have maintained an implicit preference to be left alone, a preference that remains manifest to this day. Once a policy of reprisal became a reality, however, it persisted and gradually turned into a deep hatred for white man. In general, the Indians showed far more restraint against hostility and the use of warfare than the Spaniards. See, for instance, Covey, pp. 122–33. See also, Hill (1936).

15. See Spencer (1947), p. 79, for a statement about this obsolete ceremony, which was "primarily a political gathering" that "took place every two or four years" and "continued all winter until it was time to begin corn planting." See also, Reichard (1928), pp. 108–10; Van Valkenburgh (1936), pp. 17–22; Haile (1938), pp. 26, 48; and Hill (1936), p. 18.

16. For a description of Changing Woman's home in the west along the shore of the Pacific Ocean, see Wyman (1970), p. 219. See also pp. 445–47. In Wheelwright, p. 108, Klah identifies the home of Changing Woman as "Santa Cruz, off the coast of Santa Barbara, California." I know of no other attempt to give it an exact location. For varying accounts of the migration to the east, see Wyman (1970), pp. 327–33. See, too, Franciscan Fathers, p. 428. And see Goddard, pp. 165–79.

17. This pattern of her dancing may be analogous to the cycle of her aging and becoming young again. See Wyman (1970), p. 469.

18. See Reichard (1950), pp. 163–64: ". . . the turn is not completed; to finish it would bring the patient to a starting point within a circle smaller than the original one—he would be winding himself in." See, too, pp. 118, 144 above, and note 37, p. 374.

19. There is a possible parallel in Wyman (1970), pp. 219–40. See especially pp. 239–40. See also pp. 447–51. She creates four groups and sends them to the east, but no mention is made of kinsmen.

20. See Witherspoon (1975), p. 33: "In contrast [with the distance between the sun and his children in his relationship with them], the closeness of a mother to her children is conceptualized by Changing Woman's closeness to her children in mythology and in the closeness of her objective symbol, the earth, to her children." We see further evidence of the way this closeness is conceptualized in this set of passages where literally these six original clans are made of her flesh. We also see this closeness in the name given to the Bit'anii for instance, which is generally taken to mean Within His Cover Clan, but can also be translated as Close To Her Body, according to Dr. William Morgan of Fort Defiance, Arizona, in a personal communication with me (4/5/79).

21. In Wyman (1970), pp. 447–50, Asdzą́ą́ nádleehé gives each group a set of gifts: the canes, plus a bear cub, a mountain lion (puma), a turkey,

and a porcupine. Also see Matthews (1890), p. 106: "... when they set out
their journey each clan was provided with a different pet, a bear, a puma, a
deer, a snake, and a porcupine. The Navajo word [łįį], which in this
connection I translate as 'pet', means a domestic animal of any kind, of
late years, especially a horse; it also means an animal fetich [sic] or
personal animal totem. In the myth of the Mountain Chant, a Navajo
youth is made to address his deer mask as '[shiłįį], my pet [p. 396, p. 466]. I
might, then, have given the translation of this word as totem. . . . These
passages, and others in the legend, allude in all likelihood, to the former
use of totemic clan-symbols, probably to the existence of totemic
clan-names, and possibly to a custom, not now practiced by the Navajos,
of keeping in captivity live totemic animals." On such a basis, Matthews
suggests that there is a link between the Navajo and the Indians "of
the Siletz Agency in Oregon." Reichard (1928), p. 33, takes issue
with Matthews on this point, however. She suggests that the references
to the snake, the porcupine, the bear, and so on reflect local accretions:
"May it not be then, that these insignificant details about pets
and the few localized animal-named clans in the myth are an atempt to
include in their legend all of the phenomena with which they have come
in contact."

22. It is worth observing that the Navajo creation story ends as it begins,
with a migration. But whereas the opening migration has been an
emergence from the center of the world in flight, the closing migration is a
more positive movement leading *toward* a union with distant kinsmen.
There is a great deal to be said about the Navajo "passion for geography"
and "preoccupation with locality," as Wyman (1962), p. 78, puts it. In the
speech of the Navajos, he writes, "movement is described in great details."
The Navajo "lives conceptually and linguistically in a universe in
motion." See, also, Jett; Van Valkenburgh and Walker; and Hoijer.

23. For a summary of variations, see Spencer (1947), pp. 83–84. In
Wyman (1970), p. 455, the puma helps the bear. The people accuse Bear of
being lazy before the fight, so that after it is over he tells them that he will
never assist them again. Then he goes away.

24. Obviously the name does not mean "Navajo Mountain." According
to Van Valkenburgh (1974), pp. 14, 114, the name literally refers to "the head
of the traditional female and pollen range of the Navajo Blessingway rite."

25. According to one version in Wyman (1970), p. 457, it took them
twelve years to migrate inland to their destination.

26. I postulate that this innocuously charming passage is more
important than it might at first seem to be. For it is actually a culminating
segment in a cycle of events relating how a migrant band is welcomed into
the larger group. What we actually have in Part Four—in sharp contrast
with Part One where groups are unable to establish social bonds—is the
broad acquisition of k'é or solidarity. See note 82, pp. 404–6 above. See also,

note 1, pp. 407–9. Worth repeating is a statement in Franciscan Fathers, p. 425, because it emphasizes the egalitarian solidarity that is established in Part Four, where the various clans assemble to form a cohesive tribe. And it summarizes the contrast between that cohesiveness and the lack thereof in Part One: "The numerical increase of the clans is not due to the process of segmentation of existing clans, but to one of adoption of new peoples which were met in the course of the journey to the present habitat of the tribe. Accordingly, the phratry is eliminated, in fact, it is unknown to the Navajo, who makes no such distinction. Each clan, therefore, forms a separate whole, which is socially the equal of others with whom it is perchance affiliated by consanguinity or adoption." I take the solidly egalitarian relationship among the clans to be an extension of the egalitarian relationship which Changing Woman demands in her confrontation with Sun, pp. 272–75 above. It is that sort of equality that neither First Man or First Woman could envision between them early in the story. Overall the narrative moves steadily toward a fully apprehended awareness of such equality.

BIBLIOGRAPHY

Aberle, David
1942 "Mythology of the Navaho Game of Stick Dice." *Journal of American Folklore*, Vol. 55: 144–54.

1963 "Some Sources of Flexibility in Navaho Social Organization." *Southwestern Journal of Anthropology*, Vol. 19: 1–8.

1967 "The Navajo Singer's Fee: Payment or Prestation?" *Studies in Southwestern Ethnolinguistics: Meaning and History in the Language of the American Southwest*, ed. Dell H. Hymes and William Elmer Bittle. The Hague: Mouton and Co., 15–32.

Allen, Paula Gunn
1976 "The Sacred Hoop: A Contemporary Indian Perspective on American Literature. *Cross Currents*, Vol. 26: 144–63.

American Anthropologist
1905 "In Memoriam: Washington Matthews." Vol. 7: 514–23.

Andrews, H. A., et al.
1943 "Bibliography of Franz Boas." *American Anthropologist*, Vol. 45: 67–109.

Astrov, Margot
1962 *American Indian Prose and Poetry.* New York: Capricorn Books.

Auerbach, Erich
1953 *Mimesis: The Representation of Reality in Western Literature.* Princeton: Princeton University Press.

Austin, Martha A.
1974 *Saad Ahąąh Sinil: Dual Language.* Phoenix, Ariz.: Navajo Curriculum Press.

Austin, Mary
1930   *The American Rhythm: Studies and Reexpressions of Amerindian Songs.* Boston: Houghton Mifflin Company.

1931   "Aboriginal American Literature." *American Writers on American Literature,* ed. John Macy. New York: Horace Liveright.

Aveni, Anthony F.
1978   "Old and New World Naked-Eye Astronomy." *Technology Review,* Vol. 81, No. 2: 60–72.

Barnes, Nellie
1922   *American Indian Verse, Characteristics of Style.* Lawrence: Bulletin of the University of Kansas, Vol. 22, No. 18.

Bascomb, William R.
1953   "Folklore and Anthropology." *Journal of American Folklore,* Vol. 66: 283–90.

1954   "Four Functions of Folklore." *Journal of American Folklore,* Vol. 67: 333–49.

Boas, Franz
1925   "Stylistic Aspects of Primitive Poetry." *Journal of American Folklore,* Vol. 35: 329–34.

Bolton, Herbert E.
1949   *Coronado: Knight of Pueblos and Plains.* Albuquerque: University of New Mexico Press.

Booth, Mark W.
1981   *The Experience of Songs.* New Haven: Yale University Press.

Booth, Wayne C.
1961   *The Rhetoric of Fiction.* Chicago: University of Chicago Press.

Brinton, Daniel
1881–   *Library of American Aboriginal Literature.* 5 Vols. Washington,
1933   D.C.: Bureau of American Ethnology.

Brugge, David M.
1965   *Long Ago in Navajoland.* Window Rock, Arizona: Navajo Tribal Museum, Navajoland Publications, Series 6.

Brunvand, Jan Harold
1965   *The Study of American Folklore: An Introduction.* New York: W. W. Norton.

Bureau of American Ethnology
1962 *List of Publications of the Bureau of American Ethnology with Index to Authors and Titles, Revised to 1961.* Washington, D.C.: U.S. Government Printing Office.

Burn, Andrew Robert
1937 *The World of Hesiod: A Study of the Greek Middle Ages.* New York: Dutton.

Campbell, Joseph
1949 *The Hero with a Thousand Faces.* Princeton: Princeton University Press.

Canfield, William W.
1902 *The Legends of the Iroquois.* New York: Ira J. Friedman.

Cook, Liz
1977 "American Indian Literatures in Servitude." *The Indian Historian,* Vol. 10, no. 1: 3–6

Covey, Cyclone, trans.
1961 *Cabeza DeVaca's Adventures in the Unknown Interior of America.* New York: Collier Books; reprint, Albuquerque: University of New Mexico Press, 1983.

Cronyn, George W.
1934 *American Indian Poetry: An Anthology of Songs and Chants.* New York: Horace Liveright.

Day, A. Grove
1951 *The Sky Clears: Poetry of the American Indians.* New York: Macmillan; reprint, Lincoln: University of Nebraska Press, 1964.

Densmore, Frances
1926 *The American Indians and Their Music.* New York: Women's Press.

Dorris, Michael
1979 "Native American Literature in an Ethnohistorical Context." *College English,* Vol. 41: 147–62.

Dorson, Richard M.
1972 *Folklore: Selected Essays.* Bloomington: Indiana University Press.

Dundes, Alan
1965 *The Study of Folklore.* Englewood Cliffs, N.J.: Prentice-Hall.

Durán, Fray Diego
1971 *Book of the Gods and Rites and the Ancient Calendar.* Norman: University of Oklahoma Press.

Dyk, Walter
1938   *Son of Old Man Hat: A Navajo Autobiography.* New York:
       Harcourt, Brace and Co.

Eggan, Frederick R.
1967   "From History to Myth: A Hopi Example." *Studies in
       Southwestern Ethnolinguistics: Meaning and History in the
       Language of the American Southwest,* ed. Dell H. Hymes and
       William Elmer Bittle. The Hague: Mouton and Co.

Eisenstein, Elizabeth L.
1979   *The Printing Press as an Agent of Change.* Cambridge: Cambridge
       University Press.

Fishler, Stanley A.
1953   *In the Beginning: A Navajo Creation Myth.* Salt Lake City:
       University of Utah Press. University of Utah Anthropological
       Papers, no. 13.

Fletcher, Alice
1900   *Indian Story and Song from North America.* Boston; reprint, New
       York: Johnson Reprint Corp., 1970.

Forbes, Jack D.
1960   *Apache, Navaho, and Spaniard.* Norman: University of Oklahoma
       Press.

Franciscan Fathers
1910   *An Ethnologic Dictionary of the Navaho Language.* St. Michaels,
       Ariz.: St. Michael's Press.

Freudenthal, Elsbeth F.
1951   Catalogue of the Washington Matthews Collection at the Museum
       of Navajo Ceremonial Art (Wheelwright Museum), Santa Fe:
       unpublished.

Frisbie, Charlotte Johnson
1967   *Kinaaldá: A Study of the Navaho Girl's Puberty Ceremony.*
       Middletown, Conn.: Wesleyan University Press.

Georges, Robert A.
1969   "Toward An Understanding of Storytelling Events." *Journal of
       American Folklore,* Vol. 82: 314–28.

Ginzburg, Carlo
1980   *The Cheese and the Worms: The Cosmos of a Sixteenth-Century
       Miller.* Baltimore: Johns Hopkins University Press.

Goddard, Pliny Earle
1933. *Navajo Texts.* New York: American Museum of Natural History. Anthropological Papers, Vol. 34.

Goosen, Irvy
1971   *Navajo Made Easier.* Flagstaff, Ariz.: Northland Press.

Greenway, John
1958   *Literature among the Primitives.* Hatboro, Penna.: Folklore Associates.

Grinnell, George Bird
1962   *By Cheyenne Campfires.* New Haven: Yale University Press.

Gummere, Francis E.
1901   *The Beginnings of Poetry.* New York: Macmillan Co.

Haile, Berard
1908   Creation and Emergence Myth. Manuscript Collection, Museum of Northern Arizona, Ms: 171–2–1, 171–2–2. Published as 1981b.

1932a Changing Bear Maiden. Manuscript Collection, Museum of Northern Arizona, Ms: 63–7, 63–8.

1932b Where the People Moved Opposite Each Other. Manuscript Collection, Museum of Northern Arizona, Ms: 63–5. Published as 1981a.

1938   *Origin Legend of the Navaho Enemy Way.* New Haven: Yale University Press. No. 17. Yale University Publications in Anthropology.

1942   "Navaho Upward-Reaching Way and Emergence Place." *American Anthropologist,* Vol. 44: 407–20.

1943a *Origin Legend of the Navaho Flintway.* Chicago: University of Chicago Press.

1943b "Soul Concepts of the Navaho." *Annali Lateranensi,* Vol. 7: 59–96 (Citta del Vaticano, Tipografia Poliglotta Vaticana).

1947   *Starlore Among the Navaho.* Santa Fe: Museum of Navajo Ceremonial Art.

1978   *Love Magic and Butterfly People: The Slim Curly Version of the Ajiłee and Mothway Myths. American Tribal Religions, Vol. 2 Flagstaff: Museum of Northern Arizona Press.*

1979   *Waterway: A Navajo Ceremonial Myth Told by Black Mustache Circle.* American Tribal Religions, Vol. 5. Flagstaff: Museum of Northern Arizona Press.

1981a *Women Versus Men: A Conflict of Navajo Emergence.* American Tribal Religions, Vol. 6. Lincoln: University of Nebraska Press.

1981b *Upward Moving and Emergence Way: The Gishin Biye' Version.* American Tribal Religions, Vol. 7. Lincoln: University of Nebraska Press.

Hall, Edward Twitchell, Jr.
1944 "Recent Clues to Athapascan Prehistory in the Southwest." *American Anthropologist,* Vol. 46: 98–105.

Hatcher, Evelyn Payne
1974 *Visual Metaphors: A Formal Analysis of Navajo Art.* American Ethnological Society, Monograph 58. St. Paul: West Publishing Co.

Havelock, Eric A.
1963 *Preface to Plato.* Cambridge, Mass.: Harvard University Press.

Hester, J. J.
1962 *Navajo Migrations and Acculturation.* University of New Mexico Papers in Anthropology, No. 6. (Albuquerque).

Hill, W. W.
1935 "The Status of the Hermaphrodite and Transvestite in Navaho Culture." *American Anthropologist,* Vol. 37: 273–79.

1936 *Navaho Warfare.* Yale University Publications in Anthropology, No. 5. New Haven: Yale University Press.

1937 *Navaho Pottery Manufacture.* Anthropology Series, University of New Mexico Bulletin, Vol. 2, No. 3. Albuquerque: University of New Mexico Press.

1938 *The Agricultural and Hunting Methods of the Navaho Indians.* Yale University Publications in Anthropology, No. 18. New Haven: Yale University Press.

1940 "Some Navaho Culture Changes During Two Centuries." *Smithsonian Miscellaneous Collections,* 100: 395–415. Washington, D.C.

1943 *Navaho Humor.* General Studies in Anthropology, No. 9. Menasha, Wisc.: George Banta Publishing Co.

Hill, W. W., and Dorothy W. Hill
1945 "Navaho Coyote Tales and Their Position in the Southern Athabascan Group." *Journal of American Folklore,* Vol. 58: 317–37.

Hoijer, Harry
1951 "Cultural Implications of Some Navajo Linguistic Categories." *Language,* Vol. 27: 111–20.

Hymes, Dell

1965 "Some North Pacific Coast Poems: A Problem in Anthropological Philology." *American Anthropologist*, Vol. 67: 316–41.

1975a "Folklore's Nature and the Sun's Myth." *Journal of American Folklore*, Vol. 88: 345–69.

1975b "Breakthrough into Performance." *Folklore, Performance and Communication*, ed. Dan Ben-Amos and Kenneth S. Goldstein. The Hague: Mouton.

1981 *In Vain I Tried to Tell You: Essays in Native American Ethnopoetics*. Philadelphia: University of Pennsylvania Press.

Jett, Stephen C.

1970 "An Analysis of Navajo Place-Names." *Names*, Vol. 18: 175–84.

Journal of American Folklore

1905 "In Memoriam: Washington Matthews." Vol. 18: 245–47.

King, Jeff, Maud Oakes, and Joseph Campbell

1943 *Where the Two Came to Their Father: A Navaho War Ceremonial*. Bollingen Series I. New York: Pantheon Books.

Kirk, Jeffery S., and J. E. Raven

1957 *The Presocratic Philosophers: A Critical History with a Selection of Texts*. Cambridge: Cambridge University Press

Kluckhohn, Clyde

1941 "Patterning as Exemplified in Navaho Culture." *Language, Culture and Personality: Essays in Memory of Edward Sapir*, ed. Leslie Spier, A. Irving Hallowell, and Stanley S. Newman, Menasha, Wisc.: American Anthropological Association.

1942 "Myths and Rituals: A General Theory." *Harvard Theological Review*, Vol. 35: 45–79.

Kluckhohn, Clyde, and Dorothea Leighton

1962 *The Navaho*. Garden City, N.Y.: Doubleday & Co., Natural History Library.

Landar, Herbert

1966 *Language and Culture*. New York: Oxford University Press.

León-Portilla, Miguel

1963 *Aztec Thought and Culture: A Study of the Ancient Nahuatl Mind*. Norman: University of Oklahoma Press.

Letherman, Jonathan

1856 "A Sketch of the Navajo Tribe of Indians, Territory of New Mexico." *The First Smithsonian Report*: 283–97. Washington, D.C.

Levy, Jerrold E.
1964   "Fate of Navajo Twins." *American Anthropolgist*, Vol. 66: 883–87.

Link, Margaret Schevill
1956   *The Pollen Path: A Collection of Navajo Myths*. Stanford: Stanford University Press.

1960   "From the Desk of Washington Matthews." *Journal of American Folklore*, Vol. 73: 317–25.

Lord, Albert B.
1960   *The Singer of Tales*. Cambridge, Mass.: Harvard University Press.

Lovejoy, A. O.
1948   "Milton and the Paradox of the Fortunate Fall." *Essays in the History of Ideas*. Baltimore: John Hopkins Unversity Press.

Luckert, Karl W.
1975   *The Navajo Hunter Tradition*. Tucson: University of Arizona Press.

1976   *Olmec Religion: A Key to Middle America and Beyond*. Norman: University of Oklahoma Press.

1977   *Navajo Mountain and Rainbow Bridge Religion*. Flagstaff: Museum of Northern Arizona Press.

1979   *Coyoteway: A Navajo Holyway Healing Ceremonial*. Flagstaff: Museum of Northern Arizona Press.

McAllester, David P.
1954   *Enemy Way Music: A Study of Social and Aesthetic Values as Seen in Navajo Music*. Papers of the Peabody Museum of Archaeology and Ethnology, Vol. 41, No. 3. Cambridge, Mass.: Harvard University.

McGreevy, Susan
1981   "Navajo Sandpainting Textiles at the Wheelwright Museum." *American Indian Art*, Vol. 7, No. 1: 55–61.

McNeley, James Kale
1981   *Holy Wind in Navajo Philosophy*. Tucson: University of Arizona Press.

Malotki, Ekkehart
1978   *Hopitutuwutsi/Hopi Tales: A Bilingual Collection of Hopi Indian Stories*. Flagstaff: Museum of Northern Arizona Press.

Marken, Jack W.
1978   *The American Indian: Language and Literature*. Goldentree Bibliographies in Language and Literature. Arlington Heights, Ill.: AHM Publishing Corp.

Matthews, Washington

1883   "A Part of the Navajo Mythology." *American Antiquarian,* Vol. 5: 207–24.

1884   An untitled report to John Wesley Powell. Box I, Folder 8, Item #190. Matthews Papers, Wheelwright Museum, Santa Fe.

1886a "The Gods of the Navajos." An unpublished lecture. Box VIII, Item #398. Matthews Papers, Wheelwright Museum, Santa Fe.

1886b "Deities and Demons of the Navajos." *American Naturalist,* Vol. 20:841–50.

1887   *The Mountain Chant: A Navajo Ceremony.* Washington, D.C.: Bureau of American Ethnology.

1890   "The Gentile System of the Navajo Indians from Their Creation and Migration Myth." *Journal of American Folklore,* Vol. 3: 89–110.

1891   "Marriage Prohibitions of the Fathers' Side Among the Navajos," *Journal of American Folklore,* Vol. 4: 78–79.

1894   "Songs of Sequence of the Navajos," *Journal of American Folklore,* Vol. 7:185–94.

1897   *Navaho Legends.* Boston: American Folklore Society.

1899   "Seeking the Lost Adam." *Land of Sunshine,* Vol. 10: 113–25.

1902   *The Night Chant: A Navajo Ceremony.* Memoirs of the American Museum of Natural History, Vol. 6. New York: Knickerbocker Press.

1907   "Navajo Myths, Prayers, and Songs." *University of California Publications In Archaeology and Ethnology,* Vol. 5: 21–63.

n.d.a   "Notes on Navajo Cosomology." Unpublished papers, Box III, Folder 1, Item 193. Matthews Papers, Wheelwright Museum, Santa Fe.

n.d.b   Untitled lecture on the Navajo war gods. Unpublished papers, Box VIII, Item 446. Matthews Papers, Wheelwright Museum, Santa Fe.

n.d.c   Untitled manuscript on culture heroes. Unpublished papers, Box IX Folder 2, Item 595. Matthews Papers, Wheelwright Museum, Santa Fe.

n.d.d   Untitled notebook. Unpublished papers, Item 674, unboxed. Matthews Papers, Wheelwright Museum, Santa Fe.

n.d.e Untitled notebook. Unpublished papers, Item 707, unboxed.
       Matthews Papers, Wheelwright Museum, Santa Fe.

Mills, George Thompson
1959 *Navajo Art and Culture.* Colorado Springs: Taylor Museum.

Moon, Sheila
1970 *A Magic Dwells: A Poetic and Psychological Study of the Navaho
      Emergence Myth.* Middletown, Conn.: Wesleyan University Press.

Mooney, James
1905 "In Memoriam: Washington Matthews." *American Anthropologist,*
      Vol. 7: 514–23.

Nelson, Ralph
1976 *Popol Vuh: The Great Mythological Book of the Ancient Maya.*
      Boston: Houghton Mifflin Co.

Newcomb, Franc (Johnson)
1967 *Navaho Folk Tales.* Santa Fe: Museum of Navajo Ceremonial Art.

Newcomb, Franc (Johnson), and Gladys Reichard
1975 *Sandpaintings of the Navajo Shooting Chant.* New York: Dover
      Publications.

O'Bryan, Aileen
1956 *The Diné: Origin Myths of the Navaho Indians.* Bureau of
      American Ethnology, Bulletin 163. Washington, D.C.

Ong, Walter J.
1967 *The Presence of the Word.* New Haven: Yale University Press.

1971 *Rhetoric, Romance and Technology.* Ithaca: Cornell University
      Press.

1977 *Interfaces of the Word.* Ithaca: Cornell University Press.

Ortiz, Alfonso
1977 "Some Concerns Central to the Writing of 'Indian History.'" *The
      Indian Historian,* Vol. 10, No. 1: 17–22.

Page, Evelyn
1973 *American Genesis: Pre-Colonial Writing in the North.* Boston:
      Gambit.

Park, Clara Claiborne
1981 "The Mother of the Muses: In Praise of Memory." *The American
      Scholar,* Vol. 50: 55–71.

Pearce, Roy Harvey
1953 *Savagism and Civilization: A Study of the Indian and the
      American Mind.* Baltimore: Johns Hopkins Press.

Poor, Robert Marshall
1975 *"Washington Matthews: An Intellectural Biography."* M.A. Thesis, University of Nevada, Reno.

Quasha, George, and Jerome Rothenberg
1973 *America, a Prophecy: A New Reading of American Poetry from Pre-Columbian Times to the Present.* New York: Random House.

Radin, Paul
1915 *Literary Aspects of North American Mythology.* Canada Geological Survey Museum Bulletin No. 16. Ottawa.

1956 *The Trickster.* London: Routledge, Paul and Kegan.

Raglan, Lord
1936 *The Hero: A Study in Tradition, Myth and Drama.* London: Methuen and Co.

Ramsey, Jarold
1979 *"The Teacher of Modern American Indian Writing as Ethnographer and Critic."* *College English,* Vol. 41: 163–69.

Reichard, Gladys A.
1928 *Social Life of the Navajo Indians.* Columbia University Contributions to Anthropology, Vol. 7. New York: Columbia University Press.

1944a *"Individualism and Mythological Style."* *Journal of American Folklore,* Vol. 57: 16–25.

1944b *Prayer: The Compulsive Word.* New York: J. J. Augustin.

1950 *Navajo Religion: A Study of Symbolism.* Bollingen Series XVIII. Princeton: Princeton University Press.

1975 *Sandpaintings of the Male Shooting Chant.* New York: Dover Publications.

1977 *Navajo Medicine Man Sandpaintings.* New York: Dover Publications.

n.d. *The Chant of Waning Endurance Told by Red Mustache of Kinłitchii.* Manuscript, 29–49. Museum of Northern Arizona, Flagstaff.

Revard, Carter
1980 *"History, Myth and Identity Among Osages and Other Peoples."* *Denver Quarterly,* Vol. 14: 84–97.

Roesler, Max
1978   "Enough Is Enough." *The Indian Historian*, Vol. 11, No. 3: 25–28.

Roessel, Robert A., Jr., and Dillon Platero
1974   *Coyote Stories of the Navajo People.* Phoenix: Navajo Curriculum
        Press.

Rooth, A. B.
1957   "The Creation Myths of the North American Indians." *Anthropos*,
        Vol. 52: 497–508.

Ross, Kurt
1978   *Codex Mendoza: Aztec Manuscript.* Fribourg: Miller Graphics.

Sandner, Donald
1979   *Navaho Symbols of Healing.* New York: Harcourt, Brace,
        Jovanovich.

Sapir, Edward, and Harry Hoijer
1942   *Navajo Texts.* Iowa City: Linguistic Society of America.

Schoolcraft, Henry Rowe
1844   *Oneota: Or, The Red Race of America.* New York: Burgess,
        Stringer and Co.

Sidney, Sir Philip
1890   *Defence of Poetry*, ed. Albert S. Cook. Boston: Houghton Mifflin
        Co.

Sobosan, Jeffrey C.
1974   "The Philosopher and the Indian: Correlations Between Plotinus
        and Black Elk." *The Indian Historian*, Vol. 7, No. 2: 47–78.

Spencer, Katherine
1947   *Reflection of Social Life in the Navaho Origin Myth.* University of
        New Mexico Publications in Anthropology, No. 3. Albuquerque.

1957   *Mythology and Values: An Analysis of Navaho Chantway Myths.*
        Philadelphia: American Folklore Society.

Taylor, Archer
1948   "Folklore and the Student of Literature." *The Pacific Spectator*,
        Vol. 2: 216–23. Reprinted in Dundes: 34–42.

Tedlock, Dennis
1972a   *Finding the Center: Narrative Poetry of the Zuni Indians.* Reprint,
        Lincoln: University of Nebraska Press, 1978.

1972b   "Pueblo Literature: Style and Verisimilitude." *New Perspectives
        On the Pueblos*, ed. Alfonso Ortiz. Albuquerque: University of
        New Mexico Press.

1981   "The Spoken Word and the Work of Interpretation In American Indian Religion." *Traditional American Indian Literatures: Texts and Interpretations*, ed. Karl Kroeber. Lincoln: University of Nebraska Press.

Toelken, Barre, and Tacheeni Scott
1981   "Poetic Retranslation and the 'Pretty Languages' of Yellowman." *Traditional American Indian Literatures: Texts and Interpretations*, ed. Karl Kroeber. Lincoln: University of Nebraska Press.

Turner, Frederick
1980   *Beyond Geography: The Western Spirit Against the Wilderness.* New York: Viking.

Utley, Francis Lee
1961   "Folk Literature: An Operational Definition." *Journal of American Folklore*, Vol. 74: 193–206. Reprinted in Dundes: 7–24.

Vansina, Jan
1961   *Oral Tradition: A Study in Historical Methodology.* Chicago: Aldine Publishing Co.

Van Valkenburgh, Richard F.
1936   *Navajo Common Law: I, Notes on Political Organization, Property and Inheritance.* Museum Notes, Museum of Northern Arizona, Vol. 9. Flagstaff.

1938   *A Short History of the Navajo People.* Window Rock, Arizona: U.S. Department of the interior, Navajo Service. Reprinted in *Navajo Indians III.* Garland Series in American Indian Ethnohistory: New York: Garland Publishing Co.

1974   *Navajo Sacred Places.* New York: Garland Publishing Co.

Van Valkenburgh, Richard F., and Frank O. Walker
1945   "Old Placenames in the Navajo Country." *The Masterkey*, Vol. 19: 89–94.

Waters, Frank
1950   *Masked Gods: Navaho and Pueblo Ceremonialism.* New York: Swallow Press.

Welsh, Andrew
1978   *Roots of Lyric: Primitive Poetry and Modern Poetics.* Princeton: Princeton University Press.

Wheeler-Voegelin, Erminie, and Remedios W. Moore
1972   "The Emergence Myth in Native North America." *Studies in*

Folklore: In Honor of Distinguished Service Professor Stith Thompson, ed. W. Edson Richmond. Westport, Conn.: Greenwood Press.

Wheelwright, Mary
1942   *Navajo Creation Myth: The Story of the Emergence by Hasteen Klah.* Santa Fe: Museum of Navajo Ceremonial Art.

Williams, Raymond
1976   *Keywords: A Vocabulary of Culture and Society.* London: Fontana/Croom Helm.

Witherspoon, Gary
1975   *Navajo kinship and Marriage.* Chicago: University of Chicago Press.

1977   *Language and Art in the Navajo Universe.* Ann Arbor: University of Michigan Press.

Wyckoff, Theodore
1977   "The Navajo Nation Tomorrow." *American Indian Law Review,* Vol. 5: 267–97.

Wyman, Leland C.
1957   *Beautyway: A Navaho Ceremonial.* Bollingen Series LIII. New York: Pantheon Books.

1962   *The Windways of the Navaho.* Colorado Springs: Taylor Museum.

1965   *The Red Antway of the Navaho.* Santa Fe: Museum of Navajo Ceremonial Art.

1970   *Blessingway.* Tucson: University of Arizona Press.

1975   *The Mountainway of the Navaho.* Tucson: University of Arizona Press.

Wyman, Leland C., and Flora Bailey
1943   *Navajo Upward Reaching Way: Objective Behavior, Rationale and Sanction.* University of New Mexico, Albuquerque. Bulletin No. 389

Wyman, Leland C., and Clyde Kluckhohn
1938   *Navaho Classification of Their Song Ceremonials.* Memoirs of the American Anthropological Association, No. 50. Menasha, Wisc.

1940   *An Introduction to Navaho Chant Practice.* Memoirs of the American Anthropological Association, No. 53. Menasha, Wisc.

Yazzie, Ethelou
1971   *Navajo History.* Many Farms, Arizona: Navajo Community College Press.

Young, Robert W.
1968   *The Role of the Navajo in the Southwestern Drama.* Gallup, N. Mex.: The Gallup *Independent.*

Young, Robert W., and William Morgan
1943   *The Navajo Language.* Washington, D.C.: Bureau of Indian Affairs. Reprints 1969, 1976, Salt Lake City: Deseret Book Co.

1980   *The Navajo language: A Grammar and Colloquial Dictionary.* Albuquerque: University of New Mexico Press.

Zolbrod, Paul G.
1973   "The Study of Native American Poetry." *Modern Language Studies,* Vol. 3: 38–96.

1979   "Big Giant and the Monster Slayers: An Introductory Look at Navajo Ceremonial Poetry." *Proceedings of the Seventh Congress of the International Comparative Literature Association,* eds. Milan V. Cimic, Juan Ferrate, and Eva Kushner. Montreal: Kunst and Wissen Erich Bieber.

Zolla, Elemire
1973   *The Writer and the Shaman: A Morphology of the American Indian.* New York: Harcourt Brace Jovanovich.